THE THIRD STATIST
OF SCOT

CH00967664

THE COUNTY OF
KINCARDINE

THE THIRD STATISTICAL ACCOUNT
OF SCOTLAND

THE COUNTY OF
KINCARDINE

EDITED BY
DENNIS SMITH

SCOTTISH ACADEMIC PRESS
EDINBURGH
1988

Published by
Scottish Academic Press Ltd,
33 Montgomery Street
Edinburgh EH7 5JX

SBN 7073 0503 9

Printed in Great Britain by
Bell and Bain Ltd, Glasgow

CONTENTS

PARISHES

ILLUSTRATIONS

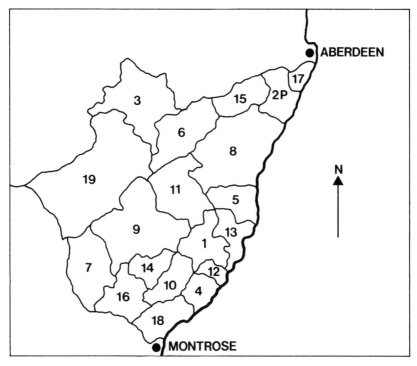

The County of Kincardineshire

1. Arbuthnott
2. Banchory–Devenick
3. Banchory–Ternan
4. Benholm
5. Dunnottar
6. Durris
7. Fettercairn
8. Fetteresso
9. Fordoun
10. Garvock

11. Glenbervie
12. Inverbervie
13. Kinneff
14. Laurencekirk
15. Maryculter
16. Marykirk
17. Nigg
18. St Cyrus
19. Strachan
P. Portlethen

The parish of Nigg was progressively absorbed into the City of Aberdeen, the final sections of the parish being transferred in 1975. Portlethen was erected as a *quoad sacra* parish in the eastern part of Banchory–Devenick.

FOREWORD

This volume of *The Third Statistical Account of Scotland* is concerned with the former County of Kincardine, and consists in the main of accounts written by the parish ministers and others in the years following the war of 1939-1945. I should like, on behalf of the Scottish Council for Voluntary Organisations, to record our thanks to the original contributors, many of whom are no longer with us, and to congratulate Mr Dennis Smith, the editor, on his work in editing the texts and providing such an interesting Introduction. These parish accounts, taken along with the Introduction, indicate the many changes in the lives of ordinary people, not only since *The Second Statistical Account* of the mid-nineteenth century, but also the rapid, even revolutionary, developments in many areas since the last war.

The Scottish Council for Voluntary Organisations and the editor wish to record their thanks for help in the preparation of this volume to The Viscount of Arbuthnott, Lord Lieutenant of the old County, and his Deputy Lieutenants, in particular Captain James Irvine-Fortescue. Their enthusiasm and local knowledge have been of assistance in checking details and presenting a balanced study of the County as it was after the war and before the local government changes of 1975.

For help in financing this volume, we in the Scottish Council for Voluntary Organisations are grateful to the Kincardine and Deeside District Council, the Grampian Regional Council, the Nineveh Trust, the MacRobert Trusts, Lord Arbuthnott and to many individual donors. We should also like to express, as we have done on previous occasions, thanks to the Carnegie Trust for the Universities of Scotland which has continued to support us in the effort to complete the series of volumes of *The Third Statistical Account of Scotland*.

ALEXANDER LAW
Vice-President
Scottish Council for Voluntary Organisations

PREFACE

The *Third Statistical Account of Scotland* was planned in 1946, and most of the parish accounts that follow were prepared between 1949 and 1955 under the auspices of the University of Aberdeen. For a variety of reasons the volume did not proceed to publication and the planned general introduction was never written. In the thirty-odd years which have passed much has changed in Kincardineshire, particularly since the discovery of North Sea oil. The accounts no longer provide a current view of the county, but they have acquired the status of historical documents in their own right, giving insights into contemporary concerns like rural electrification and the evils of football pools. It was therefore decided to print the accounts as they stood, except for the correction of a few obvious factual errors and a certain amount of grammatical pedantry from the editor. In the Introduction I have attempted both to give a brief summary of the accounts, highlighting the main social changes since the *New Statistical Account* of the 1840s, and also to indicate some of the major developments since the 1950s.

No accounts were available for two parishes among the original typescripts. I am extremely grateful to James Irvine-Fortescue of Kingcausie and the Rev. Laurence J. Matthews for the readiness with which they undertook to write accounts for Maryculter and Nigg respectively, and for the promptness with which they supplied their texts. If only all other editorial problems could have been solved so easily! Readers should bear in mind that these two accounts are of a different vintage from the rest. For answers to queries I am also grateful to Dr David Hewitt, Iain F. MacIver, Arthur F. Bryce of the Sandeman Library, Perth, and especially to H. B. Sturgeon, Regional Assessor for Grampian. At a late stage Leslie Fraser generously placed at my disposal his bibliography of material relating to Kincardineshire: this provided many valuable references (and would have saved me a great deal of work if I had learned of it earlier). In the Introduction my intellectual debt to Ian Carter will be obvious to all who know his work. Last but not least I must thank my mother, Winifred Smith, for her patience in answering innumerable questions about Kincardineshire events past and present.

November 1985   *DENNIS SMITH*

INTRODUCTION

by
Dennis Smith

On p. 84 of the Dunnottar account the Rev. John Campbell mentions that Dunnottar woods were then (November 1950) in the process of being felled. Some of the present writer's earliest memories are of playing beneath those splendid beeches, and of childish grief at their incomprehensible destruction. Now some of the trees in the replanted woods are themselves approaching maturity and provide a playground and a refuge for new generations of children.

In some ways this is a fitting image of continuity through change. The rhythms of the land endure while human struggles and human fashions pass. In the words of Lewis Grassic Gibbon, 'sea and sky and the folk who wrote and fought and were learned, teaching and saying and praying, they lasted but as a breath, a mist of fog in the hills, but the land was forever . . . ' (*Sunset song*, hardback ed., p. 97). But this contrast, setting a changing humanity against an enduring land, is at best ambiguous. While individuals and generations came and went, flitting across the face of the land, there was for centuries a pervasive and essentially stable rural culture which bound them together across the generations, shaping and limiting their actions and outlook. Despite a continuing flow of historical change people shared — and were conscious of sharing — the mental universe of their parents and grandparents. And since this culture was closely tied to the annual cycles of the land, summer and winter, seedtime and harvest, it appeared to be timeless in a double sense.

It is here that the image of continuity breaks down. Within the period covered by this Account — from the 1840s to the present — there were decisive and irreversible changes in the structure, customs and outlook of that society. A basically agricultural society which, through its links with the land, could maintain an essential continuity through change has given way to an irredeemably temporal technological society. (There are arguable analogies here with the widespread abandonment, over the same period, of the timeless rites and concepts of religion.) It is important not to distort and sentimentalise this change, particularly by confusing a level of personal experience with external developments in social history. It is common to look back on one's childhood as a time of innocence, wholeness and unchanging values, an Eden before the Fall. This image is vividly displayed in Edwin Muir's *Autobiography*, which contrasts the timeless idyll of Orkney peasant society with the social and spiritual hell of industrial Glasgow. This factually describes Muir's personal history;

but it also expresses a recurring archetype based on the universal experiences of growing up and on the necessity of adjusting to the contingency and limitation of social life. This pattern increases the danger of seeing a bygone peasant society as a lost Eden.

Nonetheless, it is clear that the nature of society has changed fundamentally. David Buchan has claimed (in *The ballad and the folk*) that the agricultural practices and social patterns of north-east Scotland remained largely unaltered between the mid-fourteenth and mid-eighteenth centuries. Then, within a couple of generations, they were transformed by an agricultural revolution and by the expansion of literacy which accompanied it. More recent research has tended to modify this picture in both directions. Early Scottish agriculture was less static and less hidebound by tradition than has often been thought; and Ian Carter's *Farmlife in northeast Scotland 1840-1914* has demonstrated that, in the north-east at any rate, peasant modes of production and peasant culture were exceptionally successful in maintaining themselves throughout the nineteenth century and even into the twentieth. It is this way of life which ended during the period under review. To quote Gibbon again, 'the ancient strange whirlimagig of the generations that enslaved the Scots peasantry for centuries is broken' (in his essay 'The land' in *A Scots hairst*, p. 77). For Gibbon, as for Carter, the First World War marked the crucial turning point, though only by accelerating forces which were already at work.

Until the eighteenth century Scottish agriculture tended to rely on the cooperation of relatively large groups, with the work of the farmtoun shared out, often by long-established custom, among tenant and subtenants, cottars and labourers. With the agricultural revolution, enclosure and improving leases, many large farms appeared with a recognisably 'modern' relationship between master and men. But alongside these 'capitalist' farms, and maintaining a complex interdependence with them, there survived a large number of smallholdings, often on poorer, marginal land which the crofter broke in from moor and bog. (In Kincardineshire there were important differences between the north and the south of the county in the fertility of the land and in the consequent patterns of landholding.) Though by no means slow to experiment with new techniques, this crofting community carried on many of the methods and values of traditional farming and did much to establish the ethos of the whole community. It placed a high value on personal independence and self-sufficiency. Labour tended to be drawn from within the family (small crofters might also work part-time for neighbouring farmers or at a home craft like weaving or sutoring). Work discipline was hard and the crofter's wife and children might tyauve for long hours without either pay or the freedom to choose their own role. Much of the economy operated at a subsistence level with cash playing a relatively minor role. But for many sons there was the incentive that, perhaps after a spell as a feed man on a muckle toun, they might save enough for a place of their own.

This way of life, with its stress on independence, individual responsibility and hard work, can be related, both as cause and as effect, to the Calvinist view of man's relation to his God, and more specifically to the position adopted in the mid-nineteenth century by the Free Kirk. Though the figures must be treated with some reserve, the religious census of 1851 suggests that in Kincardineshire the Church of Scotland outnumbered the Free Church by more than three to two in attendances. This shows the Free Church as rather weaker than the average for Scotland as a whole and may, among other things, reflect the dominance of capitalist farming as against crofting in the Howe. It would be interesting to know if these figures changed later in the century in line with political trends. As the larger farmers tended to Conservatism and the established church, so the crofters tended to Liberalism and the Free Kirk, as did the spinners in the mills, and others. Gibbon comments that Bervie 'was fell radical and full of souters ready to brain you with a mallet or devil if you spoke a word against that old tyke Gladstone' (*The speak of the Mearns*, p. 24). It may be possible to draw economic inferences from the county's parliamentary history, though other, national factors like changes in the franchise clearly played a part. From 1832 to 1865 the Hon. H. Arbuthnott held the seat for the Conservatives: apart from 1832 he was never opposed. From 1865 to 1923 the seat was Liberal, often with massive majorities. Since 1923 it has been continuously Conservative apart from a short break from 1929 to 1931.

The peasant way of life was undermined by a number of economic and technological factors. Farm prices slumped in the late 1870s: new machinery made the big farms increasingly independent of peasant skills and of the need for seasonal labour. It became harder for young men to get crofts, so weakening the incentive to toil on those which remained. All this coincided with the major changes in educational opportunities which sprang from the Education (Scotland) act of 1872. Young people became simultaneously more aware of opportunities in the cities, and better equipped to take advantage of them. This contributed to a widespread sense in the last quarter of the nineteenth century that a traditional way of life and sense of community were under threat. This was reflected in a conscious vernacular revival in Scottish poetry and also, as Ian Carter has suggested, in the contemporary enthusiasm for local history and in the popularity of Kailyard novels which stressed the harmony of community values just at a time when they were in fact being eroded. Of this period the traditionalist narrator in a George Mackay Brown story says: 'To such an extent, in a few years, had education rotted the minds of the people' (*A time to keep*, p.96).

Peasant culture might be described as rich in meaning but materially deprived. Kincardineshire shared in the rich folk culture of the north-east, providing a fertile hunting ground for the ballad collectors David Herd and George Ritchie Kinloch. These same ballads somet-imes paint a grim picture of back-breaking toil and meagre food:

> Wi your tattie poorins an your meal an kail,
> Your soor sowen soorins an your ill-brewed ale,
> Wi your buttermilk an whey an your breid fired raw
> (*The twa recruiting sergeants*)

The stark choice between a close community, at once rich in personal values and socially restrictive, and the disorientating freedom of an educated urban environment is vividly embodied in the figure of the young Chris Guthrie. Many in real life must have felt the same conflict. Some willingly left the land to better themselves. Others, one may suspect, would gladly have stayed but were driven from the land by inexorable economic forces. In either case, the county's population dropped, from 35,017 in 1851 to 31,537 in 1901 and 27,882 in 1951, with the sharpest falls concentrated in the rural parishes (See Appendix 1).

Agriculture has always been dominant in the Kincardineshire economy. Fishing enjoyed a spectacular boom in the second half of the nineteenth century, but the fishing communities, with their long history of self-sufficiency and endogamy, and their distinctive lore and customs, have tended to remain relatively isolated from the rest of society. One view of this relationship is summed up in the title of a recent anthropological study of Ferryden, just outside the county boundary: 'Stigma and separation: pariah status and community persistence in a Scottish fishing village'. Manufacturing has always played a relatively minor role, and bearing in mind the decline in weaving and rural trades like blacksmithing it may actually be less significant now than in the 1840s, though the service sector has certainly expanded considerably. Overall, there has been a decisive shift from a partly subsistence economy to a capital-intensive one, which may help to explain the apparent paradox noted by the Rev. D. W. Greenfield: 'Despite the decline in local industries, the standard of life in the village has risen greatly in living memory' (Benholm, p. 81).

One important effect has been to make the local economy and way of life less distinctive, closer to the rest of Scotland, Britain and the industrialized world in general. Greater affluence, greater mobility, the communications revolution, different work patterns and greater leisure — all have changed the way of life in ways that are at once complex and commonplace. Within the last thirty years supermarkets have tended to replace groceries, building societies and travel agents have appeared in the streets, and Chinese and Indian restaurants have sprung up alongside the Italian-run chip-shops and ice-cream parlours which now appear traditional. In Stonehaven harbour yachts greatly outnumber fishing boats: and while the fishing industry may now have passed its lowest ebb the days are unlikely to return when more than 100 boats fished out of the harbour.

The great expansion in communications has tended to make communities less inward-looking, less self-sufficient and perhaps also less cohesive. Several of the parish accounts stress the importance of the motor car in this respect, even at 1950s levels of ownership, and the influence of television over the past thirty years has probably been even more significant. Particularly since the start of the North Sea oil boom there has been a great increase in the volume and speed of road traffic passing through the county, often having no contact at all with the locals. Since the 1950s a dual carriageway has crept southwards in fits and starts from the Aberdeen city boundary, culminating in the opening of Stonehaven by-pass in November 1984, so realising a project first mooted in the 1930s. Traffic pressure in the town centre has been dramatically reduced: the long-term economic effects remain to be seen. This was followed by the opening of the Laurencekirk by-pass in June 1985, and plans are in hand to upgrade the A94 to dual-carriageway standard throughout the rest of the county. This expansion in private transport has gone hand-in-hand with a reduction in rail and rural bus services. The Deeside line fell victim to the Beeching axe in 1966, following on the closure of the Bervie branch line a few years earlier. The smaller mainline stations followed the same track, leaving Stonehaven for a number of years as the only operational station in the county. But in an interesting reversal of commuting trends (and reflecting the growth of the village) Portlethen station re-opened with considerable publicity in May 1985. Away from the trunk routes bus services have continued to decline.

At present there are three secondary schools in the county — Banchory Academy, Mackie Academy (Stonehaven) and Mearns Academy (Laurencekirk) — and 28 primary schools, including one private school at Lathallan. By a fine irony Portlethen Junior Secondary school closed in 1969, just before the oil-inspired boom in the village. A new academy is currently under construction. Two special schools, for handicapped children and mentally handicapped adults, have been built in Stonehaven. Mackie Academy moved to a new building at Ury in 1969, and this has since been extended. The old Mackie building, now re-named Arduthie, houses an expanded primary school, and the old Stonehaven Public (Fetteresso) school building has become a much-needed community centre. A recreation centre and indoor swimming pool have recently opened in the Queen Elizabeth park.

The break-up of the landed estates, which was particularly evident after the First World War, has gone further, and some of the great

houses have suffered accordingly. Of the four which used to ring
Stonehaven, for example, and survived into the 1950s, only Cowie
House is still occupied. Fetteresso Castle and Ury House are roofless
decaying shells and Dunnottar House has vanished almost without
trace. Other houses, however, like Arbuthnott, Fasque and Rickarton,
remain in their traditional family ownership. Some, like Fasque,
Arbuthnott and Muchalls Castle, have responded to changing
economic circumstances and a developing concept of heritage by
opening their doors to the public. Crathes Castle, a gem of Scottish
baronial architecture, passed into the care of the National Trust for
Scotland in 1952. Changing leisure patterns and a growing environmental concern are both reflected in the establishment of nature
reserves at Fowlsheugh and St Cyrus. At the same time the traditional
tourist industry, highlighted by the annual invasion of Stonehaven for
the Glasgow Fair, has declined with greater mobility and the trend to
touring by car.

If Kincardineshire's experience has deviated from the over-all
national trend in recent years, it is because of the accelerated rate of
change brought by the North Sea oil boom. Numerous small
factories, often involved in modern oil-related technology, have been
constructed, particularly in the north of the county between Portlethen and Nigg and on the Spurryhillock industrial estate at
Stonehaven. Large areas, particularly around Altens, have also been
taken over for storage yards and warehousing for offshore materials
and equipment such as pipelines. These developments can be seen as
part of a continuing process of technological renewal, with obsolete or
uneconomic industries being replaced. Within the last thirty years, for
example, Stonehaven has lost such traditional employers as the
networks, tannery, lemonade factory and distillery, following in the
tracks of the woollen mills and ropeworks before them. On the other
hand, many of the current developments are based on an extractive
resource with a limited future, and there are indications that some
settlements in the north of the county are increasingly used as
dormitory suburbs of Aberdeen. So it remains to be seen whether any
indigenous industries have a long-term future in the county.

House prices have risen sharply, in line with Aberdeen's, and are
now among the highest in the country. Many new houses have been
built, particularly at Portlethen and on the western fringes of
Stonehaven. Inevitably most have been built in the anonymous
modern style, cramped rows of indistinguishable rabbit-hutches, with
no reference to vernacular tradition. Fortunately this has been
balanced by some examples of sensitive restoration, as in the old town
of Stonehaven. This expansion has attracted many newcomers to the
county, and the scale of the changes can best be illustrated by looking
at some figures from the population census.

Between 1851 and 1971 the population of Kincardineshire fell from

35,017 to 26,058, a fall of over a quarter. Though this is partly accounted for by boundary changes caused by Aberdonian expansionism, it reveals a trend towards rural depopulation in line with many other landward counties in Scotland. But by 1981 the population had risen to 33,725, the highest figure since 1891. This reversal is almost entirely due to the oil boom and can be vividly illustrated by concentrating on two parishes. In 1951 Fetteresso (which includes the new town of Stonehaven) had a population of 5,696, barely altered from a century earlier: There was little change by 1961 but by 1971 the total was 6,796 and by 1981 10,086. The number of houses rose from 1,541 in 1950 to 3,803 in 1983 (while in the twin parish of Dunnottar, which includes the old town of Stonehaven, stricter housing standards saw the total fall from 512 in 1950 to 471 in 1983). The expansion in the civil parish of Banchory-Devenick, which includes Portlethen, is even more striking: the population rose from 1,264 in 1961 to 3,836 in 1981 and the number of houses from 357 in 1950 to 1,400 in 1983, increases of over 200% and nearly 300% respectively. For fuller statistics of population and housing see Appendices 1 and 2 respectively.

In total these changes have, perhaps, finally eroded the county's most striking cultural feature, its frontier position. Geologically, the Highland Fault bisects the county and the Mounth runs north-eastwards, in hills of decreasing size, to meet the coast south of Aberdeen. Until last century the Mounth constituted a real barrier to communication, with traffic, much of it on foot, having a choice of at least seven Mounth roads, all of them bad. To the south lies the Howe of the Mearns, the northerly continuation of the fertile valley of Strathmore. To the north the land is much poorer, with large areas of moor and peat-bog. To quote J. R. Allan, 'though there are pockets of good land, the rocks too often stand out of the soil and the whins wait at the dykesides to recapture the fields' (*North-east lowlands of Scotland*, p.7). Such land can only be made productive with great human effort — a feature it shares with much of Aberdeenshire — and it is noticeable that crofting remained widespread here long after large capitalist farms dominated the Howe.

For centuries the area north of the Mounth, with Aberdeenshire as its economic and cultural centre, remained relatively isolated from the rest of Scotland. The economy was largely self-contained and formed its own overseas trading links through the port of Aberdeen. The twin universities of King's and Marischal maintained distinctive intellectual traditions. The impact of the Reformation came late and in a muted form, as shown by Aberdeen's reluctance to accept the National Covenant in 1638. Later in the century the north-east was a notorious hotbed of Jacobitism and Episcopalianism. In short, there was a distinct subculture preserving unusually strong links with the past.

Kincardineshire has thus been a meeting-place for diverse influences

B

coming from the north and the south. This Janus-like position is reflected in various spheres. It is striking how evenly the books listed in the Bibliography split between those which link Kincardineshire with Angus and those which link it with Aberdeenshire and Banffshire. Equally, in the long-established scheme of church government (which was modified but not radically altered at the Union of 1929) two thirds of the county fell into the Synod of Angus and Mearns, while the six Deeside parishes belonged to the Synod of Aberdeen. Before regionalization in 1975 library services were shared with Angus while many specialist health services were provided from Aberdeen. That this was not just an arbitrary administrative border is shown by the standard dialect boundary between South Northern Scots and Mid Northern Scots which cuts through the middle of the county.

There was therefore some geographical and historical logic in the proposal by Lord Wheatley's Royal Commission on Local Government in Scotland to split Kincardineshire between the regions now known as Grampian and Tayside. But it is mark of the county's strong sense of local patriotism that this proposal met with such fierce opposition that it was quickly dropped. The subsequent creation of Kincardine and Deeside district within Grampian region preserved the county intact, apart from the transfer to the City of Aberdeen district of the remaining portions of Nigg parish, and added to it the vast rural hinterland of Deeside. Stonehaven rule now extends to the summit of Ben Macdui. This combination guarantees the predominantly rural nature of the county and, with Deeside's scenic splendour and sporting and tourist economy, adds still further to its diversity. Even within its traditional boundaries Kincardineshire compresses a remarkable variety into its 350 square miles, ranging from hill to sea, from deer forest through upland grazing and croft to rich arable land. In many ways it provides a good microcosm of modern Scotland, not least in the uncertainty of its industrial future.

One type of local culture, which it is tempting but probably misleading to call 'organic', has decayed over the past century. For all the material progress that has been made, it is clear from the lively current interest in local and family history that this is felt by many as a real loss and that there is a widespread desire for something, a sense of belonging or self-definition perhaps, to put in its place. Whether such a renewed sense of community can be constructed through conscious effort, and in the face of increasingly supranational and impersonal economic forces, must remain an open question.

November 1985

THE PARISH OF ARBUTHNOTT

by the Rev. Geo. A. Henderson, M.A.

PHYSICAL BASIS

The inland parish of Arbuthnott, situated almost wholly to the north of the Bervie, extends from near the mouth of that river to where it meets in the west the parish of Fordoun, a distance of 5 miles. With projections in the north and south, it has a length of 6 miles. In the north-west the river Forthy separates it from the parish of Glenbervie, and on the north-east Arbuthnott adjoins the parish of Dunnottar. To the east lies Kinneff. On the south Arbuthnott is bordered by the parish of Bervie and on the south-west by Garvock. Fordoun lies to the west. The parish covers an area of 9583 acres, nearly 15 square miles.

The surface is very uneven. Bruxie Hill (710 ft), on the north-eastern border, is the highest point. The Bervie flows mainly in a deep valley, so that on both sides of the river there is a steep rise. On the north side the land is all agricultural, and on the south side it is partly agricultural and partly woodland. There also the surface is broken by deep gorges, called dens, down which in times of flood turbulent waters rush into the Bervie. The soil is varied. Along the ridges on the north side of the river there is a considerable amount of clay. Higher up the soil is lighter, but in parts it is peaty and gravelly. The climate is dry and bracing. The quantity of sunshine is well above the average for Scotland, and the prevailing winds are north-east and south-east. On the whole there is good agricultural land, on which excellent crops of oats, barley and potatoes are raised. Little wheat is grown.

ESTATES

Formerly there were three estates in the parish, viz:— Arbuthnott, Allardyce and Kair. Now there are two, Arbuthnott which, during the past century, has been greatly diminished by sales of land, and Kair. The Arbuthnott family is one of the oldest in Scotland, and its ownership of Arbuthnott dates from the end of the 12th century, when Osbertus Olifard was granted a charter of these lands by

William the Lion. It was Sir Robert Arbuthnott who, on 17th November 1641, was created Viscount Arbuthnott and Lord Inverbervie by Charles I. The present Viscount is the fourteenth in succession.

POPULATION

During the past century the population of the parish has suffered a severe decline, as will be seen from the following Census figures:— (1801) 942; (1851) 1002; (1901) 698; (1911) 674; (1921) 683; (1931) 577. In 1948 it was estimated at 412. [In 1951 the Census showed 480 (244 males and 236 females).] This decline is due to several factors, including frequent depressions in agriculture and latterly mechanisation in agriculture, lack of any alternative industry, poor housing conditions and houses having been allowed to fall into disrepair and finally into disuse. There is neither working blacksmith nor carpenter in the parish, and the one-time busy meal mill is now a ruin. If a youth wishes to learn a trade he must go outside the parish. When he has completed his apprenticeship he leaves it for good. Similarly young girls, who very rarely enter domestic or farm service in the parish, seek employment elsewhere and are permanently lost to it.

PUBLIC SERVICES

Most farms have a separate water supply and frequently in dry weather suffer a shortage. Farm houses have modern conveniences and sanitary arrangements, and an increasing number are installing a private electricity supply. All other houses have paraffin lighting. All farmers have motor cars and are not inconvenienced by the absence of a frequent bus service. In 1947 a service was begun between Fordoun and Bervie, which operates twice daily both ways, with additional runs on Saturday and Sunday.

HEALTH

During the past 30 years there has been a steady development. Medical inspection, dental treatment, and the provision of milk and meals for school children have much benefited their health. The County Nursing Scheme has been a great boon. The National Health Service now operates, but it is too early to estimate its effects. The health of the parish is good, there being a marked absence of infectious troubles and tuberculosis.

HOUSING

Statistical tables supplied by the County Health Department show that of the 137 houses surveyed in the parish — 8 of them were vacant — 14 had 2 rooms, 61 had 3, 13 had 4, 12 had 5, 11 had 6, 6 had 7, and 12 had 8 or more rooms. The total number of persons living in the 129 occupied houses was 402, of whom 52 were in 2-roomed houses and 136 in 3-roomed houses. Of the 137 houses, 5 were bungalows and 132 were of cottage type (37 of them semi-detached). As regards tenancy, 27 houses were owner-occupied, 40 were rented, 1 owned by local authority, 7 were 'tied', and 62 (including 9 houses with 2 rooms and 39 with 3) occupied by farm servants. In 5 of the 2-roomed houses and in 7 of those with 3 rooms, there was overcrowding, to a total extent of 37 persons overcrowded.

It will be seen to what extent overcrowding prevails, but the most disturbing feature of the housing situation is the lamentable condition of the great majority of farm servants' houses. Many have not even a sink in the kitchen, have no water supply laid on, and depend on one outside the house — in some cases at a distance from it. Some are damp and in wet weather not rain-proof. Nearly all have only primitive sanitary arrangements. Lord Arbuthnott and one or two owners of farms have modernised their workers' houses, but much more requires to be done throughout the parish by other farm owners. These bad housing conditions account for frequent shifting among farm servants and it is notable that young married men, who, with their wives, have received a better standard of education, will not engage to farmers who do not provide proper houses.

AGRICULTURE

The following are the most notable changes during the past 50 years:— (1) The increasing use of artificial manures, especially for turnip and potato crops. (2) The increasing mechanisation of farms. On many there are now no horses. (3) Owing to war and post-war needs, the maximum amount of land has been brought under the plough. (4) The potato crops play a most important part and large quantities of seed are grown, especially for the English markets. (5) The growing number of farmers who own their farms. (6) Fixed prices have brought great benefit to the countryside. According to the Minister of Food the net incomes for farmers were four times the pre-war level, while agricultural labourers had, because of fixed minimum wages, made the biggest gains of any single class in the community. For tractor-men, minimum wages vary between 95/- and 105/- per week, and dairy cattlemen, who have longer hours and a seven-day week, receive up to 130/- weekly. The working day is 8¼ hours in

winter, with 8¾ hours in spring, summer and autumn. Perquisites and
house rents are now deducted from wages — rents range from 2/6 to
3/- per week. All overtime work is paid at 2/6 to 3/- per hour. Hence,
five years after the Second World War, there is no indication of a
slump in prices for agricultural produce, whereas two years after the
First World War the decline in prices began and continued till
agriculture became a depressed industry.

RELIGION

The parish church — the building is dealt with under Antiquities —
has a membership of about 100. The custom widely prevails that
attendance at communion services twice a year suffices for church
membership. The weekly attendance is poor, averaging about 22.
Among a considerable number of farmers, as well as farm servants,
there is a marked indifference to the church, which they neither attend
nor help to support. This is a long-standing tradition in the parish.

The Sunday School and Junior Bible Class are well attended, and
the present minister holds a monthly service in the school. The
Woman's Guild is small but active in promoting the good of the
church and helping its schemes. The Christian liberality of the parish,
considering the prosperous condition of agriculture, is poor. The most
difficult problem for the parish church is the widespread and deep-
rooted apathy of so many of the parishioners.

EDUCATION

The decline in population has led to a corresponding fall in the
numbers attending the local school, especially during the past 30 years.
This is seen from the following statistics:—

Year	School Population	Boys	Girls	Male Teachers	Female Teachers
1919	74	37	37	1	2
1931	69	34	35	1	2
1949	29	18	11	—	1

Thus, in the last 19 years, the attendance has declined by approximately 60%. The school is likely to remain a one-female-teacher
school, because it is not affected by the raising of the school age to 15.
Pupils above 12 years of age attend Bervie school or the Mackie
Academy, Stonehaven.

Both school and schoolhouse are in good order.

SOCIAL ACTIVITIES

There is a good parish hall, seated for about 200 people. A Social Club functions and has a membership of 50. Its activities are recreation, competitions, whist drives. It makes no cultural effort, such as drama, music or lectures. It has an annual Burns Supper, but generally the contributions of the members are of an inferior standard. Very few people in the parish seem to know the history or the poetry of Burns. Whist drives and dances are the usual means of raising funds for charitable objects.

NOTABILITIES

Eminent members of the Arbuthnott family were mentioned in the previous *Statistical Account*. These include Alexander Arbuthnott, who was appointed minister of Arbuthnott parish in 1567, first Protestant Principal of King's College, Aberdeen, in 1569, and in 1573, 1577 and 1578 Moderator of the General Assembly; and Dr. John Arbuthnott, M.D., whose father, Alexander Arbuthnott, became minister of the parish but had to resign his charge in 1690 because he refused to comply with the Presbyterian system, restored in 1688. Dr. John Arbuthnott, physician to Queen Anne and one of the best wits of her reign, was a friend of Pope and Swift.

William Kinloch was born in a low thatched cottage in the second half of the 18th century. He went to Calcutta, where he amassed a fortune. Dying in 1812, he bequeathed to the Arbuthnott Kirk Session a sum of £2,700 in trust on behoof of the native poor of the parish. It is known as the Kinloch Fund and the annual interest is distributed quarterly.

George Brand was born in the early 19th century, also in a humble cottage. Beginning as a herd boy, he became a mason's labourer, and in his spare time studied under the Rev. William Chrystall, the local schoolmaster. With the aid of a bursary, he continued his studies at Aberdeen University, where he graduated. For a time he was private tutor to Lord Haddo, and thereafter entering the Consular Service he became Vice Consul at St. Paul de Loando and later Consul at Lagos, where he died.

'Lewis Grassic Gibbon' was born on 13th February 1901 at Auchterless in Aberdeenshire. In 1909 he moved with his parents to the small farm of Bloomfield in Arbuthnott. He was James Leslie Mitchell, son of James Mitchell and Lilias Grassic Gibbon. He began his education at the local school and continued it at Mackie Academy, Stonehaven. From his boyhood he revealed a notable literary gift, and pursuing a literary career he wrote, along with more than a dozen other books, a trilogy of novels dealing with the rural life of the

North East, and especially of his native parish, which brought him widespread fame. These novels were *Sunset Song*; *Cloud Howe*; and *Grey Granite*, together comprising *A Scots Quair*. Scenes from these and some of his short stories have been broadcast by the B.B.C. He died on 7th February 1935 and is buried in the Kirkyard of Arbuthnott.

ANTIQUITIES

Arbuthnott House and Allardyce Castle are notable examples of early Scottish architecture. In Arbuthnott House are the family records, dating from the founding of the family. Papers dealing with these records have been contributed to historical journals.

The parish church is one of the few Scottish pre-Reformation churches still in use for public worship. It was probably on the site of this church that St Ternan built the first church, early in the 5th century. He was a native of the north Mearns, became a convert of the St Ninian mission to the north-east of Scotland, and was trained at Candida Casa, of which he later became the third President. As a missionary to the Mearns, he founded a church in Arbuthnott. Hence the original name, viz: the Kirk of Saint Ternan, Arbuthnott. It must be borne in mind that, in the Celtic Church, churches were dedicated to their actual founders and not to departed Saints.

The present chancel was built between 1200 and 1240 and was re-dedicated on 4th August 1242 by David de Bernham, Bishop of St Andrews, in whose diocese it was. It was made a prebend of the Collegiate Church of Kirkheugh, St Andrews. The chancel is lit by five small lancet windows and contains a piscina under the eastmost south lancet. Between 1500 and 1503 Sir Robert Arbuthnott built the aisle to house a portable altar. This aisle, a beautiful example of late Scottish Gothic, has two storeys. The lower one, dedicated to the Virgin Mary, has a stoup and an aumbry. It also houses a full-length recumbent effigy, probably that of the famous Hugo le Blond, one of the earliest of the Arbuthnotts, though it is also suggested it may be that of James Arbuthnott, who died in 1521. The aisle is lit by three lancets in the apse at the south end. It is supported by four buttresses, on each of which is a fine canopy and corbel. The corbel on the east buttress is beautifully carved with signs of the Passion. A circular stair leads to the priests' chamber above, which also is lit by three windows, looking west, each of which has stone seats at the sides. It, too, has a small aumbry. Formerly it housed the mortcloth, the bier, and the cutty stool, or stool of repentance, besides a considerable library, bequeathed by Rev. John Sibbald, minister of the parish, who died in 1662. Unfortunately, these relics and the library were wantonly destroyed.

It was in this priests' chamber that James Sibbald, Vicar of Arbuthnott, who died in 1507, wrote the missal of Arbuthnott, which was used at the altar in the St Mary Chapel till the Reformation. He also wrote the Psalter and the Book of Hours, designated 'Office of the Virgin Mary', which were likewise used in the Chapel. These most precious MSS. were offered for sale in London in 1897 by the then Lord Arbuthnott, whose property they were. Fortunately, they were brought back to Scotland by Archibald Coats, Paisley, who purchased them and presented them to the Free Library and Museum of his native town.

The first nave of the church was probably built soon after the chancel and rebuilt on the eve of the Reformation. In 1890 it was partly destroyed by fire and again rebuilt. Central heating and a pipe organ were then introduced. This beautiful old church is much in need of repair, little or nothing having been done for many years to preserve the fabric. Under the present incumbent, who was inducted to the church and parish in 1946, a scheme has been approved by the Presbytery and the General Trustees of the Church of Scotland for its restoration as a mediaeval church. Government permission has been given to spend £1000 for this purpose and almost all that amount is in hand.

WAY OF LIFE

There are no licensed premises in the parish. Drunkenness is exceedingly rare and crime almost unknown. The people are industrious and live simply. Generally, the farmers are frugal, keen to make money and slow to part with it. They prefer to run whist drives, dances or sales for a cause, rather than contribute personal payments.

The nearest picture house is in Inverbervie, where numbers go on Saturday nights. Dancing is the principal recreation among the young, and some of the older men engage in bowling. The young men show no aptitude for outside sports and take no part in them. Football pool betting, however, is on the increase, with no good results. Among the young of both sexes cigarette smoking is very prevalent and is increasing, despite the cost. It is rare to see a pipe smoker.

The Education Committee's rural library scheme operates in the school but, with few exceptions, the people are not readers. Outside their work they have few, if any, interests, and their main conversation is about farm stock, crops and prices. Over a long period of years, except from the Manse, the parish has not produced a university graduate.

All classes dress better than their forebears and, despite the primitive conditions of their houses, some farm servants' wives strive to keep their homes and children clean and tidy. Farm servants have a statutory week's holidays, but many farmers and their wives rarely have that break. Domestic servants are almost unprocurable for farm houses, and farmers' wives, having poultry and dairy produce to look after, in addition to their household duties, find it difficult to leave home for any length of time. They have hard work and little leisure.

January 1950

THE PARISH OF BANCHORY-DEVENICK
(excluding Portlethen)

by the Rev. E.C.P. Hood, M.A.

EXTENT

The civil parish of Banchory-Devenick was reduced in size by about a quarter in 1891 when all its Aberdeenshire part, on the north side of the Dee (between Murtle and Garthdee) was transferred to Peterculter parish by the Boundary Commissioners. This portion included the district of Cults and what is now the south-western fringe of the royal burgh of Aberdeen — Pitfodels, Mannofield, Craigiebuckler etc. The area of Banchory-Devenick parish since 1891 is 7733 acres; the length (north and south) is roughly 5 miles, its breadth mostly from 2 to 3 miles. The surface is in general between 200 and 400 feet above sea-level. The coast (4 miles) is rocky and indented. The adjoining parishes are Peterculter to the north, in Aberdeenshire, Nigg (east), Fetteresso (south and south-west) and Maryculter (west). The ecclesiastical parish of Banchory-Devenick is bounded on the north by the river Dee and on the south by the *quoad sacra* parish of Portlethen, which is the subject of a separate report.

HISTORY OF THE LOCAL COMMUNITY

In 1890 Mr John A. Henderson, Avondale, Cults published a comprehensive history of the parish. He made full use of the records of the Kirk Session for the period from 1708, which are still extant; as Session Clerk, he had easy access to them. In 1881 the Rev. Dr. Paul, a nephew of Dr. Morrison (who wrote the *Second Statistical Account*), and minister of the parish, published *The Past and Present of Aberdeenshire*, which, while not dealing specifically with the parish, gives a clear account of the way of life in the area. In 1949, the Third Spalding Club, Aberdeen, published the *Diary 1692-1710* of James Gordon, son of James Gordon, a minister of the parish and a proprietor of Ardoe. The volume is edited by G.D. Henderson and H.H. Porter. There is a monument on Tollohill, on the estate of Banchory, to commemorate a visit by the Prince Consort in 1859, after he had addressed the British Association in Aberdeen on 14 September.

LANDOWNERS

The lands of Banchory are in the possession of David Stewart Esq., a grandson of Sir David Stewart, and great-grandson of Mr John Stewart who purchased the lands from Mr Thomson's Trustees in 1872. Mr Stewart is connected with Aberdeen Combworks, founded by his great-grandfather. The lands of Ardoe passed into the possession of a limited company, Ardoe (Deeside) Limited, following the death of Mr A.G. Ogston. The mansion-house is now a hotel. Most of the marketable timber has now been felled. The garden is let as a market garden.

THE LOCAL RECORDS

These are chiefly the Kirk Session records from 1708, which (with the exception of a hiatus from 12 Dec. 1714 — 1 March 1716; 7 June 1724 — 23 October 1726; 16 Aug. — 8 Nov. 1747; 12 Aug. — 3 Nov. 1757) go down to the present day. These are in the custody of the minister at the moment, and are all in a good state of preservation. There are also a number of books belonging to the Nether Banchory Savings Bank from 1815 to 1866. Similarly the records of the Free Church are preserved from 1843

POPULATION

The population of the civil parish was 2588 in 1831 at the time of the *Second Statistical Account* (of these, 683 were in the Aberdeenshire portion and 1905 in the Kincardineshire portion, which now forms the entire parish). Mounting steadily, the total reached 3052 in 1871 and by 1891 it had risen to 3564. The Kincardineshire portion accounted for 1981 thereof, its inhabitants having decreased rapidly since 1851, when they numbered 2465. After the loss of its Aberdeenshire section (where the population kept on multiplying), the figure for Banchory-Devenick parish dropped to 1726 in 1901, to 1500 in 1911, to 1377 in 1921, and to 1335 in 1931. In 1951 it recovered slightly to 1379, but it is significant that the male population fell from 664 in 1931 to 648 in 1951 (as compared with 940 males in the same area in 1831).

EMIGRATION

The population in the delimited parish is for the most part native to it, exceptions being very few. There are two farms only where the people originated from Orkney; others belong to the parish or north-east area. Two Polish ex-servicemen, one of whom resides in the parish, married local girls, and a few local girls married English ex-servicemen and are now resident in England. On the whole, the population is engaged in agriculture, or other rural work, exceptions noted later. Movement from the parish is chiefly caused by young married people going to live in Aberdeen in order to be nearer the husband's place of work, and occasionally by farm people retiring elsewhere. There is, of course, a good deal of movement among farm servants generally, though there are exceptions. A few young men have gone out recently to Africa. One girl has married and gone with her husband to India. Another married a Canadian farmer, and is now in Canada. A young couple, both ex-service, have emigrated to New Zealand. Several young men are in regular service with the forces.

PUBLIC AND SOCIAL SERVICES

This area, from its scattered nature, has not benefited from the development of these services as it might otherwise have done. The following notes relate to the ecclesiastical parish of Banchory-Devenick:

WATER SUPPLY

Generally speaking, each farm or cottage has its own water supply from a spring with a collecting cistern, or well, led by pipes to the house. In some cases, e.g. Arnwell Cottage, Parkneuk, the water still has to be carried from a well with a pump. The supply of water in the area, apart from these springs and wells, is not large.

ELECTRICITY

Strong representations were made to Aberdeen Corporation Electricity Department before the Second World War to provide the parish with a supply of electricity. These eventually proved abortive, due to the unwillingness of the householders to meet the initial installation costs, which appeared to some to be excessive; the remainder found the whole cost, when apportioned among them, too great. It must be noted, however, that this took place when agriculture was suffering from intense depression. Electricity was brought through private enterprise to Tollohill Lodge, and Tollohill farm and three cottages in the vicinity of the lodge also benefited. The electric cable has now been taken out the South Deeside road as far as Drumduan House and the estate cottages on and near the road have benefited. Since the end of the war, a plan to cover the parish has been prepared by the North of Scotland Hydro-Electric Board and is expected to be carried out in 1952. Modern paraffin lamps, Tilley and Aladdin, are in general use in farms, cottages, the schoolhouse and manse, but a number of farms have in recent years installed small electric generating sets, which give light for house and steading, and power for milking machines.

GAS

There are no gas mains in the parish, but liquid gas in portable cylinders is used by a number of people.

SEWAGE

The number of homes with bathrooms, and with cesspools for the disposal of sewage, is small and there is no proper system of sewerage. Disposal of sewage and other refuse is a matter for each household.

ROADS

The portions of the South Deeside road, the Aberdeen-Banchory road and the Aberdeen-Stonehaven *via* Netherley road which pass through the parish are in good condition and well maintained. The others are, for the most part, narrow and, though repaired from time to time by the County Council Roads Department, seldom in a reasonable state for long. But one is not surprised, as the cost of maintenance is high, and it is this type of road that predominates in the county, which has a trunk road to maintain throughout its length.

FARM ROADS

In some cases where they are fairly level these have been improved by ashes from the electricity works in Aberdeen, but in the main they remain as they seem to have been for a very long time — extremely rough. There is one exception — the farm of Jockston, Ardoe, where the road and area around the farm buildings have been covered with tarred chips.

EDUCATION

The parish school, under the County Council Education Committee, is now approximately ¼ mile south of Broadgreens Farm. It is staffed by a Headmaster and an Infant Mistress. There are over 40 pupils, who must now leave on attaining the age of 12, to be transported daily to a secondary school at Banchory or Stonehaven. A not unimportant consequence of this practice is that it deprives the child of the influence for good that his local master used to have between the ages of 12 and 14, or, as it would now be, fifteen, and further that it makes it very difficult to get those children, when they leave school, to return to the local school for evening class work.

HEALTH SERVICES

The parish is well served by doctors from Portlethen, Cults and Aberdeen. General nursing and maternity work is handled by the District Nurse at Cove Bay under the National Health Service, while the general and special hospitals in Aberdeen are open to people from the area.

POLICE

The nearest police stations are (1) in the parish of Maryculter across the parish boundary from the Old Mill of Ardoe; (2) in the parish of Nigg at Charlestown.

FIRE

Fire service facilities are available in Aberdeen, but scarcity of water at any great distance from the river Dee makes their work extremely difficult.

POSTAL SERVICES

There is a sub-post office in Banchory-Devenick and mail is delivered to the whole parish once on week-days by small motor vans, with a second delivery to parts of the parish near the South Deeside road.

HOUSING

A survey which I made in 1948, showed that there were 104 houses in the ecclesiastical parish, of which 8 have been built by the County

Council during the present century.† It is almost certain that more
would have been built, had not the water supply been so difficult.
Apart from two houses now in more or less ruinous state, viz.
Westside Cottage and Tillyhowes Cottage (a potato and manure
store) and one known as Banchory Hillock, of which there is no
longer any trace, the number of houses is much as it was.

There are very few cases of overcrowding. By generally accepted
standards at the present time the housing is substandard. But the
number of farm houses with greatly improved cooking facilities in the
form of enclosed anthracite-burning cookers and cookers fired by gas
from portable cylinders is on the increase. Some have tiled fire-places,
but these are still the exception. In nearly every case where the people
are able to do so, the houses and gardens are cleanly and tidily kept. In
writing of the state of the buildings themselves it must not be
overlooked that in this generation the taxes upon landed proprietors
are exceedingly heavy, as are the costs of repairs to property and
improvements.

FARMS AND CROFTS

On Banchory estate these are let to tenants. There is a trend towards
working a larger area of land than was once the case. For example, the
tenant of Butterywells is also tenant of Cranhill, and has let the house
there to people not connected with agriculture in the district. The
farms are chiefly dairy farms, due to their proximity to Aberdeen. The
farmers used to retail their milk in the city, but for some years now it
has been collected by motor lorries from the farms daily. On this
estate, through an arrangement with the proprietor, those tenants who
desire to bring their byres etc. up to the standards required by the
regulations for T.T. milk are carrying out this work at their own
expense, some of them by their own labour. In the case of Arnwell
farm, the tenant has preferred to change over to poultry and pigs. For
the former he erected two large sheds composed of ex- W.D. sheds
(prefabricated buildings). The hens were at first kept in laying
'batteries', but are now on deep litter. Crops are barley, potatoes, oats,
hay, turnips, cabbages for feeding cattle. Arnwell has a small field of
strawberries, while the tenant of Nether Brandsmyres, who has
connections with a wholesale vegetable business in Aberdeen, grows a
quantity of vegetables in his fields.

On Ardoe estate, the property of Ardoe (Deeside) Ltd., the
following farms are now owned by the farmer who was previously
the tenant:— Jameston, farm and cottage, Scatterburn, farm and
cottages, Jockston and Townhead, farms and cottages. The South

† The corresponding figure for the civil parish (including Portlethen) was 357
houses in 1950.

Lodge, formerly the forester's house, is also sold to a private owner, as are two cottages at Craighead, which are now renovated and converted to make one dwellinghouse. On this estate, too, the farms are dairies, except Easter Ardoe, and the crops grown are the same as on the lands of Banchory.

MECHANISATION

Nearly every place, however small, has a tractor and modern implements. There are very few horses at work in the parish. The change-over has been made possible by the prosperous state of agriculture during the Second World War and in the post-war years, and desirable by the present regulations, which permit farm servants to have complete weekends off duty, or to claim increased remuneration in lieu. On the larger dairy farms this is a serious matter as, where the bothy system is in operation, the farmer may find himself responsible for the whole of his stock from mid-day on Saturday till Monday morning. The majority of farmers own motor cars, which are pressed into service for the farm, as well as for the convenience of the farmer and his family. All farms now have milking machines. There is a mobile threshing mill at Jameston farm, and a potato planting machine at Arnwell. Both these are hired to other farmers in this parish and in others. Combine harvesters are used occasionally, but not owned by local farmers.

OTHER CHANGES

In addition to the changes already noted incidentally, the following seem worthy of record:—

1. ARDOE HALL

Erected by A.M. Ogston, Esq., of Ardoe, an elder of the parish church congregation, and presented to the Kirk Session in trust for the congregation of the established church of Banchory-Devenick, and for the benefit of the area generally. Mr Ogston also gave an endowment of £150 to be invested for the maintenance of the building, which is of corrugated metal sheets, lined with wood.

2. ALTERATION TO ROAD JUNCTION

The heavy traffic of modern times on the South Deeside road made it desirable that the junction at the foot of the Kirkbrae should be altered in the interests of safety. The alteration was carried out in 1948 by the County Council, who purchased a portion of the glebe for the purpose.

3. LOCUS OF POST OFFICE

When the post-mistress of the sub-post office retired in 1948, the G.P.O. had the locus changed to the small general store at the cross-roads. This is the only shop in the parish.

4. ST DEVENICK'S BRIDGE

The maintenance of this bridge, which during the present century has been an increasing problem for the Kirk Session, is now, after much negotiation, to be taken over on a year-to-year basis by Aberdeen District Council. Lower Deeside District Council felt that, proportionately, the people in their area made practically no use of the bridge, and eventually declined to offer help. Taking all facts into consideration, their view is correct, as the main use of the bridge is now for walks at the week-end by the citizens of Aberdeen. There are very few members of the congregation now in Cults, which is well served by two churches of the Church of Scotland and a Scottish Episcopal Church.

LOCAL ENDOWMENTS

The parish church has endowments for stipend which amount to a total of under £300, including the rent from the glebe. Of this total approximately £200 is standardised stipend. The Kirk Session also hold funds bequeathed to them as trustees for the poor of the congregation and parish; care of graves in the parish and St Devenick's on the Hill (formerly Free Church) churchyards; upkeep of St Devenick's Bridge; upkeep of Ardoe Hall; and upkeep of the church buildings. Endowments which were held for educational purposes have now been transferred to the Education Committee of the County Council.

CHURCH HISTORY

The Disruption of 1843 resulted in a Free Church being erected in the parish, approximately ¾ mile south of the old parish church. Alexander Thomson, Esq., of Banchory, who granted the site for this building also gave sites for a Manse, with the usual offices, a schoolmaster's house and a stable for the use of those coming to church — this building is across the road from the church and is in a very bad state, modern transport having made it redundant. A small part of it, at the east end, is used as a store for tools etc. for the churchyard. There was also a small school attached to the Free Church. The rooms are still used for Sunday school, but the day school has been closed since 1863. The congregations continued as separate units till 1935. Both churches are still being used for divine service, on alternate Sundays — 5th Sundays also alternate.

The residence of the parish minister is at present St Devenick's on the Hill (former Free Church) manse. The basis of Union left the question of the manse of the parish undecided till the death of the Rev. Andrew Dickson, who retired from St Devenick's on the Hill in the interests of Union. The Old Manse was let — the surplus rent to provide part of Mr Dickson's retiring allowance. The congregation ultimately decided in favour of the Old Manse, but cannot obtain occupancy, due to the tenant choosing to use the provisions of the Rent Restriction Act.

The delimitation of the parish area has not yet resulted in a similar curtailment of the area in which members of the congregation reside. A recent investigation showed that the distribution was as follows:—
(1) Delimited parish area 226; (2) Aberdeen city 111; (3) Cults, east and west 49; (4) Maryculter, Nigg, Portlethen 82. This has two rather serious results. (1) It is difficult to achieve any sense of real fellowship in a congregation so widely dispersed. (2) Attendance at divine service is small in comparison with the total membership, and from the records there appears to be no great tradition of church attendance in the parish. It is no great assistance in this direction that the wound of the Disruption is slow to heal.

RECONSTRUCTION OF OLD PARISH CHURCH

The church was in need of extensive repairs in the 1920s. It was eventually reconstructed in 1929-30. The interior arrangements now show that an attempt was made, by removing the gallery, which was on the east, north and west; by altering the position of the pulpit and organ from the middle of the south wall to the east; by building up the entrance door in the east wall and installing a large gothic window; and by placing the pews facing east instead of south, east and west, as formerly, to make the building conform to an ecclesiastical type that was not intended by its previous architect. The four large windows on the south, and the large expanse of plain wall, relieved only by the two small (formerly gallery) windows on the north, give it rather an unbalanced appearance. The prevailing tendency today in respect of such restorations is to restore the buildings as far as possible to their original design — a more commendable practice resulting in the buildings retaining the design of their period, and therefore less likely to contain conflicting styles of architecture.

WAR MEMORIALS

In the Old Parish Church and St Devenick's on the Hill memorials to those who lost their lives in the First World War were erected. The memorial for the Second World War is in St Devenick's on the Hill — the plate being placed in that church as those who fell were mostly associated with it. It was not to the credit of the parish that subscriptions came in slowly and after repeated appeals. Eventually, it was only possible to provide a simple plaque in bronze.

YOUTH ORGANISATIONS

(a) Church: Sunday schools at St Devenick's on the Hill and in the Bothy at Ardoe Gardens. Bible Class. Girl's Association. (b) Community: (connected with the church): Boy Scouts and Wolf Cubs, Girl Guides and Brownies. In common with most country parishes at the present time, there is difficulty here in finding suitable men and women to undertake leadership in these organisations — the three organisations for girls have been under the leadership of one person for some time, but it is hoped that the position may be eased as girls take up training, for which there is opportunity in Aberdeen.

WOMEN'S ORGANISATIONS

(a) Church: There is a branch of the Woman's Guild, which is active, and meets monthly, with an average attendance of 20-35. (b) Community: There are two branches of the Women's Rural Institute, one meeting in the school, and the other in Ardoe Hall, monthly. The average attendance is the same as that of the Guild, and both branches have a number of members who do not reside in the parish.

In connection with the church, but run by an independent committee of management, a social club was begun by the Rev. M. Cunningham Wilson, B.D., who undertook a short term ministry in the Old Parish Church prior to the Union of 1935. It was then a men's club, which was in abeyance during the war. It was revived in 1946, and later a joint evening for men and women was begun. The activities are social and recreational. A small library is now supplied from the County Library. Dances are held on Saturday evenings to augment funds, and the Kirk Session have been grateful for sums donated by the club for hall improvements, including one half of the cost of installing an electric generating plant, and wiring and fittings. It is extremely unfortunate that the only suitable meeting-place for such a club is Ardoe Hall, which is situated on the north edge of the parish. This results in the club serving the Ardoe area, and also an area north of the Dee, rather than the whole parish.

The younger men and women in the southerly part of the parish attend evening classes in the school, but the attendance is not large.

YOUNG FARMER'S CLUB

A club for the young people connected with farming ran for about two years after the end of the war in 1945, but failed to keep sufficient interest to warrant its being continued.

These organisations organise variety concerts, mostly provided by concert parties from Aberdeen, dramatic shows — chiefly of the 'Scottish comedy' variety — whist drives, sales of work, etc. in support of their activities. During the past few years, the social club has been particularly active in having entertainments of rather a better order than are usually presented in country areas, and these have been very well received. Nearly all functions are very well attended and supported.

WAY OF LIFE

Generally speaking, the people in the area enjoy good health and work conscientiously. Most are employed in agriculture, and some of the farms — indeed most — are worked by the family themselves, with the assistance of one or two men. Some of the young men and women are engaged in various occupations with firms in Aberdeen, in shops, offices, stores and garages, and either cycle to work or make use of the service buses which run on the South Deeside road, the Stonehaven *via* Netherley road, and the main south road, on which there is a half-hourly service from Aberdeen and return. Nearly all, except those confined to their homes by infirmity, join in the social functions of the parish with enthusiasm. A number are now spending their summer holiday in bus tours to the Highlands and the west, and in some cases to England. Most people did not travel very far afield before the Second World War.

No serious crime has occurred during the years (five and a half) since I came to the parish, and as there is no public house in the area, or licensed premises apart from Ardoe House Hotel, cases of excessive drunkenness do not come readily to one's notice. Custom has it that special occasions — weddings, sometimes baptisms, New Year —

must be celebrated in the traditional manner — 'feet washing', the custom of blackening the feet of persons about to be married, is pursued with enthusiasm. The number of illegitimate children born, and the number of marriages which are hastened by the pregnancy of the girl, is not to the credit of the community, but the number does not seem to have varied much according to Kirk Session records of past days. The record looks a bit cleaner in the twentieth century, as the Session has ceased to 'compear' the offenders. Any 'discipline', along with a host of other duties, is tacitly left to the minister.

It is difficult to estimate how much Christianity means to the people. They do not talk readily of their faith, but parents are usually anxious for their children to have the benefit of Sunday school teaching. On the other hand, there appears to be a widespread lack of a sense of responsibility, both in parents towards the vows and duties of Church membership, and in the young people towards their organisations. Any pretext is a good enough reason for neglect of duty in these directions. But it must not be left unsaid that there is always a kindly welcome for the minister on his round of visitation, and that the church generally has the good-will of the people.

Though the people have the advantage of a daily newspaper and radio, and proximity to Aberdeen, whose entertainments they patronise, their interest is primarily and chiefly in the north-east to which they belong — apart from those who have been abroad or who have relatives abroad. Nearly all are concerned about the present unsettlement, but it seems to be a personal concern. Thanks to the schemes for National Assistance, there is no extreme poverty in the parish as it was once known. On the whole, the community appears much more prosperous, and work much easier, than it was in this parish even twenty years ago.

I have to acknowledge the valuable assistance of David Stewart, Esq., of Banchory and Leggart, who kindly revised this Account, and offered several interesting suggestions, which are included.

August 1951

THE QUOAD SACRA PARISH OF PORTLETHEN

by the Rev. Alexander Dunn, B.D.

SITUATION

The seaward side of the parish of Banchory-Devenick is known as the parish of Portlethen—*quoad sacra*—and the period covered by the present *Statistical Account* is approximately that which represents Portlethen's existence as a separate parish. The Rev. Wm. Law, who was assistant to Dr. Morison at Banchory-Devenick, was ordained as the first minister in charge of Portlethen in 1840, and the church itself was erected to full status in 1856.

The parish of Portlethen is roughly 4 miles long and extends 2-3 miles inland. Starting at the S.E. corner of the parish and proceeding north along the coast, one comes first of all to the small fishing village of Downies in the estate of Clashfarquhar, formerly owned by the Thomsons of Banchory and latterly by the University of Aberdeen. About a mile to the north lies the village of Portlethen, in the estate of that name, which was for many years in the possession of the family of Gammel. Still further to the north is the village of Findon, which at one time was the most important part of the parish. It was for a long time owned by the Menzies family before passing into the possession of the Piries.

The main Stonehaven-Aberdeen road runs parallel with the coast, about one mile from the sea. On the west side of it, six miles from Aberdeen, is a little cluster of houses known as Hillside and dominated by Hillside House, for long in the possession of the Shand family and occupied for many years by the Walker family. After 1945 it was, for a time, used as a hotel but it is now occupied by Mr. Wm. Hall, farmer.

The majority of the people in the parish, especially those who are younger, work in Aberdeen and an excellent bus service enables them to travel daily. The journey takes no more than twenty minutes and is reasonably cheap. In the parish interest is divided, as in earlier years, between agriculture and fishing, the former predominating. With the advent of the steam trawler and the fishing industry becoming centralised in Aberdeen, the old family-manned boats engaged in line fishing vanished slowly and by the time of the First World War they had almost disappeared. The villages, once so thriving and populous, declined as the younger fishermen and their families made their way to Torry or Footdee or elsewhere in Aberdeen.

NOTED CATTLE BREEDERS

On the agricultural side, the main feature of the past century has been the almost total disappearance of the small croft, absorbed into the larger farms, few of which, however, are really extensive. The largest is Mains of Portlethen, which runs to about 300 acres; most of the others are around 100 acres. As in most farming communities, business is at present prosperous, after many hard and difficult years. The majority of the farmers now engage in dairying, and with the various estates being sold in the past few years, most of the farms are in the possession of the occupiers.

One or two farmers, however, continue to concentrate on beef, notably Mr. Jas. Nicol of Clashfarquhar, who worthily maintains the reputation for 'Blacks', so long borne by the Walker family of Mains of Portlethen and Hillside House. The Walkers were undoubtedly the best known family in the district during the past century, not only because of the great renown they won in agricultural circles but also because of their interest in, and development of, the affairs of Portlethen. Mr. Robert Walker (d.1873) erected a memorial stone 'in memory of Chas. A. Ewen, schoolmaster in this district for upward of 40 years, who died 29th November, 1855, aged 64.' Mr.Walker also laid the foundations of the land valuation business, still carried on under the name of Walker & Duncan, Golden Square, Aberdeen.

The Aberdeen Angus herd of cattle is supposed to be the oldest in Scotland, a herd being in existence at Mains of Portlethen in 1780. Referring to Mr. Walker's success in the showyard, Mr. McCombie in *Cattle and Cattle Breeders* says 'It would be endless to attempt to sum up his victories — local, national and international — they are spread over such a large surface.'

Robert Walker's work and reputation were carried on with distinction by Mr. G. J. Walker, who not only excelled in the field of agriculture but proved a wonderful benefactor to Portlethen generally. He presented the church with communion vessels in 1886 and a harmonium in 1889. A new roadway to the church was built in 1897, on the advice and the plan of Mr. Walker, and in 1898 a pipe organ was also presented. Mr. Walker likewise designed the local hall, known as the Jubilee Hall, the foundation stone of which was laid in 1889. It is a spacious building over 70ft in length and has proved of immense value in the parish. A keen volunteer and crack shot, Mr.

Walker commanded the first volunteer camp in Scotland on the Hill of Clochandighter in June 1869. He was presented with an illuminated address in 1898 by the people of Portlethen in recognition of his services. He died in 1914. His son, Mr. Robert Walker, who died a few years ago, carried on the farm at Mains of Portlethen, although he himself resided outside the parish.

The fame of the Aberdeen Angus cattle is now worthily maintained by another very old Portlethen family — the Nicols of Clashfarquhar (farquhars = hollow), who carried off the supreme Championship R.A.S.E. in 1950 and the Royal Highland the same year.

Mains of Portlethen is now occupied by Mr. John Shand, one of the leading farmers in the north-east and Chairman of the N. E. Agriculture Committee. He has a noted herd of Friesians, thereby carrying on the reputation of the late Mr. James Findlay of Balquharn (i.e. the farm inside the cairn). Among other outstanding names are the Alexanders of Causeyport which is situated on what was at one time a large marshy piece of land called the Haremoss. From this moss peats were conveyed to Aberdeen, whose citizens laid a firm 'causey' roadway over the moss in 1684 and built thereon a 'port' in order to uplift toll dues. Nicol of Barclayhill, Shepherd of Cairnrobin, Begg of Mill of Findon, Ritchie of Mains of Findon, Strachan of Whitebrunt-land, Hutcheon of Bourtreebush, Watson of Cookston and Duncan of Blackhill have farmed extensively in the district during the past century, in recent years concentrating mainly on dairy farming. The farms are almost completely mechanised and few horses survive. Incidentally, it is interesting to note that no longer ago than March 1918 there were no motor lorries in the district, and only one motor car, which belonged to Mr. Jas. Findlay of Balquharn.

FISHING

The story of the fishing villages — Findon, Portlethen and Downies — is in two parts — a story of intense activity and abundant life, of prosperity and numerous families in the first half of the period covered by this *Account* — of crowded villages, of considerable numbers of yawls and smaller boats, most of which were usually run as a family concern, being manned by members of the same family who worked the boats, sharing expenses and profits, all busily engaged in line fishing and in curing. However, with the coming of the steam drifter and trawler and the general changes which resulted with the centralis-ation of the fishing industry in Aberdeen, fishing gradually died out in the villages and the fishing familes, the younger generation in particular, made their homes in that city, especially in the Torry district.

The following table gives a good picture of the changing course of events during the past century:—

		No. of Boats	No. of Fishermen
1855	FINDON	21	50
	PORTLETHEN	27	68
	DOWNIES	18	45
1881	FINDON	14	39
	PORTLETHEN	37	89
	DOWNIES	17	45
1928	FINDON	0	0
	PORTLETHEN	2	8
	DOWNIES	4	11

Most widely known by reason of its celebrated Haddie is Findon. Just prior to the First World War almost all the inhabitants of the village were engaged at the smoking and on Fridays a special van was required at the railway station in order to take the fish creels and baskets of Finnan Haddies to Aberdeen for the market. Curing was still carried on in Portlethen village by the Craig family as late as 1940, but ceased during the war and has never been resumed.

There are still many of the fishing families resident in the villages. They are easily recognised by name, the most common of which are Buchan, Main, Leiper, Wood and Craig, to quote only a few. Their houses, which are for the most part in their own possession, are scrupulously clean and tidy and very attractive, both oustide and in. They are almost all lit by electricity and have been modernised in recent years. A reminder of the old curing days is seen in the low black tarred sheds, with their tall wide chimneys, built close by the dwelling houses. There, in the wide open hearths, were placed dozens of fish, all neatly skewered, and cured in the smoke which arose from slowly burning peats, upon which, at judicious intervals, was cast a handful of sawdust. The fisher folks are exceedingly kindly and hospitable, and loyal and faithful in attendance at and support of the Church. A few of them still go out in small boats, but the main fishing interest in the district is in salmon fishing. There is a station at Findon and one at Portlethen, employing six or seven of a crew, both of which are operated by members of the well-known Powrie family.

TOLL OF THE SEA

The seas, of course, always exact their toll and the villages, especially the Downies, have known their share of sorrow and disaster during the past century. The Rev. Wm. Law, first minister of Portlethen, records in his diary for April 8th 1847: 'This day a Portlethen fishing boat was lost. It contained five men — three brothers of the name Leiper and two brothers of the name Craig, leaving five widows and twenty-eight children.' In 1848 two fishermen of the name Craig drowned off Cove. One of the most serious disasters of all took place in April 1880, when the village of Downies lost nine men by the swamping of a yawl and a boat. Six members of the Wood family went down in the yawl *Isabella* and two further members of the same family and a fisherman named Main were lost in the boat *Twilight*. A subscription list for the dependents was opened by Mr. Walker of Hillside House, which was eventually absorbed in a central fund under the chairmanship of Mr. R. W. Duff M.P. to help families not only in the Downies but also in Footdee and Newtonhill, where ten men were lost. A few years later on 20th July 1891, the Downies again suffered when the boat *Rose in June* went down with two young lads on board — Alexander Wood, aged 23, and William Main, aged 18. January 30th 1911 again saw loss of life off the Downies when the boat *Alexander and James* sank with three brothers — James, John and Andrew Wood.

Five years earlier, in the same month, Portlethen was the scene of a similar loss of life when the yawl *Sea Hawk* was overturned and her crew of six thrown into the sea. Of these men, R. Main, skipper, A Leiper and G. Main were lost. A subscription list in aid of dependents was opened by Mr. Walker of Hillside House and within a month had reached a total of over £200. The balance of that money is still administered by the church as the Boat Disaster Fund, which yields an interest of £3.10/- per annum.

Just after the First War the rocks off Findon and Portlethen were the scenes of several accidents to trawlers, which ran aground in dense fog. The result was that three new Coastguard houses were erected at Findon village, with a look-out post built on a prominent rock.

QUARRY

About the same time great things were expected by Portlethen inhabitants when Mr. Stewart, granite merchant of Aberdeen, started work at Clochandighter Quarry, in the south-west corner of the parish. Unfortunately, due either to high transport costs or the unsuitability of the stone, the work was discontinued after a few years and has not been resumed.

The only other occasion on which considerable local labour was employed was the building of the joint railway, which passes through the parish and which was completed about the middle of the last century.

THE TWO WARS

Before the First World War Portlethen had a very strong detachment of volunteers. The Walker family were especially keen in the movement and were noted shots. Due to their enthusiasm and help, an excellent rifle range was constructed near the sea close by the Mains of Portlethen. Here rifle practice took place almost every Saturday, a training which stood in good stead the large numbers of young men who were called to the colours. The fishing villages naturally supplied many men for naval and mine-sweeping duties. The call to serve was answered no less readily in the last war, when over one hundred men and women joined up from the parish. A memorial which bears the names of the fallen of both wars stands close beside the church and is visible over a wide area.

The greatest change in the parish in recent years was caused by the recent war. A radar station was set up at Schoolhill and large numbers of men and women were stationed in the parish, both at Schoolhill and at Portlethen Cross Roads. With the end of hostilities and the departure of the serving men and women the huts were occupied by the homeless. The camps were eventually taken over by the County Council and the tenancy put on a proper footing. This naturally added considerably to the population of the parish, which was at its maximum when the fishing villages were in full employ.

HOUSING

Apart from a few houses near the railway station which were built just prior to 1914 by Mr. John Watt, a local builder, and the double bungalow type houses erected by the County Council in the period between the wars, very little in the way of building has taken place. There have been no housing schemes or anything of a like nature, due mainly to the lack of a proper water supply. This defect is being remedied at the present time by the Kincorth Water Scheme, whereby the local Council are bringing water to all the villages between Aberdeen and Stonehaven. Once water and drainage are assured, building on a large scale will be entered upon in the fields near the school and station, which area is estimated as having a probable population of over 400 by the year 1970. Under the present scheme no development will take place in the villages. The chances are that the population there will gradually decline. In any case they are rather far from the main road and transport and, as most of the young people work in Aberdeen, it is not surprising that they should seek to make their homes either in that city or at least close by a bus route.

CHURCH

The first building of any note was that opened by Dr. Morison in 1844, along with a manse and offices. The foundation stone was laid by Dr. Morison on 4th July 1843, on the site of the old chapel, which had been a place of worship for upwards of 170 years. At first it was occupied by itinerant preachers, but since 1800 it has been regularly supplied by licentiates of the Church of Scotland and since 1840 by an ordained minister. In 1856 the church was erected a parish church (*quoad sacra*) with a seating capacity of 800.

The first minister was Rev. Wm. Law who, acting as assistant to Dr. Morison, was appointed preacher at Portlethen in 1827, ordained in 1840, and became minister of the parish in 1856, where he continued until applying for a colleague and successor in 1868. Mr. Law, who was originally schoolmaster at Maryculter where he is buried, was greatly respected by his congregation and much loved by his pupils, one of whom held Mr. Law in such regard that he built a ship's model and presented it to him. Mr. Law had it placed in the church, where it occupies a position of prominence even to this day. The ship, which is called *The Rev. Wm. Law*, was repainted and rigged out anew when the church was renovated in 1938, at the instigation of one of the elders, Mr. James Findlay. On his death last year, it was found that Mr. Findlay had bequeathed to the Kirk Session a sum of money, the interest on which was to be devoted to keeping the ship in good repair for all time.

Mr. Law was succeeded in 1870 by the Rev. Wm. Bruce of Finzean. A man of intense sympathy for and interest in his parishioners, and one who had more than a slight knowledge of medicine, Mr. Bruce proved a friend indeed to many in his parish both as minister and doctor and his death in 1882, at the early age of 49, was a great loss to the parish.

The Rev. Alexander Robertson Grant, M.A. exercised a most powerful ministry for the next 53 years. The manse was greatly improved and heightened, additional endowments were secured for the church and the culmination came in 1938 when Mr. Grant presented his colleague and successor with a church completely reconstructed and renovated, making it one of the most attractive and modern places of worship in the north-east. Mr. Grant was succeeded in 1939 by the present minister, the Rev. Alexander Dunn, B.D. It will thus be seen that the church of Portlethen has been the one and only charge for all its ministers — a fact which speaks volumes for the loyalty, affection and understanding of a congregation which still finds joy in going up to the House of God and in bringing to its support the service of its life and means. The church has known many benefactors. Dr. Morison, who did so much for the parish, presented the congregation with two communion cups. Two pewter plates were presented by Catherine Smith of Cookston, in memory of her parents. In 1886 Mr. G. J. Walker also gifted two cups and plates, while in recent years Mr. David Donaldson, J.P., of Whincairn, has gifted a beautiful memorial window in memory of his parents. Mr. A.G. Ritchie has presented a baptismal font, Mr. Watson of Cookston, individual cups, and Mr. Findlay, late of Balquharn, communion chairs. In addition various gifts of money have been bequeathed from Mr. Robert Shand, Miss Glashan, Miss Walker, Mr. Kenn and Mr. Findlay for various church objects.

SCHOOLS

Centralisation has been the order of the day in the scholastic line. For many years there were no fewer than five schools in the district, all of which were well attended, especially when the fishing villages were fully occupied. Thus, in 1854, we find in the parish a school at Portlethen (89 pupils), Downies (71 pupils), Findon (63 pupils), Badentoy (54 pupils) and Hillside (41 pupils), as well as a few private pupils, bringing the total number of children attending school in the parish to close on 400. Gradually, almost imperceptibly, the various schools closed down, until today there is but one school, situated near the Portlethen railway station, on the site of Dr. Morison's school, which he had built in 1829. There have been some excellent teachers in office, including Charles A. Ewen, David Silver, John Watt, Charles Meston, W. Hunter, J. Stalker, A. Gauld and T. G. Little. The school has now the status of a Junior Secondary and has been twice extended and enlarged since 1945.

ANTIQUITIES

The most remarkable piece of antiquity in the parish is a Druidical temple near the farm of Craighead. It seems to have been a place of burial. There is no trace of sculpture or inscriptions, nor of flint, knives or weapons. A few stone coffins have been found in various parts of the parish, notably at Clashfarquhar near Downies village.

The church is surrounded by a burial ground, which was under the care of the Kirk Session until 1950, when it was taken over by Kincardineshire County Council. There are many grave-stones, but all are of a late date. Thus a table-shaped stone on which a boat in full sail is represented with a crew of six, bears the name James Leiper, white fisher, and the date 1840.

WAY OF LIFE

The climate is bracing and vigorous — cold but with a fair share of sunshine and not too much rain. Crops are good and gardens not only attractive but productive; indeed, one of the features is the skill and the knowledge which the individual householder brings to his work in his own garden. The health of the people is good and death usually occurs at a fairly advanced age.

This is an encouraging parish, containing a thrifty hard-working people. They are well-read, intelligent and possessed of good sound common sense. They still have regard to the higher things of life, are sober and temperate in word and way and, for the most part, give a sincere service and support to their church and to all worth-while objects. With exceptions, the children are clean, tidy and well behaved, excellent in their attendance, not only at Sunday School but also at church. Most parents make a sincere effort to teach them to love and respect what is right and decent and honest, thereby ensuring a foundation upon which they and the parish can continue to build with hope and promise and confidence that the best is yet to be.

June 1952

THE PARISH OF BANCHORY-TERNAN

by the Rev. T. Gemmell Campbell, M.A.

The parish is often called Upper Banchory in the older writings, as distinguished from Nether Banchory (Banchory-Devenick). It has been usual to associate the name 'Banchory' with the old church site beside the river, a very beautiful site before the railway was made. The name has its two occurrences on Deeside and also several in Aberdeenshire, in compound forms like Edinbanchory. There are several occurrences in the Highlands as Banchor, and in Ireland and Wales as Bangour and Bangor. The name has, however, not been explained; at least, all efforts to reach a derivation appear conjectural. Beannchar, plentiful in Ireland, is translated by Joyce (*Place-names of Ireland*) as 'pinnacle'. The same word is translated by Watson (*Celtic place-names of Scotland*, 1926) as 'horncast', and he points out that at Banchory-Ternan on Dee the river forms two broad sweeping symmetrical horns. As to the form Banchory, Banchory-Ternan was of old Bennchar; other place-names vary between Banchor and Banchory.

As for the saint's name Ternan (A.D.431), probably A.P. Forbes, Bishop of Brechin, gives us all that is known in his *Kalendars of Scottish Saints*. What has come down to us of the memory of S. Ternanus or Terrenanus confirms the inference which the scanty remains of the Pictish language suggest regarding the connection between that race and the rest of the Celtic family. There seems no reason to doubt the tradition that this saint was the High Bishop of the Picts, yet distinct traces of him are found in Ireland. He is the Torannan or Mo-Thoren of the *Kalendars*. In the east, Torannan is specially connected with Banchory-Ternan on the Dee, and this is the reason why he is styled 'abb Benncair' — abbot of Bennchar — in the note in Gorman and in the *Martyrology of Donegal*, edited by J.H. Todd. The *Breviary of Aberdeen* devotes 6 lections to his history and may be regarded as authentic, so far as it relates to his parentage and his baptism by S. Palladius. The legend is that S. Ternan was born of noble parents in the province of Myrnia and S. Palladius, divinely warned, baptised him. Hearing of the fame of S. Gregory the Great, he betook himself to Rome to submit himself to his discipline. After seven years the Pope raised him to the episcopate, and sent him back to his own country to preach the gospel to the unbelievers there. A bell, given him by the Pope, miraculously followed him till he reached Albania. Of his book of the gospels, the volume containing S. Matthew was preserved at Banquhory. His head was also preserved there and the skin of the part where he had been tonsured and anointed existed 1100 years after, and had been seen by the compiler of the Aberdeen *Martyrology* about 1530. He was the contemporary of S. Macharius, and a most devout lover of solitude (*Mart. Aberd.*). The miraculous bell, called the Ronnecht, alluded to in the legend, was preserved at Banchory-Ternan till the Reformation. A monstrance containing his relics was in the treasury of the Church of Aberdeen (*Regist. Episcop. Aberd.*, ii, p.185). Thomas Innes places his seat of episcopal government at Abernethy in Strathearn (*Civil and Eccl. Hist.*, p.187).

EXTENT

Occupying the north-west corner of Kincardineshire, Banchory-Ternan was partly in Aberdeenshire till 1891, when the Boundary Commissioners transferred to the County of Kincardine its Aberdeenshire portion (on the estate of Leys). Banchory-Ternan is the only Kincardineshire parish that extends to the north of the Dee, which divides it into two unequal parts — the larger and wider, roughly deltoid in form, to the north; the smaller and narrower tapering southward from the river. The northern and southern ends of the parish are 9 miles apart, the eastern and western extremities over 8 miles apart. The land area is 20,083 acres, of which the burgh of Banchory accounts for 545 acres. From 150 to 250 feet above sea-level along the Dee, the surface rises to over 1500 feet on the Hill of Fare to the north, and to over 800 feet (Craig of Affrusk) to the south. The Feugh joins the Dee opposite Banchory. The adjoining parishes are:— Midmar (to the north), Echt (north-east), Drumoak (east), Kincardine O'Neil (north-west), Birse (west) — all these being in Aberdeenshire; Strachan (south-west) and Durris (south-east and south) in Kincardineshire.

NATURAL HISTORY

In the last few years the great amount of timber felling has naturally reduced the number of woodland birds, such as the goldcrest, long tailed tit, coal tit, etc. However, it is gratifying to know that the bullfinch seems to be increasing and in spring 1950 the flocks of lapwings are larger than since the devastating winter of 1946-47, when the plovers suffered great losses. The great spotted woodpecker is increasing in the parish despite the diminishing timber, but so far there

D

are no records of its smaller cousin, the lesser spotted woodpecker. Among the birds of prey, that rare and interesting bird, the honey buzzard, was seen in Crathes woods in 1949. There is no doubt that the increased use of artificial fertilisers on farm lands has led to a decrease in many passerine birds — obviously ground treated with chemical fertilisers cannot contain the 'humus' and insect life found in land 'dunged' as formerly. Indeed, it is very clear that this is causing more centralisation of the flocking birds in winter. Formerly, almost every field had its quota of bird life — now fields are often deserted, but when one comes to a district where the crofter still uses animal manure one will find more birds than before. It is gratifiying to record the rapid growth and progress of planting by the Forestry Commission. Here, animals and birds are finding cover that for some years has been lost to them and in another two or three decades the animal and bird life should be greatly increased. Curiously enough, far more foxes are about than for many years, but the badger is still very rare.

BOTANY

Perhaps the rarest plant in the parish is the charming little *Linnaea borealis*, very occasionally found in pine woods. Linnaea crawls along the ground with tiny pinkish-white and sweetly scented bells hanging down from an erect flower stalk, an inch or two high. The plant is said to resemble Linnaeus in its ways — being shy and retiring and avoiding the 'limelight'. The blue Lupine (L. *Nootkatensis*), of American origin, is believed to have been brought to Deeside by Queen Victoria from Windsor Castle in the forties of the last century. On some reaches between Banchory-Ternan and Park it has covered large stretches of shingle (for it can sprout and grow from the very sand) with its lovely foliage and handsome spikes of flower. V.J. Buchan Watt deals fully with the natural history of the parish in the *Book of Banchory*.

HISTORY OF THE LOCAL COMMUNITY

Banchory as we know it today dates from the year 1805. In that year the first sod in what is now the burgh area was cut in Bellfield to prepare for the erection of the first 'stane and lime' house in Banchory, for a feuar named William Shaw, postmaster. This feu extended from opposite Brae Villa to the Douglas Arms. The second feuar was John Watson, a native of Braemar, who in 1807 feued a strip of ground in what is now High Street. The building presently known as the Dee Valley Cafe was the house in which John Watson lived and died. This feu extended from Corsee to Towerfield, backwards to Rosebank and westwards to Rosehill on Mount Street. John Watson, whose ambition was to make Banchory the 'most beautiful, populous and important place on Deeside' has been described as its 'greatest benefactor'. His dream of the day when Banchory would become a suburb of Aberdeen was virtually realised within a century. He was the founder of the John Watson Guild. The third feuar was William Ewan, whose ancestor, Ewan Macdonald, was one of two men who escaped the massacre of Glencoe and came to reside on Deeside. William Ewan's grandson was the late Baillie Alexander Ewan, for many years agent of the North of Scotland Bank in Station Road. The ground feued stretched from Arbeadie or Ewan Place northwards by Schoolhill and Ramsay Road. He farmed the whole of the land now occupied by that area. The oldest house remains only in the foundation of the tall house behind the garden at Ewan Place. William Ewan was a councillor and did much for the progress of Banchory. To the enterprise and vision of these three men whose surnames are still household words, enshrined in the names of houses and streets in the town, the present burgh of Banchory owes its origin.

LOCAL GOVERNMENT

Special praise, however, must be accorded to the second of these feuars — John Watson, who anticipated the formation of Banchory into a burgh by the inauguration of a Town Council. All residents in the district were eligible for membership by the payment of an entrance fee of 2/6d and thereafter an annual tax of 1/-. The affairs of the Council were managed by a Provost, Baillies, Town Councillors and a Dean of Guild. These officials were elected annually by the membership, known as Burgesses of Guild, but each election was preceded by a 'heckling meeting', at which candidates had to bear the brunt of a severe interrogation as to their claims to hold office. The first Provostship was offered to John Watson, but he declined it in favour of Mr. James Torry. The Town Council did much to improve the social conditions of the inhabitants, such as the lighting of the streets with gas in 1867 — free of charge — until street lighting was taken over by the Commissioners of Police in 1885; the inauguration of a Coal Fund, disbursed yearly for the deserving poor of the parish; and the erection of a Town Hall in 1873. This has since been extended to include a large airy hall with commodious stage and gallery, capable of seating 500 persons; a smaller hall with accommodation is also provided for a married hallkeeper.

With the adoption of the Lindsay Act in 1885, the shadow Town Council had to make way for a popularly elected Board of Police Commissioners, but it re-constituted itself into a corporate body under the name of 'The John Watson Guild'. That body still administered certain charities but its 'temporal sovereignty' was restricted to the Banchory Town Hall. (The Town Hall was recently transferred to the Town Council under an agreement entered into between the two bodies).

The County Council was set up under the Local Government (Scotland) Act 1889. Its powers were greatly extended under the Local Government (Scotland) Act 1929. The Parish Council for the parish of Banchory-Ternan ceased to exist at 16 May 1930, most of its functions, including poor law, going to the County Council and the remainder to the District Council. The functions of the District Council are minor and include such matters as maintenance of rights-of-way and allotments and parish trusts, except trusts relating to the poor, to churchyards and to burial grounds. The area of the Upper Deeside District Committee, which covered the parishes of Durris, Strachan and Banchory-Ternan, is now covered by the Upper Deeside District Council. Up to 1929 there was only one County Councillor for the parish, but by an Order of the Secretary of State in that year, the parish was split into two Electoral Divisions, Banchory-Ternan North and Banchory-Ternan South. The boundary between the two areas is the railway line. The burgh itself has 3 representatives on the County Council.

The Town Council today consists of 9 members — namely the Provost, two Baillies, Treasurer, Dean of Guild and three Councillors. The officials consist of Town Clerk, Town Clerk Depute, Burgh Treasurer or Chamberlain — all part-time offices, together with the Burgh Surveyor, who is in full-time employment. Provosts of Banchory have been: John P. Bisset, John Blacklaws, Dr. James McHardy, Donald Munro, James M. Burnett, Charles R.F. McIntosh, William D. Horne, Alexander Durward — all of them public-spirited and progressive men.

CASTLES AND ESTATES

Several changes have occurred in the land holdings of the parish, and of the eight estates only two remain in the hands of the original families.

1. CRATHES CASTLE (estate of 12,025 acres)

Crathes Castle, pleasantly situated on the north bank of the Dee, about $2\frac{1}{2}$ miles east of Banchory, is the seat of the ancient family of Burnett of Leys, the Loch of Leys being the site of the original home of the family. On 28 March 1323 the lands of Leys were granted by King Robert I to Alexander Burnard of the Farningdound Burnards in Roxburghshire and since then have been held continuously by the family. Inheriting the Barony of Muchalls in the Mearns, in 1646, Sir Thomas obtained an Act of Parliament which transferred the Barony of Leys to this shire — thus the anomaly of the county boundary which exists to this day. Maj.-Gen. Sir James L. G. Burnett, the present owner, is the 13th Baronet and the 25th Laird. Crathes Castle, built between 1533-96, is a magnificent example of the L-plan (from late 14th century onwards), of the finest Scottish baronial design, elaborately decorated within and without. Early in the 18th century a new wing, the 'laigh house', was built and there have been more recent additions. In 1951 the Castle was handed over by Sir James and Lady Burnett to the National Trust for Scotland and the Scottish Gardens Committee (of the said Trust) has, at their suggestion, decided to establish a propagating centre there. Crathes, which is world-famous for its collection of shrubs and flowers, will be able to provide a wide variety of plants for use in developing and improving other gardens owned by the Trust.

2. TILQUHILLIE CASTLE

This lies about 2 miles south-east of the town, was the ancient home of the Douglas family and dates from 1575. Originally the lands belonged to the Abbot of Arbroath, but in 1479 they passed into the hands of the Douglases by the marriage of David Douglas, grandson of James, the second Lord of Dalkeith, to Janet, heiress of Walter Ogston of Tilquhillie. With the exception of a period of some 45 years when Mr. H. Lumsden of Aberdeen and subsequently his trustees were proprietors, the property has remained in the hands of the Douglas family. Tilquhillie Castle, built on the Z plan, semi-fortified and a good example of the Scottish mansion of the 16th century, is now used as a dwellinghouse by the tenant of the farm. The present owner is Major Sholto Douglas, who resides at Feugh Lodge.

3. BLACKHALL CASTLE

Approached by a long wooded avenue, Blackhall Castle stood on the south bank of the Dee some 2 miles west of Banchory and was built by Mr. J.T. Hay about 1884. The estate of Blackhall belonged for long to the old family of Russell, whose crest — a goat, life size, with the motto 'Che Sara Sara' (What will be, will be) — cut out in stone, adorned for many generations the top of the principal entrance gateway beside the bridge. This was, however, removed to Finzean half a century ago. Recently, the castle was sold to the Forestry Commission, who now use part of the farm lands for a nursery for

their young coniferous plants with which in due course they will plant
the hills denuded of their timber to supply the wants of two World
Wars. The Castle itself has been entirely demolished, the stones being
carted away by a contractor for use in the building of houses
elsewhere.

4. INVERY HOUSE (estate of 1808 acres)

On the Feugh, about 1¼ miles from the town, stands the mansion
house of Invery. The proprietor from 1807-17 was Mr. Skene of
Rubislaw, a life-long friend of Sir Walter Scott. And it was here in
the 'Gothic Room' that part of *Marmion* was written. Major James
Kerr is the present proprietor.

5. BANCHORY LODGE (estate of 1800 acres)

On the north bank of the Dee and commanding a magnificent view
of the Falls of Feugh, with Scolty and Tilquhillie in the background,
stands Banchory Lodge, for generations the property of the Burnett
family and their connections. The present handsome mansion house
was restored and enlarged in the 18th century by Gen. William
Burnett, a cadet of the House of Crathes, who after a brilliant military
career as equerry to Kings George III and IV, retired here and proved
a kind and considerate landlord. He devoted himself to the development of agriculture in the district. The last proprietor was Mr.
T.W.B.R. Bentinck, for the estate has now been broken up and the
mansion has reverted to its former use as a hotel. The property of
Banchory Lodge, which included Ardbeadie etc., was formerly
known as Cobleheugh — an inn with practically the only transit
across the Dee prior to the erection of the bridge in 1798.

6. INCHMARLO HOUSE (estate of 985 acres)

This stands about a mile west of Banchory. The lands, originally
church property, fell into the hands of the powerful family of Douglas
of Glenbervie. They were acquired in 1650 by James Douglas, a
younger son of Douglas of Tilquhillie, who soon succeeded to that
estate also. Built by Mr. John Douglas, the house was for almost a
century the property of the Davidson family, until it was purchased
by Mr. C.T. Cox. On the latter's death, the estate was divided into
three.

7. RAEMOIR HOUSE (estate of 4750 acres)

At the foot of the Hill of Fare on the south side, about 2¼ miles to
the north of Banchory, Raemoir House was originally erected by Mr.
John Hogg. In 1816 it was acquired by William Innes, a most
indulgent and enterprising landlord. Early in the 1920s the estate
changed hands from the Innes family to the first Viscount Cowdray,
who leased to a London company the house, which is now a
residential hotel with a high reputation.

8. GLASSEL HOUSE

Formerly the property of Mrs. Mitchell of Glassel, this is now
owned by an important breeder of Shorthorn cattle, Dr. Salvesen,
who also takes a keen interest in the famous rock garden there which
was made by his predecessor about the beginning of the century.

THE RISE OF BANCHORY

The development of Banchory — and for that matter of the Dee
valley — as a health and holiday resort had its real origin in the
selection of Balmoral as a royal residence, in the late forties of last
century, by a Royal Commission under Sir James Clark. Inquiry as to
rainfall and climate generally revealed that the valley of the Dee was
one of the driest parts of Scotland and that the climate was excellent
and the scenery unsurpassed. This selection secured for Upper Deeside
a fame that attracted visitors from every quarter of the country and
even from overseas, and in particular contributed largely to the choice
of Banchory as the site of the first sanatorium in Scotland. Besides, the
vast pine forests enriched the health-giving air by the quantity of
ozone given off, while the number of hours of sunshine on Deeside
during winter months exceeded that of the south of England.
Banchory's climate shows:— Mean temperature: January 38.7; July
59.9. Average temperature for June, July and August and September,
57.3. Mean annual rainfall 21.3 ins. Mean annual sunshine: 1397 hours.
Nordrach-on-Dee Sanatorium, founded by Dr. David Lawson in
1899, flourished and achieved a world-wide reputation, many distinguished people being patients. This did much to put Banchory on the
map and was a formative influence in increasing its trade and
developing its popularity.

The rise of Banchory was greatly promoted by the Deeside
Railway, opened in 1853 from Aberdeen to Banchory, and later
extended to Aboyne and Ballater. Soon the Highland villages, with
their 'but and ben' thatched cottages, disappeared. The enterprise not

only bore fruit in the agriculture and industries of the district, but created wholly novel conditions as well, and tended greatly to extend and enhance the importance of the burgh, capturing its timber trade and encouraging excursion traffic. The first royal journey was made on October 13, 1853, when Queen Victoria and the Prince Consort were leaving Balmoral for London. The royal party drove to Banchory. At the old station great preparations were made. A triumphal arch, with a crown in the centre, had been erected at the station entrance, and the platform covered with crimson cloth. The Queen was received on the platform by Mr. James Innes of Raemoir and the chairman and directors of the Deeside Railway, and a great crowd assembled. For the next seven years Banchory continued to be the arrival and starting point for the royal trains.

POPULATION

The population of the civil parish increased by about 1000 in each half of the 19th century, viz. (1801) 1,465; (1851) 2,462; (1901) 3,449. In 1951 it was 3,692, little short of the maximum (3,710) recorded in 1921. Census figures from 1891 onwards are:—

Year	Parish	Burgh	Landward
1891	3188	1400	1788
1901	3449	1475	1974
1911	3377	1633	1744
1921	3710	1776	1934
1931	3335	1690	1645
1951	3692	1958	1734

While the population of the burgh shows, for the most part, a steady growth, that of the landward area seems to fluctuate between two constants, reaching its lowest ebb in 1931. The rolls of the rural schools confirm this.

SEX DISTRIBUTION

In 1951 the male population in the parish numbered 1743 (as compared with 1516 in 1931 and 1690 in 1921), while females totalled 1949. Each Census reveals a preponderance of females, but the proportion is fairly well maintained. Percentage of male to female (= 100%) population in 1921 was 83.6%; and in 1951, 89.4. (In 1841 the corresponding percentage was 91.9). In the burgh the preponderance of females is more marked (1103 females to 855 males in

1951), but the disproportion of the sexes has lessened in recent years, the percentage of male to female (= 100%) population being for 1921 — 69.7; 1931 — 72.4; 1951 — 77.5

IMMIGRATION

About 20% of the population were born in the parish, 30% in the county and 50% outwith. Those born in the parish may seem relatively few, but it should be remembered that the majority of children belonging to Banchory are born at Torphins Maternity Hospital, Aberdeenshire — only a very small number go to Aberdeen. For example, the total number of births registered in the burgh in 1949 was 8, while those corrected for mother's residence was 36.

There is a large residential population in Banchory. It comprises retired civil servants from different parts of the world, some of whom reside permanently in Banchory, seeking warmer climes in the winter from time to time; together with people from varied walks of life who have retired from business in different parts of Britain; and those who still have business interests and travel to and from Aberdeen. Occasionally work brings in outsiders, such as ex-servicemen who have married local girls and found employment locally. These categories together represent the 50% born outwith.

Banchory is unable to provide adequate scope and opportunity for all its young people; consequently, those bent on making their way in the world, or following the call of a University career or profession, must seek the city. The various industries provide the main economic opportunity, together with the shops that line High Street, while hotels, boarding-houses etc. employ fairly large staffs. Quite a number of farmers' sons follow in their father's footsteps, and a large number of businesses carried on in Banchory today have been handed down from parents to children. In the employment of Paterson's sawmills are members of the third and fourth generations of the same families, whose fortunes have been continuously linked with those of the business. Very few have migrated.

ROADS

The most important highway in the parish is, of course, the North Deeside road, route A.93, which follows the line of the river fairly closely and was originally the turnpike road to Braemar.

Parallel to it and communicating with it by Raemoir road (A.980) there is the main Aberdeen-Lumphanan road, which serves a large part of the parish and runs for 5 miles along the southern base of the Hill of Fare, past Raemoir and the ruin of Cluny Crichton Castle

(1606). Passing under the Deeside railway between Glassel and Torphins, it keeps along the south side of the railway to Lumphanan.

Another important highway in the parish is the South Deeside road, route A.943. Leaving the town on the south, it crosses the Bridge of Dee and the Bridge of Feugh — that strong and interesting little structure set amidst the most romantic scenery — and follows the river closely to Aberdeen. It is only less important than the North Deeside road for quality and convenience, while it is superior to it, on the whole, for its charming scenery and outlook. Branching off to the south, about a mile downstream, is the Slug road (A.959) which twists and twines its way over Cairn-mon-Earn and thence down through stern solitary country to the county town of Stonehaven (16 miles from Banchory).

There is also the road which runs up the Feugh (B.974) leading to Strachan and over the Cairn-a-mounth to Fettercairn (17 miles distant). Finally, there is the road (B.977) which strikes north-eastwards from Raemoir for Kintore and the north. The total mileage of highways for which the County Council is responsible in the parish is 53.13 outside the burgh and 2.57 inside the burgh. All the classified roads are tar-macadamised and it is the policy of the County Council to bring the few unclassified roads which are not so surfaced up to this standard. All these roads are widely used by omnibuses, transport vehicles, private cars and those on pleasure bent.

TRANSPORT

Up to 1848 a small coach plied between Aberdeen and Banchory and took so long to accomplish the journey that a man walking for a wager took only 15 minutes longer.

The railway from Aberdeen to Banchory was opened on September 7, 1853, and the ordinary service began on the 8th. The old station was east of the present one, with a passenger overhead bridge but a level-crossing only for vehicles. The original train services consisted of 3 passenger trains in each direction. First and Third Class accommodation only was provided, fares 3/3d and 2/2d; no smoking allowed; running-time one hour. The Deeside service reached its maximum that year with no fewer than 11 daily trains to and from Banchory, together with 2 extra trains on Wednesdays and Saturdays and late evening trains on Saturdays as well. Thus great efforts were made to encourage excursion traffic.

The railway was opened originally under the Deeside Railway Act 1852, but it was under the Great North of Scotland Railway Act 1898 that a widening and improvement of the railway between Park and Banchory was carried out in 1903. This involved the complete re-organisation of the lay-out of the railway, including a new station —

the present one — on a different site, together with engine and carriage yards.

After the First World War the Government sold a large number of military vehicles, and this gave a tremendous fillip to motor transport. The change to road transport was also hastened by the railway strike of 1920. This strike, and that of 1926, did a great deal of damage to the railway industry, for they taught the public that there were other and perhaps more dependable methods of transport. For nearly 10 years after amalgamation, no serious effort was made to meet the new competition or to improve relations with the general public.

The pioneer of road passenger services between Aberdeen and Banchory was the Bydand Motor Services, which from 1923 to 1933 ran an hourly single-decker bus, accommodating 14-20 passengers. No real effort, however, was made to maintain a regular frequency until the advent of the Road Traffic Act 1930. During the period 1928-30, a rival entered the field. The L.N.E. Railway operated a single-decker bus, with seating capacity for 30, every two hours. Time-keeping was a very important factor in the railway-operated road services and for the first time Deeside had a regular frequency. The Bydand operated what were known in those days as 'pirate' buses at the L.N.E.R. times and all sorts of practices were attempted, some of them dangerous, to prevent the L.N.E.R. from getting passengers.

In 1930 W. Alexander & Sons Ltd. inaugurated an hourly service, with 35-seater single-decker buses. Alexander's which was then a unit of the S.M.T. Group, absorbed the L.N.E.R. road services in 1930 and acquired the Bydand Motor Services in 1933. 48- and 53-seater double-deck vehicles were introduced on this route in 1934. In 1948 the S.M.T. Group was acquired by the British Transport Commission. The above all operated on the North Deeside road.

Commencing in 1924, and still in operation, is Strachan's Deeside Omnibus Service — a 3 hourly single-deck bus accommodating 32. This service operates between Aberdeen and Braemar, and proceeds via the South Deeside road between Aberdeen and Banchory. Today Banchory is well serviced by buses, and trains are so sparsely used that they do not work economically. The station is inconveniently situated; buses pass right through the town.

POST OFFICE

An old record says that in 1841 there was a Post Office, a wooden building located in Watson Lane. Later it was moved to Dee Street. The present Post Office was built in 1910 and was raised to a salaried Post Office. The present Postmaster is the fourth since 1910. In olden days the staff consisted of 2 town and 3 rural postmen and mails were conveyed to and from the station by horse-gig. The staff now comprises 4 indoor officers, 1 postman Higher Grade, 2 town postmen, 7 rural postmen and a junior postman — the new designation for boy messenger. The Postmaster is also responsible for the staffing and welfare of the 4 staff on the Telephone Exchange. The rural postmen cover a radius of 15 miles by cycle and motor van. In 1930 motor cycles were introduced for remote deliveries, but were ultimately found to be detrimental to the health of the drivers. In 1940 they were withdrawn and replaced by motor vans, which afforded protection to the drivers and also enabled them to keep letters and parcels dry in inclement weather. The present Post Office, modernised in 1938, is now classed as one of the most up-to-date offices. It is proposed to build a new Post Office in the near future on the spare ground west of the Town Hall.

TELEPHONE

Telephone communication between Aberdeen and Banchory was completed on Saturday April 12, 1897, with about 6 subscribers. The exchange was in a room in Mrs. Russell's property in High Street and among the first messages to be transmitted was one to the 'Aberdeen Journal'. The exchange was removed to its present site adjoining the post office in 1923. Today there are over 260 subscribers, and practically half of these rent business lines.

WATER SUPPLY

(1) The burgh

Prior to 1887 the inhabitants relied for water supply on natural sources, such as wells and springs. In that year, however, the Police Commissioners constructed reservoirs and other works for a system of water supply. The operations were commenced in 1886, the engineers being Messrs. Jenkins and Marr, Aberdeen, and the contractor Mr. John McPetrie, Torphins. The supply was of a purely gravitational character and was conveyed from a spring at the foot of the hill of Caerloch, about six miles distant from the town. Two reservoirs were provided, one at the top of Mount Street for the high service, and the other somewhat further down for the low service. The former was capable of holding 28,000 gallons of water and the latter 75,000 gallons. The total cost of the new system was between £3000 and £4000. In the years 1903, 1924 and 1925 further works were carried out for the augmentation of the supply and at the present day, when water supply runs low, water is obtained from the main Aberdeen supply.

(2) LANDWARD

As a result of the present local government administration the supply of water to houses and farms has greatly improved, although a fair number of the inhabitants have still to draw water by hand from wells. The farming community have in many cases taken advantage of the grants given by the Department of Agriculture for introducing piped supplies of water to farm and cottar houses.

ELECTRICITY

The first public supply of electricity was introduced in the burgh in December 1932 by the Grampian Electricity Supply Company, under the Scottish Highlands Electricity Special Order 1932. Initially the source of supply was two diesel driven alternators, which were dispensed with in 1934 when the Deeside 11,000 volt line was completed and energised by the Grampian Company. Power for this line was generated at Loch Tummel and Loch Rannoch hydro-electric stations. Apart from the burgh, several of the larger houses and other premises in the parish were connected, among them being Crathes Castle, Inchmarlo House, and Glen o'Dee Sanatorium (then Nordrach on Dee). Within the burgh the demand for electricity has steadily increased, both for business and domestic premises. Coinciding with the introduction of the supply, the public lighting system was converted from gas to electricity and officially switched on by the reigning convener, the late Dr. Cran, on 1 December 1932. A ready supply of power assisted the burgh when it was found necessary to augment the water supply by tapping and pumping water from the Aberdeen city aqueduct. There are now approximately 600 consumers in Banchory.

It is expected that supply will be made available in the Bridge of Feugh, Auchattie and Crathes localities in the very near future and other similar communities will be catered for at a later date. The North of Scotland Hydro-Electric Board was nationalised on 1 April 1948.

GAS

In 1845, when the Deeside Railway was first mooted, a meeting of local residents was held in the Burnett Arms Inn, for the purpose of forming a company 'to manufacture inflammable air or gas from coal and for the sale of coke, tar and other products derived therefrom'. The Banchory Gas Light Company Ltd. came into being then, but did not actually commence operations until 1853 when the construction of the works was begun, the Deeside Railway having reached Banchory. Many delays were encountered, but the building of the works was completed and gas issued for the first time in October 1854 to a few consumers near the works.

At the end of the first year the number of consumers was 46 and the gas sold 187,000 cu.ft. Since then, as the town has grown, the mains have been extended to provide an adequate service for all parts. The following are the statistics for 1950:—

Number of gas consumers in burgh.. 516
Amount of gas manufactured — approximately......... 12,000,000 cu.ft.
Domestic (cooking mainly).. 8,444,000 cu.ft.
Commercial (business premises, shops, hotels, etc.)....... 2,096,000 cu.ft.
Industrial (potato crisp factory) .... 583,000 cu.ft.
The balance is used for works purposes.

SEWERAGE

At present there is no scheme of sewerage and sewage disposal in the parish outside the burgh. Within the burgh, the main sewers run straight into the River Dee. The County Council, however, have in view proceeding with a full sewage disposal plant — 100% purification — at Silverbank, covering the existing sawmill and other properties there and a new housing scheme of 40 houses which the Council propose to build on the present Market Hillock stance.

STREETS

High Street, which is part of the North Deeside road, and the principal street, extends for over a mile, but all the business premises are concentrated within the space of some two hundred yards. To the north of High Street, rising one above the other and running parallel to it, are Arbeadie Terrace, Watson Street, and Ramsay Road. To the east is Arbeadie Road and Schoolhill, on which stands the Academy. To the north of Schoolhill lies Woodside of Arbeadie. This area has been considerably extended by the erection, by the local authority, of new houses after the First and Second World Wars. This area comprises Woodside Crescent and Road and Arbeadie, Deeview and Raemoir Roads.

To the west of the above-named streets, and separated from them by Mount Street or what was known as Chapel Brae, is Corsee Road which, rising westwards for about a mile, terminates at the Glen o' Dee Sanatorium. Westwards from the top of Mount Street is another housing scheme, comprising Burnett Road and Terrace.

To the south of High Street are Dee Street, leading to the South

Deeside road, and Kinneskie Road, leading to the golf course. Bridge Street, which is parallel to High Street, connects these two.

CLEANSING

Within the burgh refuse is collected twice per week by tractor and covered-in trailer. In the landward area, apart from a small number of houses near the burgh, no special arrangements are made for disposal of refuse. Waste paper is collected once per week. The refuse is taken to a rubbish tip north-west of Upper Arbeadie Farm. The highways are kept very clean and tidy.

STREET LIGHTING

Gas was first used for lighting the streets of the burgh in 1867. A sum of 10/- per lamp per annum was the charge made. This included the cost of lighting by lamplighter, and the illumination was provided by fish-tail burner, i.e. naked flame burner. By 1914 the streets were lighted by incandescent gas. This remained until 1932, when electricity was introduced. Today the streets of the burgh are well lighted. There is no lighting outwith.

POLICE

The first act which enabled counties to establish and maintain a paid constabulary was passed in 1839 and the first policeman was stationed at Banchory in 1840. His duty was to maintain order, keep the peace, and attend the market and fairs. Today a sergeant, whose house forms part of the Police Station (which has 3 cells), and 2 constables are responsible for the parishes of Banchory, Strachan and Durris. In the early days there was no real traffic. Today however its regulation is a very important part of police duty, and even more onerous is the enforcing of Orders under the Diseases of Animals Act. At present the tramp has practically disappeared from the area, and on the whole Banchory is very well-behaved.

FIRE SERVICE

There is an efficient fire service for the needs of Banchory-Ternan parish and beyond. The engine is kept in premises in Mount Street, north of West Church Hall.

HOUSING

Banchory today is a place of many mansions, up-to-date hotels and boarding houses. Almost every house in the burgh has a garden. Indeed, it is a garden city in miniature. The total number of houses in the parish is approximately 1030 — 600 in the burgh and 430 in the landward area. Houses range from 2 to 5 rooms, while there is also quite a number of the residential type with 6 or more rooms. The latter are occupied mainly by retired people and represent about 50% of the housing accommodation. The average is one room per person, excluding the larger residential houses. Since the Second World War the number of badly housed families has been considerably reduced and while there is ample scope for improvement in the conditions of life, there are few, if any, really bad cases of over-crowding.

TYPES OF HOUSE

On the High Street the area has been closely built up and many of the houses are of the tenement type; elsewhere, apart from a small number of blocks, the houses are mainly after the cottage style, merging into detached residential dwellings. There is no particular style prevalent and apart from the tenement blocks the houses are mainly two-storeyed. Water is laid on in all but a few isolated cases, and in the burgh the majority of houses are connected to electric or gas supply. Outside the burgh, very few houses have electricity. Most of the cottages and all local authority houses have ample gardens, with a good supply of flowers, fruit and vegetables. There are about 6 market gardens with mixed produce.

RENTALS

Houses of the residential type are owner-occupied, the remainder are rented. The assessed rentals vary considerably. On the Corsee Hill area they are around £60 p.a., in the Ramsay Road and Watson Street area £40, and elsewhere, anything from £10-£40. The rents of local authority houses (exclusive of rates) are:— 3-roomed £26 per annum; 4-roomed £31; 5-roomed £36. Banchory Town Council early realised that the rents of their houses could not remain at the pre-war level because of present day building costs and with foresight increased the rents. The farms in the parish are mainly tenanted.

NEW HOUSES

Since 1918, 150 houses have been built by the local authority and 10 are under construction at the moment. Since 1945, 34 permanent houses and 20 prefabs have been erected. The County Council have built 10 prefabs on the outskirts of the burgh. The influence of building societies has been negligible.

Details of new houses built since 1918:

1. Monearn Terrace — built 1922, 6 blocks of flatted houses (4 houses per block), stone built and three rooms per house.

2. Burnett Road & Terrace — built 1928, semi-detached stone-built bungalow type, 26 houses, three rooms per house.

3. Mansefield Place — built 1932/33, semi-detached stone-built bungalow type, 12 houses, three rooms per house.

4. Loanhead Terrace — built 1935, three blocks of flatted houses (2 houses per block), stone built, three rooms per house.

5. Woodside Crescent — built 1937, forty three-, four-, and five-roomed houses (cottage type) in blocks of twos and fours, all stone-built.

6. Arbeadie Road — built 1946, 4 blocks of cottage type flatted houses (2 houses per block), brick and harled, five rooms per house.

7. Deeview Road — built 1946, 22 houses of the same type as Arbeadie Road, in blocks of twos and fours, four rooms per house.

8. Woodside Road and Raemoir Road — temporary houses — built in 1946, 20 prefabricated type houses, three rooms per house.

9. Leys Road (County Council) — temporary houses — 10 prefabricated type houses, three rooms per house.

10. Woodside Road — 10 houses in course of construction in 1950, built of bricks and harled over, cottage type, semi-detached, four rooms per house.

These houses all have bathrooms and kitchenettes; where a house is referred to as a three- or four-roomed house, the kitchenette is in addition and is not classed as a room. All these houses have back and front gardens.

In a most worthy sense the tenants are house-proud and take a very keen and profitable interest in their gardens.

HEALTH SERVICES

A hundred years ago the health of the people lay in the hands of the doctor, and doctors were few in number and had widely scattered practices. The famous Dr. Francis Adams was the first resident doctor in Banchory. Doctors McHardy and Cran were two wonderful family doctors, who brought healing and help to the sick for over 50 years. In those days an appeal to the specialist was rare, and there was no district nurse to help the doctor, who had to care for all cases of sickness and accident in the homes of his patients. For a radius of 20 miles around Banchory they travelled in those early times, by foot, by 'boneshaker' and 'safety' bicycle, by gig, on horseback and later by motor car.

E

What a sharp contrast today! The parish is now served by 3 doctors and a district nurse, all resident in Banchory — the district nurse with a car at her disposal — 3 dentists, 3 fully qualified chemists, and a child welfare clinic. The schoolchildren are regularly examined medically and dentally by the doctors and dentists appointed by the county Education Committee. There are maternity hospitals at Torphins — where most of the births take place — and also at Aberdeen. Pre-natal and ante-natal care is given. In Aberdeen are the Sick Children's Hospital and the Infirmary.

It was not until 1921 that a modified scheme for dental inspection and treatment of schoolchildren was started in Kincardineshire. The first part-time dental surgeon for the schools in the Banchory area was appointed in 1924.

Tuberculosis and the relatively high infant mortality rate both show a steady decline, while the figures for Kincardineshire compare very favourably with those for the country as a whole. Child welfare clinics were started in Banchory early in 1940, clinics being held at fortnightly intervals. On 8 January 1951 these clinics commenced weekly sessions.

The introduction of immunisation against diphtheria has effected an enormous change in connection with that disease, so deadly to young children. Facilities are now provided for the immunisation of all children from the age of 6 months upwards.

On 5 July 1948, the National Health Service came into being. Certain duties were then laid upon local authorities: (1) midwifery (domiciliary), health visiting and home nursing; (2) care of mothers and young children; (3) vaccination and immunisation; (4) prevention of illness, care and after care: (5) domestic help scheme; (6) mental health. The health of the community has thus vastly improved.

SANATORIUM

The first sanatorium in Scotland — Nordrach-on-Dee, founded by Dr. David Lawson — was opened at Banchory in 1899. The sanatorium flourished until 1935, when it was sold and became the Glen o' Dee Hotel. In 1945 the Scottish Red Cross decided that their main objective in the post-war years was to be the care and treatment of ex-servicemen and women suffering from pulmonary tuberculosis. In pursuit of this objective they acquired Tor-na-Dee sanatorium at Milltimber and also the building at Banchory which had formerly been Nordrach-on-Dee. Those two institutions, under the joint name of the Red Cross Sanatoria of Scotland, were to be reserved entirely for ex-service cases. The building at Glen o' Dee required much alteration and reconstruction to bring it into line with the require-ments of a first-class tuberculosis hospital, and it was not until

December 1948 that the first patients were admitted. Its total bed capacity is 78 and it has a modern X-ray department. In 1949 a new kitchen block was completed and a few months later an occupational therapy department and a laboratory were ready for use. On August 10, 1949 the official opening ceremony was performed by Her Majesty the Queen.

THE RED CROSS

This was started in Banchory before the First World War by Dr. G. Cran and a very strong V.A.D. was maintained, which was responsible for a bed in the Red Cross Hospital at Rouen. When the war ended Banchory started a men's Red Cross detachment which became responsible for the maintenance of a Red Cross post at the Aboyne Games and Braemar Gathering of the Clans in September each year, as well as casualty duties at local games, agricultural shows, etc. From time to time lectures on first-aid, nursing, chemical warfare, gas, etc. have been given. In 1932 the Banchory men's detachment went to Edinburgh to compete with other Scottish county teams for the Scottish Cup. This they won by 45 points and so went to London for the Stanley Shield competition.

AGRICULTURE

Life on the farm has undergone tremendous changes in the last hundred years, and some of the romance has gone from the harvest-fields with the coming of mechanisation. The improvement of implements alone has been a major factor in the changes. Among others there are implements for digging the potatoes — once a laborious job for man and his graip — and machinery as well for dressing the seed-size potatoes from the ware-size. The seed potato industry is a fruitful one in this whole north-east corner of Scotland. The smaller size of the farms in our district is not very suitable for the latest tool of the farm — the combine harvester

Besides the potatoes, the main crops grown are oats, barley and turnips on the arable land. On the rough hill pasture of the Hill of Fare (Raemoir) and Scolty there is grand grazing for sheep. Animal feeding has undergone a marked change. Quite a number of well-known and up-to-date T.T. dairy herds in the parish assure Banchory of a supply of clean, healthy milk. The surplus is sent to Aberdeen to a milk pool, run by the Milk Marketing Board. Prime fat cattle are now produced in the space of two to two-and-a-half years, compared with the four years required at the end of last century, due to the better feeding methods. In the late 19th century and the beginning of this century, these fat cattle, sheep and pigs went to market to be auctioned and sold to the highest bidder. Now they go to market, certainly, but they are graded according to their quality of fatness by competent farmers appointed by the Ministry of Food for this purpose.

Horse-breeding, once an essential and remunerative part of farm life, is now practically non-existent, the horse having been ousted from its useful place by the tractor. Today, however, pig and poultry rearing has come into its own. In the late 19th and early 20th century the farmer looked on the hen as a liability on his farm, not an asset. Now in 1950 that is entirely changed, and the hen and her produce give him the quickest cash crop on his farm, the pig following a close second in quick cash returns.

The liberal use of so-called artificial manures too has made a tremendous difference to the cropping. We now have better crops, and crops much earlier harvested, as a result of their use.

The advent of the machine age has made changes in the life of the farm servant as well — and for his betterment. He has shorter working hours, bigger pay, his half-day off weekly, and his annual holidays to bring him into line with other tradesmen, and rightly so. Nevertheless the 'drift' from the land to the city continues. This is due in no small measure to the fact that, so far, few of the cottar houses have any of the conveniences so essential to the upbringing of a modern family. Families are smaller, with smaller numbers attending the schools. This drift to the city continues in spite of the fact that, in each district of the parish, a hall has been built for the use of the local community, and at Crathes, Raemoir, Tilquhillie and Inchmarlo there are flourishing social and whist clubs and strong branches of the Scottish Women's Rural Institutes.

The Mill of Hirn is the only meal mill in the district and here the miller is kept busy. About 25 years ago the Mill of Raemoir was converted into two dwelling houses, as was the smithy there; the smithy at the Hirn does very little now, but the blacksmith is kept quite busy at his forge in Banchory. This again is due to the mechanisation of farm implements.

The farms used to be well surrounded by trees, but the urgent need for timber in the two World Wars has practically denuded them. Nevertheless, the planting of trees has begun again, witness Blackhall estate, and in years to come we may hope these woods will grow up as beautiful as ever. The pony and trap used to be the farmers' sole means of conveyance to kirk and market, but now practically every farmer has his own motor car. This is a great asset to both old and young. A Junior Agricultural Club thrives in the parish and these cars take young lads (and lasses too) to neighbouring farms to learn to judge the various kinds of breeds of stock in their proper type.

The life of the farmer's wife has changed considerably too. Domestic staff on the farm are just out of the question. But with the advent of modern cookers and other labour-saving devices, she gets her work done and can always find time to accompany her better half to town on market days, and to be an active member, possibly an office-bearer, in her local branch of the S.W.R.I. Electricity has not come to the landward parts of the parish yet, but the Hydro-Electric Board brings it nearer daily. Practically all the dairy farms have electric plant of their own — generated by an engine — and in these the electric milking machine is in use. The farms in the parish are mainly situated on the east and north side of the Crathes and Raemoir (Dunecht) estates. Within the burgh, the farms include: Lower Arbeadie — 26 acres — assessed rental £36.9.0d; and Upper Arbeadie — 44 acres — assessed rental £62. Both are owner-occupied. It also includes a part of New Banchory Farm, which is tenanted only, and is being encroached upon for building purposes. Outwith the burgh, there are some 52 crofts, most of which are only some 5 acres in extent, and approximately 73 farms, whose acreage varies from 20 to 200 acres. Most of the farms are average-sized, with 60 to 75 acres.

LEASES

Farm lands are at a premium and when offered to let often fetch from £3 to £4 per acre. The average rent per acre would be approximately £2. Landlords are tending to take over farms in order to work them themselves, as and when they fall vacant, because farming today is enjoying an era of prosperity. In this parish many farms are run on a year-to-year lease. Where leases are entered into, they are usually of 14 years duration, with a mutual break at 7 years. The Agricultural Holdings (Scotland) Acts are giving farm tenants an ever increasing security of tenure.

AGRICULTURAL STATISTICS

The landward area of the parish at present is 19,538 acres and the agricultural statistics as at 4 June 1950 are as follows. The total area under crops and grass is 6,967 acres. Of these, 408 are permanent grass, leaving 6,559 acres normally arable. Of the latter figure 2,763 acres are in temporary grass, leaving 3,796 acres under actual cultivation. Rough grazing amounts to 2,338 acres. The acreages of the principal crops are:- barley 320 acres, oats 2,307 acres, potatoes 297 acres, turnips and swedes 763 acres.

SHOW

Worthy of note in this connection is the Deeside Agricultural Association, the objects of which are to encourage the breeding, rearing, fattening, etc. of farm stock, by holding shows and granting premiums; and generally to promote the prosperity of agricultural matters in the district. The oldest premium book is dated 1820, and from it it is evident that the Association was in existence before that time. It is interesting, and perhaps surprising, to note that in that year £5.5.0d was offered as first prize for stock shown, whereas in 1950, despite a tremendous development of the show in every respect, the corresponding first prize was no more than £1, although the expenses of the exhibitors must have increased ten-fold. In common with other shows, the organisers have to rely mainly on the afternoon gate for the sports programme to clear expenses. It can only be concluded that in 1820 the subscribers must have given very generous support before they were able to pay out such prize money with, presumably, very much smaller attendances. There were, of course, fewer classes. The gate now is around the 6,000 mark, but the Association has a very serious obstacle to overcome — lack of adequate space; otherwise the show has tremendous possibilities. At present it is held at Bellfield Park, Banchory, but prior to 1913 it took place at the Market Stance, beside the Silverbank Sawmill. One important change across the years has been the inclusion of the S.W.R.I. with their industrial sections, the entries being sometimes over 700. The show is still confined to members residing in the area, which embraces most of the Deeside and neighbouring parishes.

INDUSTRIES

One of the chief industries of Banchory in the old days — stone quarrying — has now ceased. At one time the quarries at Craigton and Raemoir were a hive of industry, hundreds of men being employed. These quarries supplied granite blocks for the building of houses, etc. as well as for monumental work. Most of the buildings in Banchory have been built of the red granite stone quarried at Craigton and Raemoir. Many fine Cairngorm crystals were found in the Craigton granite. The sawmill, owned by the late Mr. C. Fraser, at Inchmarlo, and the bobbin mills at Invercannie, belonging to Messrs. Bremner — employing many men — were both closed down many years ago, the latter firm being transferred to Aberdeen. Many men were once employed in the large repair and engineering shops erected at the station for the making of coal waggons and cattle trucks. Today, the sheds still stand, but the work has long since been transferred to Inverurie.

Sawmilling in Banchory still flourishes. The firm of Messrs. A. & G. Paterson Ltd has carried on this valuable work for almost 100 years at Silverbank. It was not until the railway to Banchory was nearly ready for opening in 1854 that the mills were erected, with sidings on the new line. It was in the early forties of last century that woods were first purchased on Deeside and floated down the river Dee from Banchory. On the river bank below the sawmills one can still see the old stones with iron rings for tying up the timber rafts. In 1881 the company brought down the last raft of logs on the River Dee. The present generation of employees has in many cases sprung from the hard and intrepid race of lumber-men who accompanied these rafts on the perilous journeys down the river. In the employment of the company are members of the third and fourth generations of the same families whose fortunes have been continuously linked with the business.

During the two World Wars the company took a very active part in supplying timber for the war effort. Their products found their way as pit props and mining timber to all the Scottish coalfields, and the Admiralty, War Office, Air Ministry, railway companies and shipyards received valuable contributions. The sawmills were completely remodelled. More modern mechanised methods were introduced, and modern drying kilns erected. A large canteen for the operatives was installed. A forestry section has now been established at Banchory for the planting of trees, which are being raised on the company's own nursery. The present Chairman is Robert Cassels Paterson, grandson of one of the founders. The local manager, Mr. J. Gove, has been in the service of the company since 1909. A. & G. Paterson's sawmills constitute the largest industry in Banchory, employing about 120 hands, some 20 of whom are women, and have been most beneficial to the parish. The workers take a genuine interest in their occupations and appreciate the lectures arranged during the winter months on various aspects of their trade and timber technology generally.

Duncan's sawmills, Invercannie (originally 3 mills — (1) turning mill (2) meal mill (3) sawmill) were worked by John Duncan 130 years ago. Later they branched out to manufacture cloth boards and became a cloth manufacturer, putting boards in boxes, tweed, etc. in later years, 17 men being then employed. The mill was taken over by Mr. J.S.Duthie for some years, and in 1941 passed into the hands of Messrs. Rosowsky and Blumstein, who carried it on as a sawmill under fellers, carters, etc. The timber was brought down from the woods and converted into squares and battens and consigned to the south. Unfortunately, owing to the shortage of timber in this locality, the sawmill has been forced to close down. Here too the workers were most conscientious during the war period, and were complimented on their production by the Board of Trade.

Summer visitors provided another industry, as witness the editions of *Banchory and Round About*, with its attractive house registry sections. This must have been a very important source of revenue. Today however, with easy travel by car, bus and rail, it is not so profitable as once it was. Hotels are also aware of the change.

The aerated water factory in Bridge Street (carried on for many years by Messrs. D. Russell & Sons and later by the late Mr. C. Ewen) is now out of existence and is used as a factory for the manufacture of cooked foods. This was founded in 1938 by Dr. D. Forbes, M.D., and commenced in Banchory in July 1949. It provides fish cakes, meat cakes and potato crisps. Further developments in mind include oatcakes, mealie puddings and soups. 14 women are employed as friers. The present output is 1500-2000 tins per week, there being 2 dozen packets of potato crisps in each tin. The area served covers Deeside, Donside and as far as Inverness, Orkney and Shetland.

DEE LAVENDER

Of recent years the desirability of establishing new light industries in the north of Scotland has been apparent. One of these, the cultivation and distillation of lavender and the manufacture of lavender water, has been undertaken in Banchory. The founder of this small industry, A.R. Inkster, M.P.S., a native of the north-east, was employed for some years in a manufacturing laboratory in China, where he occupied much of his spare time in research and study of the essential oils, devoting himself particularly to lavender and its allied perfumery compounds. He conceived the idea of growing the shrub in the light sandy soil of Deeside, which is particularly suited to the purpose. A new company, Ingasetter Limited, was formed with the main object of developing the lavender industry. After some years of experimenting, three varieties are now being cultivated on a commercial scale on the outskirts of Banchory, making a very pleasant and colourful picture when in bloom. The flowers are harvested and distilled, a small modern factory near New Banchory having been built for this purpose, and the essential oil is collected and stored until matured. It is recognised that this locally produced oil is of a very high quality from the perfumer's point of view. It is blended with certain other flower perfumes to develop and enhance its distinctive bouquet, matured again in alcohol, and the resultant Dee Lavender — the completed toilet water — is sent to all parts of Britain and also enjoys a considerable export market. Experiments are being continued, not only with lavender, but also in the examination and treatment of other locally-grown plants in the perfumery industry, and it is realised that a considerable field for research exists in this sphere.

THE BURGH SHOPS

High Street is the main shopping centre where provision merchants, butchers, bakers, chemists, newsagents, fruiterers, tailors, shoemakers, hotels, cafes, drapers, a painter, a jeweller, a radio engineer, a dentist, an ironmonger, a garage and a post office adequately supply the needs of the local community. Here too, are the offices of the Town Clerk, the Clydesdale and North of Scotland Bank, the Customs and Excise and the Ministry of Labour and National Service. There are of course other shops in various parts of the burgh, and vans serve the people in the landward area. Thursday is the early closing day.

During the past 50 years there has been very little change in the number of shops. But there has been a considerable improvement in their appearance, most of the fronts having been modernised. Most of the businesses carry on trading as in years gone by, but there are certain exceptions. With the passing of horse-drawn transport, all the saddlers' shops have been closed, and in most cases the motor garage has taken the place of the smithy, although one still remains in Raemoir Road. It is interesting to note that a large number of the businesses now carried on in Banchory have been handed down by fathers and mothers to sons and daughters over a long period of years. This is especially noticeable in the case of butchers, bakers, shoemakers, tailors, painters, joiners and grocers. Whereas, in older days, the shopkeepers depended for their living on trading with residents, they now derive a large part of their yearly overturn from passing trade, Banchory being a popular resort for visitors. On 7th July 1947 the Northern Co-operative opened a branch in High Street with departments for grocery, bakery, hardware, butcher and fish goods. Sales amount to £40,000 per year for Banchory and district, the latter supplied by their vans

BANKS

The first bank to open for business in Banchory was the North of Scotland Bank in 1846, in premises now occupied by the Co-operative Society. In 1874 a branch of the Town and County Bank was opened at the corner of Raemoir Road in a house presently owned by Adams. Later it was removed to its present position, at the corner of Arbeadie Road. In 1908 these two were amalgamated. A third bank — the Union Bank of Scotland — entered the field of business but was closed in 1942. Today Banchory has two branches of the North of Scotland Bank — since 1950 the Clydesdale and North of Scotland Bank.

HOTELS

Of the 8 hotels, five are mentioned in the *Automobile Association Handbook*, viz Raemoir, Tor-na-Coille, Banchory Lodge, Burnett

Arms and Ravenswood (unlicensed). The others are the Douglas
Arms, Banchory Hotel and Station Hotel.

ECCLESIASTICAL

Banchory-Ternan is in the Presbytery of Deeside, which meets at
Aboyne on the first Wednesday of February, August and October and
last Wednesday of March, April and November. There are 4
handsome churches in Banchory — two Church of Scotland (East and
West), St Ternan's Episcopal Church and a Roman Catholic Chapel.
The present East Church, formerly the Old Parish church, was built in
1824, replacing the previous edifice, which stood in the churchyard. It
is a Gothic building with a tower and had 1250 sittings. This number
was considerably reduced when the central pulpit and side galleries
were removed and a new chancel built at the north end. The entire
woodwork is of light oak. Morning worship only is conducted in the
church. During the winter the evening service is held in the church
hall, situated at the junction of Arbeadie Terrace and High Street,
while in summer country services are conducted.

At the Disruption in 1843 the Free Church group seceded and the
Rev. William Anderson A.M. who as parish minister prepared the
Second Statistical Account, 1842, went to be its first minister. For a time
the congregation worshipped in what is now the masonic temple,
until a church was built at Loanhead. The garden of the Station Hotel
was the site of the original Free Church, and part of the foundation
stones can still be seen there. Immediately westwards was the original
Free Church manse — still the manse of the West Church. On
September 5, 1880 a new Free Church — the present West Church —
was opened in the heart of the town at a cost of £3,000, with 700
sittings. It is Early English in style and of pink and white granite, with
a spire 100 feet high. The woodwork is of pitch pine. When a pipe
organ was installed in 1922 a side pulpit replaced the central one.
Some of the stonework from the original church was used to build the
church hall, part of the old pulpit being still preserved there.

In November 1877 the United Presbyterian Church was formed in
Banchory, when the Independent Church — now the masonic temple
— was purchased for £700, with a manse then let at £16. At the
union of the U.P. Church and the Free Church of Scotland in 1900,
the former Free Church became known as the South United Free
Church and the former United Presbyterian Church as the North
United Free Church. Both maintained their individuality till 1918,
when the North and South congregations formally united to form
Banchory United Free Church, the South Church becoming the place
of worship of the united congregations, while the North Church was
to be used for congregational purposes or disposed of as the united
congregation might decide.

At the union of the churches in 1929 the former Old Parish became known as Banchory-Ternan East Church of Scotland, and the former United Free Church as Banchory-Ternan West Church of Scotland, where morning and evening worship is conducted every Sunday throughout the year, while in summer country services are held in the parish. The minister of the West Church is chaplain to the Glen o' Dee Sanatorium and with the help of the choir conducts a service for the up-patients there every second Sunday, which is relayed to all bed patients throughout the hospital.

The East Church has 1162 members and the West Church 454, the total Christian liberality being £1862 and £1240 respectively. St. Ternan's Episcopal Church, erected in 1851, is an Early English granite edifice, with nave and chancel, 4 stained glass windows and a very high-pitched open timber roof.

About the year 1930, a Roman Catholic chapel was erected in the west end of the town as the result of an endowment left by Mr. Leslie of Auchinove. There is no resident priest — one travels from Aboyne.

EDUCATION

BURGH SCHOOLS

A century ago the Church was responsible for the administration of schools and so the parish school was built opposite the parish church and was called St. Nicholas. Following the Disruption in 1843, a Free Church school and schoolhouse were erected at Loanhead. The building survives today as the Station Hotel. On October 6, 1873 the Free Church school was re-opened as Loanhead Public School, under the School Board of Banchory-Ternan, there being present 22 girls and 41 boys. After the passing of the Scottish Education Act in 1872, the schools at St Nicholas and Loanhead were closed and the new Central School at Schoolhill was opened on September 16, 1878. Extensions of east, west and south wings were added in 1907 and 1908, in which year the school's status was raised to higher grade. In 1911 came the union of the Reid and Burnett School with the Central School. The Lady Burnett School, founded in 1750 and endowed by Lady Burnett of Crathes Castle, was rebuilt in 1858 and further endowed by the Rev. Dr. Reid, Free Church minister, when it became known as the Reid and Burnett School. It was a most successful school of some 130 girls and boys. Ultimately, however, it was sold for £700 to the town council for burgh buildings and the schoolhouse became the house of the Burgh Surveyor.

Further extensions to the Central higher grade school were carried out in 1913 and 1925 when the school, now under the Kincardineshire Education Authority, was raised to secondary status. Since then it has

provided courses leading to the award of the Scottish Leaving
Certificate. In 1936 new buildings, consisting of 2 infant rooms and a
gymnasium with dressing rooms and spray baths, were opened. In
1947 four H.O.R.S.A. huts were erected in the playground, three of
these providing accommodation for 44 pupils in the infant and
primary classes while a fourth is equipped with technical machines and
metalwork benches for 14 pupils. To relieve the congestion, the
Committee recently purchased St Leonards, the residence of the late
Mr. T. Walker Hector, which will provide large class-rooms and an
excellent school garden. The school, now known as Banchory
Academy, has at present 600 pupils, of whom 270 are in the primary
and infant departments and are taught by 8 teachers. In the secondary
school there are 23 teachers, exclusive of the Rector. The Academy
provides secondary education for the whole of Upper Deeside. The
'house system', with 4 houses — Kerloch, Monearn, Morven and
Scolty, all named after hills in the district — has been introduced and
makes for keen and happy rivalry. These include pupils from Primary
VI upwards to Secondary VI, who compete for cups — scholastic,
music festival, sports, etc.

RURAL SCHOOLS

Several schools survive in the rural areas of the parish. It was at
Tilquhillie School that the sons of the famous Dr. Francis Adams of
Bellfield were trained. They forded the Dee daily to get there. The
school was closed about 1930, owing to complete depopulation.
Raemoir had two schools — at Kinnerty and Bockton — but both
were closed when the new school was opened at Raemoir. Today
there are 6 primary schools, the present number of pupils in each
being given in brackets:- Crathes (32); Cross-roads (39); Inchmarlo
(19); Raemoir (45); Strachan (81); and Woodlands (36). All have two
teachers, with the exception of Crathes and Inchmarlo which have
only one, and Strachan which has 3. For comparison the peak figures
were: Inchmarlo, 120 pupils in 1885, with staff of 4; Durris Crossroads, 106 pupils in 1876, with staff of 2; Raemoir, 80 pupils in 1910,
with staff of 2, which shows a decided decrease in the number of
pupils attending. In the case of Inchmarlo, this was largely due to the
transfer of local industry to Aberdeen; in other instances the causes
were: (1) rural depopulation; (2) the recent centralisation at the age of
12; and (3) smaller families.

SCHOOL MEALS

Opposite the Academy in Schoolhill a canteen, recently erected,
provides an ample two-course lunch for 5d. Special decreasing figures

of 4d for a second child and 3d for a third and subsequent children are set for members of the same family in attendance at the same school. Rural schools are supplied by van service. This canteen service for both local and travelling pupils must have reacted considerably on family life.

TRAVEL

The Education Committee meet their obligations regarding transport under the Education Act by (a) paying travelling expenses if the pupil resides more than 3 miles from school; and (b) paying the cost of board and lodging for the whole or part of a session if, in the opinion of the Committee, the pupil's home is so remote that daily travelling would involve hardship to the pupil.

PARENTS'-TEACHERS' ASSOCIATION

Parents today are definitely more interested and more education-conscious. A Parents'-Teachers' Association, drawing for its membership on the whole parish and beyond, was formed in 1947. Membership stands at over 300. In addition to educational debates, teaching demonstrations are a feature, showing the parent exactly how the child is being taught and what is being taught. From such contacts there is assuredly a much closer link between parent, teacher and child so that each is aware of the various problems affecting the other. Last year the Association raised £85 for the purchase of an up-to-date edition of the *Encyclopaedia Britannica*.

The raising of the status of Banchory Central school in 1925 to Senior Secondary with multilateral courses, has definitely stimulated interest in and desire for higher education. This has resulted in a large increase in the staff and roll at Banchory, while the rolls of the landward schools have fallen. This reduction has been further accentuated by the provisions of the 1945 Education Act, which encouraged the centralisation of all post-primary pupils at Banchory.

RECREATION

The burgh has two public parks. The Burnett Park is at the west end of the town, at the junction of the North Deeside road and Glassel Road. At the entrance the old Cross stone, which marked the centre of the market in the early days, has been erected. Here are excellent facilities for cricket, football, skating and curling, amid beautiful surroundings. Bellfield Park, which provides a natural setting for so

many games and public gatherings, was recently gifted by Dr. Wilson
Park, Bellfield, Mr. William Emslie, Town Clerk, and the late
Provost Charles R.F. McIntosh. There is also the King George V
playing field, situated between the north and south avenues, leading
from Dee Street westwards to Banchory Lodge Hotel. The new
entrance, in course of erection, is almost directly opposite the Scout
Hut.

The recreation grounds in Dee Street consist of a bowling green,
tennis courts, and a putting lawn. These were opened in 1903 and are
most attractively situated. The grounds are controlled by a Committee elected by members and full use is extended to visitors.

GOLF COURSE

Some three minutes' walk from High Street is the 18-hole golf
course, opened on 1 July 1905 by Sir Thomas Burnett, Bt., at a cost of
£1000. Set amid beautiful Highland scenery, it is bounded on the
south by the Dee in one of its most entrancing stretches, with the hills
of Scolty and Tilquhillie rising beyond. The total length of the course,
which is on two levels, is 5000 yards. Lunch and high teas are served
to visitors during the season in the circular tearoom or on the
verandah of the club house. An open tournament for amateurs is held
in August. The course is open on Sundays.

ANGLING

Banchory, as the seat of the best salmon fishing, provides a great
attraction for the real angler. The Dee, once a highway for timber
traffic, is an ideal salmon river, as it flows through a granite formation,
the gravel of which is just what the salmon require for their spawning
beds. In the seventies of last century sportsmen came regularly to the
Dee and paid from £20 to £30 a month per beat, but the angling
rents have risen tremendously since then. Today some of the hotels
rent stretches for their guests, and sometimes a day's fishing may be
obtained through the courtesy of the proprietor. During the last 50
years various changes in the habits and size of the salmon have
occurred. Years ago there were magnificent autumn fish, averaging
over 20 lbs., with spring fish under 10 lbs. Now practically no fish
come as far as Banchory in autumn. One man caught only 2 fish in
eight weeks. But there is a magnificent spring fishing — 8 lbs on an
average. No explanation has yet been deduced to account for the
change, nor yet for the fact that salmon and sea-trout all pass the
mouth of the Feugh up till June but go up the Feugh in great numbers
thereafter.

Another curious thing is that while there has been a dying-out of black-game on middle Deeside, there has been an increase in the number of capercailzie. The Blackhall shooting had a record bag of 62 killed in one day. This would be about 1920.

YOUTH ORGANISATIONS

The 2nd Kincardineshire Boy Scout troop and Wolf Cub pack was formed in 1917; the present strength is 20 scouts and 15 cubs. The Girl Guide company and Brownie pack, founded soon after, has today 10 guides and 25 brownies. The First Banchory Life Boy team (formed in 1944) has 52 members and 1st Banchory Boys' Brigade (formed 3 years later) has 40 members. Banchory West Church Youth Club (1944) has a membership of 40. Banchory Children's Theatre (1948) has 25 members. The Army Cadet Force has a total membership of 18. Of these 10 are attached to Banchory Academy, the remainder to the Drill Hall. There is also a Junior Agricultural Club.

WOMEN'S ORGANISATIONS

The East Church Women's Guild has 100 members and the West Church 33. The Scottish League of Wives and Mothers has some 20. The Scottish Women's Rural Institute has a branch at Banchory (135) and also branches at Crathes, Raemoir, Inchmarlo and Tilquhillie.

MUSIC

Banchory has a Pipe Band and also a Strathspey and Reel Society (16).

SPORTS CLUBS

Badminton clubs comprise the Banchory Club (20), the Teachers' Club (15) and Banchory West Church Youth Club (20). The Cricket Club is meantime in abeyance, pending the returfing of the Burnett Park. There are two football teams — Banchory Football Club and the Thistle Football Club. Other clubs are the Bowling Club (40), the Curling Club (25), the Tennis Club (40), the Golf Club (250) and the Kincardineshire Drag Hunt (25).

SOCIAL AND EDUCATIONAL

The Bridge Club has a membership of 20. Banchory Academy has a flourishing Former Pupils' Association and in 1947 a Parent-Teacher Association was formed. The F.P. Association is in process of installing a war memorial in the Academy.

FRIENDLY SOCIETIES

The St Ternan Lodge of Freemasons, no. 443, founded in 1865, purchased the U.P. Church after the First World War for a temple. There have been 31 masters and the present membership is 450. There is also the St Ternan Chapter, no. 521, which was founded in 1922 and meets in the temple. There are 7 principals. The Society of Oddfellows (524), Feugh Lodge, no. 2852 of the Loyal Order of Ancient Shepherds (500) was formed in Banchory on April 4, 1925.

POLITICAL PARTIES

There are two political parties in Banchory today, the Liberal-Unionists and Labour. The Junior Unionists are no longer active.

ALLOTMENTS ASSOCIATIONS ETC.

An Allotments Association operates and also a Bee Keeper's Association. Deeside Agricultural Association is dealt with under Agriculture.

BRITISH LEGION

At a meeting held in the town hall on April 23, 1919, it was unanimously resolved to form an Association under the name of 'The Banchory and District Discharged and Demobilised Sailors' and Soldiers' Association', to be affiliated to the Aberdeen Association and the Scottish Federation. The membership was never very large, and when eventually it was decided to wind up the Association all funds were merged into a benevolent fund under the charge of a small committee. Their work, carried out so quietly, conscientiously and gratuitously, is recalled with pride and gratitude, not only by ex-servicemen but by the people of Banchory in general. About 1934, it was decided to form 'The Banchory and District Branch, The British Legion (Scotland)', the objects and work of which were similar to those of the old Association. In striking contrast the new branch has a huge membership of 450 — one of the largest in the British Isles in proportion to population. In being affiliated to the British Legion

Plate 1. The kirk of St Ternan at Arbuthnott, the best-preserved pre-Reformation church in the country. (*Photo: By permission of Kenneth M. Hay and the Trustees of the National Library of Scotland*).

Plate 2. Banchory High Street in the late 19th century. (Photo: By permission of the George Washington Wilson collection, Aberdeen University Library).

(Scotland) it is much more powerful. Since the close of the First World War, the ex-servicemen of the parish and district have cherished the memory of their fallen comrades by attending Remembrance Services held alternately in the East and West Churches and Gordon Memorials where wreathes have been laid.

Since the branch was formed, 4 members have been appointed life members of the British Legion (Scotland) in recognition of long and faithful service, viz: Messrs J. Anderson, A. Durward, W. Hendry and J. Martin. In addition, Mr J. Abel, who lost the sight of both eyes when on service overseas in the Second World War, has been appointed a life member.

GORDON HIGHLANDERS

The 5th/7th Gordons meet in the Drill Hall — erected about 1905 — and have today some 20 Territorials.

WAR MEMORIALS

Banchory gave generously of her sons in the First World War, and those who made the supreme sacrifice are commemorated by the burgh War Memorial, situated in the Square, and the fine granite monument to the Gordon Highlanders farther west on the North Deeside road. The names of their comrades who fell in the Second World War have recently been added.

LOCAL FOLKLORE

In the early days of last century, superstition was rife. Stone throwing and cloddings have much in common. The witches openly cast stones. The cloddings took place by the instrumentality of an unseen agent, usually supposed to be in league with Satan. Here at Banchory, about the middle of last century, a clodding occurred which caused great commotion. Let William Baker tell what happened, in 'The De'il at Baldarroch' —

> Afore the fire folk couldna' sit for fear,
> For peats and clods cam' bunging ben the flear;
> The Parson cam' and gained the house wi' prayer,
> But still the clods were thuddin' here and there.
> The spoons an' dishes, knives an' forks,
> They frisked aboot as light as corks,
> An' cups an' ladles joined the dancing,
> An' thro' the house they a' gaed prancing.

F

Eventually suspicion fell on a young servant girl. Calling on her, the minister and Mr Burnett, brother of the Laird, found her washing potatoes in a tub. By a quick movement of her hand they noticed that she could make the potatoes squirt through her fingers and scatter all over the floor. On her being ordered by the minister to remove her hands from the tub, the confusion ceased. She was finally summoned to Stonehaven with an accessory, but there is no record of the verdict pronounced.

In those days it was believed that the Mineral Well, about a quarter of a mile from Craigton, had health-giving properties. A sufferer from any disease could be instantly cured by depositing a pin or a button in the well and then partaking of its water. Belief in malevolent water-spirits was also prevalent in those times. Many were the weird stories told by James Humble, the ferryman at Coble Heugh (Banchory Lodge) of the mysterious water-kelpie which haunted the pool there. 'The Green Lady' is the name given to one of the private apartments on the upper floors of Crathes Castle. The various figure subjects painted are accompanied by a wealth of quaint proverbs and scriptural texts on the joists. The room is so called because it is believed to be haunted by the spirit of a female figure clothed in green, carrying a baby in her arms, though she has not made her appearance during living memory.

ANTIQUITIES

Banchory has not yet been surveyed and reported upon by the Royal Commission on Ancient Monuments. Several monuments, however, have been scheduled for protection under the Ancient Monuments Acts 1913 and 1931. A list of these is as follows:— 2 stone circles, 600 yards E.S.E. and 800 yards S. of Eslie, near Banchory; Glassel stone circle in Dam Wood; Mulloch Wood stone circle ('Nine Stanes'). These archaeological remains, together with the Druid Stone near Inchmarlo Cottage and the numerous microlithic or pigmy flints, first discovered in 1906 by Miss Hilda M.L. Paterson, F.S.A. Scot., on the river terraces near her own home at Birkwood, as well as at Knappach, Maryfield and Beltcraigs, are evidence that the region was inhabited long before the Christian era. It is obvious that the locality around Birkwood was used as a camping site by the Tardenoisians, and evidence that the flints were made on the spot was found in the abundant flakes and cones. In a long cist discovered on the farm of Clashfarquhar, Banchory, 2 urns were found, of which one was a beaker and the other a food vessel. There is only one other instance of such an association on record in Scotland, namely in Berwickshire. Some three miles from Banchory, at Cairnton, there are remains of an ancient fort or camp, which may be either Pictish or Roman in origin.

Only two relics of the Monastery of St Ternan — the burgh's patron saint — remain still at Banchory. One is an equal-armed and wheeled cross, resting on a shaft, carved in relief on a stone now inserted in the garden wall of the East Church manse. The other is a slab with two incised Celtic crosses built into the Tilquhillie vault in the churchyard. A third, the famous Ronecht Bell or 'songster', in all probability survived down to our time, only to be destroyed, alas, through callous neglect; for some years previously to 1875, when a pathway was being made from Banchory Lodge to the railway station, what is described as a small square bell was unearthed. This can hardly have been other than a hand bell of the well-known Celtic type, and its disappearance is much regretted. Two Celtic sculptured stones, not associated with ecclesiastical sites, have been found at the Mill of Crathes. Both are incised. One is an equal-armed and circled cross, the other a shafted cross.

In the early days the market centre was marked by a stone with a cross, which stood somewhere near the site of the present East Church. Today it stands at the entrance to the Burnett Park. Worthy of note are the bell and watch tower (or mort-house) in the churchyard. The bell was taken from the old church, which stood in the churchyard, and placed in the watch-tower. Inscribed on the bell are the words, 'Petrus Ostens, Rotterdami, me fecit A° 1664. Soli Deo Gloria' — Peter Ostens or Peter of Ostend made me at Rotterdam in the year 1664. To God alone be glory. The bell bears a detached floral ornament of a small rose and leaves, with the figure of a recumbent ox. The watch tower was erected as a safeguard against the 'resurrectionists', who from 1711 onwards were notorious.

The Loch of Leys, probably dating back to the 14th century, was the early stronghold of the Crathes family, built on a crannog. The foundations show a structure of indeterminate type. An attempt at drainage was made about 1865, but the lakelet referred to in the previous *Statistical Account* still persists, though its surface is almost entirely hidden by plant growths; the loch is, therefore, not extinct. The drainage cut leading to the Burn of Bennie passes through a thick cover of drift and descends 5 feet or more into rock. The level of the loch before artificial drainage was at least 245 feet. The natural outflow by Burn of Bennie has made a deep cut in the 'drift barrier'. Relatively to the size of the Loch, the spreads of sand and gravel on both north and south sides are very extensive; the old shore-line is there clearly defined, but less so in other parts. In some shallow openings near the old north shore the sands have evidently been bottomed, judging by the numerous boulders on the floors of the pits. Antiquarians have explored the crannog, but further examination of this interesting site seems desirable (*Proc.Soc.Antiq.Scot.*, vol. I, pp.26-27). The previous *Account* refers to the old name of this place as 'gow' or 'goo' house, perhaps from the number of gulls which build their nests on the island. V.J. Buchan Watt cannot accept this derivation of the name. In the glossary of *Johnny Gibb of Gushetneuk* — the classic of N.E. Doric — 'gow' or 'goo' means 'old' or 'ancient'. This is obviously the meaning of the 'goo' house at the now dry Loch of Leys. A mile or so eastwards is Kilduthie, believed to be the site of an ancient chapel dedicated to St Duthus.

Crathes Castle contains several pieces of ancient furniture, pictures (including five Jamesones) and other family heirlooms of considerable value and interest. Chief of these is the 'horn of Leys', made of ivory, with four gilt bands, the two centre bands being adorned with carbuncles and crystals. This horn has belonged to the family from time immemorial and is believed to be the badge of office of the first Laird, who had been King's forester at Drum before that domain was granted to the Irvines. Of its history nothing is known, but the horn is portrayed on the heraldic stones dated 1553 and 1596. Here too, there is the massive and elaborately adorned oaken four-poster bed of the 12th laird, Alexander Burnett, who completed the castle, and his wife, Katherine Gordon of Lesmoir; it shows their portraits, coats of arms and monograms, and bears the date 1594. There is also a carved wardrobe — another piece of old oak furniture — bearing the initials of the 1st baronet and his first wife, Margaret Douglas of Glenbervie. The original charter by David II to Alexander Burnard, 17 November 1358, confirming the charter by Robert I to the same Alexander of Kellienclerach and the Cardneys, 28 March 1323, is also preserved in the castle.

Queen Mary's Well and the 'Queen's Chair' are still pointed out on the Hill of Fare, but it is more than doubtful that Mary Queen of Scots was ever nearer than Aberdeen.

UNUSUAL PLACE NAMES

As in most parts of Scotland, the older place-names within the parish permit of only tentative conclusions as to origins. A few can be pronounced upon with fair confidence.

The stream called the *Canny* has an old name (with Invercanny, 'confluence of Canny', which is the last occurrence of a genuine 'Inver'-name as you come down the river). It is Kanyn in old documents. *Coble Heugh*, later Banchory Lodge, and now Banchory Lodge Hotel, indicates the croft or 'parcel' of land given to the ferryman who kept the 'coble' or large shallow boat in which passengers were ferried across the Dee. The old ferry of Banchory was there and in those days the ferries, like the market stances, were perquisites of the lairds. So a man was put there to work the boat and collect the dues, and he was given a croft adjoining. Heugh means the steepish bank of a river. The same name, Cobleheugh, occurs further up the river at the site of the former Boat of Dinnet. *Corrichie* might be *corrfhiadhach (aidh)* — deer corrie. The battle of Corrichie (October 28, 1562) was fought in a great hollow or corrie in the heart of the Hill of Fare. *Crathes* is the same name as Crathie, further up the valley, with the English plural 's' attached, a frequent occurrence. *Glassel* is *glas-choille*, green wood. *Hill of Fare* — the earliest known form of the name, 'Mont de Fair' occurs in the Register of the Great Seal of Scotland, 1598. In Gaelic, *faire* means 'watch' or 'watching'. This may be right, but it is a conjectural reading, to be adopted only with reserve. *The Hirn* is old Scots, meaning a corner or something like that. *Inchmarlo* representing an older Inchmarloch, would probably be *innis-meirleich*, thieve's island or meadow. *Kinneskie*, now the golf course, seems most likely to be derived from *ceann-eascain* — top of the marshy place. *Knappach* is from cnap, a little hill. The *Leys*, the old name of the estate, is Scots for lea ground. *Raemoir* is the 'big rae', rae meaning an enclosure of some kind. Today, in dialect, 'ree' is used for an enclosure for hens or the like. *Tilquhillie* is *tulach-choille*, hillock of the wood.

Some ancient names, like *Brathens*, *Feugh*, and others, may be said pretty well to defy the investigator.

LOCAL RECORDS

There has been no report by the Historical Manuscripts Commission. The local reports are as follows:—

CHURCH RECORDS

(a) *Banchory-Ternan East Church of Scotland*, formerly the old parish church. Kirk Session minutes dating from 1699 to 1861 in 3 volumes are lodged in the General Assembly Library and Strong Room, Tolbooth Church, Castlehill, Edinburgh; the remainder in 3 volumes dating from September 1861 to the present — the last still in current use — are in the custody of the Session Clerk, Mr A.E. Gowan, Schoolhouse, Banchory. Records prior to 1660 were destroyed by fire, as noted in the report to the General Assembly in 1889.

(b) *Banchory-Ternan West Church of Scotland*, comprising the former Free, United Presbyterian, North and South United Free Churches.

The following minute books are in the possession of the Kirk Session and except where otherwise stated are lodged in metal boxes under lock and key in the vestibule of the church there.

Kirk Session records:—
(i) *Banchory Free Church*: Minutes dating from August 8, 1843, the first

meeting after the Disruption, to May 1, 1901, in 8 volumes. There is, however, no record for the period Sept. 28, 1883 to April 22, 1885.

(ii) *South United Free Church*: one volume from June 6, 1901 to June 18, 1918.

(iii) *U.F. Church and Banchory West Church of Scotland*: Two volumes from July 14, 1918 to date, in possession of the Session Clerk, Mr P. Thomson, Sunningdale, Raemoir.

(iv) *North U.F. Church, formerly U.P.*: No trace of anything before 1879. One volume, Jan.8, 1879 - May 20, 1918.

Records of Deacons' Court, Congregational Boards, etc.:—

(i) Banchory Free Church Deacons' Court: minutes from Jan. 1843 to July 1918 in 7 volumes.

(ii) North U.F. Church Managers' minute book: one volume, from Feb. 23, 1909 to June 24, 1918.

(iii) Banchory U.F. & Banchory-Ternan West Church of Scotland Deacons' Court & Congregational Board: five volumes, from July 14, 1918 to date.

Baptismal Register:—

For Banchory Free Church, South U.F. Church, U.F. Church and now West Church — one volume from June 3rd, 1891 to date in custody of the minister at the West manse, Banchory.

TOWN COUNCIL RECORDS

There are no old charters and papers affecting the burgh and the records of the Town Council are all contained in minute books. From 1887 to 1910 these records are contained in scroll minute books, written by hand. From 1911 to the present time the minutes have been printed and bound and to date there are eleven volumes. These minute books and the prior ones are all lodged in the office of the Town Clerk.

It is worth recording that a coat of arms for the burgh was drawn up by the Lyon King of Arms in 1939 through the generosity of Mr James M. Burnett, Provost at the time.

SCHOOL RECORDS

Seven school log books, dating from 1869, are kept in the Academy. The official school records, however, are in the keeping of Mr Alexander Jenkins, Director of Education for the County of Kincardine at his office — 'Viewmount', Stonehaven. These consist of the following:—

(i) *School Board records*: (1) Minutes from 1873 to August 1919, five volumes; (2) Ten letter books; (3) Sixteen ledgers, cash and abstract books; (4) Two scroll minutes.

(ii) *School Management Committee records*: Two box files from July 1930 to June 1948. The gap between 1919 and 1930 cannot be explained. The School Management Committee (now defunct) was to a large extent successor to the School Board.

HERITORS RECORDS

Minute books and other papers from 1829 are lodged at the Record Office, H.M. Register House, Edinburgh.

PRIVATE RECORDS

(a) For a report on the muniments of Sir James Horn Burnett, Bart., of Leys, Crathes Castle, Kincardineshire, see Hist. MSS. Com., 2nd Rep., xix, 197; and National Register of Archives, Scottish Record Office, H.M. General Register House, Edinburgh.

(b) Twenty writs, 1328, 1359, 1600-1700 of the estate of Raemoir were deposited in 1949 in the Record Office, H.M. General Register House, Edinburgh.

LOCAL ENDOWMENTS

1. RELIGIOUS

(a) Banchory-Ternan East church has total endowments of £399.7.1, made up as follows:— £212.8.8 — standardised stipend; £360.8.0 — glebe money; £126.10.5 — local endowment held for stipend of minister.

(b) Banchory-Ternan West church has total endowments of £130, made up as follows:— £80 — Lynnwood Trust; £50 — allocated by the Church and Ministry Department when the stipend of East Church was standardised.

2. EDUCATIONAL

In the list of endowments in the county of Kincardine that were, by Order in Council, to be held and administered by the Governors of the Kincardineshire Educational Trust under the Educational Endowments (Scotland) Acts, 1928 and 1935, there appear the following with relation to Banchory, viz:—

(a) Hunter's Bursary Fund, Hunter's Medal Fund, Hunter's Prize

Fund — founded by James Hunter, merchant, Banchory, by trust disposition and settlement dated 22/6/07 and codicil dated 15/7/10.

(b) Reid and Burnett Endowment — founded by Alexander Reid, M.D., and Alexander Burnett, indweller and agent in Edinburgh, under Section 33 of the Educational Endowments (Scotland) Act, 1882 approved by the Scottish Education Department on 22/2/93.

(c) Reid and Burnett Endowment — founded by Sir Thomas Burnett of Leys and Alexander Reid, M.D., Mrs. Catherine Burnett or Skinner and Dame Margaret Burnett of Leys, under section 33 of the Educational Endowments (Scotland) Act, 1882, approved by the Scottish Education Dept. on 24/2/90. as amended by decrees of Court of Session dated 5/11/95 and 17/3/11.

In the K.E.T. Scheme, 1935, Section 29 sets forth that the governing body shall make certain special payments, including payments annually to the County Council — (1) of £5 to purchase silver medals (Hunter) to be awarded to pupils in the parish of Banchory-Ternan for regularity of attendance and good progress; and (2) of £7 to purchase books (Hunter prizes) to be awarded as prizes to scholars attending Banchory Secondary School.

Section 30 further sets forth that scheduled bursaries shall be awarded on certain conditions — (1) Hunter bursaries, tenable at Banchory Secondary School and awarded to pupils in the area comprising the parishes of Banchory-Ternan, Strachan and Durris. (2) Reid and Burnett bursaries, tenable at Banchory Secondary School and awarded to pupils in the parish of Banchory-Ternan.

3. CHARITABLE

The County Council hold two trusts for the poor of the parish. One is the Leys Mortification and the other is the Mary Ann Thomson Fund. In addition there are four bequests, the total interest on which amounts annually to £45 (approx). This money is distributed at Christmas to the inhabitants of the burgh selected by the Town Council. The names of the bequests are — The Sutherland Bequest, The Gordon Bequest, The Anderson Bequest and The Philip Bequest.

NOTABLE MEN

During the first half of the 19th century the most learned physician in Britain, and probably in Europe, was Dr. Francis Adams, M.D., LL.D. (1796-1861), born at Lumphanan and first resident doctor in Banchory. By the sheer force of his intellect, by the extent and exactness of his erudition, he became the cherished friend of many famous scholars; & he left in his own profession no equal in the combination of honest, deep and broad learning, with practical sagacity and enlightened experience. He was the author in large part of Dunbar's Greek Lexicon and of a translation of Hippocrates. A fine granite monument to his memory stands at the south-west corner of Bellfield and bears an inscription written by Sir William Geddes.

James Scott Skinner, born in Banchory in 1843, was a noted composer of Scottish music and violinist. He composed his famous Strathspey 'Miller o' Hirn' in the Ewans' house at Ewan Place. A tablet inset in the wall on High Street opposite Dee Street marks the place of his birth. His brother Alexander, was a noted teacher of dancing and his portrait hangs in the small Town Hall.

General Sir William Burnett of Banchory Lodge, who was a good and just landlord, served in the campaign in Flanders in 1793, and commanded the 14th Regiment in the attack on Porto Rico under Sir Ralph Abercromby in 1797. The round tower on Scolty, some 60 feet high, was erected to his memory.

The Rev. George Hutchison, D.D., minister of the parish church from 1846-1894, was elected Moderator of the General Assembly of the Church of Scotland in 1877.

The Rev. Robert Reid, M.A., was minister of the Free Church for fifty years 1843-1893 and was Clerk to the Presbytery of Kincardine O'Neil for nearly forty years.

Dr. George Cran, M.B.E. (1852-1938), a successful doctor and all round sportsman, gave distinguished service to his profession and to the community for over half a century. For his valuable and gratuitous war-work during the First World War he received the M.B.E. He rendered long and valued service on the Town Council and was for many years a magistrate.

In his time, John Watson was a man of note, being the second feuar in Banchory and the founder of the Town Council. To his foresight and encouragement Banchory owes much of the popularity it now enjoys as a holiday and health resort.

No trader on Deeside was better known than James Hunter, merchant. Of 'glib' tongue and rare wit, he was exceedingly diligent in business and amassed a considerable fortune. In 1911 he bequeathed the sum of £1030, the income from which was to be used for payment of bursaries to pupils of Banchory School. Aberdeen University and local charities also benefited.

Donald Munro, who was for nine years Provost of Banchory, began his working career at eight years of age when he left school and started at the sawmills of Messrs. A. & G. Paterson Ltd. at 5/- per week. He rose to be Director of the firm and Convener of the county. During the First World War he founded the North of Scotland Home Timber Merchants' Association in order to increase the drive for home timber. At this time, too, he and his wife raised £1,000 for benevolent funds and he was invested with the O.B.E. He was a wonderful organiser and ready to help in every good cause — local and otherwise.

When Charles Murray, C.M.G., LL.D., died on 12th April 1941 at the Lythe, Banchory, Scotland lost a pioneer in modern vernacular poetry and South Africa one of its pioneers in administration. Born at Alford on September 28, 1864, he went to South Africa in 1888 where practically all his poetry was written. The last and only poem Murray wrote during his retirement in Banchory was 'Ae year's bairns', addressed on 24 October 1940 to his friend Dr. J.F. Tocher.

David Lawson, M.A., M.D., F.R.S.E., a pioneer in the treatment of tuberculosis, founded in 1899 the first sanatorium in Scotland at Nordrach-on-Dee, Banchory. Inspired by the work of the celebrated Dr. Otto Walther at Nordrach in the Black Forest in Germany, he gave up general practice in Somerset to devote his life to this branch of medicine. A committee of prominent physicians was formed in Edinburgh, the geographic and climatic conditions in Scotland were carefully studied, and 25 acres of woodland at Banchory were selected as the site. While embodying many of the German ideas, the Scottish sanatorium was entirely different in design and many improvements were made. From the first a staff of qualified nurses was in residence. A laboratory for clinical research work was provided and by 1901 an X-ray Department was opened. Ten more years were to elapse before any other sanatorium in Britain possessed an X-ray department and so it was that all the pioneer work in the application of Röntgen rays to the diagnosis and treatment of chest disease was carried out at Banchory. In 1902, research was begun on X-rays, and a year later Dr. Lawson, at the invitation of the Royal Medical Society in London, delivered a lecture on the use of Röntgen rays in the diagnosis of lung and pleural diseases. This lecture, recorded in *The Lancet* in 1903, was the first publication of its kind in this country. For his work in this field Dr. Lawson was made a Fellow of the Society. In 1918 Dr. Lawson acquired the Deeside Hydropathic at Milltimber, near Aberdeen, now known as Tor-na-Dee, and adapted it to the treatment of phthisical diseases. Nordrach-on-Dee flourished and achieved a world-wide reputation. How many, in sanatoria all over the world today, owe the possibility of their ultimate cure and recovery to the patient endeavours and pioneer work of this skilful Scotsman!

Maj.-Gen. Sir James Lauderdale Gilbert Burnett of Leys, 13th Baronet, C.B., 1932; C.M.G. 1919; D.S.O. 1915; Colonel of the Gordon Highlanders since 1919; member of the King's Bodyguard for Scotland, was born on 1 April 1880. He has been Vice-Lieutenant since 1944 and J.P. of Kincardineshire and owns 13,400 acres. His recreations are fishing and shooting. He resides at Crathes Castle.

Well-known to old residenters was John Moir, who kept a small shop at the Bridge of Feugh. Although belonging to the pathetic fellowship of the blind, he was of a very cheerful disposition. He advertised his wares in verse, on a blackboard which stood outside his shop. A collection of his rhymes and verses was printed in Aberdeen by G. & W. Fraser under the title *Feugh Spray* and sold by the author, 1903.

James C. Hadden, born in Banchory in 1861, attained distinction in music and literature. Appointed organist of St. John's Parish Church, Edinburgh in 1889, he was a member of the staff engaged by Leslie Stephen on the *Dictionary of National Biography*. *A Life of Handel* and *A Life of Mendelssohn* came from his pen in 1888.

WAY OF LIFE

One cannot but remember with gratitude the many public-spirited and progressive men who have rendered notable service to the community across the years. Greater interest by the people generally in civic affairs seems, however, to have been taken in earlier days, when 'heckling meetings' were all the go. Since 1945 there has been no municipal election and very great difficulty was experienced in finding persons to fill casual vacancies on the Council, and on one occasion there were fewer nominations than seats to fill. This could be interpreted as due to a general feeling of confidence in the local administration, but undoubtedly it is the case that a good deal of apathy prevails. At the moment the Council is endeavouring to bring home to the ratepayers some sense of their responsibility, and hopes are high that in 1950 there will be a keenly contested election. Fortunately, party politics play no part whatever in local municipal affairs.

Regarding the sense of community, here again one feels that it was much stronger in former times. Today the tenants of local authority houses may feel a sense of community but, strangely enough, have never made any attempt to form any association among themselves until requested to do so by the Town Council. Many factors have been at work across the years. Some 50 years ago all contact with the outside world was closed at 7 p.m. when the last train left for Aberdeen, and Banchory was then a self-contained community; the people had to provide for their own leisure hours and so learned the art of entertaining themselves. There were many simple amusements, such as Scott Skinner's dancing class, the singing class, the berry market, the dambrod (draughts), cards and barn dances, etc. There were no passive entertainments such as mass football-watching, wireless and cinema. Thus a sense of 'togetherness' prevailed and the people knew one another better. But today Banchory's proximity to Aberdeen, with a plentiful and quick service of buses, if not trains, till within an hour of midnight, while in many respects an advantage, has no doubt made for a lessened interest in local community life. Many seek the city for their pleasures and amusements, as well as to fulfil their daily calling there.

Family life, too, has been impaired owing to the facilities afforded by easy travel. Time was when the family, much larger then than now, was a real social unit. Members had greater opportunity of being together, and were more dependent on one another. At present, there is a growing independence of one another and even of the parents, whose authority is not so strong as once it was. Few families find their entertainment at home; more spend their leisure time outside. Moreover, it was once the accepted thing for a country girl, on leaving school, to go into domestic service at one of the 'big houses'. That is a thing of the past. Now she is more likely to seek employment in a shop or office locally, take a clerical post in town, or train for a business or nursing career. The day of the domestic servant has gone and the 'big houses' have to manage with skeleton staffs.

RELIGIOUS OBSERVANCE

The practice of church-going was much more widely observed then than now. Older residenters can recall the streets black with folk on their way to kirk. The family pew has almost disappeared, and parents tend more and more to entrust to the Sunday School the religious instruction of their children — a lack, surely, of parental responsi-bility. In former days, too, much of the cultural life of the people was centred in the church, where dramatic clubs, debating societies, choral singing and magic lantern shows were popular. Sunday was spent for the most part in a reverent way, and in most homes religious exercises, including the Shorter Catechism, were a regular feature, though perhaps not always as inspiring as they might have been. Nevertheless, they wove religion into the warp and woof of daily living, and their total effect across the years has been mighty in the moulding of character and shaping of destiny. The younger generation, alas! know nothing of the inspiration of those days, nor yet of their Shorter Catechism. We have grown accustomed, perforce, to smaller con-gregations, to an increasing secularism, to Sunday trippers and Sunday golf, and in consequence to an ever-widening gulf between religion and the people.

While religious apathy is manifest, there is no active hostility to the church or the Christian faith. Intense religious emotion is not frequently marked in the life of the parish, and evangelistic services, once carried on by the Davidsons of Inchmarlo, have long been discontinued. Yet all is not lost; to many, still, religion is of supreme importance, they love their church and serve it with devotion and zeal. All honour to the faithful few in every congregation. Today there is no ecclesiastical tension, as in the days that followed the Disruption, when the parish and Free Church ministers were at loggerheads and, rather than pass each other, would seek refuge in a house or turn into a side street. What exists today between the former parish and Free Church members is a certain feeling of rivalry — perhaps a healthy rivalry — which in due time, of course, will die out.

The minister, once the most important and awe-inspiring person in the parish, plays a much humbler role today. Education is more widespread, and the doctor, the teacher, the lawyer and the minister no longer provide the exclusive leadership of their neighbourhood. Much of the feeling, too, of aloofness is gone, and the minister today is human and approachable, interesting himself in all the affairs of his people and parish. Church discipline has lapsed, and the stool of repentance is not even a memory.

Crime in Banchory is negligible; the citizens are law-abiding and there is very little drunkenness. Still, football coupons find their way into a good many homes, while the predatory proclivities of boys prove troublesome, especially in the season of mellow fruitfulness. Stolen fruit, it seems, still tastes the sweetest.

SOCIAL LIFE

The Town Hall, the church halls, the Drill Hall and Scout Hut provide ample facilities for social life. The various organisations are ceaseless in their activities and certainly give colour and, in some cases, cultural development to those who participate. Organisations for women, such as the Women's Rural Institute, with its popular demonstrations of leatherwork, dressmaking, cookery, home hints, etc., are certainly well supported. Further, they meet a much-felt need in providing a respite from the daily round at home. Two things here are worthy of note. First, the lot of the country housewife today is much easier than it was yesterday. What with gas and electricity, inside sanitation and new grates, Aga and Esse cookers, and labour-saving devices of all kinds, her work is immeasurably easier. Further, married women today enjoy a much greater freedom from domestic duty than before. Many of the younger ones have their regular 'night out' at the Guild, the Rural, or in town, and all because father looks after the children. Men are much more domesticated than previously. The care of the children is no longer entrusted wholly to the mother, and rightly so; the father also plays his part.

The British Legion has done much in recent times to foster the spirit of community. It now provides 3 film shows in the Town Hall every week. It initiated and organises the annual Gala Week with its sports, competitions, amusements, and crowning of the Gala Queen. It has purchased property in the High Street with a view to the erection of a proper cinema. Moneys raised from whist drives, dances, etc., which appeal so irresistibly, are handed over to charity, nor are the needs of their unfortunate comrades in the Second World War forgotten. While interest in lighter entertainment abounds, especially among the young, societies for the promotion of literary, musical, dramatic and the more cultural activities seem to have a very transitory life.

CLOTHES

The clothing worn today is much more hygienic than formerly. It was impossible for the air to penetrate the many layers of clothes once worn. The health of a child wearing 7 undergarments must have suffered immeasurably. 'Sabbath clothes' are a thing of the past and even at funerals ordinary garments are worn by the majority.

Work, for the most part, is undertaken in a conscientious way. Shopkeepers and their assistants are cheerful, friendly, willing to help and anxious to please. The advent of the machine age has greatly improved the lot of the farm labourer and saved him much laborious toil. Still he continues to sow and reap, in sunshine and in shower. The worker today has his half-day off weekly, as well as his annual holidays, and while he receives much higher wages, the cost of living, it should be remembered, is correspondingly higher.

LANGUAGE

Our language has changed, as other things have changed. The 'mither' tongue is fast dying out and that is a pity, for to the true Scot, it is so much more expressive than English. It is doubtful if the young people of today would know half of the strangely-sounding words of 'The muckle spate o' twenty-nine', by David Grant.

CONCLUSION

Time marches on and nothing remains the same. But the people today, if quiet and undemonstrative, are kindly, friendly and sincere, and the standard of morality, on the whole, is good. And yet one feels that, with all the progress and improvement, notable and worthy as it undoubtedly is, the quantum of happiness is no greater today than it used to be. There is more leisure, but less home life. There is more activity, but less contentment.

(undated: ca. 1950)

THE PARISH OF BENHOLM

by the Rev. D.W. Greenfield, M.A.

GEOGRAPHY

The parish (spelt Benholme in the first and second *Statistical Accounts*) lies on the main Dundee-Aberdeen coast road, which passes half a mile above the fishing village of Johnshaven. The old road, which can still be traced, passes through Benholm, which is near the centre of the parish and about a mile inland. Here there was formerly a road inn. Samuel Johnson and John Wesley passed this way. The adjoining parishes are St Cyrus to the south-west, Garvock to the north-west and Bervie to the north-east. The coastline (about 3 miles) runs north-eastward from the Grip or Narrows, a few hundred yards south-west of Johnshaven, along the Haughs of Benholm (where the Benholm Burn enters the North Sea) to near Gourdon. The parish church and manse, a school, public hall, and the old graveyard are at Benholm. Over 3 miles in length (north and south) and mostly 2 to 3 miles in breadth, the parish has an area of 4892 acres.

The whole coastline consists of long reefs of black rock, stretching out to sea, and covered at high tide. The coast is dangerous to shipping. Formerly Johnshaven had a coastguard-station and a life-boat, but both have been given up, the latter since a gallant attempt at rescue in which some of the crew and the boat were lost. There is a rocket-apparatus, whose crew recently won the award for the most gallant deed of the year in that service. The crew stood by for three days in a high gale before effecting a rescue off Montrose bay. At a look-out station a cone is hoisted as a gale warning. A good tidal harbour at Johnshaven, formerly the property of Miss Scott of Brotherton, now belongs to the County Council. From the coast the land rises abruptly behind Johnshaven, affording it protection from the north wind, and giving it a mild winter climate, suitable for the growing of early cabbages. The farms nearest the coast are among the best in the county and grow good wheat. Inland is mainly moorland.

GEOLOGY

Certain aspects of the geology of the parish are dealt with in the *Transactions of the Edinburgh Geological Society*, Vol. XIII, Part 1, in an article by the Hon. Editor, Robert Campbell, M.A., D.Sc. In this article special attention is directed to boulder clay in the Benholm Burn, on the east side of which, about a mile inland, is a 'Potters' field', where there must have been a pottery, and to the Cove Hill, a short distance south of the Narrows, Johnshaven, where there is also an exposure of shelly boulder clay.

According to Dr Campbell, the black boulder clay 'can only represent the bottom moraine of an ice sheet which had passed over the floor of the North Sea. In the earliest ice movement in north eastern Scotland, the Scottish and Scandinavian *mers de glace* coalesced and moved together along the coast of Kincardineshire from the north-east or north-north-east This conclusion is supported by the character of the included stones in the shelly boulder clay, and by its occurrence over 200 feet above sea level and $1\frac{1}{2}$ miles from the sea in the Burn of Benholm. From Aberdeen to Inverbervie the lower layers of the North Sea ice were deflected by the high cliffs which bound the coast. South of Inverbervie the cliffs give place to a flat foreshore with wide developments of raised beaches. There, obviously, the North Sea ice was able to deposit its bottom moraine at the Horse Crook, at the Coldwell Brae and at Cove Hill, and to invade the deep pre-glacial hollow between Gourdon Hill and the Hill of Stone of Benholm, where west of Upper Birnie there is again a thick accumulation of the shelly boulder clay.

'At Horse Crook and near Upper Birnie there are exposures of interglacial deposits. The interglacial peat at the Burn of Benholm is of particular interest. It was formed after the North Sea ice had retreated and before the advance of the later ice sheet from Strathmore.'

FLORA AND FAUNA

Botanically, the parish is of less interest than that of St Cyrus. Among the more characteristic coast flowers are Geranium sanguineum, Bloody Cranesbill and Cochlearia officinalis, Scurvy-grass. Brotherton gardens, though situated on the coast, used to be famous, as were the long stretches of snowdrops and daffodils planted in the grounds.

Most of the commoner gulls, including the cormorant, may be seen along the coast. Oyster catchers are particularly numerous and may be observed near at hand from the pleasant grassy path which stretches from Johnshaven to Gourdon. Seals make an occasional appearance in pursuit of salmon.

ESTATES

The estates of Brotherton and Benholm are well wooded, but the Lady's Wood on Stone of Benholm has been cut down. The principal

Plate 3. Crathes Castle: a fine example of a north-east L-plan tower-house.
(*Photo: By permission of the Royal Commission on Ancient Monuments, Scotland*).

Plate 4. Dunnottar Castle. (*Photo: By permission of the Royal Commission on Ancient Monuments*).

Plate 5. Dunnottar Castle. (*Photo: By permission of Van Werninck Studio, Montrose*).

estate is Brotherton, which belonged till recently to Miss Scott. Brotherton House is being used temporarily as a private school. The Benholm estate has also changed hands and the castle, whose tower is the oldest part of the building, is falling into decay. During the Second World War Brotherton House served for a time as a maternity hospital.

CHANGES

Two wars have taken their toll of life, and in the Second World War the men of the Merchant Service suffered heavily. No permanent dislocation, however, has been caused in the life of the parish. Such gradual changes as have occurred will be summarised.

POPULATION

Between 1801 and 1851 the population of Benholm parish rose from 1412 to 1641. By 1901 it was back to 1426. The maximum recorded by census was 1648 in 1841. In the present century the figure fell rapidly:— (1911) 1276; (1921) 1170; (1931) 1092. In view of the lack of employment and smaller families, the decrease is not surprising. A number of houses are occupied by retired people, most of whom have some local connection. There are about 15 shopkeepers. (The 1951 census showed a further drop in the population to 1028, there being 476 males and 552 females).

HOUSING

Johnshaven lies round the harbour, and sloping up towards the main road. The houses look to the sea, and have been built at various periods, with a surprising number of wynds and pends. The typical fisherman's cottage is solidly built of stone, having two or three rooms, but there are many variations. The Council houses have, from an aesthetic point of view, changed the appearance of the village, which formerly toned in well with the grey of the sea. The old houses are mostly owner-occupied, and are generally kept with great pride. Baths are rare, and water closets have often only been recently introduced. The principal faults in most of the old houses are lack of light and inadequate facilities for baiting. Most of the cottages have gardens, and many of these suffer from infertility, owing to the annual planting of potatoes in the same plot. The County Council houses are of the usual type. None has special facilities for baiting.

WATER SUPPLY

Johnshaven is supplied from two springs, which are stored in a large tank above the village below the main road. The supply is just adequate. There is no water supply for the parish.

ELECTRICITY

The main streets of Johnshaven and most of the houses are lit with electricity from the Grampian supply. A few of the larger farms have light and power from this scheme. There is no gas.

CLEANSING

Rubbish is collected in Johnshaven. The present method of dumping it on the foreshore, to the west of the village, is unsightly.

HEALTH SERVICES

These are shared with the rest of the county. Patients are sent to Aberdeen Royal Infirmary or Stracathro Hospital, and fever and tubercular cases to Stonehaven isolation hospital. There is a nurse in Johnshaven, and the country district is served by a nurse shared with adjacent parishes.

FARMING

In the landward part of the parish the changes have been those common to country districts. The townward drift of the population is seen in the abandonment of small hamlets. On the farms themselves there is always a demand for labour. There is little continuity of tradition. Farms change hands, farm labourers move around. The wages of the farm labourer have improved even in relation to the cost of living, but some of the cottar houses are damp and even without an inside water supply. The Benholm hall is not yet adequately equipped to serve as a Community Centre.

INDUSTRIAL DECLINE

In Johnshaven there is still a strong community life and a continuance of tradition. Industrially there has been a steady decline. Within living memory the village was a thriving place. Fifty years ago it had a population of over 1000. A linen mill offered employment to the women and in addition to inshore fishing there was a herring-curing yard. Owing to the change of habit of the herring, which now seldom visit this port, the curing industry has been given up. The linen factory has also been closed.

FISHING

The number of boats is steadily decreasing, though inshore fishing is still profitable. Cod is caught by line or net. The rocky bottom favours crab and lobster catching. Farther out, on a sandy bottom, plaice and sole are caught with the seine net. The cost of gear and especially of boats, the growing reluctance of the women to bait the line, and the competition of the trawlers have contributed to the decline of inshore fishing.

Though Johnshaven is unlikely to become a holiday resort, owing to the absence of sands, all available rooms are let for August and September, and this is a considerable source of income to the village. Increasingly the men have found employment as salmon fishers, working under various companies, some of them going as far north as Wick. Formerly most salmon fishers went to sea in the winter, owning their own boats, and some, at the conclusion of the salmon fishing season, joined the herring fleet at Yarmouth; some, too, found employment on the land. Now, however, most are willing to work for contractors at various unskilled jobs.

Despite the decline in local industries, the standard of life in the village has risen greatly in living memory. Half a century ago large families were the rule, and when storms made fishing impossible, as they may do for several months, people had to subsist on salt herring, potatoes and oatmeal. Tuberculosis was common, but those who survived were healthy, independent and intelligent.

OTHER EMPLOYMENT

The women and girls of the village mainly find employment in factories or offices in adjacent burghs. In the case of factories working the three-shift system, this entails considerable hardship, as they have to walk half a mile in all weathers to the bus which takes them to their work. Night work in factories contributes to the break-down of home life. For those who work at a distance the home is little more than a dormitory.

ECCLESIASTICAL

The church life of the parish reflects the prevailing trend of church life in Scotland. Where there were formerly three Presbyterian denominations worshipping in the parish — Johnshaven had a Free Church and a United Presbyterian Church — there is now a united Church of Scotland (Benholm and Johnshaven), retaining places of worship in both centres. Owing to generous benefactions by the Misses Myers, daughters of a fomer minister of the parish, provision has been made for the upkeep of the Benholm manse garden and also for the augmentation of the stipend to about £500. The few Episcopalians in the parish worship at Inverbervie or Montrose.

While there is still, as in many fishing villages, a strong religious tradition in Johnshaven, and notably hearty congregational singing, church attendance has steadily declined. In the last *Statistical Account* it is stated that the average attendance in Benholm (before the Disruption) numbered over 640 in the summer. It may be questioned if today it is over 100. On the other hand, there is now a strong Woman's Guild. The present membership of the united congregation is 400.

EDUCATIONAL

There are 2 schools in the parish, one at Benholm and one at Johnshaven. At one time there were seven. The present school at Johnshaven was formerly a Free Kirk school, built shortly after the Disruption in 1843. Both schools are for younger children — up to the age of about eleven or twelve, the older children being conveyed by bus to Bervie Central School or the Mackie Academy at Stonehaven. The standard of intelligence among the fisher children is generally above the average. I have seen no bad results of inbreeding as, for the most part, the Johnshaven fisherfolk intermarry with those of Gourdon. Few children proceed to the universities. Schools are now better equipped than they were, and the headmaster or headmistress has still a great influence in the community. Elementary education is probably much better than it was. The number of those receiving good secondary education and obtaining good posts, notably in the merchant service and banks, has declined.

RECREATION

Facilities for organised recreation have been increased notably by the Wairds Park, gifted by Miss Scott of Brotherton, in which there are a pavilion, tennis courts, a putting green and a football pitch. Football is the most popular sport. There are two halls in Johnshaven, belonging to the Good Templars and the Freemasons respectively. Neither is adequately equipped for a Community Centre. The Good Templars, once a flourishing body, are now defunct, but St John's Lodge of the Freemasons has an ancient history and still maintains a large membership.

The only youth organisations at present in the village are the Boy Scouts and Girl Guides. There is a branch of the Young Farmers' League in Benholm. Other organisations are the Women's Rural Institute in Benholm and Johnshaven, and a branch, under Inverbervie, of the British Legion. While concerts, if given by local performers, whist drives in aid of charities, and dances are well attended, there is no recreational centre for the village, and picture houses outside the parish are largely patronised.

WAY OF LIFE

In general, the life of the parish shows continual change. As in the fishing village depicted in Scott's *Antiquary*, matriarchy was, until recently, the rule among the fishers, and after the death by drowning of a son or husband, the mother or wife took to bed for a stated time. Many of the old customs are dying out. 'Old Yule' is little kept. Weddings, in which the bridegroom, attended by his friends, went out to meet the bride with her processions of maids, are now often celebrated more conventionally in church. It is still unlucky to use the word 'salmon', to touch iron, or for a minister of religion to pass while the lines are being baited. Funerals are often held on Sundays, and an invitation is issued to every house. Only the men attend.

The speech of the fishermen, though not so distinctive a dialect as that of Gourdon, owing to greater admixture of other elements, has yet changed little. The speech of some of the fisherwomen is very beautiful in its clear enunciation. The necessity of being heard against gales may have something to do with this.

Though the life of the village is less homogeneous than it was, strong local feeling can easily be aroused, particularly at the time of a general election. There seems as yet to be little cultural advance as the result of improved education. A marked change is in the independence of the people. Johnshaven, formerly self-supporting, now lives largely on government aid. The increased well-being of the people may be illustrated by the fact that a clothing society, which continued for many years, has now been given up. But this is not due to any increased productivity or thrift, though this latter is still a strongly marked characteristic of the people.

Agriculturally, the parish may continue to flourish, especially on the better farms, but unless some local industry is established the community life of Johnshaven is likely to diminish. It will become more and more a haven for the retired.

October 1949

THE PARISH OF DUNNOTTAR

by the Rev. John C. Campbell, B.D.

NAME

The meaning of Dunnottar is still under discussion, but the etymology which best fits the lie of the land is the fort (*Dun*) on the low ground (*O-Tir*). This defines well the promontory on which Dunnottar Castle is situated and which is likely to have been used as a strong point from the dawn of history.

PHYSICAL BASIS

The parish has roughly the shape of a triangle, with its apex in the Old Town of Stonehaven and its east and north sides the North Sea and the River Carron respectively. The base runs from a point 5 miles inland to the sea at Crawton Bay, about 4 miles to the south of Stonehaven. The principal natural features of the landscape are the great cliff and bird sanctuary known as Fowlsheugh and the woods of Dunnottar, which fan out from the outskirts of the town, southwards for a couple of miles between the River Carron and the main road to Perth. This amenity is likely to disappear at an early date, as the trees have been bought and are to be felled.

From 200 feet above sea-level in the coastal area the surface rises westwards to over 400 feet, the highest point being Carmont Hill (774 ft) on the Glenbervie border. The landward area of Dunnottar parish is 7734 acres. Stonehaven (mostly in Fetteresso parish) has a burghal area of 457 acres. The neighbouring parishes are Fetteresso (to the north), Kinneff and Catterline (S), Arbuthnott (SW), Glenbervie (W).

LOCAL HISTORY

Dunnottar has a place in national history through the founding of a church and missionary settlement by St Ninian, through the events associated with Dunnottar Castle from the time of Wallace to the siege of the castle by Cromwell's troops, when the Regalia of

Scotland were rescued and hidden in Kinneff Church, and also through the sufferings of the Covenanters imprisoned in the Whigs' Vault. The story of the internal affairs of the parish may be taken up where it was left by the second *Account* (1842).

ESTATES

The estates have all changed hands during the last 100 years. Dunnottar estate was entailed by the proprietor mentioned in the last *Account*, Lieutenant-General Forbes. In 1901 one of his heirs disentailed it and it was bought by Mr William H. Ritchie, who died in 1944. Mr Ritchie, who was unmarried, left it to his nephew, Mr David A. Ritchie, whose home is in New Zealand, but who was at that time in this country on war service. The estate was sold by him to Mr G.W. Fletcher of Ilkley Hall, Yorkshire, who died about two years later. The estate was then divided between the Cairngorm Investment Company Ltd., who own the house and part of the woods and parks, and the Kapemi Investment Company Ltd., who own the rest of the estate. The house is at present uninhabited and has a derelict appearance. The woods are in process of being felled.

The Dunnottar Castle estate was sold in 1919 by the proprietor, Commander J.W. Guy Innes, to the late Viscountess Cowdray, who began the systematic restoration and excavation of the castle ruins. A lodge was built at the approach to the castle on the main road to Dundee, where the custodian and estate officer resides. The present owner of the estate, Lord Cowdray, visits the estate from time to time and has had some plantations of trees made to give shelter to game.

The lands of Barras, part of which is in Dunnottar parish, passed in 1943 from the Trustees of Donaldson's Hospital, Edinburgh, to Mrs Louise Carnegie, widow of the late Mr Andrew Carnegie. At her death in 1946 they went to her daughter, Mrs Roswell Miller. At the same time the lands of Fetteresso, a small part of which lie in Dunnottar parish, passed into the same hands.

The farms on all these estates are rented by tenant farmers. Since the death of Mr William Ritchie in 1944 there has been no resident landed proprietor in the parish.

LOCAL GOVERNMENT

The Old Town of Stonehaven, which lies wholly in the parish, was a Burgh of Barony. The original charter of the Burgh was lost and the Sheriff Court Book for 1626, in which it was copied, was either burned or destroyed or carried away by the English in the time of Cromwell. The town was governed by a board of Managers elected by the feuars of the Old Town, to which body the Superior elected

Bailies. This body met in the Old Tolbooth until 1879, when a meeting is recorded in the Court House in the County Buildings. When the Town Council of Stonehaven, as at present constituted, first came into being on 28th October 1889, it took over the government of the whole burgh, meeting in the present Town Hall. Until recently some of those former Managers were still alive and enjoyed the distinction of their now honorary title.

In 1856 the Registration District of Dunnottar was constituted, coinciding with the bounds of the parish. An entry in the Kirk Session minutes of that year gives an inventory of church records handed over to the Sheriff Substitute, to be transferred to Register House at Edinburgh. This marks the passing of the function of registration from church to state. In January 1935 the separate Registration Districts of Dunnottar and Fetteresso were united in one District of Stonehaven and the Dunnottar Registrar moved out of the parish into new quarters as Registrar of the Stonehaven District.

The Parish Council of Dunnottar ceased to exist on 16th May 1930, most of its functions being transferred to the County Council, except those administered by the Stonehaven District Council, which now covers the area of Dunnottar, Fetteresso, Glenbervie and Kinneff.

The County Buildings, situated in Dunnottar parish, were the headquarters of the county police from 1890 to 1949, during which time three Chief Constables of the county police had their office there. In 1949 the police forces of Kincardine, Aberdeenshire, Moray, Nairn and Banff were amalgamated, and since that time Stonehaven has no longer the distinction of a Chief Constable with headquarters in Dunnottar parish.

The principal civil distinction remaining to the parish of Dunnottar and the Old Town is the Town Cross in the High Street, at which Royal Proclamations are still made with the appropriate pomp and ceremony. The ecclesiastical parish of Dunnottar continues, with its boundaries undiminished.

THE FISHING INDUSTRY

The most noteworthy development in the last hundred years is the rise and decline of the fishing industry. An episode attended with great expectations and recollected with pride and regret, it deserves special mention. From the middle of last century onwards fishermen began to come into Stonehaven from small hamlets along the coast, attracted no doubt by the advantages of the harbour and the facilities of a large centre, until by about 1890 the fishing industry dominated the life of the town. There was a winter fleet of fifty to sixty yawls, which went to the haddock fishing. In spring bigger vessels went to the great line fishing for cod and other large fish. The busiest time, however, was the herring season, when the harbour was filled with boats from all parts of the country and even from Cornwall and France. It is estimated that about six hundred fishermen would be in the town at this season and Stonehaven is reckoned to have been the biggest herring fishery on the east coast of Scotland at this time. Besides fishermen, many coopers, carters and fish workers thronged the town, as well as curers, buyers and exporters. Local records reveal expectations of a great development of the industry and its ancillary trades. In a circular, dated 1899, about renovation of the parish church, Dr Barron, the minister, is still able to write that, in view of planned improvements in the harbour, it is believed that a fresh impulse will be given to its (Stonehaven's) expansion, greater in all probability than any hitherto experienced. Those who remember those days recall how herring barrels used to line the whole length of the High Street and the walls of corner houses were worn by the bosses of many carts scraping them as they turned the corners of the narrow streets. There is a persistent tradition that Stonehaven was considered, along with Peterhead, as a possible site for the convict prison and that a breakwater would then have been built across the bay. But these expectations were doomed to disappointment. About the turn of the century, with the rise of the trawling fleet centred on Aberdeen, the fishing began to decline. The herring also left the coast. In 1914 there were only twenty line boats and eighteen larger ones. During the First World War the industry experienced a boom, owing to the absence of trawlers. But since 1918 it has decreased steadily. A contributing factor has also been the disinclination of the women to share the drudgery of baiting the hooks. The seine-net now, for the most part, replaces the line. The younger men have been forsaking the calling of their fathers. At present there are not more than half-a-dozen local boats and the small fishing village of Crawton, at the south end of the parish, has been deserted since 1913 and one hardly now discerns the sites of the former dwellings.

The harbour was also used by larger vessels in the coastal and continental trade. When the fishing was at its height there were some half-dozen sailing ships carrying cargoes of coal and potatoes and other goods. Some of these went as far as Sweden and Russia with cargoes of herring, returning laden with timber. More recently two locally owned steam vessels were engaged in the coastal trade until 1939, when they were disposed of. Since then fishing craft alone use the harbour, which had been enlarged before the First World War and which has recently been made more secure by the erection of a boom at the entrance to the inner harbour, ensuring calm water during the heavy storms of winter and spring.

As an epilogue to this record of the fortunes of the fishing and coastal trade in Stonehaven it may be added that in 1934 the Lifeboat Station was closed down and shortly after that the last lifeboat was sold and taken away.

A NOTABLE PERSONALITY

The most outstanding personality in the parish during the last hundred years was the Rev. Alexander Silver, Minister at Dunnottar from 1844 to 1884. A man of strong character, he left his mark on an earlier generation. So many anecdotes are told concerning his words and deeds that he is become an almost legendary figure. He is particularly remembered for his encouragement of thrift and as founder of the Stonehaven Savings Bank, which is now a branch of Aberdeen Savings Bank.

SECOND WORLD WAR

During the Second World War the parish was left in comparative peace and quiet, except for occasional alarms due to passing raiders. It may be worth recalling that in the spring of 1940 some Norwegian refugees reached Stonehaven harbour in an open sailing boat. In the early summer of 1940 a German raider was shot down in the bay of Crawton. The only substantial damage suffered by the town was caused by one of our own mines. In November 1944 violent storms swept a number of mines away from their moorings. Most of them exploded harmlessly on lonely beaches. One, however, floated into the inner harbour and remained there for most part of a day. The inhabitants of houses near the harbour were evacuated to the Rest Centre and late in the afternoon the mine, bumping against the harbour piers, exploded, doing considerable damage to nearby property and breaking many windows throughout the town. Fortunately, no one was killed or injured.

POPULATION

The population figures for 1901 and at each census for the past hundred years are as follows:— (1801) 1975; (1841) 1873; (1851) 1949; (1861) 1828; (1871) 2102; (1881) 2498; (1891) 2739 (maximum recorded); (1901) 2533; (1911) 2255; (1921) 2197; (1931) 1987 (958 males: 1029 females); (1939) 1637 (National Register). (The parish total at the 1951 Census was down to 1514 (712 males: 802 females).

These figures show that the population has risen and fallen with the rise and decline of the fishing industry, which may be regarded as one of the main factors affecting the population. Two other contributory factors are (1) the gradual decrease in the landward population and (2) the restriction of the size of families, which are not so large as formerly.

The follwing figures indicate the distribution of the population between burgh and landward areas:—

	BURGH	LANDWARD
1921:	1587	610
1931:	1425	562
1939:	1092	543

The figures for 1939 are from the National Register, but may be taken as relatively reliable, as this parish was not very much affected by evacuation. It was a receiving area, but comparatively few evacuees were billeted in Dunnottar. The decline in the landward population may be attributed to three main causes. Firstly, there is the depressed state of agriculture, which continued up to the early thirties. During that time many people left the land. Secondly, there is the great increase in mechanisation on the farms, which has reduced the numbers of permanent farm workers. Thirdly, families are rarely more than two or three where they were from six upwards before. As regards the burgh area, apart from the causes noted above, the sharp drop in the population between 1931 and 1939 coincides with the transference of large numbers, and especially of large families, from the Old Town to the new housing area at Brickfield, in the parish of Fetteresso. Since that date it may reasonably be forecast that there will be some increase in the burgh population, both through the building and occupation of new tenements in the Old Town and also through the reletting of condemned properties there in order to cope with the present housing shortage. A partial cause of the decline of population in the burgh area is also the disappearance of nearly all local industries of any considerable size. (The burgh bounds of Stonehaven were extended in 1946. The population of the entire burgh rose from 4185 in 1931 to 4438 in 1951, females outnumbering males by 2503 to 1935).

The figures for the parish as a whole reflect, on a smaller scale, the tendencies observable in the figures for the whole of Scotland as regards the relative distribution of sex and age, but the percentage drop of the population in the parish between 1921 and 1931 of about 9 per cent is much greater than that for the country as a whole for that period, which is barely 1 per cent, whilst between 1931 and the National Register of 1939 there is a drop of 17 per cent in the parish, as compared with an increase of a little over 1 per cent in the figures for the whole country. This decrease is abnormal and largely due to the transference of population noted above.

In the landward area about 50 per cent of the farmers were born in the parish and some farms are held by sons of the second and third generations. The majority of the other farmers have come in from nearby parts of the county. The farm servants, with few exceptions, come in from other parishes, mainly from the north east. They change more frequently since the control of engagements order was cancelled. In the burgh portion, while a large majority of the population belongs to the Stonehaven district and the county, a reasonable estimate does not suggest that much more than a half have been born in the parish. The prevalence of certain family names is evidence of a stable core of the population and also of a degree of inter-relationship. The same is to some extent true of the country area.

PUBLIC SERVICES

In common with Fetteresso, Dunnottar parish benefits by the usual public services available for the whole burgh. The town has an excellent water supply and there is water in almost every house. Electricity, supplied by the North of Scotland Hydro-Electric Board, is used for street lighting and an ever increasing number of people have it installed for lighting and other domestic uses. Gas, supplied by the local Gas Company, nationalised recently, is much used for cooking. The sewage is carried away into the sea, where the movement of tides and currents ensures that it is never cast up on the beach again. The streets are a model of cleanliness and good repair.

In the landward area each farm has its own water supply, but on Dunnottar Castle estate the enterprise of the proprietor has provided a common water supply for a number of farms which were inadequately provided for. Electricity is available through the hydro-electric scheme, but most farmers prefer to make their own supply, regarding as too high the rates charged by the Hydro-Electric Board. As yet there is only one farm in the parish served by this scheme. The main roads are in good order, but are hardly wide and straight enough for modern road transport. The side roads are only passably good, as the surface is quickly worn by the considerable traffic of cars, vans and lorries going between the farms. All parts of the parish are within easy reach of bus and train services, which provide rapid and convenient travel to all the larger centres of business, industry and entertainment. The whole parish also shares with the Stonehaven district the statutory nursing, medical and hospital services.

HOUSING

Old town

There are approximately 389 houses in the burgh area of Dunnottar parish. The bulk of them are in the Old Town, where they grew up, crowded together and with narrow lanes and wynds. The main street, the High Street, is, however, wide, straight and of good appearance. In the Old Town most of the houses are two and three storey tenements or old houses divided up into flats or apartments, some with two and most with three rooms each. In the back streets are some single-storey houses, with a garret, divided into ends having three rooms each. All the new building in the Old Town has been done by the local authority. It takes the form of tenèments or semi-detached houses with three to four rooms each. There is one block of houses built in a crescent, with two-storey houses of three to four rooms each. Building throughout is of stone. In all new buildings up-to-date sanitation is provided, and in most of the older houses it has been installed. Lighting is either by gas or electricity, and the tendency is to replace gas by electricity, except for cooking. The majority of houses in the Old Town have no gardens and what there are consist of very small plots and borders.

Overcrowding, according to a survey made in 1935, was 10 per cent. Since then there has been much building and shifting of population but, owing to the housing shortage since the war ended, there are still a number of cases. On this account some houses previously condemned and untenanted have been let again, though this only mitigates the trouble very little. As housing development in the Old Town has taken the shape of rebuilding on the sites of demolished houses, it has not created an entirely new community. Nevertheless, by raising the standard of comfort, convenience and amenity it has given a new sense of pride in the Old Town and a desire to see it all rebuilt in such a way as may retain its former character and raise the standard of living in it.

Beyond the Old Town some private building took place between 1900 and 1934, resulting in two new streets — Dunnottar Avenue, on either side of the main road south, and Victoria Street running parallel to it. The houses there are mainly semi-detached houses and bungalows, varying in size from four to eight rooms. They have small gardens at the back and facing the street are flower beds. Of the houses in the burgh portion of the parish, 45 are owned by the local authority and the rest by private owners.

LANDWARD HOUSES

In the landward portion there are 123 houses, between forty and fifty of which are farm houses, the remainder mostly cottages attached to farms and crofts, half a dozen new houses for land workers built by the County Council, a few private houses, and a mansion house at Dunnottar. A great improvement has taken place in the standard of comfort and convenience in farm houses during recent years. New and up-to-date grates are installed in kitchens and living-rooms. Sanitation and water supply are being brought into line with modern standards. Bathrooms have been added in many houses. Calor gas is often used for cooking. Some of the farms have electric light, in most cases using their own plant. Otherwise modern paraffin lamps are used. The installation of telephones in farms is increasing and already the majority have this convenience. The cottages are all brought up to the standard required by the Health Department, and some have been rebuilt. They are lit mostly by paraffin lamps, but the four new houses recently finished for the County Council are wired for electricity, although not yet linked up to the current. The Manse, up till now lit by paraffin, is to have electric light installed in the near future.

AGRICULTURE

The most important and thriving industry in the parish is farming. Farms vary in size between 80 and 350 acres arable, but most of them are between 100 and 200 acres. One farm has over 500 acres of hill pasture. Crofts are from 12 to 30 acres in size. Rentals run to £1 or £1.10/- per acre, though it is reasonable to suppose that, in the case of a change of tenant at the present time, a considerable increase would be likely. By 1930, at the time of the depression, tenants could not be found for a number of the farms. These were then let as out-farms, along with larger places, and used mainly for grazing. Since the end of the 'thirties all farms have got tenants and the industry is prosperous. The improvement is due to the Government policy of aiding agriculture and to the needs of the war and post-war years.

HORSES

The most notable change in the industry in recent times has been the decrease in horses. In 1793 the *First Statistical Account* reports that there were 188 work horses in the parish. In 1939 there were still 163, but by 1949 the number had fallen to 75, and in the present year it is likely to be smaller. The primary reason for this is the increased use of tractors, of which there are 64 in the parish. In addition to that, there must be reckoned the scarcity of men willing to take a horseman's job, which ties them up at nights and over weekends. The prevalence of grass-sickness for a time may also have influenced farmers to change to tractors, owing to losses incurred and high insurance premiums. A result of this is that there is no longer a smiddy in the parish, although formerly there were two. Blacksmith work is now done in some of the garages in the town or neighbouring parishes. Today, modern equipment is used for every kind of work. Two years ago the first combined harvester was introduced.

LIVESTOCK

In 1939 there were 3917 sheep, but in 1949 the number recorded is 877. This drop is due to the ploughing up of pasture during the war, and the policy of a large arable acreage continues. There are two dairy farms and the total number of milk cows in all farms was 112 in 1949, an increase of 28 on 1939. The milk marketing scheme has put an end to the casual sale of milk at farms generally. The number of pigs has increased from 54 in 1939 to 235 in 1949, a result of the wartime demand for more home-fed bacon. In the early 'thirties there were two large poultry farms, with upwards of 2,000 and 5,000 poultry respectively, besides smaller flocks at all the other farms. The need for more plough land and the scarcity of maize for feeding put an end to these. There is still, however, a considerable quantity of poultry — in 1949, 9338 hens and 7983 pullets, a slightly lower figure than in 1939. Ducks, geese and turkeys are also reared in smaller quantities, and a few years ago very high prices were being paid for them.

CROPS

The largest cereal crop is oats, the acreage of which increased from 1211 in 1939 to 1623 in 1949. Barley comes second with 745½. A small amount of wheat is grown. The potato acreage is 263. This again is due to Government policy and subsidies, the normal acreage being little more than half that. A certain amount of crops are grown for silage, turnips for winter feeding, and also some sugar beet. Grass for pasture is scarce and has reached abnormal prices — £10 to £15 per acre during and since the war years. In spite of this the number of beef cattle fed has increased and beef of very high quality is produced.

FARMING ENTERPRISE

The agricultural community is very much awake to the opportunities of the time. A keen interest is taken in the scientific improvement of land, and every means of increasing production and efficiency is examined and, if feasible, tried. The farmers form an enterprising, intelligent and progressive section of the community. The flourishing condition of the industry, in spite of increased costs and wages, is reflected in the higher standard of living on farms, both among farmers and farm servants.

OTHER INDUSTRIES

The fortunes of the fishing industry have been dealt with in the history of the parish. The only industry of any size remaining is the manufacture of fishing nets. This industry, begun about 1860 in a factory in the Old Town, has in the course of time moved out to a large new building on the southern outskirts of the town. The proprietors are now Messrs J. and W. Stuart, a Musselburgh firm. Occasionally some finishing work is given out to be done in homes. The factory gives employment to about 60 workers, mostly women and young girls, and has not been idle for many years. During the Second World War nets for military purposes were made. Its principal product now is herring nets. A flax mill, which once employed as many workers as the net factory, was closed down during the War and has since been completely dismantled. The building now houses a toy factory, which is connected with a sawmill in the parish. This, however, is seasonal work and the number employed is very small.

Those members of the community who are not absorbed locally in the building and allied trades travel into Aberdeen to work. Others leave the town altogether to seek their living in busier centres. During the summer months there is a certain amount of tourist trade. All who can do so let their rooms to visitors and a considerable income is realised in this way. The hotels also are very busy at this time. The Mill Inn, formerly the coaching hotel in Stonehaven, mentioned in the last *Account*, has recently been altered and redecorated, and after a period of inactivity has become busy again under new ownership. The recent installation by a local garage of a filling station at the entrance to the hotel has restored to it, in some degree, its former position as roadside hostelry. Beside the Mill Inn stands the former meal mill, which was sold two years ago and is now reconstructed and converted into the local egg-grading station.

SHOPS

The shopping centre of the burgh has shifted from the Old Town to the Market Square in the New Town, so that there has been no development in this direction in the parish. Some old shops have been closed down. There still remain grocers' and bakers' shops, which do a good trade and maintain their clientele, drawn from all parts of the town. In some cases their trade has been extended by the use of vans. One or two shops selling stationery and fancy goods are busiest during the summer season and one home-made confectionery shop would do a much larger trade but for the limited sugar ration.

CHURCHES

The principal church is the parish church of Dunnottar, with a membership of 1000. Of these, two-thirds live in the town and one-third in the country. There are 24 members of Kirk Session. The charge was formerly in the Presbytery of Fordoun, but in 1929, at the union of the former United Free Church with the Church of Scotland, it was transferred to the Presbytery of Aberdeen, to which the former United Free charges as far south as Stonehaven had belonged. In 1903 the old church was reconstructed under the inspiration of Dr Barron, minister at that time. A nave and chancel were added, making the old rectangular building into a beautiful cruciform church. There are six stained glass windows in the choir, a large one in memory of a Calcutta merchant connected with Stonehaven, and the others forming a group commemorating twenty-nine men from the congregation who fell in the Second World War. The memorial to the 61 men who gave their lives in the First World War consists of wooden panelling round the choir walls, on which their names are inscribed in letters of gold. At about the same date as the reconstruction of the church, part of the glebe was sold and made into a new cemetery surrounding the church building. It is beautifully situated and kept in fine order. The congregation has also a smaller church in the town, known as St Bridget's, built in the time of Dr Barron, in 1886, and obviously intended for the needs and expected development of the then growing fishing population. It is used for evening services from October to May and for the Sunday School and other meetings.

The congregation of Scottish Episcopalians numbers upwards of 400. The original church was in the High Street, on the site now occupied by grocer's and baker's shops at numbers 19-23. It was built in 1737, but never consecrated. It was demolished in 1879. The foundation stone of the present church, St James', situated just inside the northern boundary of Dunnottar parish in Arbuthnott Street, was laid in 1875 and the nave was opened for worship in 1877. The chancel was opened in 1885 and the church was consecrated in 1889. A baptistry was added and consecrated in 1906.

A small Roman Catholic Chapel, in Arbuthnott Place, was built in 1873 by a Mr Hepburn, at that time proprietor of Rickarton House and estate. It was more of the nature of a family chapel, for there was not then, nor is there yet, a Roman Catholic community in the town, but only a few individuals and families from time to time. This chapel has its largest congregation when summer or weekend holidays bring Roman Catholic visitors into the town.

EDUCATION

In 1873, a year after the first Education Act came into force, a census taken by order of the School Board reveals the following state of education in the parish as regards children between the ages of 5 and 13:— educated at home, 11; educated at school, 221; have been at school for a period of 3 to 6 years, 46; have been at school for a period

H

of 3 months to 2 years, 35; have never been at school, 77; total, 390.
At that time the following schools existed in the parish. In the Old
Town were the Parish School, where the Drill Hall now stands, and
the Episcopal School, built in 1851. In the landward area there was a
school, on the present site, at Brackmuirhill, controlled, according to
the School Board minutes, by the Governors of Donaldson's Trust
(Edinburgh) and the proprietor of Dunnottar Castle estate. The west
side of the parish was served by Dykeneuk School, just across the
boundary in Fetteresso parish. A small number of children from
Dunnottar went to Donaldson's Free School, also in Fetteresso parish.
Dunnottar and Brackmuirhill schools were taken over by the School
Board. Dykeneuk was closed down and in conjunction with Fetteresso
School Board a new school was built nearby on the land of Tewel
Farm, to serve the needs of children in that area. The Episcopal School
was enlarged in 1897 and, although the Dunnottar School Board
wished to take it over, it remained under the control of the Episcopal
Church until 1939, when the school was closed and the building taken
over by the Education Authority.

In the Old Town the present Dunnottar School was built in 1889 to
meet the needs of the increasing school population. For the same
reasons Brackmuirhill was later altered and added to. Primary subjects
were taught in these schools, and in Dunnottar, for a time, navigation
as well as technical subjects was taught to the older boys. There were
also, until the school-leaving age was raised in 1945, a few post-
primary classes at Dunnottar, but the older pupils attending these have
now been transferred to Mackie Academy in the New Town. The
staff of Dunnottar, which is now a primary school, comprises 7
teachers and a headmaster. Brackmuirhill is a one-teacher primary
school. The school population in the parish has much decreased
through the same causes as have affected the population as a whole.
The number at Brackmuirhill has been affected also by the growing
tendency of children near the bus routes to come into Dunnottar for
their education. The following figures may be added for
comparison:—

1900		1950	
Dunnottar School (290)			
Episcopal School (115)	405	Dunnottar School	219
Brackmuirhill School	98	Brackmuirhill School	17

Generally speaking, education is eagerly desired by parents for their
children and the copious provision to meet its expenses is taken full
advantage of. The children themselves enjoy school life, for the
curriculum is more varied and attractive and the teachers less
formidable than the dominies of former days. The relations between

home and school are harmonious and studiously fostered, and between church and school a spirit of co-operation and mutual goodwill exists. A recent expression of this is the custom now established of holding a school service in St Bridget's Church for pupils of Dunnottar at the end of each term. The bodily refreshment of the children has been improved by the milk scheme and also by the recently established school meals service, which is especially appreciated in the country school, where children come long distances and remain at school all day.

Adult members of the community attend in small number the lectures organised by the Workers' Educational Association, and evening classes arranged by the Education Committee meet with a fair response, particularly where instruction in practical arts and crafts is given. Many of the younger people travel to Aberdeen to attend classes necessary to them in their trade.

VOLUNTARY SERVICES

The voluntary services cover the town and district of Stonehaven as a whole and are not confined to one parish. The people of Dunnottar share in the activities of the many voluntary organisations which have branches in Stonehaven. The catalogue of these would include: Church Guilds and Fellowships; the three main political parties; Rotarians; Freemasons; Old Age Pensioners' Association; Youth Clubs, Scouts, Guides, Territorials; Red Cross Society; Ex-Service Men's Association; Shepherds' Friendly Society; Arts Society; Chamber Music Club; Choral Union; Three Churches' (Junior) Choir; Dramatic Societies; Burns Club; Football, Golf, Tennis, Badminton, Swimming, Rifle, Darts, Bowling and Quoiting Clubs. Trade union organisation is based on Aberdeen. There is no Young Farmers' Club in the parish, but many of the young farmers play a leading part in the clubs of adjacent parishes.

The chief difficulties facing youth organisations are the problem of finding leaders and adequate hall accommodation. The Rifle Club is said to be finding it difficult to attract new members from the younger generation, who prefer the Darts Clubs sponsored by licensed premises. The extension and development of these many different forms of group activity has been one of the most remarkable features of post-war life in the community.

LOCAL ORGANISATIONS

The organisations which have a special link with Dunnottar parish are five in number. The *Territorial Association* has a drill hall in the Old

Town. There has been an infantry company here since early in the century, but since the last war it has fallen off and now there are only eleven territorials in the district. This is partly due to the introduction of compulsory military service. *St Kieran's Club* for girls between the ages of fourteen and eighteen and a Boys' Club for the same age-group use the old Episcopal School building for their meetings. A lodge of the *Loyal Order of Ancient Shepherds* was founded in Stonehaven in 1890 and is the friendly society to which most working men in the town belong. It has a hall in the Old Town, which is let out for the use of many organisations. The *Swimming Club* of Stonehaven had its origins in the Old Town and its headquarters in a hut at the harbour, in which practices, races and galas were held. Since the building of the new swimming-pool in Fetteresso parish most of its activities are held there, though a gala is still held occasionally in the harbour. In the landward area a *Quoiting Club* continues to maintain a vigorous existence during the summer months and in recent years has been successful in winning cups and shields in the Northern League.

LOCAL USAGES

The most distinctive custom still alive in the Old Town is the practice of swinging fireballs on Hogmanay. Before midnight young men in the town gather in the High Street with fireballs made of wirenetting containing tarry chips and other inflammable material. On the stroke of twelve these are set alight and are carried up and down the High Street and swung round by the wire ropes to which they are bound. Large crowds from the town and country round gather to watch this method of bringing in the New Year. Sometimes minor burns are received by the participants or bystanders, but as a rule no harm is done. The practice was suspended for security reasons during the two world wars. The custom is not of long standing and appears to have arisen during the second half of last century among fishermen and other mariners. Whether it is connected with or originates from any of the more ancient fire rites in the North East is unknown.

When the fishing was at its height in the nineteenth century many of the fishermen celebrated Old Yule on the 5th of January and went to sea on New Year's Day. This custom met with opposition among the fish buyers, who did not find it convenient or desirable to deal with a catch on New Year's Day, and the observance of Old Yule gradually died out.

Another curious frolic which was in vogue towards the closing years of last century may be recorded. It was known as the barrow-rowin, a form of wheelbarrow race. At this time excavations and improvements were being carried out in the harbour and it was mainly labourers engaged in work there who competed in this race.

On Old Yule, when the tide was out, competitors, being blindfolded, had to wheel their barrows along the shore inside the harbour from the south to a fixed mark on the north side. When the tide was full the race was run on the north wall of the harbour, known as the Old Pier. The wanderings and watery mishaps of the entrants appear to have occasioned much merriment. This practice died out before the beginning of the present century.

Before the Second World War the custom of washing the feet of the bridegroom (and sometimes of the bride) before a wedding was occasionally followed, in this parish as elsewhere in the North East, but it has now practically ceased.

DIALECT

A great many of the dialect words in use in the parish are common to the Mearns and the North East generally. The following words locally used by fishermen may be recorded: *pallach* or *pallachie*, a young crab; *gowdie*, a gurnet or gurnard; *buckie*, a whelk; *plingie*, a young seagull. The following verbs are also in common use:— *chaav*, to strive, to toil; *daachil*, to dilly-dally; *ramscootir*, to beat severely, to confound. Many other words and expressions common to the North East dialects are in use and persist in spite of the school English which has not been able to displace the more forcible and picturesque expressions of the local speech.

HISTORICAL MONUMENTS

The following buildings and places of historical interest are situated in the parish.

(i) DUNNOTTAR CASTLE

This building is preserved in excellent condition and kept open for visitors by the proprietor of the Dunnottar Castle estate, Lord Cowdray.

(ii) THE MARISCHAL AISLE

This is the burial place of George, Earl Marischal, founder of Marischal College, Aberdeen. It was restored from a state of ruin by Aberdeen University in 1914 and is now maintained by Dunnottar Kirk Session.

(iii) The covenanter's stone

This is a plain rectangular grave stone in Dunnottar Churchyard marking the spot where are buried some of the Covenanters who died in imprisonment in Dunnottar Castle in 1685. It was here that Sir Walter Scott met Robert Paterson, as recorded in the introduction to *Old Mortality*.

(iv) The old tolbooth

This building, situated on the Old Pier in Stonehaven, was originally used as a store by the Keiths. When the Sheriffdom was transferred to Stonehaven in 1607 it became the court house and gaol until 1767. It is associated with the imprisonment of Episcopal clergymen for holding illegal services in the district. The question of its maintenance as a historical monument is at present under review by the Town Council of Stonehaven.

(v) Old houses

The old house at 51 High Street is said to have been a town residence of Sir George Ogilvie of Barras, the defender of Dunnottar Castle against the Cromwellian troops. On the opposite side of the street the house at No. 56, west of the Old Water Gate, dates back to the early 18th century. It is one of the houses in which Episcopalians met for worship at the time when they were forbidden to preach. At the farm East Mains of Barras are preserved the bell and some of the carved stones from the house of Sir George Ogilvie, which formerly stood nearby. The gravestone of Sir George Ogilvie and his wife is preserved inside Dunnottar Church. Behind the farm of Clochnahill the now almost invisible site of the house occupied by the grandparents of Robert Burns is pointed out.

(vi) War memorials

Mention may be made of the War Memorial to men of Stonehaven and district. Situated on the Black Hill, overlooking the harbour, it can be seen from all parts of the district and from far at sea. It takes the form of a shrine containing a monolith and stones bearing the names of the fallen of the two World Wars. In a piece of rough grazing in the glebe, near the east wall of Dunnottar Cemetery, there grows an oak tree, now of considerable size, planted in 1919 in honour of parishioners who fought in the First World War. It is locally known as the Peace Tree.

ENDOWMENTS

The following endowments are applied in the parish. The capital sum is given in each case. 1841: Jane Walker's Bequest (£100): for the poor of the parish. 1844: the Isobel Donaldson Bequest (£200): to provide a money gift for poor persons in the parish. 1858: the Anne Brebner Bequest (£50): to provide comforts for necessitous sick. 1861: the William Duthie Trust (£1210): originally to provide meal for poor persons, now commuted to a money payment. 1869: the Clementina Fraser Bequest: residue of the estate divided between provision for the poor and education. 1877: William Cockie's Bequest (£500): for the soup kitchen, coals for the poor and the education of farm servants and labourers. 1878: Walter Napier's Bequest (£25): to provide coal for the poor of the Old Town. 1938: John Milne's Trust (£500): left by John Milne, aerated water manufacturer, for the funds of Dunnottar Church.

The Trustees for the above funds are the Kirk Session of Dunnottar, with the exception of the portion applied to education (since 1936 administered by the Kincardineshire Educational Trust, created by the Educational Endowments Act) and the William Duthie Trust. The latter names as Trustees the Minister of Dunnottar and the Provost of the Old Town, but as the latter office is now obsolete the minister of the parish is sole trustee.

Some of the funds from John Beattie's Trust, William Duncan's Trust and Martha Napier's Trust are also available for poor people in the Old Town. On these trusts a minister and elder from each church and congregation in the town represent the interests of the different parishes. In 1841 money was subscribed for a soup kitchen, which since 1891 has had premises in the Old Town. The need for it has passed away and it has not functioned since 1946. The funds are under the care of a local committee. Of such charitable bequests generally it may be said that the extreme need which they were designed to serve no longer exists, though they are none the less welcome to those whose incomes have not risen to meet the rising cost of living and particularly of coal.

WAY OF LIFE

There is a strong and healthy local patriotism, but this springs more from natural affection for the place of one's birth and breeding than from a sense of its importance in the present and prospects for the future. It partakes of a family feeling, and many a young man who wandered far during the war will say that he saw many fine sights but none finer than the Old Town of Stonehaven. A sense of continuity with the past, partly due to the fact that some families, both in town and country, have been here for several generations and also to the witness to the past in ancient buildings and local traditions, helps to develop this special attachment. As the community is a small one, the people of Dunnottar live comparatively close together, have been to the same schools and churches and know one another personally, so that the community feeling is born of familiar faces as well as familiar places. This is true also of the landward part of the parish, and it is appropriate to remark here that the relations, social, business, cultural and family, between burgh and landward districts are so close that they may be regarded as one community. At the same time this local patriotism is qualified by the feeling that the place has nothing to offer young and enterprising persons, and the remark is often heard that there is nothing for anybody in Stonehaven, or that the town is becoming a dormitory for Aberdeen.

Within the community, particularly in the burgh, there are still vestiges of a distinction between those born and bred in the parish and incomers. This may have its origins in the consanguinity and exclusiveness of the former fishing community, but time, change and marriage alliances dilute the thickest blood, and while there is still a core claiming kinship with the old families, the feeling of apartness has almost disappeared. There is a certain rivalry between the Old Town and the New, the two being separated geographically by the River Carron, historically by their different development, and economically by the fact that the higher income groups tend to reside in the New Town and the lower in the Old. This rivalry is not, however, bitter and between the schools and churches provokes a friendly interest and desire to excel.

These geographical and economic groupings are transcended by the intermingling of all sections of the community in the numerous fellowships and societies of a social, recreational, cultural and educational order which have been noted earlier. During the winter months in particular there are few who do not enlarge the circle of their interests and friends by sharing in one or more of these organisations. One of the most recent and happy of them is the Old Age Pensioners' Association, which draws many keen members from Dunnottar parish. It has given to the older people a new interest in life and a recognised place in the community. These various activities, in which the people spontaneously entertain and instruct themselves, form one of the most significant and promising developments in the life of the community in recent years.

The main source of happiness, however, continues to be home and family life, although the family desired is now much smaller than in former days. Parents take a great interest in the welfare, education and progress of their children, using all the facilities available for this purpose. The children themselves often have an abundance of pocket money and toys, and the reading of comics and a regular visit to the cinema are common ingredients in their mental diet. The traditional games and amusements associated with different seasons of the year have not been ousted by any of these modern substitutes. The common ambition of families is to have a house and door of one's own, and it is to be regretted that so many young married couples have to begin, and for long continue, their married lives in a sub-let room or a condemned house. Although it is a truism, it may be said that if there were sufficient houses a principal and potent cause of bitterness and discontent would be removed from the life of the community.

A fair proportion of the population takes advantage of the reading provided by the County Library. There is a healthy interest in acting and drama. The mass of the people share with the country as a whole the standardised entertainment of cinema and wireless programmes. The menfolk go in large numbers to Aberdeen and further afield to see football matches. The womenfolk go thither on shopping expeditions. Dancing goes on all through the year, both in the more sociable and artistic patterns of Scottish country dancing and the quadruped meanderings and sinuous shuffles of the modern ballroom. The dances held by different bodies during the winter season are recognised social functions. Young men of the district sometimes proceed from one dance to another on the same night, travelling considerable distances by bicycle, bus and even taxi, to indulge in this pastime. The profits of such dances are frequently devoted to charitable objects. With dances are often coupled whist drives. The majority of the people who attend these do so for the pleasure of the game and the social intercourse, but a minority, known locally as professionals, go in the hope of winning some of the prizes that fall to the highest scorers. There are also a number of bridge clubs that meet regularly during the winter for serious card play.

Holidays are taken by all sections of the community. Many go away for a change of air, some travelling as far as the Continent. At local holidays, on half-days and on Sundays during the summer, many take the opportunity of touring the Scottish countryside by bus, car and bicycle. All sections of the farming community now take a holiday break and get away from the daily round. Hardly a year passes now but one or two people are visiting relatives in the Dominions or the United States or receiving visitors from there. Thus the horizon of interest and outlook is enlarged. The adequate public transport and increased use of cars and motor bicycles puts the rural area within easy reach of town and city, so that in the matter of entertainment, recreation and social activities, burgh and landward areas may be regarded as one. There is abundant facility for the sports of bowls, golf, tennis and swimming, and a certain amount of football is played, although for the latter accommodation is not sufficient.

For some time a parish picnic was held in Dunnottar in the

landward part, at which sports and games were organised for adults as well as children, and in the evening dancing boards were laid and a band, made up of local talent, played whilst the young people danced far into the summer night. Since before the war this function diminished in scope to a picnic for the children at school. One occupation which is widespread in town and country is the filling up of football coupons, and in the majority of homes this must provide one of the main reasons for interest in the postman's knock. Apart from that, the amusements and leisure pursuits of the community do much to enrich the minds and enlarge the outlook of the people and afford an opportunity for exercising gifts and talents that would otherwise lie unused, as well as furnishing a link with the larger world and its interests.

While leisure is thus used and enjoyed there is plenty of will to work. No one likes to be idle, and the worst memories of many a working man are of the years of unemployment. Seldom, if ever, did one hear of the young man, demobilised at the end of the last war, taking full advantage of the long leave granted on that occasion. A week or two was sufficient. The desire to get back to regular work was too strong. There are always big squads of men ready to go out to work additional hours at the seasonal activities of hoeing turnips, harvest and potato lifting. The need for larger earnings to meet the rising cost of living is an important motive for working, but this is qualified and weakened in some degree by the reflection that the more you earn the more you must pay in income tax. Older men brought up in a more exacting school may criticise the younger generation for a lack of sense of vocation and interest in their job. But if this is true it is not due to any defect of character or capacity in the younger men but to the standardised conditions and techniques of modern labour. There is abundant evidence of ability and initiative in the leisure activities of the young people.

The church makes its influence felt through its members, who are often in leading positions in the various bodies and organisations of the parish. At the same time it may be said that, while nearly everyone in the parish has a church connection, active interest and participation in congregational life is confined to a minority, and attendances at services, apart from Communion and special festivals, are small. Though family life is cherished, it cannot be said that religion is the avowed and conscious basis of it. The Bible is no longer systematically read. The family pew is no longer an institution. Parents seldom mark by their presence the day when their children are welcomed into full communion with the church. It is doubtful if grace is said before meat in more than a small number of homes. The Sabbath tradition with its public recognition of religion has broken down, and no comparable common religious observance has taken its place. Religious instruction of a direct kind is largely left to day school and Sunday school. The latter takes in hardly a half of the available child population. The Sunday school leaving age has dropped to 12 or 13, and Bible classes are poorly attended.

Yet, if there is only a meagre appreciation of the church as a living fellowship, there is a general acceptance of it as a institution catering for those interested in religion. The link with it is sometimes of a utilitarian order. Like the Infirmary, it is to be kept up because you never know when you may need it. It has also the important function of enshrining and consecrating the memories and ties of home and country which are dear to every human heart. At the same time those who form the kernel of the congregation are loyal, keen and, on the whole, well informed about the nature and aims of the church and devoted to its principles and traditions. While a number still join the church because they feel that a church connection is useful to have, an increasing number do so because of some real conviction. It is becoming more common to have baptisms and weddings in church. Funerals are largely attended by men, and indeed for many the main form of pious observance is to show in this way that respect for the dead which signals both the dawn and the twilight of natural religion.

As regards the outlook for the future, in an age when religious conviction is weak and moral idealism has suffered some decline, it is natural that this should be of a practical and terrestrial order. Despite the shadow of fears that are common to the whole world, the aims and hopes of the people lie in the direction of the improvement of their material comfort and the enrichment of the life of the community by the strengthening and development of existing trends and organisations. There exists an altruistic and natural desire to provide a better life and opportunity for the coming generation. This is not envisaged in utopian colours by this sober and practical people. They look for more halls and space for club organisations, for greater recreational facilities, in fact for a community centre. They would like to see better school accommodation and equipment and perfected domestic, industrial and transport equipment and appliances to raise the standard of life. The rural section of the community look for the maintenance of the farming industry on a foundation which will ensure a good living for all concerned. All are anxious to see the development of public services, such as electricity supply, telephone services and housing, to cover the countryside. But the dominant and outstanding desire is for more and better houses, and the principal cause of sickness of heart among people in the present is the repeated deferment of hopes for a speedy and adequate solution to the local housing problem.

November 1950

THE PARISH OF DURRIS

by David B. McKelvie, M.A.

EXTENT

An inland parish on the northern border of Kincardineshire, Durris today is the same in size as it was at the time of the *Second Statistical Account* (1838). Its length (E. and W.) is 6 miles, towards the middle of the parish, and 3-4 miles in the north and south; its breadth averages about 4 miles. The land area is 15,317 acres, nearly 24 square miles. The northern border is the River Dee, which separates it from Drumoak parish in Aberdeenshire. To the east Durris adjoins the parishes of Maryculter and Fetteresso; to the south lies Glenbervie; to the south-west is Strachan parish, and to the west and north-west, Banchory-Ternan. The parish is traversed by the Sheeoch Burn. The surface is hilly, rising from 100 feet above sea-level beside the Dee to over 1200 feet in the south, on the lower slopes of the Grampians.

LANDOWNERS

The last proprietor mentioned in the *Second Statistical Account* was Mr Anthony Mactier, owner of Durris estate, which covered the whole parish except Corsehill farm. His successor was Dr James Young, the widely known paraffin oil manufacturer, and founder of the shale oil industry, who bought the estate in 1871. Dr Young is remembered not only for his scientific work in mineral oil, but also for his intimate friendship with David Livingstone, the African missionary and explorer. Mr Henry R. Baird became the next proprietor in 1890, and it was he who interested himself in silviculture, and planted many acres of hill land in the parish. He died in 1929 and in 1930 the estate was sold to Mr Alfred G. Johnston, tile manufacturer, of Tilbouries, Drumoak, while Mr Douglas M. Baird, son of the late laird, retained the mansion house, the home farm and Upper and Nether Balfour farms. In 1948 Upper Balfour was sold to a farmer. The Forestry Commission acquired 4,000 acres of woodland from Mr Johnston. Alterations were made to Durris House in 1948. The impressive portico was removed, as well as the large drawing room, and replaced by a plain, simple main entrance, with long vestibule and glass verandah.

ANGLING

The salmon fishing on the Durris part of the River Dee extends to approximately 6 miles and includes many first-class angling pools — Castle Pool, Long Pool, Hut Pool and the Keith Pool. Salmon is now a luxury selling at over 7/- a pound. The Sheeoch Burn, a Dee tributary, affords first rate sport in brown trout fishing.

POPULATION

After mounting rapidly from 605 in the year 1801 to 1109 in 1841, the population of the parish dropped slightly to 962 in 1851, but equalled the 1841 record in 1861. Since then the total has fallen at each Census without a break. By 1901 it was down to 884 and the figures for the present century are:— (1911) 872; (1921) 810; (1931) 731.

To this day Durris has no centres of population large enough to be called villages; it is a parish of farms, crofts and hills, with clusters of houses or hamlets at Kirkton, Woodlands, Denside and Crossroads. The steady decrease in the population is probably due to agricultural conditions. At this present time the total might be around 730. Owing to the wide use of mechanical contrivances in agricultural work, fewer farm servants are now employed, but the population has been maintained by the addition of about 30 forestry workers.

(Actually the 1951 Census showed a further decline to 664. Of these 353 were males as compared with 374 in 1931.)

ROADS AND COMMUNICATIONS

The last *Statistical Account* states that there was no post office nearer than Banchory. However, on 1 June 1886 was opened the Durris Post Office at the Kirkton shop. It is a sub-post-office, and with the exception of the issuing of money orders, it transacts all kinds of post-office business. Three postmen cover the district, and one delivery of letters and parcels is made daily.

Running along the northern edge of the parish is the South Deeside road, which crosses the Dee at Banchory and links Aberdeen to Royal Deeside. Along this road, for over a quarter of a century, regular services have been available to Durris for business and pleasure at the various town centres. In addition a special bus, begun 2 years ago, starts from the Kirkton of Durris at 10 o'clock each morning for Aberdeen. For years the return fare to Aberdeen was 1/6d., but within recent weeks the fare has been increased to 1/10d. Previously, travel to and from Aberdeen was by the Deeside Railway, opened in 1853, at first with its terminus at Banchory and later extended to Ballater. The railway does not pass through the parish, but runs along the north bank of the Dee, within easy reach of Durris at Park and Crathes stations.

The Slug road from Stonehaven to Banchory cuts across the parish from its summit (757 feet) beside Cairn-mon-Earn. A new road, structured roughly but passable for motor traffic, was completed by the Forestry Commission during the recent war to facilitate the passage of fire engines and equipment to fight plantation and forest fires. Because of its winding and steep course over the hills it has been locally named the 'Burma Road'. This road begins near Meikle Tulloch farm, on the Woodlands to Lochton road, and mounts the hills in a southerly direction, passing Pitcowdens till it reaches Strathgyle.

HOUSING

A few 3-roomed wooden houses for forestry workers were constructed in the early 1940s and 2 blocks of brick houses, 2 storeys high, each containing 4 homes were built in 1947 on the Woodlands road near Woodlands School. The latter have modern conveniences, with the exception of electric light, each home containing a living room, kitchenette, 3 bedrooms, bathroom and W.C. Unfortunately, this tenement type of building rather clashes with the simple beauty of the countryside, especially with the modest one-storey houses alongside. The rent, including rates, amounts to little over £28 per year.

ELECTRICITY

The electric cable of the North of Scotland Hydro Electric Board passes through the east part of the parish, but so far only Durris House, the farms of Upper and Nether Balfour, Bogenraith and the Home Farm are linked up with this power. So distant are the prospects of obtaining the Board's electricity that most farms are installing private plants for generating electricity.

AGRICULTURE

Agriculture is still the most important industry of the parish. Arable land extends to approximately 7000 acres. There are over 20 farms each with an acreage of between 100 and 280 acres, and about 30 farms having under 100 acres each of arable land. In addition, a number of crofts are worked by tenants, such as forestry workers, roadmen and sawmill workers. Since the 1838 *Account* vast changes have taken place in modes of agriculture. With the introduction of the tractor horses for farm work are now the exception, as farmers have little use for them. The petrol or paraffin-driven tractor completes speedily and satisfactorily almost all operations — ploughing, land-rolling, seed sowing, and conveying produce to and from the farm. An acre can be ploughed in two or three hours when a tractor and double plough is used, whereas to do the same work by horses a day and a half was usually required. This mechanisation of all farm work, including the milking of cows by electric power, has so speeded up the work that fewer workers are employed.

Startling, too, is the steep rise in wages to £5 a week for a farm hand, £12 a week for a dairyman and his wife, and over £5 for a shepherd. But these high wages are somewhat offset by the fact that the usual perquisites of free house, coal, meal and milk are no longer granted. Usually, 2/6 per week is the rent for a cottar house with no water, 5/- where water is available in the house, and 7/6 when a bathroom is provided. Coal, meal and milk have to be bought at current prices.

Black-faced sheep are the usual breed in Durris. The largest single flock, numbering about 700, is at South Brachmont farm, with its extensive hill pasture. During the Second World War much land, previously thought unprofitable, was broken up to provide additional food for the nation. Financial help from the government was given. Two new crops successfully tried out during the war were sugar beet and flax, but these are no longer grown.

Conditions of work for farm servants in Durris have also not escaped the general tendency for improvement. The week is now one of 5½ days — no work after noon on Saturday, so that the livestock must be attended to by the farmer, or at his additional expense, till Monday morning.

To attract more young people to farming, and at the same time to encourage more food production, there was formed in 1945 a Durris Junior Agricultural Club, familiarly known as the J.A.C. Over 60 people (male and female) are members and organised monthly meetings take place, when farming topics are discussed. Experts from Aberdeen Agricultural College lecture on all phases of farm work, including livestock and the maintenance of farm machinery. The scientific facts thus presented, combined with practical experience, should eventually lead to better farming in the parish. Great enthusiasm featured this novel venture at the beginning, and fortunately keen interest is still maintained. Competitions with other Clubs in judging the merits of horses, cattle, sheep and pigs keep the young farm workers alert, and many prizes have come to Durris. Skill in practical work is shown in the annual ploughing and hoeing matches.

AFFORESTATION

Within the last twenty years a new and active industry has arisen — afforestation, employing at present about 30 workers. Growing of trees interested Mr Anthony Mactier, the laird mentioned by the Rev. R. Copland in 1838, and it was he who in addition introduced to Durris many foreign specimens of trees. One might call him the pioneer of tree planting. His mantle fell on the shoulders of Mr H.R. Baird, laird of Durris from 1890 to 1929, who experimented with tree planting, growing extensively such trees as Douglas fir and Menzies and Sitka spruce. He probably foresaw the vast possibilities of silviculture on the hills of Durris. Then in 1930 came the Forestry Commission, who acquired 4,000 acres of woodland, cut down the matured trees during the Second World War, and have now replanted most of this vast area. The soil and climate of Durris have been found very favourable to the rapid and sturdy growth of all types of conifer trees.

ECCLESIASTICAL

The present parish church, built by the side of the Dee at Kirkton in 1822, was the only place of worship till 1856, when a Free Church was erected on the road between Kirkton and the Slug Road, about a mile from the parish church. In 1897 important renovations to the parish church were carried out by the heritors. The gallery round the church and the centrally situated pulpit, along with the outside stair at the east gable, were removed. A new porch of stone and lime was built at the west door, with a vestry attached, and an inside stair leading to the reconstructed gallery. The pulpit was placed at the east end, and a passage was made down the centre of the church. New comfortable seats of modern design, facing one way, were installed, as well as suitable accommodation for choir and organ. The church was heated by a hot water system. A new window was made in the north wall to light the gallery, and a new walk round the church.

In 1933, after the Rev. Robert Spark, M.A., minister of the parish church, retired, having completed a ministry of 50 years in Durris, the union of the two churches was consummated and the United Free (originally Free) Church (the last minister being the Rev. Dr Rankin) then ceased to be a place of worship. The united congregations number 400. The stipend is the minimum of £450 per year.

EDUCATION

There are two schools in the parish, each capable of accommodating 90 pupils — Woodlands School (in the east) and Crossroads School (in the west), both built in 1876. They replaced the Central School at Kirkton, and the two side schools at Brachmont (east) and Dhualt (west). Both schools provide primary education to the age of 12.

Thereafter the pupils proceed to Banchory Academy for secondary education. At present the schools have approximately 40 pupils each on the registers, and as the leaving age has been raised from fourteen to fifteen years, most parents are keen to give their children a good secondary education. This transference of country scholars to a town secondary school may unfortunately lead to the depopulation of country districts, given the attractions of employment in the towns and cities. Even in Durris this tendency is apparent. To arrest this drift from country to town the County Council has erected 2 blocks of modern houses (already mentioned) and a beginning has been made to modernise the cottar houses.

School dinners, consisting usually of 2 courses, were introduced by the Education Committee at the beginning of the Second World War at a daily charge of 6d for the first child, 5d for the second, and 3d each for the others in a family. Approximately 80 per cent of the scholars take the school dinners. Those living near the school usually dine at home. About the same percentage take the third of a pint of milk supplied daily free of charge. The result of these schemes is a definite improvement in the health of the scholars. The dinners are made at a modern equipped kitchen at Banchory Academy, catering not only for Durris schools but other rural schools. Previously the Durris schools were supplied with dinners as an obligement by Aberdeen Town Council, who had converted the out-buildings at the Durris Home Farm into a modern kitchen for supplying Aberdeen schools. Long before these two organised dinner schemes, the two local schools (since 1933) had run their own soup kitchen under a parents' interest committee, providing one course, usually soup, with an occasional meat course.

CHARITIES

One might truly say that there are no really destitute poor in the parish. However, the Kirk Session distributes individual sums varying from £1.10/- to £5, mostly to widows, spinsters or families suffering from hardships. These monies represent the interest from capital sums known as the Hogg Fund, the Lady Fraser Fund, the Thom Fund and others.

LOCAL RHYMES

When Cairn-mon-Earn puts on her cap,
The folks of Dores will get a drap.

This couplet, as old as Durris itself, refers to the fact that when Cairn-mon-Earn (1245 feet), the highest hill in Durris, has mist on its summit, the folks of Dores (old name for Durris) will have showers of rain.

Another homely Durris rhyme is:—

> Lime, lime without manure
> Mak's baith the fairm and fairmer poor.

WAY OF LIFE

The way of life of the Durris people has vastly changed in the last 50 years. No fairs are held in the parish, and if the Rev. R. Copland of the 1838 *Account* were alive today, his heart would rejoice that there are now no inns in Durris, although a few years ago a licence to sell porter and ale was granted to the grocer's shop at Lochton.

Peats are not used so widely as in former years. Prices are high, usually £2 and over per cart load. Coal is brought to the door by motor lorry from Aberdeen and sells at the high price of £5 a ton for English coal and £4.15/- for Scotch coal.

Telephones are installed in most farm houses and in the two schoolhouses, a change from the time over a quarter of a century ago when the post office and Durris House were the only telephone centres. Now two telephone kiosks are in full operation — one at the Kirkton shop (opened 12 August 1938) and the other at Denside shop (opened 11 April 1950).

There are two smiddies, one at Denside, the other at Lochton. A third one, at Crossroads, has not been in use since the death of the smith over twelve years ago. Horse-shoeing is almost a job of the past, and the blacksmith has had to learn new techniques in the repair and maintenance of farm machinery. At Denside Smiddy a petrol pump was installed a few years ago, a pointer to the future kind of work of the smith.

Social gatherings, concerts, barn dances and rural sports are now less frequent, owing to the ease of travel by bus to Aberdeen, where the cinema, theatre and football, wrestling and boxing matches provide a poor substitute for former country pleasures. The Durris Dramatic Club, whose activities were suspended at the beginning of the recent war, has not been resuscitated, and unfortunately the two Durris social clubs have become defunct. Dancing seems to have supplanted all these activities. It is hoped to restart the Durris Horticultural and Industrial Show this year (1951). It was suspended in 1940 owing to the war. The Women's Rural Institute, which celebrated its 25th birthday in December 1950, is strong in Durris and the members bravely try to recapture the atmosphere of the past rural life.

March 1951

THE PARISH OF FETTERCAIRN

by the Rev. Charles L. Hunter, M.A.

GEOGRAPHICAL BACKGROUND

The parish of Fettercairn lies along the south side of the eastern Grampians and forms the south-western corner of Kincardineshire. It is bounded on the north-west by Strachan parish, north-east and east by Fordoun, south-east by Marykirk; and on the south by Stracathro and west by Edzell, both in the county of Angus. Its utmost length from north to south is about 8 miles, its breadth, except at the tapering north and south ends, is 3 or 4 miles, making a land area of 14,844 acres, or 23¼ sq. miles. The detached portion (1120 acres) of Edzell parish on the Kincardineshire side of the North Esk river was transferred to Fettercairn by the Boundary Commissioners in 1891.

The parish may be described as one-half hilly and one-half level. At the southern border the surface declines to 115 feet above sea-level, rising to 1698 feet at Hound Hillock, close to the northernmost point of the parish. The village of Fettercairn stands 220 feet above sea-level. It is 11 miles north-east of Brechin and 12 miles north-west of Montrose.

NAME

From the tenth century down to the present time the name of the parish has appeared in no fewer than twenty different forms. In the tenth century it was 'Fotherkern' according to the old chroniclers, and 'Fother' probably gives a clue to the meaning of the word. The writer of the first *Statistical Account* says '*Fetter* signifies a pass, and *Cairn* a heap of stones; and there are two large cairns at the top of the mountain, and many small ones lower down, near to which, according to tradition, a great battle was fought, from which it is probable that the district got its name.' Dr Cameron, the author of *The History of Fettercairn*, rejects Mr Foote's derivation as 'fanciful' and 'unscientific'. He suggests that *Fother*, *Fether* or *Fetter* means the jutting ridge or ridges, and *Cairn* the hill upon which stood Fenella's Castle. The site of Fenella's Castle, however, the traditional scene of the murder of Kenneth II, is disputed. Dr Cameron favours *Greencairn*, about 1½ miles west of the present village, but one is more inclined to the view of the late J. Crabb Watt, K.C., in *The Mearns of Old*. Following Bishop Forbes of Brechin, he says that *Bother* or *Fother* denotes a road — the main road to the north — and *Cairn*, 'The great road of the Cairn o' Mount'.

HISTORY OF THE COMMUNITY

In a rural community the most important changes that call for notice are those associated with agriculture and the tenure of land; consequently, 1923 is an outstanding date. That year marked the passing of the Agricultural Holdings (Scotland) Act, which gave agricultural tenants security of tenure. According to the terms of this Act, if a landlord desired a change of tenant, he was obliged to give the tenant due notice, usually one year in advance; and if the tenant on leaving the farm could prove any loss through having to quit, he was entitled to compensation from the landlord equal to at least one year's rent. Further, under the same Act, a tenant on quitting was entitled to claim compensation for improvements he might have made in the fertility of the land which he occupied under lease. This process of providing the tenant with greater security of tenure was still further encouraged by the 1931 and 1948 Agricultural Holdings (Scotland) Acts.

During the last half-century some of the estates have been broken up, as many owners find it impossible to carry on under the increasing burdens of taxation and estate duties. Frequently the sitting tenants have bought their farms, thus reducing the number of large estate owners and considerably increasing the number of owner-occupiers.

During the First World War farmers were encouraged to crop as much as possible, but at that time horses were the principal source of power, and agricultural tractors, as we know them today, were just being introduced. Thus the increase in cropping land was somewhat restricted. Since those days farmers have become more mechanically minded. This has meant the rapid decline in the number of horses on the farm, but at the same time it has facilitated more intensive cultivation of the land.

During the depression between the wars, marketing schemes were introduced to deal with agricultural products such as milk and potatoes. Today, practically all agricultural produce is sold through a Government-controlled market. This has given the farmer a guaranteed price for his products,and, as a further incentive to increase productivity from the land, the Government in recent years have offered subsidies or grants.

With the increased acreage of the potato crop it has been necessary to obtain the assistance of organised labour for potato lifting. This labour is provided to a large extent by school children, and the local schools are closed for what are known as 'tattie holidays', so that the older pupils may assist with the securing of the crop.

Under present-day conditions farming is a prosperous business, and workers are now receiving wages which compare very favourably with those of other industries. These wages are controlled by statute. There is no doubt that agriculture is now on a much sounder footing than ever before.

CHANGES IN LANDOWNERS

With the exception of the estates of Fasque and Fettercairn, which are still held by representatives of the families named in the previous *Account* (1837), the land of the parish has passed into other hands. The name of Gladstone has been associated with Fasque for the past 120 years. The present proprietor is Sir Albert Gladstone, Bart. The Fettercairn estate has descended from Sir John Stuart Forbes, Bart., to his grandson, Lord Clinton.

When Balmain was sold about thirty years ago, most of the tenants purchased their farms, and the proprietors gifted to the parish a park adjoining the village, which a local committee has laid out for recreation purposes. The Burn and Arnhall estate was bought by George Herbert Russell, Esq., in the early twenties of the present century. He was a well-known and successful breeder of Aberdeen Angus cattle, and acted as Chairman of the Kincardineshire Agricultural Executive Committee during the war years. Keenly interested in the provision of better rural houses, he led the way at The Burn and did a great deal to improve the estate. Only the outbreak of war prevented him from carrying further plans into effect. The Air Ministry purchased 362 acres and later requisitioned an additional 513 acres for an aerodrome; and the 18th century Georgian mansion house, which had been modernised and largely remodelled, was given over and used as a convalescent home in connection with the military hospital at Strathcathro.

THE BURN

A few years ago Mr Russell sold the estate to Mr H.J. Kennoway, retaining the mansion house and the policies. He has generously gifted the mansion to the Dominion Students' Hall Trust as a residence for students of the British Commonwealth. The residence is to be used for holiday purposes, and for periods of private study and reading. It will provide a common meeting-place for both Scottish and overseas students, and give the latter an opportunity to gain a knowledge of the traditions and customs of our country and our people. With the house the generous donor gifted a handsome sum of money as the nucleus of a fund to enable the scheme to be launched.

The Burn, which will be administered by the Dominion Students' Hall Trust, has the approval of the Scottish universities, and the committee of management includes a representative from each of them. In the words of the Earl of Selkirk, 'the whole scheme brings to Scotland a unique opportunity of making a direct contribution to a noble far-seeing project'. The house is now open, with accommodation available for about thirty students. It is proposed that the Forestry Commission should take over the woodlands and also care for the river-side paths, thus ensuring the amenities of the residence. The setting is ideal. Mr H.J. Warden, in his *Angus, the Land and the People*, said of it 'There is perhaps no residence in Scotland surrounded by so picturesque, so romantic, and so beautiful scenery as The Burn'.

POPULATION

In 1801, when the first government census was taken, the population of Fettercairn parish was stated to be 1794; in 1851 the total was slightly less, viz. 1741; in 1891 the population was down to 1376; in 1901 the figure rose to 1390. There had been an alteration to the parish boundary since 1891, the Balfour section having been disjoined from Edzell and annexed to Fettercairn. The census of 1911 gave a population of 1301; that of 1921 returned the figure to 1325; and in 1931 the number had fallen heavily to 1087. (In 1951 the total jumped to 1323 — back to the level of 1921 — but this is plainly due to abnormal conditions at the time of the census. In 1931 there were 560 males to 527 females: in 1951, while females increased only by 29, males increased by 207.)

The depopulation may be accounted for by the gradual change that has taken place in the conditions of agricultural employment: with the introduction of improved machinery and implements, and with tractors displacing horses to a large extent, fewer men are employed in farm work.

MIGRATION

Farm servants are a migratory class and few of them are natives of the parish or of the county. For the most part, they have worked their way south from Aberdeenshire, and there is a coming and going between Kincardineshire and Angus. Formerly the term markets ensured that a married man was likely to remain on a farm for at least a year, and a single man for not less than six months, but with the present-day method of engagement — a month's notice on either side — flittings tend to become more frequent. This has an unsettling effect on family life and is most detrimental to the children's education.

WATER

Throughout the greater part of last century the village had no public water supply. Shortly after the death of Sir John Stuart Forbes, in May 1866, steps were taken to provide a suitable memorial, and in 1869 the Forbes Memorial Fountain was erected, for which a supply of water was granted by Sir Thomas Gladstone of Fasque from a spring on the farm of Nethermill. A few years later the local authority formed a special district to supply water to the village. For a long time this supply has been regarded as very inadequate and at present engineers are engaged in bringing a fresh supply from Bogindollo on the Fasque estate. This, it is estimated, will give sufficient water, not only to the village of Fettercairn, but to the neighbouring villages of Luthermuir and Marykirk.

LIGHTING

In 1847, thanks to the enterprise of two blacksmiths in the parish, gaslight was introduced into the village. In 1852 a joint stock company was formed to take over the plant and carry on the business, and for a number of years the company had a fair measure of success. By 1879, however, the cost of paraffin was cheap, lamps were greatly improved, and the consumption of gas had fallen. In consequence the concern was wound up with a call upon the shareholders, and the company dissolved.

Lighting by paraffin lamps was general until 1938, when electricity was made available by the North of Scotland Hydro-Electric Board. Now the benefit of electric light and power is enjoyed, not only in many of the houses in the village, but in a number of the farmhouses and cottages.

CLEANSING

The County Council provides the services of the cleansing department for the collection of ashes, refuse, etc. once a week in the village.

HOUSING

Dr Cameron, in his *History of Fettercairn*, has a chapter on 'Modern Buildings', in which he mentions 'The Royal Arch', built to commemorate the visit of Queen Victoria and the Prince Consort in 1861, the 'Forbes Memorial Fountain' (1869), and the Public Hall (1890). There is not much to record about building since that date. A few houses have been built, some re-conditioned and modernised, and at the time of writing the County Council is building 8 houses in the village for 'agricultural workers'. Judging by the number of applicants for the houses in course of erection, it is quite obvious that here, as elsewhere, there is an urgent demand for houses. Considerable improvement on many of the farm cottages has been effected, some having every modern requirement — bathroom, hot and cold water, and electric light.

The village attracts a number of visitors during the summer months, but apart from the hotel, there is a lack of suitable accommodation. With the development of the recreation park and an improvement in the housing position, its popularity as a holiday resort would be enhanced.

LOCAL INDUSTRIES

When the writer went to Fettercairn parish forty years ago the sources of employment were more numerous than they are today. There were six blacksmiths in the parish; today there is a smithy in the village and another, conducted by the village smith, on the Burn estate. There were three meal mills; today there is one. The freestone quarry on the Fasque estate is no longer worked; the woollen mill at Arnhall was burnt out and never rebuilt. There is no saddler, no shoemaker, and no tailor's shop. The baker, the butcher, the chemist, and 3 general merchants supply the needs of the community, and if these cannot be met within the parish, a frequent bus service conveys the shopper to nearby towns. Three carpenters provide openings for boys wishing to serve their apprenticeship as joiners.

Fettercairn distillery gives work to some 20 men, and during the war years the aerodrome offered work to a number of men in the village. Domestic service does not attract girls on leaving school. Some have found employment in the local shops, some have taken up nursing, and others have gone to offices and shops elsewhere.

Agriculture is the dominating industry and has been dealt with earlier in this *Account*.

THE PARISH CHURCH

The coronation of Queen Victoria took place on 28th June 1838; and in the *Montrose Standard*, a week later, a local correspondent, under the heading of 'Fettercairn', reports:— 'Our little village was not behind in the general rejoicing on Thursday night. Although we did not follow in the wake of some of the neighbouring towns in *founding* public buildings, the day was employed in *pulling down* part of our church to make way for a handsome steeple and additional church accommodation about to be erected by the munificence of several of our public-spirited proprietors'.

The church was built in 1804, and a transept was added in 1838. It is interesting to note the reason given for the building of this church. It was built, says the Kirk Session record, 'in consequence of the old one being too small to accommodate those who wished to attend'. The times are strangely altered, and the years have brought many changes in customs and in the ordering of the church's worship. From the Kirk Session records we learn that in 1858 it was resolved to discontinue the practice of collection by ladles, except on special occasions, and instead to substitute plates at the doors of the church. In 1867 the second Communion service was introduced; in 1880 the practice of sitting during the time of singing and standing at prayer gave place to the present method; and in 1886 the organ was used for the first time in the services of the church.

No one can read the former *Statistical Accounts* without being impressed by the hard conditions of life which prevailed. This hardness affected all aspects of life, the religious not excepted. Now conditions are very different. The standard of taste and of comfort, as of education, has been wonderfully heightened, and the desire is strong to make beautiful the sanctuary where prayer is wont to be made. Accordingly, in 1926, an extensive scheme of renovation was completed at a cost of over £6000. The building was greatly improved and the church enriched by many gifts, which are a distinct aid to the seemly and reverent offering of divine worship.

OTHER CHURCHES

After the Disruption in 1843, a congregation of the Free Church was formed and a church erected. A succession of 5 ministers served the charge until the congregation united with that of the parish church in 1930.

St Andrew's Episcopal Church, at Fasque, was built by Sir John Gladstone, Bart., and consecrated in 1847. A chancel was added by his son, Sir Thomas, in 1869. It, too, has had 5 incumbents, but the charge is now linked with that of St Palladius, Drumtochty, and served by its Rector.

CHURCH HALL

The building of a church hall has proved of great benefit to the parish, providing a meeting place for the various church organisations, and also for other social agencies.

RECORDS

The Kirk Session records, dating back to 1676, are deposited in the Church of Scotland strong room in the General Assembly Hall, Edinburgh.

BEQUESTS

Since the benefactions mentioned in the previous *Account* the following bequests have been made. To the Kirk Session:— Brown Bequest for General Church Purposes, £861. Molison Bequest, £129; Miss Jessie Hill's Bequest, £155; Mrs Hoult's Bequest, £204 — all to the poor. Mrs. Hoult's Bequest £102, for the Sunday School Picnic Fund. Mrs. Callum's Bequest: at her death in 1846 Mrs Callum left to the parish and Free Church ministers of Fettercairn £50 each, with the annual interest to provide bibles for the aged poor, and Sunday School requisites for the children in attendance. Since the union of the Churches the bibles have been given to the first communicants.

The Gladstone Bursaries: Sir John R. Gladstone of Fasque left £800 to provide Bursaries of £15, £10 and £5 annually to pupils on the roll of Fettercairn school who are going on to post-primary education. The Trustees are the parish minister, the headmaster of Fettercairn school, and the factor of the Fasque estate, so long as the property remains in the Gladstone family.

Sir John also left a sum of £50 to the public property committee, and Mrs. Hoult £200 to the same committee for the upkeep of the public hall.

EDUCATION

There are 2 schools in the parish. The staff in the village school consists of the headmaster and 3 assistants. The number of children on the roll is 119. The school at Inch of Arnhall is in the charge of a lady and is attended by 24 pupils. Pupils over twelve years of age are transferred to the junior secondary school at Laurencekirk and those who are going on to higher education take the secondary course in Brechin High School.

The Education Committee of the County Council arranges for transporting pupils travelling to Laurencekirk, grants bursaries and, in necessitous cases, free meals in the school canteen. The provision of free milk and dinners at a moderate cost is a great boon to children attending the country schools, whilst the frequent visits of the doctor, dentist and school nurse have done much to promote the physical well-being of the younger generation.

LIBRARY

An excellent selection of good literature is sent out to the schools from the County Library, and of this full advantage is taken. A supply of books is also sent to the Library in the public hall.

SOCIAL ACTIVITIES

The recreation park offers facilities for various games. Football, cricket, tennis, bowling and curling are enjoyed in their season, while badminton is played in the public hall during the winter months. The hall, built in 1890, has accommodation for 400 people. It is frequently filled to capacity at popular concerts, and is greatly in demand for dances and other forms of entertainment.

Brownies, Girl Guides and the Army Cadet Force cater for the youth of the community. A strong and healthy branch of the Women's Rural Institute has a good record of fully twenty years to its credit. St Mark's Lodge, No. 1313, of the Ancient Order of Freemasons has celebrated its twenty-fifth anniversary.

FETTERCAIRN FARMERS' CLUB

The former *Account* recorded the establishment of the Club in the year 1826. It has had a long and honourable history, promoting agricultural interests in every way, furthering research, and not forgetting the claims of the Benevolent Fund on its liberality. The membership is drawn from Fettercairn and the neighbouring parishes in Kincardineshire and the county of Angus.

On the first Wednesday of August the Club has its annual show of stock, which is the outstanding social event in the parish. The weather is almost invariably fine and the quality of the exhibits in every section of a high order, and accordingly the show attracts a very large number of visitors. This year, 1949, the Club held its 117th show in the park, kindly given year by year by Lord Clinton, and it is estimated that the number of people attending exceeded 5000. There were large entries for all classes except horses. Particularly popular was the W.R.I. marquee, which housed 600 entries, representing 16 Institutes. The Club holds its root and seed show, dinner and business meeting in December.

Last year a Junior Farmer's Club was formed, with much enthusiasm. It has had a successful session of lectures, debates and outings, and has entered teams for various stock-judging competitions.

An evening class in agricultural book-keeping, conducted by the manager of the North of Scotland Bank, has a large attendance.

WAY OF LIFE

With the various changes that have taken place in local government in the course of the years, perhaps it would be correct to say that there has been a loss of 'civic consciousness and civic pride' in country parishes. The Parish Council and the School Board evoked considerable interest in the community, and whatever be the admitted gains of centralisation, there seems to be a good deal of apathy about public administration and the conduct of parochial affairs.

The wars have had an unsettling influence. There is a marked decline in family life, and, as the advertisements in the weekly newspapers indicate, a keen demand for amusement and entertainment.

In the former *Accounts* of the parish, the writers stated that the people 'give regular attendance upon public worship on the Lord's day.' 'Divine service is well attended by all ranks.' Today! *O tempora! O mores!* Church-going has sadly declined, but it is not the be-all and end-all of religion. There is much indifference, there is no hostility; and the last hundred years have witnessed a great advance in Christian activity in country parishes. In former days the church's outlook upon life was of a very narrow and provincial character and the various agencies which are now regarded as the natural outlet of Christian activity were scarcely dreamt of. With the experience of forty years behind him, the writer gladly bears testimony to the generous and ready support the people gave, not only to church schemes but to everything that was promoted for the good of the community.

December 1949

THE PARISH OF FETTERESSO

by the Rev. W.C. Bigwood, B.D., J.P.

FEATURES

The parish of Fetteresso stretches some 6 or 7 miles to the north and north-west of Stonehaven and some 5 or 6 miles to the west. It includes the new town of Stonehaven, the former fishing village of Cowie, the villages of Muchalls and Newtonhill and the estates of Fetteresso, Ury, Rickarton, Netherley, Cowie and Elsick. The landward area is 26,833 acres and the area of Stonehaven — partly in Dunnottar — is 457 acres. Fetteresso is bounded on the south by Dunnottar, on the west by Glenbervie, on the north-west by Durris, and on the north by Maryculter and Banchory-Devenick; to the east there is the North Sea. The coast line here is rugged, with cliffs rising in places to well over a hundred feet, deeply indented where the sea has worn away the softer portion of the cliffs into gullies and ravines. What little stretches of beach there are, are mainly shingle. The beauty of the rock scenery around Muchalls in particular has drawn many artists. It is the only scenery praised by Robert Burns in his travels — 'a good deal romantic', he says. The encroachment of the sea in Stonehaven Bay has led to the decline in the village of Cowie and is now presenting the Town Council with a major problem. A recent engineers' report has revealed that the high-water mark of ordinary spring tides has advanced over sixty feet since 1935.

GEOLOGY

Geologically, the parish is of particular interest because the Highland Boundary Fault, which runs diagonally across Scotland, begins in it at Garron Point, traversing the southern part of the parish. It was not till after the publication of the *Second Statistical Account* (1842) that the existence of the Fault was appreciated — about 1855, while the full term, Highland Boundary Fault, seems first to have been used by Geikie in the annual report of the Geological Survey for 1895 (Anderson — 'Geology of the Highland Border' — *Trans. Roy. Soc. Edin.*, vol. 61, 1949, p.481). A full description of the rock formation and also of the remarkable suite of fossils found in Craigeven Bay $1\frac{1}{4}$ miles to the north-east of Stonehaven, is to be found in Campbell — 'Geology of S.E. Kincardineshire' — *Trans. Roy. Soc. Edin.*, vol. 48, 1913, pp.923–960.

The presence of the Fault makes it a transitional area. To the north are the same metamorphic rocks with igneous instrusions as the rest of the lower-lying north east peneplane. South of the Fault are found the great sedimentary rocks of the Old Red Sandstone (Devonian) variety, which form a rich belt of soil southwest of Stonehaven. Actually, Fetteresso contains very little of the true Devonian rocks, since a belt of Silurian rocks, about a mile and a half broad and seven miles long, stretches inland from Stonehaven, dividing the schists and gneisses of the north from the Old Red Sandstone of the south. The transitional aspect is seen in the building stone of the parish. While Stonehaven, which is south of the Fault, is largely built of Old Red Sandstone, the houses to the north of the town, in Rickarton, Cookney, Muchalls and Newtonhill, are mostly built of dull grey stone — schist, gneiss or granite.

SOIL AND SURFACE

Of greater importance is the type of soil produced. The underlying geological formations have a great effect on the farming of the area, since the soils depend on disintegrated rocks for their mineral constituents and quality. In the parish the underlying rock is predominantly metamorphic. This has produced a soil which is neither deep nor naturally very productive. It is of a thin, gravelly, acid nature and although at the end of the 18th and the beginning of the 19th century great tracts were reclaimed from moorland, moss and bog under the enlightened policy of such proprietors as Barclay of Ury and Silver of Netherley, the northern part of the parish has still rather a bleak and poor aspect.

About half the area of the parish is under cultivation. The remainder is moorland, woodland, waste land and hill country. There has been very considerable deforestation during the past eighty years and today even the picturesque and old hardwoods of the estates are being felled. The Forestry Commission have, however, started reafforestation. The parish is undulating, rising to its highest points in the west and north-west area in Trusta Hill (1051 feet), Craigneil, Bawdy Craig and Meikle Carewe, all over 800 feet. The Carron forms the southern boundary, separating Fetteresso and Dunnottar. The Cowie, rising in the high ground to the west, flows most of its course through the parish to enter Stonehaven Bay just north of the town. Both rivers have occasioned considerable damage when, in spate, they have overflowed their banks and flooded the lower-lying parts of the town.

The most recent occasion was at the end of October 1945, when the Cowie broke its banks, undermined part of the recreation grounds, and seriously threatened the bridge which carries the main road north from the town. Considerable expenditure has been incurred in building retaining walls to prevent a recurrence of this danger.

HISTORY OF THE LOCAL COMMUNITY

The new town of Stonehaven was begun in 1759, when the then proprietor of Ury purchased the Links of Arduthie. He planned the new town with broad streets at right angles to each other. The street names — Barclay Street, David Street, Robert Street, Allardice Street, etc. — perpetuate the close connection between the town and the Barclays of Ury. For more than a century the new town was confined to the low ground adjoining the beach, but in the latter half of the nineteenth century it began to spread westwards over the high tableland towards the railway. The closing years of the nineteenth century and the opening years of the twentieth saw the building of the substantial dwelling houses to be found in Gurney Street, Bath Street, Arduthie Road and others. The period following 1919 marked the beginning of building by the local authority. The main housing scheme, that of Brickfield — the site last century of a brick-field — was begun in 1935 and is still under development; it brings the houses right up to the railway just to the south of the railway station. And the latest extension of the burgh boundaries in 1946 brings a stretch of the railway between the viaduct at Kirktown of Fetteresso and Glenury viaduct, as well as the station, situated about three-quarters of a mile from the Market Square, within the burgh.

THE RAILWAY

Work was in progress on the laying of the railway in 1847 and on October 30, 1849 the line was opened from Dubton, near Montrose, to Limpet Mill, about 3 miles to the north of Stonehaven, and the first passenger trains were run on November 1, passengers coming off the train at Limpet Mill and completing the journey to Aberdeen by coach. By April 1, 1850 the line was completed into Aberdeen and opened for passenger traffic. The royal family first travelled south from Aberdeen by train on October 13, 1853 — their train left Aberdeen at 12.46 and arrived at Stonehaven at 1.15. The Queen and her suite alighted and entered the station, where 'an elegant and substantial luncheon had been provided by Mr. Douglas of Douglas Hotel' (*Aberdeen Journal*, Oct. 19, 1853). This became the usual practice in the early journeys from Balmoral.

The work on the railway brought many labourers — the *Aberdeen Journal* says Highland, local tradition Irish — into the neighbourhood, and there was more than one disturbance in the town. The most serious took place on Old Christmas Day, Jan. 5, 1848, when a company of labourers, some 200 to 300 strong, gathered in the Square, armed with bludgeons, knives, pickstaffs and branches cut down in Dunnottar Woods. Their grievance seemed to be rising prices in the shops and a feeling that the townspeople were hostile to them. Houses and inns were attacked and anyone they met in the street who could not speak Gaelic (so the *Aberdeen Journal*) was assaulted. One young man in from the country was so severely handled that he died that night. The next morning assistance was summoned from Aberdeen; twenty men from the 93rd Highlanders were sent out and eleven of the ringleaders were arrested. At the subsequent trial in the High Court of Justiciary in Aberdeen four were convicted, of whom one was sentenced to transportation for seven years and the other three to terms of imprisonment varying from twelve to eighteen months. The story of the riot is told in a poem, published in 1850 by James Walker, Mains of Cowie, though there are differences in detail between his account and that of the *Aberdeen Journal*.

THE BURGH

Mention must be made of the part played in the town's development by a Party of Progress formed about 1858 by a number of alert members of the community binding themselves together to improve the condition of the county town. Their ideas were at first ridiculed and strenuously opposed in the Parochial Board, the then public health authority, but they ultimately had their way, and water and sewerage systems were installed at a cost of about £14,000, systems which have stood the community in good stead. In 1892 Stonehaven became a police burgh and the commissioners who had till then managed local affairs were replaced by a Town Council of twelve. Various local government acts since then have transferred some of the Town Council's responsibilities to the County Council, on which the Town Council is represented by three of its members, and have added others, notably since 1919 housing. The burgh rates have been fixed for 1950-51 at 14/10½d in the £, as compared with 11/6 for the preceding year, while the county rate is 12/-, as compared with 9/5.

ESTATES

If the story of the part of the parish which includes the new town of Stonehaven is one of growth and development, the story of the rural areas is one of partial decline. Of the estates that are mainly included in the parish, Netherley, owned by H.O. Ritchie, Esq., in whose family it has been since 1901, remains largely intact. Elsick, with its model home farm, has been vastly improved by the present Earl of Southesk, to whose maternal ancestors, the Bannermans, it has belonged since about 1387, and the old castle of Muchalls, built about 1620 by the Burnetts — the 'gyte covenanter' of Spalding — is still in good order, with its famous ceiling. But the estates of Fetteresso, Ury and Cowie have been broken up, and only in the case of Cowie is the mansion house occupied by a member of the family who formerly owned the estate. Ury affords a good illustration of the changes that a century has brought. For nearly two hundred years it was in the possession of the Barclay family. On the death of Captain Barclay-Allardice it was left to his daughter, but the debts were so enormous that everything had to be sold to satisfy the creditors. It was purchased by Alexander Baird of Gartsherrie in 1854. The old house was pulled down and replaced by the present building in 1858. In 1874 the neighbouring estate of Rickarton was also bought by the Baird family, and is now occupied by Viscount Stonehaven. The Ury estate was sold in 1946. The timber in the policies has been cut down, completing a process begun during the war years. The house itself has been purchased by the Education Committee of Aberdeen City as a holiday school for city children, but so far the scheme is only in its initial stages and the house stands empty, as it has done for the past six years.

Fetteresso Castle and estate remained in the possession of the Duff family till 1944, when the bulk of the estate was sold to Mrs. Andrew Carnegie. The Forestry Commission have taken over a considerable stretch of land in the Swanley area, and are replanting with coniferous trees. The woodlands around the castle have been cut down and what was a few years ago fine wooded parklands is now open and bare. The castle is now used as a guest house.

DECAY OF CROFTS

Along with the break-up of the estates has gone the decline of the rural districts. This is particularly noticeable in an area like Rickarton. Croft after croft has fallen into decay. The arable land has been added to neighbouring farms or allowed to revert to rushes, and the homesteads have fallen into ruin or almost wholly disappeared. The War Department have taken over a considerable stretch of moorland in the district and are to use it as a training area.

COASTAL VILLAGES

Of the coastal villages, Newtonhill and Muchalls are now used mainly as residences of Aberdeen business men and elderly retired people.

K

The roofless ruins of the Kirk of Cowie standing on the high ground overlooking the sea are a familiar landmark to passers-by on the road or on the railway, and the four walls of the original parish church at the Kirktown of Fetteresso still remain; the bell was removed from the west gable of the building a year or two back and is at present in the vestibule of the parish church. The story of the Kirks of Cowie and Fetteresso is told in an attractive brochure published by the late Rev. J.B. Burnett, D.D., minister of the parish from 1905 till 1943. The old burial grounds surrounding both buildings are now virtually closed for interments except in the case of very near relatives of those who had ground in them. The new burying ground at Broomhill was opened in 1903.

The war memorial on the Black Hill, in the neighbouring parish of Dunnottar, keeps in remembrance the men of Stonehaven and district who gave their lives in the two world wars, as do also the memorials in the several churches and the memorial outside Mackie Academy. Reminders of the Second World War are the concrete blocks still to be seen on the foreshore at Cowie, and the tangles of barbed wire to be found along the course of the Cowie River, part of the defences that were put up in 1940 when there was considerable threat of invasion.

POPULATION

The population of Fetteresso parish rose steadily from 3687 in 1801 to 5720 in 1851 — a total which has never been equalled since. By 1901 the figure gradually fell to 5409. During the present century the population recorded by Census has fluctuated as follows:— (1911) 4961, (1921) 5700, (1931) 4919. It is possible that the 1951 figure will show an increase, as the new housing scheme in Brickfield has brought up many families from the Old Town (the part of Stonehaven in Dunnottar parish).

(The 1951 Census recorded 5696 — almost the same as in 1921 and little less than 1851. Females increased from 2680 in 1931 to 3091 in 1951, males from 2239 to 2605. The population of the burgh of Stonehaven advanced from 4185 in 1931 to 4438 in 1951, females numbering 2503. In 1891 the population was 4500, of whom 1946 lived in the Old Town.)

PUBLIC SERVICES

The past hundred years have seen a wide extension of public and social services. A century ago the town depended for its water supply on wells, supplemented by water piped from the Ewen Burn by a private company. In 1887 the reservoir at Elfhill was opened, the occasion being marked by a march of local schoolchildren to the reservoir, an occasion for which they were trained by the sergeant of the local Volunteers. This supply was augmented with a bigger supply from the Cowie at Hobseat, in the neighbouring parish of Glenbervie, in 1934. Electricity, now supplied by the North of Scotland Hydro-Electric Board, is becoming widely used; the streets in the town are lit with it and its use is also extending to the rural areas. Gas manufactured by the former Stonehaven Gas Company still continues to be used for lighting, heating and cooking. A progressive group during last century planned and laid the excellent sewage system, and under the Town Council the streets are kept clean and tidy. A rubbish collection scheme has recently been introduced into the rural areas by the County Council.

HOSPITALS

Prior to the National Health Service (Scotland) Act 1947 there were two Nursing Associations, one for the town and one for the landward parishes of Dunnottar and Fetteresso, each with its own district nurse and each run very efficiently by local committees. Of hospitals, there are the Isolation Hospital, the James Mowat Home and Woodcot. The Isolation Hospital was built in 1901 by a combination of 7 local authorities and opened in August 1903 as an infectious diseases hospital, serving practically the whole county. It passed to the County Council in May 1930, was extended with the addition of a cubicle block in 1936, and passed from the County Council to the Secretary of State at 5 July 1948. It is now administered by the Board of Management for Kincardine Hospitals, under the general control of the North-East of Scotland Regional Hospital Board. As there are many fewer cases of infectious diseases than formerly, while tuberculosis is a serious problem, the hospital is now used solely for tuberculosis, and cases of infectious diseases in this area are taken to the City Hospital, Aberdeen.

In his will the late James Mowat, at one time provost of Stonehaven, left his house, Carron Lodge, to be used as a nursing home for persons permanently resident in Stonehaven or elsewhere in the county of Kincardine — 'suffering from medical or surgical ailments, unable without undue strain to pay the charges of ordinary nursing homes, but able to pay for the attendance of doctors or surgeons chosen by themselves and also to pay to this intended Home such moderate rates for their nursing and board, as will, coupled with the help to be given by me, produce such a revenue sufficient for its expenditure. It is my desire that the intended Home shall be strictly reserved so far as practicable for the persons whom I wish to benefit and that the charges shall be kept sufficiently moderate to be within their means.' Along with the house there was left an endowment of £14,000. A matron was appointed in 1927 and the Home was opened. An operating theatre was added in 1931 and various additions have been made to the house to accommodate nurses. Maternity cases were also admitted. Since the Home came under the Hospital Board the theatre has been closed and the Home is now used for maternity cases and medical cases, particularly elderly people. A moderate charge is made for medical cases.

Woodcot was built by a combination of thirteen of the Parochial Boards in the county in 1867. The first cases were admitted on 18 August 1867. They were five ordinary poor. During the first year 116 ordinary poor were admitted. Originally, the main block had only two storeys and the porter's lodge was a single-storey building. The House Committee proceeded with the work of constructing additional dormitories in 1896. This was probably the construction of the third storey in what had previously been attic space. Additions to the porter's lodge were carried out in 1913. Prior to 1926, the Governor's accommodation was in the centre of the main building, but in that year it was decided to proceed with the construction of a Governor's house, thus freeing the accommodation which he occupied in the main building for other purposes. The work started in 1928. Under the National Health Service (Scotland) Act, 1947, the institution, by that time under the control of the County Council, passed over to the Secretary of State at 5 July 1948. The type of case is very much as before. The old people and the mental defectives in the institution are the responsibility of the County Council and they pay the Board of Management part of the cost of accommodating them there. The sick, including lunatics, are hospital cases proper and are the financial responsibility of the Board of Management, acting for the Secretary of State. 'Casuals' or 'vagrants' are still accommodated in the lodge premises, but they are now called 'persons without a settled way of living'. These persons are the responsibility of the National Assistance Board, but the County Council is the agent of the National Assistance Board for this purpose. The officers of the hospital are as before, but the Governor is called the 'Superintendent'. It is interesting to note the salaries of the officials at the opening of the institution in 1867 — Governor £60 per annum and Matron £30 per annum, both having in addition house accommodation, fire and light, and the 'ordinary rations of the house'. The Medical Officer had £30 per annum, the Chaplain £20, and the Secretary £15.

HOUSING

The number of inhabited houses in the parish is 1541; of these 1009 are in the burgh, 97 in Newtonhill, 54 in Muchalls, 37 in Cowie, and 344 in the landward area. The houses in the burgh reflect the different periods of building. There are one, two and even three storey houses in Allardice Street, Barclay Street and Cameron Street, occupying the sites of earlier buildings and incorporating parts of them. Some few in Barclay Street were condemned and replaced with council houses, others condemned have been reopened to meet the housing shortage since 1945. There are the substantial stone-built villas that mark the building of the late nineteenth and early twentieth century. There are the less substantial bungalow type that characterise most of the private building since 1919 and the council houses which have come to be erected in increasing numbers, so that approximately one-quarter of the houses in the new town are council-built and council-owned. Most of the houses have some garden, many of them walled, and there are only a few with no garden at all. The following figures, supplied by the Burgh Surveyor, show the extent and the nature of the new building since 1919:

Number of houses built by the local authority at Brickfield, Barclay Street, Rodney Street and Fetteresso Terrace between 1919 and 1939 — 4 two-apartment; 132 three-apartment; 44 four-apartment; and 14 five-apartment. Number of houses built by private enterprise between 1919-1939:— approximately 30.

Number of houses built by the local authority since 1945 at Brickfield:—

	3-apartment	4-apartment	5-apartment
Temporary	35	—	—
Cruden (Non-trad.)	—	10	—
Traditional	—	20	2
Total	35	30	2

Number of houses built privately since 1945 — seven.

The encroachment of the sea at Cowie has led to the disappearance of at least a row and a half of houses. With the exception of 4 new houses for the coastguards, whose headquarters are in the village, there has been no new building, and the surviving houses are old and without adequate modern conveniences. At Muchalls several of the old houses have been reconstructed and a few modern bungalows have been built, and the County Council are meantime erecting 8 traditional houses. Bungalows have also been built at Newtonhill, and since 1945 15 temporary houses of the Arcon type and 8 Swedish timber houses have been built by the County Council. The rural areas have seen the disappearance of many of the old cottages, while attempts have been made to modernise a few. Four Swedish timber houses have been put up at Tewel for rural workers, and a beginning has been made with traditional-type houses, four of which have been completed and are now occupied above Redcloak, and 8 more are still under construction at Farrochie.

AGRICULTURE

Agriculture bulks largely in the economy of the parish, approximately one half of its area being under cultivation. The following figures, supplied by Mr Gordon Watt, B.Sc., the county agricultural adviser, show the nature of the crops grown and the acreage under cultivation in the years 1939 and 1949 —

	1939 (Acres)	1949 (Acres)
Wheat	12	49
Oats	$3346\frac{3}{4}$	$4658\frac{1}{2}$
Barley	598	$541\frac{3}{4}$
Potatoes	$259\frac{1}{4}$	$643\frac{3}{4}$
Sugar Beet	$2\frac{1}{4}$	17
Turnips	$1512\frac{1}{2}$	1474
Other Cultivation	69	$120\frac{1}{4}$
Total Tillage area	$5799\frac{3}{4}$	$7504\frac{1}{4}$
	(Nos.)	(Nos.)
Horses	477	284
Dairy Cattle	1160	1044
Beef Cattle	3591	4255
Sheep	10490	6331
Pigs	454	696
Poultry	33043	55810

The number of tractors as at 1st January 1950 was approximately 140.

FISHING

The fishing has largely declined. There is some salmon fishing off the beach at Stonehaven, but Cowie has no longer any fishing boats. The Muchalls disasters referred to in the *First Statistical Account*, when two boats with their crews (each six men) were lost within ten years of each other, led to the village of Muchalls at the Broad Shore being deserted as unlucky. Finally a new village was built at Stranathro, $\frac{3}{4}$ mile north of the old site. It had no good harbour facilities and the inhabitants gradually departed from the old fishing ways. Further north along the coast, at 'the Skateraw', some men are engaged in salmon fishing and when nothing else is doing they go white-fishing or set creels for crabs and lobsters.

OTHER EMPLOYMENTS

There is no large industry in Stonehaven. A tanworks, which at the close of last century employed about a hundred men in tanning still carries on, though with fewer hands and on a more restricted basis, being confined now to tanning on a small scale and dressing leather of high quality, for which there is, however, a limited demand. Glenury distillery employs a few men, as does a lemonade factory which was begun in 1846. A depot of British Road Services, Alexander's bus depot and the various garages give employment to mechanics and drivers. Some more men are employed by the railway and by the Forestry Commission. The local trades employ a few men as journeymen and apprentices. For women and girls there is the net factory; shops, offices, and the hotels and boarding houses, particularly during the busy summer months, employ others, while the buses have women and girls as conductresses. Since 1945 there has been a considerable addition to the staff of County Council officials. The different County Council departments are accommodated in offices in Evan Street, at Viewmount and at the Briars. All these forms of employment are not sufficient, however, to absorb the whole available labour force in the town, and it is reckoned that some 300 men and women travel daily to Aberdeen to work. While some of the country tradesmen have disappeared the smiddies have been adapting themselves to the new mechanised farming, and where horses were once shod, tractors and the other complicated implements of modern agriculture are now handled. Within recent years in the parish designs for many new agricultural implements have been patented, the latest being a spring device on the plough to enable it to negotiate boulders in the soil.

HOLIDAY RESORT

No account of the industry of Stonehaven would be complete without reference to the summer visitors. Since the latter half of the nineteenth century Stonehaven has become increasingly popular as a holiday resort. In the 1890s it was the practice, on a fixed day in the month of August — apparently August was the peak period of the holiday season — to take a census of the visitors in the town. This was done by a committee under the direction of the Burgh Treasurer. Here are the figures for four consecutive years:— (1895) 1266; (1896) 1212; (1897) 1249; 1898) 1433. More interesting still are the details of the census taken on 8 August 1898:—

Ladies	633
Gentlemen	337
Children under fourteen	298
Maids	165
TOTAL	1433

Of that number, 390 came from south of the Border, 30 from abroad, 191 from Edinburgh, 197 from Glasgow, 234 from Aberdeen and 391 from the rest of Scotland.

No such census has been taken in recent years, but the following changes in holiday customs are to be noted. The peak holiday period in Stonehaven is now July, particularly during the Glasgow Fair fortnight, and the preponderance of visitors are from Glasgow and the south-west of Scotland. It is also to be noted that, while fifty years ago the general practice was to rent a house in the town and bring one's family and household staff, today people coming on holiday stay at one or other of the many hotels or boarding houses, into which some former dwelling houses have been turned. This change seems to have come after the First World War. While the hotels keep open during the winter, though with reduced staffs, the boarding houses close down at the end of the season, i.e. sometime in the month of September, and re-open around Easter or a few weeks later. A further change in holiday habits may be coming. Recently a camping site has been opened where caravans may be parked and this is being increasingly used. The town has also been attracting large numbers of day visitors and picnic parties, particularly at the weekends. It is also a popular camping place for Boys' Brigade companies and Scout troops. In recent years the Town Council have appointed an entertainments manager during the summer months, and have also engaged the services of a dance band during the same period.

SHOPS

Stonehaven is well supplied with shops, a few of them old-established businesses going back practically a century in the same family. Some are branches of Aberdeen shops, among them the Northern Co-operative Society, which has fairly extensive premises and a large membership. Motor vans serve the country districts. The weekly market on Thursday brings many of the farming community into the town that day. There are branches of the North of Scotland and Clydesdale Bank, the Bank of Scotland, the Commercial Bank and the Union Bank, and the original Stonehaven Savings Bank is now linked up with the Aberdeen Savings Bank. There are 11 licensed hotels and public houses in the town, and 3 in the landward part of the parish, and there is one local cinema, with changes of programme three times a week. The close proximity to Aberdeen and the frequent and cheap bus service — half-hourly, return fare 2/- — offer an inducement to some to shop and seek their entertainment there.

CHURCHES

There are 5 churches over and above the parish church. Cookney, first built as a Chapel of Ease, was erected into a parish *quoad sacra* in 1859.

This building was replaced by the present church in 1886. Rickarton Church was built and erected into a parish *quoad sacra* in 1872, with an endowment provided by a legacy from Mr George Thomson, one time minister at Fetteresso and writer of the *Second Statistical Account* of the parish. The South Church in Stonehaven, originally a congregation of the Free Church begun in 1843, and united with the former North Church, originally United Presbyterian, in 1927, entered the Church of Scotland at the Union of the churches in 1929. Bourtreebush, begun as a preaching station from Maryculter Free Church in 1876, and raised to a full charge in the Free Church in 1882, is now also a congregation of the Church of Scotland. There is one congregation of the Scottish Episcopal Church, St Ternan's, Muchalls, with a chapel (St Michael's) recently opened in Newtonhill. In addition, there is a group, the Apostolic Church, which meets in the Liberal Rooms, Arbuthnott Street.

Changes have taken place in the church worship, for example, the introduction of the organ — in 1876 the kirk session of the parish church 'taking into due account the great degree of unanimity found to prevail as to the use of the instrument in the public worship, cheerfully resolved to introduce it into the service of the sanctuary' (Session minutes) — standing while singing, introduced into the parish church about the same time, the use of hymns, and the use of individual cups for the Holy Communion.

In 1926 the parish church and manse passed from the hands of the heritors to the General Trustees of the Church of Scotland, their maintenance now being a charge on the congregation. In 1946 the manse, with its extensive grounds, was sold, and a smaller, more convenient and more modern house in Bath Street was purchased in its place. Consequent to the Union of the churches in 1929, Fetteresso, Cookney and Rickarton were transferred from the Presbytery of Fordoun and synod of Angus and Mearns to the Presbytery of Aberdeen and synod of Aberdeen.

EDUCATION

There have been extensive developments in education. In 1876 Stonehaven Public School was opened to take the place of the parish school, situated opposite the church. It came to supersede other schools, among them Donaldson's School, the Free Church School, Cowie School and others. It was characterised in the inspectors' reports in the 1880s as a 'mixed school', combining secondary with elementary instruction, presenting pupils for the Leaving Certificate and sending up candidates to the Aberdeen University Bursary Examination. The school opened with 236 pupils; by 1887 the number had risen to 529; in 1903 the attendance of older pupils was beginning to be affected by the growing popularity of Mackie Academy; in 1909 the roll stood at 400, in 1920 271; and now, in 1950, as an elementary school, it has a roll of 263, under a headmaster and 5 women teachers, as compared with a staff of 4 men and 3 women in 1881 and 3 men, 4 women and 5 pupil teachers in 1901.

In 1893 Mackie Academy was built out of a Trust fund created by William Mackie for secondary education. It was managed by a Board of Governors as a 'higher grade school' until 1919, under a scheme prepared under the Educational Endowments (Scotland) Act; in 1919 it was transferred to Kincardineshire Education Authority, and in 1930 to Kincardine County Council. The original building was largely destroyed by fire in 1929; the school was rebuilt on the same site and opened again in January 1932. It is now classed as a multilateral school, having a primary section (fee paying), a junior secondary department drawing pupils from Stonehaven and the neighbourhood, and a senior secondary department meeting the needs of the whole southern section of the county, as well as districts lying to the north of the town. Pupils travel to Mackie Academy daily by bus and by train. The following figures show the school's development:— (1893) 111; (1920) 269; (1930) 291; (1940) 374; (1950) 634. The present staff consists of the rector, 15 men and 17 women teachers. Other schools in the parish, with their present numbers are:— Tewel (52), Rickarton (34), Cairnhill (45), Netherley (35), Cookney (29), and Muchalls (41). These are all elementary schools, administered by the Education Committee of the County Council.

SOCIAL ACTIVITIES

A wide number of voluntary social services exist. It is hardly possible to do more than catalogue them here. For the young there are a Boy Scout troop, a Wolf Cub pack, a company of Girl Guides and Brownies, a unit of the Army Cadet Force, Youth Fellowships in the churches, and various youth clubs in the town. Social clubs at Tewel and Rickarton provide recreation for the people in these districts, and for women there are branches of the W.R.I. in the rural areas, e.g. at Rickarton, Cookney and Netherley, and a flourishing branch of the Townswomen's Guild in Stonehaven. Women's Guilds in the churches play an important part in maintaining the various congregations.

Music is catered for by the Stonehaven and District Choral and Orchestral Society, which holds weekly practices throughout the winter months and aims at giving two concerts each season; by the Stonehaven Chamber Music Club; by the Three Churches Junior Choir, which trains young people in choral singing; and by the recently re-formed Stonehaven Pipe Band, which gives weekly performances during the summer. For drama, there are the Ury

Players and the Stonehaven Dramatic Club; for art, the Stonehaven and District Art Society, which arranges monthly lectures and holds occasional art exhibitions; for dancing, a Scottish country dancing class and a modern ballroom dancing class. Weekly lectures are provided by a local branch of the W.E.A.; and the memory of Burns is kept alive by the Stonehaven (Fatherland) Burns Club.

A lodge of the Freemasons had its headquarters in what was formerly the North Church, in Ann Street, and a chapter of the Eastern Star was started in the early summer of this year and meets meantime in Fetteresso Church Hall. The Rotary Club has its weekly lunch on Wednesday. For old age pensioners a Pensioners' Association exists, and for ex-servicemen of both wars, an Ex-servicemen's Association. Politics is represented by a branch of the Liberal Association, a local branch of the Labour Party and a recently formed Liberal-Unionist Association, which meantime takes the place of the Unionist Association. There is a branch of the Red Cross.

RECREATION

For outdoor recreation there is a sporting eighteen hole golf course, situated just over a mile to the north of the town, and a Men's and Women's Golf Club. Football is played in Cowie Park by the Stonehaven Football Club and some junior teams. Newtonhill has also its football club. The once flourishing Thistle Cricket Club, founded in 1859, has disappeared and the cricket pitch situated close to Cowie House has reverted to cultivation. In 1885 the recreation grounds were opened and provide facilities for bowling, tennis and putting. In August each year a tennis tournament is held, which draws competitors from near and far. An open-air swimming pool was opened in 1934 and attracts thousands each summer. It has come to replace the former bathing from the beach. Fishing is to be had in the Cowie and the Carron and there is a local Angling Association. For indoor recreation there are several badminton clubs, a darts league made up at present of fifteen teams, a miniature rifle club and bridge clubs, while whist drives and dances, run both in town and country for all and sundry purposes, provide social outlet and recreation. A good deal of overlapping occurs among those various organisations and on the whole the numbers are not large. They are dependent generally on the zeal and enthusiasm of a few.

ANTIQUITIES

Places and features of antiquarian interest include the ancient camp at Raedykes, mentioned in the two previous Accounts. The site was surveyed and partly excavated by Dr George Macdonald in 1914. A full account of this will be found in the *Proceedings of the Society of Antiquaries*, 1916, pp.327-48. The nature of the entrenchments, particularly the protection of the entrance by traverses, led Dr Macdonald to the conclusion that the camp was a Roman one, though whether the builder was Agricola or Lollius Urbicus or Severus he leaves undecided. Crawford, however, in the *Topography of Roman Scotland* (1949), pp.130ff., identifies the camp with that set up by Agricola and Raedykes as the scene of the battle of Mons Graupius.

Two standing stones at Kempstonehill seem to mark the site of some battle. An old legend has it that they mark the distance which one of the combatants ran after his head had been cut off. There is an Ogham stone at Auquhollie, one of the fourteen to be found in Scotland. Kinnear, in *Kincardineshire* (Cambridge, 1921, p.73), says of it: 'The writing is in some part much worn and doubtful, but it has been deciphered and translated as follows:— "F (a)dh Donan ui te (?n)." "(Here) rests (the body of) Donan, of the race of . . . "'.

The *Second Statistical Account* noted the finding of a tumulus, which was conjectured to be the burial place of Malcolm I. The more likely conjecture now is that it was the burial place of a lady of the Bronze Age, c.3000 B.C.

WAY OF LIFE

The bicycle, the motor bicycle, the bus and motor car have done much to break down the isolation of the countryside, and the improved rates of wages paid to agricultural workers have put those means of communication within the range of most. Few farmers but have their own car, and it is not unknown for a farmservant or a woodcutter to have a car too, but the bicycle and the bus are the main means of transport and are widely used. Women's Rural Institutes and social clubs do much to bring people together. Both in the town and country, whist drives and dances are a feature, particularly of the winter months, though in Stonehaven dances are held all the year round. The cinema has considerable appeal. There are those who make a habit of going to every change of picture, but the number of such does not seem to be large and the majority of people are content with a weekly or even less frequent visit. Cigarette smoking is widespread among young and old, men and women, and football pool betting would appear to be the same — the weekly coupons are generally to be seen behind the clock on the kitchen or living-room mantelpiece. Dancing is popular, both modern and Scottish country dancing, while at least three bridge clubs meet weekly in hotels throughout the winter months. Most homes have their radio. It is worth noting the strenuous lives of some of the apprentices, travelling daily to work in Aberdeen and returning there to evening classes on as many as three evenings a week.

The lack of any considerable industry means that there is no great opportunity for young people, and many of them have to find employment elsewhere. Within the past half century there has been a good deal of emigration, particularly to Canada and the United States, and now Australia and New Zealand are attracting some of the younger folk. The drain of the younger men and women from the town and the coming-in of retired people is more and more tending to make Stonehaven a town of rather elderly people.

A significant change is the almost complete disappearance of 'the maid' from houses, her place being taken by what daily help can be had. Even that is difficult to get, particularly in the summer months when hotels and boarding houses make big demands on the available domestic labour. In the country it is more difficult still to get household help, and keeping a maid in a farmhouse is now largely a thing of the past.

In spite of family allowances the big family is the exception and the average is two or three children. There is still a good deal of home life. Children are given a greater freedom than even a generation ago, though there are signs among the younger parents of a desire to exercise more control. Children are certainly given much more money to spend. Women are coming to take a greater share in public life — the present Treasurer of the burgh is a woman and so is the Burgh Chamberlain — but not in any numbers, and the councils, town and county, are still mainly the preserve of men and controlled by them.

Improved rates of pay have led to better standards of living. On the whole the population of the parish is well clothed and well fed. The consumption of meat, butter and eggs is limited mainly by the fact that they are rationed, that of fruit and vegetables by their high price — as much as 1/1 being paid for a turnip or a cabbage in the scarce season and 1/6 for a lettuce. There is an almost universal use of tinned or precooked foods — tinned soups, meat, peas and beans, packets of cereals, chipped potatoes and potato crisps. In fact, there is no longer much distinction between the working classes and those of a better social standing. A good deal of home-baking is done and great pride is still taken in this domestic art, the many sales of work and whist drives bearing witness to the housewives' skill. The housing situation stands in need of very considerable improvement. The health of the parish is good. Thanks to better sanitary conditions and to immunisation, the frequent epidemics of scarlet fever and diphtheria — one such epidemic of a virulent type of fever in the 1880s caused almost a panic in the town — have disappeared.

The community is, on the whole, very law-abiding. The principal offences in the local courts are infringements of lighting orders, failure

to stop at halt signs and motoring offences. There is little flagrant
juvenile delinquency.

The parish is well provided with charitable funds, e.g. Beattie's
Trust, Duncan's Trust, the Farquharson Bequest, the Munro Fund, the
Martha Napier Fund, More's Fund etc. Some of these are administered by the Kirk Session and some by Trustees, of whom the
minister of the parish is generally one. Few people, however, now
fulfil the original conditions of the trusts.

Churchgoing does not bulk as largely in the life of the people as it
did a generation or two ago; ordinary congregations are small, except
on Communion Sundays and for special occasions, e.g. Harvest
Thanksgiving and Christmas services. Though religious observances
seem to be in eclipse, the services of the minister are still in demand for
baptisms, weddings and funerals. The custom of having baptisms in
private houses is disappearing and most baptisms are in church and in
face of the congregation. Weddings are almost all celebrated in church
too, a change that has come about within the past ten years. They are
followed by a reception and a lunch in one of the hotels. The usual
day, meantime, for a wedding is Saturday. Funerals are, on the whole,
largely attended. If it is women one sees at a wedding, it is men one
meets at a funeral. The practice of wearing deep mourning is passing
and often in notices of deaths there is an intimation 'No flowers.'

A feeling prevails that traditions and customs which have been
maintained for centuries seem to be passing away, whether for good
or ill it is hard to tell. Possibly it is part of the worldwide process of
standardisation.

December 1950

THE PARISH OF FORDOUN

by the Rev. J.D. Bissett, M.A.

INTRODUCTION

The parish of Fordoun, or Fordun, as it was formerly spelt, can lay claim to being as historically interesting as any parish in Scotland. Across it marched the Roman legionaries, who built one of their northernmost camps within its bounds, manning also an outpost a few miles off to keep watch on the pass that led from the lands of the Celts *via* the Cairn-na-mount. By a singular coincidence, within yards of all that remains of their camp site, an aerodrome was built where aeroplanes landed and took off in their missions against modern enemies in the Second World War. To this parish came one of the earliest Bishops known to have brought the Gospel to this land, building here his tiny wattle settlement and chapel, which for centuries was to be a scene of pilgrimage for kings and peasants alike. Eleven centuries later, a baby was born in the parish who was later to be burnt at the stake as the most notable of the Reformation martyrs. Here the priest of the ancient chapel dipped his goose quill into his ink-horn to write the first history of Scotland. Within sight of the Roman camp, the great English lexicographer, with his faithful Scottish henchman, dined with his host, one of Scotland's distinguished philosopher-judges. Two of Scotland's kings came to an untimely end within its boundaries, and another surrendered the Scottish crown to that English king who carried away the Stone of Destiny, which not till this year of grace 1951 returned to its own land, and then only for a few weeks. Here in a lovely glen, hidden in the hills, a castle was built on an older foundation by one who became a pillar of a remarkable sect and one of the self-styled Twelve Apostles, raised up, as they believed, to usher in the millennium. And in the Second World War this same castle became a little bit of Norway. Fordoun, ancient and modern, has, it must be admitted, enough in it to arouse interest, however lacking in some other respects that make localities notable.

TOPOGRAPHY

Fordoun lies at the north-eastern tip of the great valley of Strathmore, which from Brechin to near Stonehaven is known as the Howe of the Mearns. It is divided into two parts, the howe or low-lying agricultural part, and the hill country, the latter containing not a few hill farms but mostly forest or heather-clad hills, which form a spur of the Grampian range known as the Mounth. In extent it is roughly 10 miles west to east, and 8 miles north to south, with a land area of 26860 acres or 42 sq. miles. The Grampian range forms its north and western boundary, separating it from the parish of Strachan, to which access is made by the ancient Cairn-na-mount track, in recent years become a well-made metalled road providing an exciting short-cut to Deeside and the north, rising precipitously to a height of almost 1500 feet. On the south-western side lies the parish of Fettercairn. On the south are the parishes of Marykirk, Laurencekirk and Garvock and on the south-west Arbuthnott; while on the north-east is that of Glenbervie, the homeland of Robert Burns's paternal ancestors.

Within these bounds are two prominent hills, the great round mount of Finella (1358 ft.), separated from the Mounth by a deep glen called Strath-Finella, better known as the Glen of Drumtochty, and the Knock Hill (717 ft.), which overlooks the Bervie Burn and the ancient house of Glenbervie. Smaller eminences are Gilbert's Hill, which looks down upon the Roman Camp and the only village of any size in the parish, Auchenblae; and the Hareshaw Hill, brother to the Knock, on top of which for many centuries Paldy's Fair, in memory of Palladius the early Bishop, took place. (It came to an end in 1913).

Of rivers of any size there are none; but a stream known as the Luther (pronounced like mother) burn arises among the hills above Drumtochty Castle, and winds its way down a deep cutting past Auchenblae into the Howe to join the North Esk below the North Water Bridge. Several smaller burns join it, such as the Ferdun burn, which comes down from the Cairn-na-mount, and the Dourie burn, which forms the boundary between Fordoun and Fettercairn.

At the western end of the Glen of Drumtochty is a very pretty artificial lake, Loch Saugh, fed by a burn which comes down a ravine called Friar's Glen, and which finds an outlet into the Ferdun, below the experimental farm at Glen-saugh. This loch, stocked with Loch Leven trout, provides excellent fishing, for which permits are to be had from the farm manager.

Needless to say, wonderful views of the mountains of Royal Deeside are to be had from the summit of the Cairn-na-mount; while from the Finella and the Knock the eye carries across the rich agricultural Howe to the Garvock Hill above Laurencekirk and southward to the hills of Angus, or eastward to the blue waters of the North Sea with its passing ships.

Plate 6. The Royal Arch in Fettercairn, erected to commemorate the visit of Victoria and Albert in 1861. (*Photo: By permission of* The Press and Journal).

Plate 7. A street scene in Fettercairn. (*Photo: Scottish Ethnological Archive, National Museums of Scotland*).

Plate 8. Muchalls station in the late 19th century. *(Photo: By permission of the George Washington Wilson collection, Aberdeen University Library).*

ESTATES

As has been noted under Agriculture a vast change has taken place in the ownership of the land. The chief proprietors are Lord Clinton of Fettercairn, on whose land the ruins of the palace of Kincardine stand; Sir Albert Gladstone, Bart. of Fasque, who owns the mansion of Phesdo; Sir James Caird of Glenfarquhar estate (now, in 1952, belonging to the Forestry Commission); the Forestry Commission; Mr. A.C. Badenoch Nicolson of Glenbervie; and Mr. J.M. Burnett of Monboddo, the only representative of the old line of estate owners.

NOTABLE HOUSES

There were in early times several baronies in the parish, with their castles or less pretentious houses. Almost all have gone or have been rebuilt. Two Castletons recall the palace of Kincardine and the barony of Mondynes. The home of the Wischarts or Wisharts is now a respectable farm house, though the ancient doo-cot nearby is evidence of a former glory. Here it was that George Wishart, the martyr, was born, and his martyrdom at St Andrews on 1st March 1546 is commemorated by a granite monument erected in 1850, near the front door of the parish church. The inscription is in the form of a scroll, which twines round the granite column, with the unfortunate result that the reader is made dizzy before he reads to the end. Another reminder of the family is now gone; Wishart's Wood, on the southern slopes of Finella, was cut down during the First World War and is now pasture land.

The castle of Glenfarquhar, the home of the Falconers, who at the beginning of the 18th century became the Earls of Kintore, has long since disappeared. Kintore Street and Inverurie Street, the names of the lower and upper sections of Auchenblae's single street, keep the memory of the former lairds green. In its stead is Glenfarquhar Lodge, built by Sir Sidney Gammell at the head of the winding glen of that name. This is a charming chalet-like lodge, in the midst of beautiful spruce and larch woods, with a large walled garden full of fruit trees. It has already been said that the Forestry Commission have purchased it. The most striking house in the parish is, of course, the castle of Drumtochty built by George Harley Drummond, a London banker, who bought the estate in 1810. This castellated Gothic mansion stands on a shelf on the northern side of the glen, embowered among evergreen rhododendrons and azaleas which, blooming in early summer, give it a perfect setting. It may be worth while noting that Drummond, who sold the estate in 1822 to Major Gammell, shortly after took a leading part in the religious revival that swept the country at the beginning of the century, and at his house at Albury the sect known as the Catholic Apostolic Church was founded, Drummond

being no.3 on the list of the Twelve Apostles, raised up, as they
believed, to usher in the millenium. As the new Apostles could not be
succeeded, the Church has now almost completely died out. The most
interesting period in the castle's history was its occupation by
Norwegians from 1940 to 1946. Men, women and children slipped
out of their Nazi-occupied country in little boats, and for them the
Norwegian government bought the castle, which they fitted up as a
school and hostel. King Haakon visited the castle in 1943 and planted a
tree in front of the dining hall. The last Norwegian left in 1947, when
it was sold, to begin a new life as a boys' preparatory school.

One other house in the parish, also at one time a castle, deserves
notice, namely Monboddo. It first appears in history as early as 1156;
but the earliest portion of the house now existing is dated 1630. In
1866 the house was enlarged by the addition of a very imposing wing,
surmounted by a tower. For 300 years it has been the home of the
Burnett family, the best known of whom became a Judge of the
Court of Session in 1767 with the name of Lord Monboddo. He was
one of the most remarkable literary men of his time. In 1773 Dr.
Samuel Johnson and Boswell, on their tour to the Hebrides, finding
themselves near Monboddo, could not pass without calling on the
judge. The magnetism of his conversation, Johnson wrote, easily drew
us out of our way, and the entertainment which we received would
have been a sufficient recompense for a much greater deviation. The
low-ceiled and panelled dining room where the learned and witty
conversation flowed remains as it was then. It was in Lord
Monboddo's townhouse in Edinburgh that Robert Burns was welcomed by the literati of the capital, and there is a family tradition that
Burns visited Monboddo on his way south from Aberdeen and his
ancestral home country. Among his poems is a very touching elegy on
Lord Monboddo's daughter, the 'heavenly Burnet' as Burns called
Eliza; a portrait of her, presumed to be by Raeburn, hangs in the hall.
Three other portraits are of historical interest; one of Lord
Monboddo's father, wearing the armour he fought in at Sheriffmuir
in 1715; one of Monboddo's only son, whom Johnson examined in
Greek and found 'proficient' and who died at the age of 12; and the
third, a charcoal drawing of Lord Monboddo by Reynolds.

CLIMATE

There are no temperature data for the parish. The range of hills
without doubt shelters the parish from the cold north winds and its
southern exposure lays it open to the heat of the sun. June is the driest
month of the year. From January to May the average monthly rainfall
is 2.5 ins., which rises in the rest of the year to 3.3 ins. The average
annual total from 1881 to 1915 was 33.2 ins. An interesting mark on

the old mill in the village records that, on 5th June 1902, flood water from the Luther and Back burns rose 3½ feet above the level of the street. But since 1931 the wettest year was 1946, with 39.97 ins.; and the driest 1943, with 28.07 ins. In November 1951 there was over 9 ins. of rain, while October had only 1.07 ins. With the advent of snow-ploughs, the roads are never long blocked with snow. The early months of 1947 were exceptional, the repeated heavy falls defeating the ploughs for several weeks.

POPULATION

In 1831 the population was 2238 — much the same as in 1801 — and until 1881 it stood at over the 2000 mark. In 1851 it reached a maximum of 2386. Since then it has declined, until it reached its lowest in 1931 with 1560. At the latest census (1951) it has risen a little to 1647 (838 males: 809 females). It seems possible that it will remain about this figure, for there are no industries to attract any influx. Auchenblae has 465 persons of all ages; but though a few new houses have been built, quite a number of the older houses are occupied by elderly people who have retired, or are widows or widowers, and so the population is not increased. In this small community, over 70 are old age pensioners.

COMMUNICATIONS

Little of the road system of 100 years ago remains. Portions still continue in use, winding picturesquely up and down the hills, indicative of a more leisurely age. These, coming from Laurenckirk, Inverbervie, Drumlithie and Stonehaven, naturally converge on Paldy's Kirk, or the Kirk of St. Palladius, the centre of the parish. But new roads have taken their place. The main trunk road to the north, running almost in a straight line from Laurenckirk to Stonehaven, forms roughly the south-eastern boundary of the parish. From it two roads branch into the heart of the parish — the southern being the old road from Laurencekirk; the northern, from Fordoun railway station, 2 miles from Auchenblae. Another road runs west to Fettercairn, while a northern road leads from Auchenblae to Stonehaven, *via* the Glen of Glenfarquhar. A branch climbs the shoulder of the Knock of Drumlithie. A very picturesque road goes through the Glen of Drumtochty, passing the Castle and Loch Saugh and joining the Fettercairn-Banchory road at the Clatterin' Brig. This road, with its masses of rhododendron and hillsides clothed with virgin forest, is a much favoured route for trippers in summer.

The railway made its appearance in the middle of last century. The station bears the name of the parish. Owing to the increase in bus services its use as a passenger station has greatly decreased. Travellers for the south must to go to Laurencekirk or Stonehaven. But a considerable business in agricultural imports and exports is done, chiefly in seed potatoes, of which 7,000 tons are railed every year. The annual revenue amounts to £30,000.

A bus service links this parish with Laurencekirk and Stonehaven, both by the trunk road at Fordoun Station and by the Glenfarquhar road. A less frequent service runs to Inverbervie. Taxis are available both at Auchenblae and Fordoun Station. A carrier service, now under British Road Services, runs daily from Auchenblae to Aberdeen via Stonehaven.

POSTAL SERVICE

The main post office is at Fordoun Station, from which mails are taken by motor-van to a sub-post office at Auchenblae. From the latter there are two daily deliveries and two despatches. Mail is delivered in the country district by van and in the village of Fordoun by postman. The telephone service has an automatic exchange. There is a kiosk in Auchenblae and another on the main road at Fordoun Station. Near the latter there is also an A.A. telephone box.

VILLAGES

The parish took its name, which is of Gaelic origin, meaning anterior or prominent hill, from the hamlet which must have clustered round the settlement of St Palladius. Of the chapel of the saint, built in 1244, and of which only the four walls remain, more will be said. But on the site of the hamlet only the parish church, with its churchyard, the manse and a farm called the Kirkton, formerly the parish inn, now stand. A little schoolroom adjoins the churchyard but, now modernised, is used as a school dining hall.

On a rising hill across a deep ravine stands the village of Auchenblae, which arose some 500 years ago. It is connected with the parish church and a fine new school and schoolhouse by a very substantial bridge spanning the Luther, known locally as the Litter. At the foot of the hill, on either side of the road leading to the village, are a number of houses, which include one of the old mills, now a store, a large garage, smithy, carpenter's shop, bank and a village hall. The road turns sharply left and climbs steeply up the hill, forming the only street of the village. On either side are well-built houses, shops and the two hotels. Halfway up, the street widens, and a grassy plot, with trees on the west side, gives the name of the Square. A fountain in polished

granite stands here, but has long belied its name. The village street
continues on the level of the hilltop until it reaches the road to the
glen. The post-war shortage of houses has added 4 wooden Swedish
houses, each for two tenants, and 11 prefabricated houses. The
numerous shops supply practically all modern needs; while bakers',
grocers' and fish vans from nearby towns make up the deficit.

Looking down on the village from Gilbert's Hill is a war memorial
to 43 men who fell in the First World War and to 14 in the Second.

The only other village is that at Fordoun, acclaimed the prettiest in
Kincardine. This also has been enlarged by 4 'Cruden' houses for eight
agriculatural tenants. Besides the hotel, there are 3 shops, a carpenter's
shop, smithy, garage and what was a large cattle market, now closed.
There is a fine hall, built as a war memorial, with tennis courts and
playfield adjoining.

INDUSTRIES

Less than a century ago the parish, then (as still) predominantly
agricultural, could boast of industry in the technical sense. A lint mill
was established on the banks of the Luther at Auchenblae and
employed as many as 50 spinners. Owing to the cost of freight, both
of the raw material and coal, which had to be carted from Inverbervie
9 miles away, the venture fell through. The mill then became a
distillery, but again costs were an obstacle, which even the attractive
name of Drumtochty whisky could not overcome. A repair shop for
motors and tractors now occupies the site.

The enterprising lint mill owner built a gas plant for the works and
for such villagers as were courageous enough to adopt this novel
lighting for their dwellings. But the cost per therm, a measurement
which they could never understand, was far in excess even of the
modern national scale, and the undertaking had to be given up.
Within these past few years, the hydro-electric company has linked up
Auchenblae, and the houses that still use oil are becoming fewer every
year. Many of the farms are connected with the grid; last year it
reached the Castle, and the forestry houses in the Glen expect to be
connected soon. Most outlying farms have their own generating plant.

For many centuries three meal mills flourished in the parish, serving
the three estates that comprised it. Now only one, Pitrennie, remains,
and its main business is the supply of poultry food — a sad comment
on the disuse that has befallen the porridge pot. Whereas in the past
part of the wages of farm servants was paid in meal, now only two
farms continue the practice.

For travellers and holiday makers the Redhall Hotel (licenced) at
Fordoun Station has 12 beds. Of the two hotels in Auchenblae, one
(the Drumtochy Arms) was recently gutted by fire. Many of the
villagers take in boarders in the summer season.

AGRICULTURE
(This section has been contributed by Mr. Gammie, Cairnton).

Fordoun is probably the most important agricultural parish in the whole county of Kincardine. There is a large breadth of really good clayey loam, varying to light loam, and cultivation has reached a very high standard.

CROPS

The following are the crops grown, the figures in brackets being those given in the previous *Statistical Account* (1837):—

Wheat 371 (40) acres. Average yield 6 qurs. (3) per acre
Barley 653 (1760) acres. Average yield 7 qurs (3½ per acre)
Oats 3,188 (2732) acres. Average yield 7-10 qurs. (4½), per acre.
Potatoes 1,277 (283) acres. Average yield 10-11 tons (20 bolls) per acre.
Turnips and Swedes 971 (1410); Sugar Beet 11; Cabbage, Kale for stock 18; Rape 50; Vegetables for human consumption 4 acres; other crops 17; bare fallow 14 — total tillage area 6,524 acres.

In addition to this there are 4060 acres of rotation grasses, 817 of permanent grass, 11,224 of rough grazing. This brings the total of all crops and grass and rough grazings up to 22,625 acres (11,330).

LIVESTOCK

The numbers of livestock on farms and holdings over one acre in June 1950 were as follows, the corresponding figures for 1837 being given in brackets:— horses 47 (391); cattle 3,444 (4,195); sheep and lambs 7,295 (3,815); pigs 1,444 (778); poultry 21,472 (10,080). To this must be added perhaps hundreds more owned by domestic poultry keepers, as they are called, which may have been included in the old number.

The agricultural and machinery census of 1950 records 140 tractors in the parish. There are 2 combines.

REVIEW

During the past 35 years great changes have taken place affecting the system of land tenure. Economic conditions brought about the sale of many of the larger estates within the parish. This has resulted in a large proportion of the holdings being now owner-occupied units.

With increasing scientific knowledge applied to agriculture and the use of new varieties of grains, potatoes and turnips, a very much greater yield per acre is now produced. Cultivation is for the most part mechanised, as is evident from the number of horses — 47 for the whole parish. Such a number would have represented the draught power used on three farms about 30 years ago. To the village smithy still come horses for shoeing, some of them from far outwith the parish, their local smiths declining the job or even having lost the art. The 'mighty man' has to be rather a mechanical engineer with an acetylene welder, and the ring of the anvil is almost gone. The prevalence of grass sickness in horses — a virus disease particularly virulent in the district — may have hastened the change-over. The persistent losses over a number of years of our best types of draught horse was becoming a very serious matter to the farming economy. With the coming of the Grampian electricity supply to the parish several years ago, the benefits accruing to agriculture are almost incalculable. Most farm buildings have been modernised to meet the needs of the times. In many cases stables, no longer used as such, have been remodelled as potato stores or implement sheds.

HOUSING

The standard of farm houses in the parish is very good, and most of the farm cottages have been either modernised or replaced by new ones.

The bothy system for single men on the farms was traditional. A separate building, with kitchen accommodation and sleeping quarters, was provided, and a woman cleaned and tidied up daily. Perquisites were given in the form of milk, meal and potatoes etc., and the men preferred to make their own meals. War conditions and rationing brought to an end a system which was gradually dying out, and now the single workmen are boarded out, with the married workmen as a rule.

LABOUR

Records show that the number of workers in agriculture in the parish totals 241 (292 in 1837). Labour is none too plentiful, and in a potato growing area such as this extra casual labour is needed at peak seasons. The release of schoolchildren for helping with potato-lifting in the autumn has been a customary thing in rural schools for a long number of years. Now the recent centralisation of schooling away from country areas has involved a greater percentage of non-agricultural children in this matter of 'potato holidays', with the result that it has become a very controversial matter. Here about 100 boys have been coming from as far away as Glasgow, being accommodated in part of the Royal Air Force camp; and apart from the help to the national economy they give, the benefits they receive in fresh air, good food, an insight into country life and about 2/- per hour for their labour, one cannot doubt, are real and worthwhile.

Women labour for farm houses is almost unprocurable, despite the fact that conditions compare favourably with town situations. While pigs and poultry were formerly a side line of the women folk on the farm, that in many cases no longer holds good. The increase of the pig population in the parish to 1444 head goes to show that this is now one of the important main parts of the farm stock. Poultry numbers swelling to well over 20,000 in the parish also indicate that this is now a full-time job on many farms, particularly the smaller ones. Hatching of chickens is no longer haphazard; accredited poultry farms, of which there are 2 in the parish, supply clean, healthy pullets to the henwife.

WAGES

The Agricultural Wages Act provides that the minimum (1951) is £5.14.— average per week — equal to the half-yearly wage, according to the last *Statistical Account* — but most workers are paid well over the minimum wage in cash and perquisites in this area.

GLENSAUGH

An experiment of much interest and undoubted value to the farming community was begun in 1943 when the North of Scotland College of Agriculture purchased the farm of Glensaugh, at the west end of Drumtochty Glen. With its staff of experts, its laboratory and a large steading, reconstructed last year, it seeks to probe into the diseases and problems that face hill-farmers. The following account of its work was supplied by Mr. George Jamieson, manager of the farm until the end of 1951.

The initial objects of the College at Glensaugh were :— (1) the control of tick-borne diseases; (2) improvement of hill pastures; (3) the home wintering of ewe hoggs.

1. *The control of tick-borne diseases*

With the depressed times in agriculture and larger rents being obtained from shooting rights than from grazing tenants, our hills in general, all over Scotland, deteriorated very much. The management of hill grazings passed from the shepherds to the gamekeepers, and what suited the gamekeepers did not suit the shepherds. The herbage on moors became very rough and unpalatable, and the stocks of both sheep and cattle became very much depleted. In the majority of cases there were no cattle and in many cases the sheep too had disappeared. One could have naturally expected that when the stocks on the hills had been so reduced, the incidence of disease would have been much less; but this was not the case and the spread of tick-borne disease became very alarming in some districts. Many high-lying farms in the neighbourhood became infected with tick and the College acquired the farm at Glensaugh in the autumn of 1943 to investigate the problem.

It has been found that tick eggs require about 80% moisture to hatch out satisfactorily and, where the heather is rank and the herbage rough, there is generally an undergrowth of moss retaining the moisture, making the conditions ideal for the tick. It can thus be assumed that the management of our hills is associated to a greater or less extent with the incidence of the disease. The problem of Glensaugh was tackled at the outset by carrying out experimental work on the better use of insecticides and the use of new insecticides, not hitherto used in the manufacture of sheep dips. Results thus obtained have been promising and further experimental work is being directed along those lines. Difficulties nearly always crop up in experimental work, and here it is impossible to have rigid control, since wild beasts and birds act as hosts for the tick and contribute to their spread over larger areas. The ultimate aim of this work is to reduce the mortality in the stock and an improvement in this direction can be seen both in the adult stock and the lambs on the farms.

2. *Pasture improvement*

This work has had a two-fold aim:— (i) the general improvement of the hill has a bearing on the disease problem, as already mentioned; and (ii) the improvement of the grazing to increase the stock-carrying capacity. In (ii) the improvement can be carried out in various ways:— (a) by ploughing, cultivating, fertilising and reseeding; (b) surface cultivation, fertilising and seeding; (c) fertilising and seeding only; (d) fertilising to improve the quality of the natural herbage; (e) burning the heather and cutting of brackens; (f) the introduction of cattle to our hill grazings. Where ploughing can be carried out, we undoubtedly get the best results, but unfortunately this method is very expensive over large tracts of hillgrazings, and something with less capital outlay and less ambitious results has to be considered. A quick improvement can be got by burning off the herbage and trying to retain this herbage in sweet condition by encouraging the finer leaved grasses to grow. This can be done by the introduction of cattle to our grazings. Cattle are less selective in their grazing habits than sheep and they eat off the rougher material and allow the finer plants a chance to develop. By this method we can increase the quality of our grazing and its stock-carrying capacity. The higher lying farms in the parish are admirably suited for stock rearing, having a considerable acreage of arable land attached to the hill farm. There is generally plenty summer keep on the hills and the low land is necessary to produce winter fodder.

Some useful work can be seen on Glensaugh on pasture improvement and stocking problems which could be applied to many hill farms throughout Scotland to advantage.

3. *Hogg wintering*

It has been the usual practice in the district for many years to winter the ewe lambs being kept for stock ewes on the lowlands during the first winter. The normal quality of the hill pasture is not sufficient to grow the body to a size to make a good breeding ewe. The problem of finding this winter grazing has been made very difficult with the extra ploughing programme forced on arable farmers during the war years. Since price guarantees have been given to the farmer for arable crops, the situation is not likely to change very much in the near future. Something of good quality had to be found as a substitute for the loss of this winter keep.

An area of heather land (37 acres) was ploughed up at Glensaugh and adequately manured and seeded with a good grass seed mixture to test if hoggs could be wintered on the hill. The area has successfully wintered 80 hoggs for the past seven years and the sward, at the moment, shows little sign of deterioration. The area has been given what is considered good management, being grazed with cattle in the summer and kept clean for the sheep in the winter. Periodic dressings of fertiliser are applied to keep the soil balance right. It has been found that the hoggs can be wintered at home to mature into equally heavy sheep as those wintered on low country. On a tick-infested farm like Glensaugh there is perhaps an added advantage of home wintering. When sheep are removed for a period of six months on to pasture free of tick, it is possible they lose some of their natural immunity to disease carried by tick infection, and on their return to the hill the mortality tends to be higher than in the home wintered hoggs.

Since the original work has now been well knit into pattern, it has been possible to investigate other problems in more detail, and work is meantime in progress on:— the intestinal worm burden of sheep at various ages; the quality of wool on our native types of blackfaced sheep; the dentition of various types of blackfaced sheep; breeds and crosses of cattle most suitable for rigorous hill conditions; crops most suitable for winter feed; and different methods of securing crops. Those problems are all of great interest to the hill farmer today, and the neighbourhood is lucky to have such an experimental farm in its midst

FORESTRY
(Contributed by D.H.Bird Esq., lately Forestry Commissioner, Drumtochty).

Although the parish is mainly an agricultural one, it also contains some very good forest land. It is fortunate that these lands were owned by lairds who were very keen foresters, so that full use was made of afforestable ground. The estates concerned were Drumtochty, Glenfarquhar and Fettercairn. Small blocks of timber were also planted on Phesdo and Monboddo estates; but the Drumtochty estate formed the largest forest, covering Drumtochty Glen, the eastern and northern slopes of Strathfinella, and the eastern and western slopes of Annahar. The main block of timber on the Fettercairn estate is Hunter's Hill, a name which takes us back to the days when Fettercairn Castle was the seat of kings and earls, who had their royal deer park there. On the Glenfarquhar estate the wooded area is mainly on the banks of the Bervie Water. Paldy Wood, on this estate, takes its name from Paldy Fair, which was held on the Hareshaw Hill. Drumtochty was acquired by the late Sir Sidney Gammell's forebears in 1822, when some of the lower slopes in the glen were planted. Planting continued during the Gammells' occupation. This estate was sold in 1916, when all but the very young plantations were felled and used mainly for war purposes, leaving the hillsides bare and desolate.

The glen was grazed by a sheep farmer for a short period and acquired by the Forestry Commission in 1926, when planting commenced at the rate of 100 acres per year, gradually rising to 250 acres. The previous crop, which consisted mainly of Scots Pine, Larch and Spruce, remained the main species, but the Forestry Commission introduced into the glen less common and more exotic species, such as Sitka Spruce from the Pacific Coast of Canada, Douglas Fir from the Rocky Mountain region of Canada, Japanese Larch and Hybrid Larch, which is a cross between Jap Larch and European Larch and which originated in the Dunkeld Forests, Perthshire. The Drumtochty Castle kitchen garden was turned into a forest nursery by the Commission, and most of the above species used were raised from seed there. The planting was completed during 1938-39 and now extends to 3500 acres.

Close by the former stables of the castle are the office, sawmill and a hostel which accommodates 11 of the 28 forestry workers. Small thinnings are sold to local farmers for fencing and larger timber is disposed of to Aberdeen and district timber merchants. In the near future increasing quantities will be available as pit props. A very fine specimen of Sitka Spruce is to be seen at the side of the Glen road not far from the sawmill. It is over 100 years old and 116 feet high, and contains approximately 700 cubic feet of timber.

In old maps the lower slopes of Finella that lead down to the Howe

are marked Wishart's Wood. It probably belonged to the Wisharts of
Pitarrow. The wood has now gone, having been cut down during the
First World War, and is now arable land.

Since the above was written, the Commission has purchased from
Sir James Caird the estate of Glen Farquhar, of which 3,000 acres is
agricultural land, and 3,000 moorland suitable for afforestation.

WILD LIFE

Under forestry it might be noted that on Finella Hill roe deer are
found in fair numbers. Capercailzie are numerous, and the lesser game
birds, grouse, pheasant and partridges, plentiful. There are occasional
foxes in the district, and the last badger was killed near Templebank,
at the foot of Finella, in 1946. Red squirrels are seen about the castle.

ECCLESIASTICAL

The parish may be said to owe its origin to St Palladius, and the chapel
bearing his name was 'the mother Church of the Mearns'. The
presbytery was called the Presbytery of Fordoun, but the ancient
primacy was forgotten in the new name of Brechin and Fordoun at
the reunion in 1929.

Information about St Palladius comes from three sources: from
Prosper of Aquitaine in Gaul, i.e. France, who was a contemporary
and wrote of him in A.D. 455: from Irish writers who, though they
could have known little of Scotland, yet write of him as being at
Fordoun: and from John, priest of Fordoun in the 14th century, the
writer of the first historical record of Scotland, later known as the
Scotichronicon. All these unite in saying that St Palladius was sent by
Pope Celestine in A.D. 431 to the believing Scots, who at that period
were the inhabitants of Ireland. But in the ten intervening centuries
much had happened, and John of Fordoun made the mistake of
thinking that it was to Scotland Palladius had been sent, a mistake
which gave rise to much of the doubt and confusion that has
surrounded the Saint. The writer of the last *Statistical Account* was one
of many who refused to believe that Palladius was never at Fordoun.

The present Librarian of Aberdeen University, however, Dr W.
Douglas Simpson, a historian and archaeologist of recognised authority, writing this year to me, says:— 'I have been led to go very
thoroughly into the whole of the evidence about St Palladius. I am
now convinced that the traditional account of his coming to Scotland
after the failure in Ireland and of his death at Fordoun is reliable and
that we should accept the main facts of the story as handed down by
later medieval writers. Some of the most ancient Irish documents have

recently been re-examined and it seems to me that they put the matter now beyond question. The whole story also fits in, in a very interesting manner, with other recent discoveries of the trend of early missionary enterprises in the Strathmore corridor'.

Dr Simpson intends shortly to publish the result of his research, and judging from a recent sermon on St Palladius, it should be as convincing as it was interesting. It may be confidently accepted, then, that St Palladius came to Fordoun soon after 431 and died here about 450. His day is the 6th July. The site of his chapel early became the scene of pilgrimage, and it was while making a pilgrimage, or immediately after, that in 994 King Kenneth II met his death at the hands of Finella, daughter of the then earl of Angus. A sculptured stone, depicting a hunting scene and presumed to commemorate the event, stands in the present chapel. The chapel as it stands today was built and consecrated by David de Bernham, Archbishop of St Andrews, on the 17th October, 1244. Another Archbishop, Chivez, had the bones of the saint, or what were supposed to be his, collected and enclosed in a jewel-encrusted casket. In the turmoil of the Reformation it disappeared. The chapel, too, suffered and with the building of a parish church a few yards away it fell into disuse and became for a time a carpenter's shop. When the present parish minister, the Rev. Angus McLeod, came in 1937 he found the roof partly fallen in under the weight of massive slates. The session court had the whole roof taken off and the top of the walls and gables cemented. So it stands open to the sky and to all weathers, deserving a bettr fate.

Dr Simpson's interest in the Saint led him to ask Dr F.C. Eeles, Secretary of the Central Council for the Care of Churches, to visit and report on the chapel; which he did in 1950. Replying to Dr Simpson, Dr Eeles wrote:

I have examined this building and find that it is in the form of a small church. It has a plainly chamfered round-headed west doorway and a smaller one on the north side. On the south side are three small plainly chamfered square-headed windows. There are no windows in the ends or on the north side. In the east wall on the inside is a monumental recess, with a large roll-moulding on a semi-circular arch. No effigy or inscribed stones remain, but it has the appearance of a 17th century insertion; this may well have weakened the wall behind, and this would account for the mending in brick of a large crack in the centre of the east wall. There is the pointed arch of a 13th century piscina in the east wall on the south of this recess, and in the north wall near the east corner is a plain aumbry, which may be of the same date.

The structure appears to be a 15th or early 16th century

reconstruction of a 13th century chapel, of which nothing is now visible save the aumbry and piscina. It is roofless, but on the whole in structurally good condition, but the interior is very neglected, full of weeds, and disfigured by a kerb and iron railing round a burial enclosure, which contains a large altar tomb. Some remains of the old roof are lying in the chapel and there are interesting monuments against the wall.

Dr Eeles recommends that an approach be made to the Ministry of Works to have the chapel taken over and cared for as an Ancient Monument, and this Dr Simpson is undertaking. Below the floor of the chapel is a burial vault; when it was constructed is uncertain. It seems to have belonged to the lairds of Monboddo, but is no longer used. Another interesting link with St Palladius is the well in the grounds of the Manse. It is of undoubtedly ancient construction and may easily have been the well of the Bishop and his house.

The present parish church, built in 1830, is well described as 'an elegant structure', with its tall square tower at the west end. A gallery runs round three sides of the interior, so that some twelve hundred persons can be seated. The furnishing is good and substantial. The stipend is fully endowed. Nominally, all living in the parish are members; but that the parish has not escaped the general decline in regard to spiritual things is evidenced by the present number of communicant members, 560, compared with the 1234 given in the last account. Partly it may be due to the depopulation of rural areas; yet the average attendance at the half-yearly communions is 350. There is a Sunday School attended by about 100 children. The minister also conducts service fortnightly at the memorial hall at Fordoun.

The only other church in the parish — since the United Free (originally Free) Church union with the Church of Scotland — is the Episcopal Church, dedicated to St Palladius and situated in Drumtochty Glen, about 1½ miles from Auchenblae. It was built in 1885 by the Rev. James Stewart Gammell, grandson of the first Gammell who bought the estate from the London banker, Harley Drummond. For some years service had been conducted by the Episcopal minister of Drumlithie, 6 miles away, in a room at the linen mill. Mr. Gammell, who had been a vicar in the north of England, decided to have a place of worship on the estate, and built the church near the east gate to the castle.

Built to the design of Pirie and Clyne, architects, Aberdeen, it is in the early English style of architecture. It consists of a nave, seating 100, and an apsidal chancel, lighted by seven lancet windows. East of the small south transept is a round tower, above which hangs the bell on an open platform, surmounted by a short stone spire. High on the south wall of the south transept is a white marble figure of a bishop in cope and mitre, with pastoral staff in his left hand, while his right hand is raised in blessing upon all who pass along the glen. Beneath are the words 'St Palladius'. The whole presents a striking and most unexpected picture in the glen, and the open door attracts visitors in hundreds for far and near.

There are about 60 members, with 40 communicants. A very fine Rectory was provided by Mr. Gammell on a hill nearer Auchenblae, and the stipend, as well as the organist's salary, was endowed. For the past few years the Rector has been responsible also for the charges of Drumlithie, Fasque and Lochlee, old historic congregations that in the course of the years have declined to vanishing point.

SCHOOLS

The parish at one time enjoyed a plethora of schools. The parish church, the Free Church and the Scottish Episcopal Church each had their establishments. There were, in addition, several privately run schools in the country district, whose teachers at least had good intentions, if little else, e.g. one was at the Clatterin' Brig, where the main preoccupation of the master was cock-fighting and 'celebration' thereafter. All have now gone, except those provided by law. The largest is at Auchenblae, which has a staff of a headmaster and 4 female teachers, all graduates. In this year (1951) there are 80 boys and 66 girls, ranging from the age of 5 to $12\frac{1}{2}$ years. On passing the promotion test they proceed to the Mackie Academy, Stonehaven, or the Junior Secondary School, Laurencekirk, whichever is nearer their home. At Castleton, half-way between Auchenblae and Fettercairn is a school staffed by a master and a lady teacher, with 20 boys and 17 girls. About 2 miles along the trunk road from Fordoun Station there is Cocketty school, with a headmistress and 16 boys and 13 girls. Some 30 children at Fordoun attend Redmyres school, which is a few hundred yards away in the parish of Laurencekirk.

The past few years have seen great advances in care for the well-being of the pupils. Gone are the days when children from outlying homes carried their 'pieces' and a bottle of milk for lunch. Now the local authority provides school meals, eaten in a warm dining-hall under the supervision of the teachers. The doctor visits the schools at least once a month and the district nurse weekly. The scheme for a visiting dentist has so far failed. The parish church minister is chaplain to the schools. The removal of advanced pupils to town schools may be inevitable, but the advantage to a rural community is a controversial matter. In 1947 another educational venture sprang up in the parish, when Drumtochty Castle was sold by the Norwegian Government and opened by Mr. R.S. Langlands, M.A., as a boys' preparatory school. With a staff of young qualified masters and mistresses, this school has had excellent results, sending pupils, who sit the common entrance examination, to famous public schools in Scotland as well as England. In its secluded glen, with its fine playing fields, the 80 pupils of the school lead a happy and healthy life.

RECREATIONS

The village hall at Auchenblae, built in 1870, caters for indoor meetings and entertainments and is a commodious and well-appointed building. The Women's Rural Institute is a strong and active body of over 80 women. The parish church Woman's Guild also meets here. Dances and whist drives are popular, and a cinema visits once weekly. There must be few houses in the parish which do not own a wireless set, battery or electric.

Outdoor games are well catered for. In the valley formed by the Luther, in a part called the Den, there are tennis courts and a bowling green. Near the hall an artificial curling pond has been laid down, and electric lighting permits enthusiasts of the 'roaring game' to continue late at night. About the beginning of the century the laird of Drumtochty gave the village a recreation field on the high ground west of the village, which in 1950 was levelled and a football pitch marked out. An old railway carriage serves as a dressing-room. A keen football team takes part in the Kincardineshire Association tournaments, though hitherto with indifferent success. Part of this field was taken over by the county some years ago for a new cemetery, when the churchyard at the parish church became inadequate. There is also a nine hole golf course on the east of the village. For boys, a Boy Scout troop has given way to the Government-sponsored Army Cadet Corps, for which a large wooden hall has been erected. Girl Guides and Brownies cater for the girls. Each has a yearly training camp under canvas.

An interesting activity of long standing is the Dramatic Society, which regularly produces plays for the community near and far. This enthusiastic society had the honour of producing the premiere of a world-famous repertory play, *Campbell of Kilmohr*, which was written for it by the Rector of the Episcopal Church, the Rev. J. Ferguson. Others written by him for the Society include *The Scarecrow* and *King of Morven*. His thrilling spy story *Stealthy Terror* gives a good description of the Glen of Drumtochty. Fordoun Station also has a strong Dramatic Society, and the W.R.I. is active there, as well as at Castleton school. At the latter is a Men's Club, with over 50 members.

Phesdo House, in the west end of the parish, was leased in 1950 by Sir Albert Gladstone Bart. of Fasque to the Scottish Youth Hostels Association and is open in the summer months. Some fifty beds are provided for young people.

Church libraries have given way to the County Library. Boxes of

Plate 9. Stonehaven harbour: a late 19th century view, with the Tolbooth on the right. (*Photo: By permission of* The Press and Journal).

Plate 10. Stonehaven harbour: foreign trawlers unloading during a strike of Aberdeen fish porters. (*Photo: By permission of* The Press and Journal).

THE HARBOUR, STONEHAVEN

Plate II. Stonehaven harbour in the late 19th century. (*Photo: By permission of the George Washington Wilson collection, Aberdeen University Library*).

books arrive from Montrose at the public school weekly and villagers are kept up to date with the latest publications. There are also two private book clubs. Newspapers and magazines are supplied by two shops, one of which deals with Sunday papers, of which 80 dozen are sold each Sunday. To the queue at the door the church bell tolls in vain.

ANTIQUITIES

Brief reference must be made to the three most interesting historical remains in the parish. First in date comes the Roman Camp, situated on the farm of Mains of Fordoun, a short mile south of the parish church. It is a clearly delineated rectangle of 500 by 300 yards, or $1\frac{1}{2}$ acres in area, surrounded by a moat still to be seen though now very shallow. Beech and spruce firs were planted on it fifty or sixty years ago, so that it is better known as the 'craw widdie'.

At the west end of the parish stood the palace of Kincardine, from which the county took its name. All that remains is part of the foundations, so well did the spoilers do their work when they required stone for farm buildings and walls. Still, one gets the impression that it must have been a powerful stronghold on its rising ground, overlooking the Howe and completely blocking the exit from the Cairn-na-mount. Here history tells us that many kings resided — indeed, that it was perhaps the earliest royal abode in Scotland; that it was from here that King Kenneth II went on his pilgrimage to St Palladius Chapel and was foully murdered by Finella, daughter of the earl of the Mearns; that, within its walls, 200 years later, John Baliol drew up the scroll surrendering the crown to the English King, Edward I, the repercussions of which act are still heard over the Stone which Edward took along with the crown. Kincardine's glory vanished when the county court was moved from it to Stonehaven in 1600.

At the eastern extremity of the parish, on high ground overlooking the railway and the main highway, is a blue granite monolith, about 6 feet 6 inches high and 10 feet in circumference, which on some maps is called the 'Court Stone'. It is in a field of Mains of Mondynes, which is the modern version of Monachedlin or Monathethun. Tradition gives it that it was on this place that King Duncan II, son of Malcolm Canmore by his first wife, was murdered by his half-brother Edmund in 1094. The name 'Court Stone' suggests that it marks the place of the courts of the barons of old. But it may well have the former association, the site being the ideal one for a camp, with a wonderful view of the Strathmore corridor; and the story is that Duncan was murdered at night in his bed. The lease of the farm, which is on the Glenbervie estate, contains among its terms one under which the tenant is bound to white-wash the Court Stone once a year.

M

WAY OF LIFE

A bird's eye view of the parish gives us a picture of a stretch of country that is almost half lowland and half highland; the lowland a rich agricultural country, from which an industrious farm community reaps rich harvests; the highland moorland, but more and more becoming valuable forest land. It is a parish of contrasts, each with its beauty and charm. The people are kindly and neighbourly. There are none of the old 'poor' class; old age pensions and public assistance have abolished poverty. Drunkenness is also a thing of the past. Education and better housing conditions have contributed to this. A great boon to the aged sick and to nursing mothers has been the provision of a district nurse. The birth rate in the parish seems at first sight to have dropped by half; but the reason is that under the Health Service mothers go to maternity homes in Stonehaven or Montrose.

There seems to have been a drift of people down from Aberdeenshire; it is remarkable how many on the farms in Auchenblae have come from the north. In speech there is no difference. In the church at Auchenblae, as in Aberdeenshire, the alphabet ended in 'epersaean', that is, the ampersand. Of the family names given in a list 100 years ago, very few are now known in the village.

Fordoun, home of the first historian of Scotland, has not been without more modern historians, whose books are mines of interesting information. Jervise's *Memorials of Angus and Mearns* alludes to the parish. Cramond's *Annals of Fordoun* is a remarkable compilation of facts from earliest times down to 1894; while Mollyson's *Parish of Fordoun: chapters in its history* gives a 'popular' account of the parish down to 1893.

March 1952

THE PARISH OF GARVOCK

by the Rev. Peter H. Nicoll, B.D.

TOPOGRAPHY

The parish of Garvock in southern Kincardineshire is situated on high ground between Laurencekirk on the west and Benholm on the east, while it is bounded on the south by St Cyrus, south west by Marykirk and on the north by Fordoun (for a short distance only) and by Arbuthnott. The best way to reach it is to climb up about two miles on an excellent road which runs from the burgh of Laurencekirk to the main east-coast road from Dundee to Aberdeen, a distance of about 6 miles; or one can ascend on a lesser but longer grade from the St Cyrus end and three miles will bring one into Garvock. The parish is 6 miles long, from the Mill of Garvock in the north to the Craig of Garvock on the south with a breadth of 2 or 3 miles and an area of 7975 acres. Most of it lies open to view, on a shallow plateau, which rises on the western side to a height of 800 feet, which height forms Garvock Hill. This hill is really a long range of high ground overlooking the Howe of the Mearns. When the aforesaid road from St Cyrus reaches the summit, it descends more abruptly to Laurencekirk by a perfectly engineered and winding highway, which is a favourite walk with the folk of the burgh. Halfway down the slope one passes the boundary of Garvock into Laurencekirk parish.

It is remarkable how little known to the modern 'hiker' Garvock Hill seems to be, and yet from at least a mile of its grass and heather top one's eyes can range over a vast and beautiful panorama of rural prosperity on the west to a still vaster seascape on the east, the long blue stretches of the North Sea matching the varied green of the Mearns, backed by the first ranges of the Grampians. Both these ample and fascinating vistas are spread out away beneath one's feet, giving a feeling of space, height and freedom, which adds to the charm of the scenery. At the highest spot of this ridge stands the Johnston Tower, a sturdy outlook tower about 40ft high, built a hundred years ago by the proprietor of Johnston estate. From the top of the tower, with a good glass or a good imagination — opinions differ! — one can, on a clear day, espy the Bass Rock and the Lammermuir Hills, far to the south over the sea.

HISTORY

The history of Garvock can be told, as far as it is known, in a few pages, for it has been mainly a quiet steady record of daily toil through the generations. The former large estates have been cut up into single farms and tenants have become owners. Men like the Earls of Kintore and the Earls Marischal formerly owned most of the land. One relative of the latter family, a Robert Keith, owned the estates of Bradieston and was also Provost of Montrose in the 17th century. His sculptured burial-stone, with his coat of arms and initials, is built high up into the western wall of Garvock church and dated 1666. The present church, plain outside but attractive inside, was built in 1778 after the previous one had stood for exactly one hundred years. The parish provided two Bishops for the Episcopal Church. The first, David Mitchell, had an adventurous career, becoming a Canon of Westminster and finally Bishop of Aberdeen, and dying in 1663. The second, John Strachan, son of the farmer at Redford, became Bishop of Brechin and died in 1810. At the Forty-five Rebellion, the Jacobite troops, on their way south, comandeered the minister of Garvock to be their chaplain, but he seems to have escaped within a week, for he was soon back in his manse.

Another son of Garvock deserves honourable mention. James Grewar, striking out for himself overseas, became ultimately Mayor of Kimberley in South Africa towards the end of the 19th century. At his death he left to the Kirk-Session of his home parish a legacy of £2000 to provide such financial help as would enable suitable scholars to proceed to a university. The bequest was accepted and faithfully administered till the Educational Endowments Act of 1928 handed it over to the County Council Education Committee. It seems regrettable that by such legislation the names of public-spirited benefactors are apt to be lost to posterity.

The only historical item which has survived in a wider world is the legend of the Sheriff's Kettle, quoted in one form in Scott's *Tales of a Grandfather*. The story is that certain of the local nobility, in the reign of King James I, went to court in Edinburgh, complained bitterly to His Majesty of the local Sheriff — a man called Melville — and got the impatient and jocular reply: 'Sorra gin the Shirra were sodden and suppit in broo!' Under pretence that they had the royal permission in these words, four men — Arbuthnott, Barclay of Mathers, Straiton of Lauriston and the Laird of Pitarrow — invited the hated Sheriff to a hunt in Garvock forest, waylaid him at a prepared spot, threw him into a caldron of boiling water, each taking a cup of the 'broo', and then fled from the vengeance of the King. One sought sanctuary in Lindores Abbey. Another, Barclay, of whom the King swore that he would give him dwelling neither on land or water, built the strong little fortress, now called the Kaim of Mathers, out on a steep cliff overhanging the waves, just north of St Cyrus village. The Kaim is indeed neither on land nor sea and its ruins are incredibly strong and nearly inaccessible. The place where this barbarous deed was said to have been done is marked on modern maps as Sheriff's Kettle and lies in a small ravine, with a tiny burn, on a farm called Browniesleys — so called, it is said, because of the fairies that came to haunt this sinister spot.

POPULATION

The population of the parish varies round about 250, showing a marked decline during the present century. In 1801 it was 468; in 1851 it was 457; and in 1871 it was up to 476. Then the figure began to fall and by 1901 it was only 368. The 1911 Census registered 371 and that of 1921 showed 376, but in 1931 the total dropped to 320. (In 1951 the population numbered 259 — 140 males and 119 females — the lowest for any Kincardineshire parish). This decline is due mostly to the coming of the mechanical binder and then of the tractor. No longer are so many workers required. Those who advocate the return of people to the country should realise that there is no present prospect of work for a returned population. Rural housing is useless without regular and convenient work.

HUMAN ASPECT

The parish, it will be realised, is secluded and rather isolated, because it lies just between, and well elevated above, the two great streams of traffic and population — the coastal main road to Aberdeen and the middle main road from Glasgow and Perth. This gives it an atmosphere of quietness and independence which is refreshing or soporific, according to taste. There are mere patches of woodland, mainly round farm homesteads, with the result that in dull weather the parish looks bare, while in sunshine it presents an open radiant picture. The social human aspect of Garvock can be estimated from the fact that there are not more than two dwellinghouses built together in the whole area of 12½ square miles, and such dwellings are farm cottages. There is no business whatever save farming, if we except one very quiet smithy, which is combined with a croft. There is now no tailor, no wright, no shop, as there were years ago. There is no great St James's Fair, attracting hundreds of people and lasting several days, as there was a century ago on Garvock Hill. There is no public-house, no hostel.

COMMUNICATIONS

The amenities of Garvock have been distinctly enhanced in the last few years by a bus service, which runs from Fordoun to Inverbervie and continues diagonally up to Garvock and down over the hill to Laurencekirk, returning by the same route. This service is twice daily and thrice on Wednesdays and Sundays, so that the housewife can now easily get down for shopping, the more advanced children to school at Laurencekirk and the whole community to the cinema there or to any other form of social entertainment. So small is the population — about 250 all told — that it must be hard to make a bus pay and, of course, the bus serves only one central part of the parish. But whatever the convenience it is open to dispute whether it is in the best interests of such an upright, industrious community of agriculturists to come into close contact with the modern habits and pleasures of a town community. Happily Laurencekirk, 3 miles away, is only a true market-town and its interests and entertainments are healthy, cheerful and beneficial.

HOUSING

Agriculture is the sole interest here and it is flourishing. The unflagging industry of the people richly deserves the prosperity which has now come to this industry from causes well-known — urgent demand for food, both bread and meat, enhanced wages for all grades of farm-workers, and steadily improved cottages. The reconditioning of the cottages during the last few years has been an immense boon to the worthy workers, giving them, as a rule, water inside and sometimes a bathroom. But improvement must go on, for families of from 6 to 10 are still crowded into three-roomed cottages without bathrooms and occasionally without water inside. It is absurd to reflect that the very workers who most need ample water conveniences, owing to the nature of their work, are provided with the fewest. The miner, in this respect, has now come into his own, but the land-worker still awaits his deserts. It has also to be remembered by all town-dwellers that the small farmer and cottager have the everlasting irksomeness of lighting, heating and cooking all by oil or coal-oven. This adds decidedly to the toil of the household. In Garvock there are now only six farms equipped with electric power, installed by the owners. These owners are 'big' farmers.

FARMING

With the exception of four or five, all the farms are very moderate in size, roughly from 90 to 200 acres, and in Garvock, with less than half-a-dozen exceptions, every farmer owns his land and works as hard at it as any of his tractor men or cattlemen. Many farmers employ only one worker, some two, some only an occasional Displaced Person from a camp 5 miles away, and only four employ more than two full-time workers. The soil is mostly heavy, inclined to be damp, and exceedingly rich in stones which, however, local opinion favours as being beneficial in providing a sort of natural drying and draining. There are 3 dairy farms, all the others bearing the usual rotation of crops, with the exception of wheat, which is grown to a limited extent on the lower levels. There are still hundreds of acres of rough pasture covering the long ridge of hill. It embraces a rather desolate valley of heather, just below Johnston Tower on the east, and an extensive elevated shoulder of moor, varied with whin and broom, towards the northern end of the range. Sheep in considerable numbers find pasture on these uplands. There has been, in recent years, a steady intake of moor by tractor and plough, so that cattle and sheep are now feeding on good grass where once were only scrub and heather. This process will almost certainly go on.

WOODLAND

In the past few decades the long narrow belts of timber which once ran here and there in the district have been felled, leaving useless tree-stumps and very little edible grass. This is an ugly and wasteful feature of the parish. These stretches ought to be replanted, even if the Government has to step in. A certain amount of woodland is necessary everywhere to retain moisture, build up new soil, provide periodic timber, and to adorn the countryside.

CHURCH

In Garvock the one centre of cultural and religious life has naturally always been the church. It was founded by Sir Hugh le Blond, the first of the Arbuthnotts in the neighbouring parish, in 1282, as recorded in the charters of Arbroath Abbey. His pious patronage and gift included pasturage for 100 sheep, 4 horses, 10 oxen and 20 cows. For over 600 years Catholic priests and then Protestant pastors have continued on that foundation, to maintain the light of Christianity in this place. One has only to read the *New Statistical Account* of Garvock by the Rev. John Charles in 1836, to appreciate the wide and profound learning of some at least of the incumbents. Practically every adult in the parish is a communicant and although here, as elsewhere, church attendance is irregular and even scanty, the church and its minister are looked to as the one source of light and guidance in the higher life of the people.

SCHOOL

The parish school offers the only place for social meetings, and it is of course a small one, with about 25 to 35 pupils. The school is one mile from the church and manse, which are pleasantly situated beside a well-wooded den with a burn, just a quarter of a mile from the top of the Hill. Parishioners find it rather a climb from the lower levels to the church, and from the farther ends of the parish it is three or four miles distant.

SOCIAL ACTIVITIES

There is no Rural Institute in Garvock. The Women's Guild of the church is the only social agency. It organises occasional whist-parties and dances for church and charity. These social meetings are eagerly looked forward to, while the minister gives occasional lectures and addresses of a cultural nature, fully attended (in the school-room) and heartily enjoyed. There is also a committee which provides for a Christmas and a summer treat for the children of the parish. Such is the simple social organisation of this quiet rural parish and it is ample, for the people are far too busy to indulge in more, and their work is not something to get through and be paid for, it is their real life interest.

WAY OF LIFE

As to the character of the people, in its moral aspect, the present writer, with experience of many parts of Scotland and in different countries overseas, will permit himself to say that if the world were composed of such as these in Garvock there would be hardly need for prisons or police, sword or shell, even if a black sheep be sometimes found in the flock! In many previous generations, when the Kirk-Session ruled the parish, its records bear witness that the chief fault of the community was a rather reckless anticipation of the marriage tie on the part of the young people. Things are today vastly improved in that respect in Garvock. The Kirk-Session was also the sole dispenser of education and charity, and again the records testify that it did so with thoroughness and acumen within the limits of prevailing conditions. Today there is no need for such charity and the very word has vanished from use. Wages are four times what they were fifty years ago and added to them are family allowances and all the benefits of our new health and insurance legislation. Poverty, as a cause of suffering, is unknown. The farm-workers are well-dressed, well-shod and well-mannered, and show a dignity and self-respect which poverty in the old days made difficult. Every farm-house and nearly all the cottages have a radio-set installed and nearly every farmer has his motor car. This, with better travelling facilities and higher school education available to the brighter pupils, has wrought a big change in the civilisation of the people. Their contacts are far more numerous and their outlook broader. Their hard work, demanding as it does patience, skill and considerable knowledge, renders them immune to and contemptuous of plausible political panaceas, for these will not pass the test of growing good crops and good beef. There is no spirit of discontent or restlessness here, but the people do share with other rural communities the strong dissatisfaction with a system which sells all the finest meat produced in these regions to southern markets, leaving only what they call a few old cows to feed the very people who have produced that prime beef.

In conclusion, it should be said that the chief needs of Garvock are an assured 'water-supply, electric light and power, and farm-roads maintained from the rates. If food is a first necessity for the whole community, the community should provide proper exits for that food. The present farm-roads are mostly deplorable. These necessities, when supplied, have been well-earned by the hard-working, food-raising, thriving people of this parish.

September 1949

THE PARISH OF GLENBERVIE

by Alexander Murray

FEATURES

The parish of Glenbervie takes its name from the river Bervie, which bounds it in the south for over four miles. The parish was formerly known as Overbervie, a name which also carries its own meaning. Glenbervie lies in the centre of the county of Kincardine, with Durris parish to the north, Fetteresso and Dunnottar to the east, Arbuthnott to the south-east, Fordoun to the south-west and Strachan to the north-west. Its length, from north to south, is about 6 miles and at its widest it stretches 5½ miles. The area is 15055 acres, roughly 23½ sq. miles. From 300 feet above sea level in the south-east corner, the surface rises westwards and northwards to heath-clad ridges that skirt the Grampians, reaching 1289 feet at Leachie Hill. The banks of the Bervie are in many places very picturesque. Running between Glenbervie and Fordoun, where it has its source, the river has little tree shelter till it rounds Glenbervie House amid wooded slopes and a rich profusion of wild flowers, ferns, etc. The Bervie has long enjoyed a reputation as a trout-fishing stream.

DISTRICTS

The parish may be divided into three districts. (I) That which lies along the side of the Bervie Water. The soil here is on the whole productive and comparatively early; since the last *Statistical Account* (1838) was written, this district, in common with other parts of the parish, has shared in the general improvement which has taken place in agricultural methods. (II) The district on the south-east, commonly known as the Kames, was covered with wood plantations, but during the First World War this was cleared out and only the beech hedges that surrounded the plots remain. (III) The northern district is naturally of a colder and less productive character, lying as it does close to the Grampian range. The advance made within the last 50 years in every respect has been very marked.

ESTATES

The Drumlithie estate, formerly held by the trustees of the late John Millar Esq. was disposed of, farm by farm, the first holdings being sold to the sitting tenants in 1921 and the last holding in 1951, also to the sitting tenant. The late Arthur Badenach Nicolson of Glenbervie, the principal heritor, purchased West Kinmonth and Broombank farms, along with the crofts of Milton Park, Burnhead and West Newbigging, making practically a straight line in the eastern side of his estate. Upper Kinmonth, which was included in the purchase, was sold later to the sitting tenant. The most attractive spot in the parish is without doubt around Glenbervie House. Some very fine old trees adorn the lawn in front of the house and also the drives. The house itself nestles cosily under the shadow of the Knockhill, by the side of the Bervie Water. Since 1918, the plantations have been depleted and many have disappeared, leaving only bare stumps to tell the tale. Up to the present there is no sign of re-planting. Wood will be scarce for a number of years to come.

DRUMLITHIE

Drumlithie, the only village in the parish, is situated in its south-eastern corner and dates back to the beginning of the seventeenth century. A derivation of the name for which there is some warrant is Lithie = water (cf. Leith). Today there is a road leading northwards from the village to the Kinmonths which is popularly known as the Watery Bawks. The most characteristic feature of the village is the steeple, which was built in 1777. It consists of a circular tower, surmounted by a belfry, on the top of which is a weather cock. The belfry was a gift from Robert Dyce Smith, for a long time postmaster in the village. The bell was rung during the days of the handloom weaving to regulate the hours of labour. It was the custom for years to ring the bell in summer at 6 a.m. and 10 p.m. and in winter 7 a.m. and 10 p.m., but the restrictions applied during the War brought this to an end. Its only use today is to warn the inhabitants when the water supply is to be cut off, or to mark the wedding of a son or daughter of the village. The care of the steeple now rests with a locally appointed committee.

POPULATION

The population of Glenbervie parish is only half of what it was a century ago. From 1204 in 1801 the total rose to 1296 in 1841, since when each succeeding Census showed a greater or less decline until

1951 recorded a very slight recovery. In the second half of the 19th century the figure dropped from 1239 in 1851 to 870 in 1901. Thereafter the totals were:— (1911) 779; (1921) 759; (1931) 644; (1951) 688. Males had no share in the increase in 1951. Whereas in 1931 they outnumbered females in the parish by 330 to 314, females in 1951 outnumbered males by 336 to 322.

TRANSPORT

Drumlithie is well served with travelling facilities. A bus passes through the village daily between Aberdeen and Brechin, every two hours (arriving from Aberdeen 8.30 a.m. up to 9 p.m.; from Brechin 8.20 a.m. till 11 p.m.) On Wednesday and Saturday a late bus leaves Stonehaven (7 miles away) at 10.40 p.m. for the convenience of those attending the Picture House, which is greatly supported. We have also a daily carrier from Aberdeen. In addition, there is the railway for both passengers and goods. The passenger service has been considerably cut, as most people travel by bus. Bakers' vans call on Monday and Thursday from Auchenblae, Tuesday and Saturday from Laurencekirk, Tuesday, Wednesday, Friday and Saturday from Stonehaven; a butcher's van on Wednesday and Saturday from Auchenblae.

LIGHTING AND WATER

Less than half a century ago, the lighting in the village was greatly improved by the addition of new paraffin lamps, erected upon metal standards. In 1903 a new water supply was introduced, with a copious supply from the Kinmonth farm. Sanitation in that year was considered too costly an undertaking, but in 1949 the County Council prepared a scheme which was approved and the work was pushed forward with all speed. All houses have water laid on, hot and cold; bathrooms were introduced in most homes.

In 1949 the village committee decided to introduce electric light and it was switched on in many of the houses on Hogmanay night, to the great delight and comfort of the inhabitants. The year 1950 — thanks to our ambitious village committee — saw electric light provided in the streets; from funds in hand it was decided to erect 16 standards at various points throughout the village.

HOUSING

Since 1919 some 26 new houses have been erected in the village, some by the County Council and some by private enterprise.

SHOPS

There are in the village 3 grocers' shops — one licensed — one hotel, 2 joiners, one blacksmith, one tailor, one shoemaker, 2 coal merchants and one poultry dealer, who employ workers. All of these seem to do a lucrative business. The Post Office has two rural postmen. The telephone was introduced first in the Post Office and today it is in all business premises. The Post Office is under Montrose and carries out all post office work including pensions, Savings Bank, etc. There are two petrol filling stations. Drumlithie is a colony of 'lairds'; most of the householders bought their properties when the estate of Drumlithie was put on the market.

AGRICULTURE

A great advance has taken place in agriculture in recent years. Farms have been mechanised and all farm machinery improved, most of the implements being made for the tractor. Threshing is done on the farms, by oil engines and tractors. Up-to-date mills have been installed. Very little water power is used and dams, which were a common sight at farms, have all disappeared. Consequently should any fire arise the lack of a water supply is obvious. On holdings where 3 pairs of horses and an odd horse did the work — and quite a few of these were in the parish — two tractors can be seen at work in one field, ploughing, sowing and reaping. The horse population is diminishing every week and the scene at the smithy has changed, the smith being more of an engineer with all these modern methods.

LIVESTOCK

According to the Agricultural Census on 14th June 1951, the number of livestock in the parish was as follows:— horses 57; cattle 1771; sheep 4792; pigs 252; poultry 18,701, all showing an increase in numbers except horses. The farmer gives every attention to poultry, and many have accredited hatcheries. Pigs have proved a very lucrative investment. Eggs are collected by van or taken by car to the grading stations at Stonehaven and Laurencekirk which give a good remuneration for the poultry keeper's labours.

CROPS

The area under potatoes is 262 acres, a considerable increase since 1914 when farmers grew from 2½ to 3 acres for their own use and their married servants. Kerr's Pink and Majestic are the varieties most popularly grown and meet a ready market at £11:10/- per ton. Arable land tillage and rotation grasses total 5,451 acres; permanent grass, 677 acres; rough grazings, 5,553 acres. Crops grown include corn, barley, turnips, kale and hay.

It may not be amiss to give the Fiars prices for the 1951 crop: oats, per quarter, £3:17/8¾ without fodder, £4:9/8¾ with fodder; barley £7:13/3 without fodder, £8:3/3 with fodder; wheat £5:18/7 without fodder, £6:11/7 with fodder; oatmeal, per boll of 140 lbs £3:2/11.

Dairy farming is carried on by Mrs Badenach Nicolson of Glenbervie at her up-to-date farm Milton Park, where she keeps a splendid herd of attested Ayrshire cows. Milk is also despatched from Broombank, Newmill and Tannachie to Aberdeen.

SCHOOLS

Glenbervie Public School with 3 teachers has a roll of 95 children. To the north, Brae of Glenbervie School with 2 teachers carries a roll of 37 children. When the children attain the age of 12 years they are transferred to Mackie Academy, Stonehaven, until the leaving age.

CHURCHES

The parish church, built in 1826, is a commodious building. The minister at that date was Rev. James Drummond, who was succeeded by his son-in-law Rev. William Gordon, who in turn was followed by his son Rev. Patrick Lindsay Gordon. As parish ministers they were beloved and were welcomed in every home. The parish was unique in that it had grandfather, father and son, all in the same church.

A Free Church was erected in Drumlithie about 1843, and on 5th December 1844 Rev. Andrew Glen, upon the unanimous call of the congregation, was ordained and admitted as the first pastor. The church building proved very unsatisfactory, having been rushed up too rapidly and with insufficient inspection. Attempts to improve it and render it watertight failing, it was taken down and entirely rebuilt. The new building was opened on 15th September 1850. In 1848 an additional piece of ground was feued and a manse built. On the Communion Sunday, 26th July 1863, Mr Glen was stricken down in the pulpit. He was carried into the manse but never rallied and died a few days afterwards. Rev. James Cameron, a native of Udny in

Aberdeenshire, was ordained minister on 10th March 1864. He died in May 1875 after an efficient ministry of fully eleven years. Following a vacancy of some eight months Rev. Robert Masson Boyd, a native of Kilmarnock, was settled on the 15th December 1875. Mr Boyd's ministry lasted for 30 years. He died on 10th October 1905, deeply regretted by the whole parish and district. He was succeeded in the now United Free Church by Rev. John Rose, a native of Nairn, who latterly received a call to Cawdor Church, Nairn. Rev. Robert Pollok Watt, of Edinburgh, was then appointed minister and remained so until 1929, when he retired to Banchory to further the Union of the two congregations.

Rev. Patrick Lindsay Gordon, Glenbervie, was minister of the two churches until his death on 17th August 1948 after a ministry of 54 years, a highly esteemed and devoted minister of the parish. The congregation of Glenbervie had a difficult task before them. The manse at Glenbervie had to be gutted, a new roof put on, and all the interior remodelled, with new grates, painting and papering, the cost of which was borne from the money left by the heritors in the hands of the General Trustees in Edinburgh. The Session introduced electric light and plant into the manse. A further burden fell upon the congregation when the manse water supply failed. An adequate supply has now been introduced from Burnhead to augment the existing source. Rev. Alex H. Bone was appointed minister to the charge and was inducted on the 24th August 1949. He conducts worship in the two churches on alternate Sundays. Worship is also held monthly in the Brae School, Glenbervie. The number on the Communion Roll at 31st December 1951 was 335 communicants and 18 young communicants, while eleven were admitted by certificate. The number who communicated at least once a year was 216. The manse at Glenbervie is beautifully situated, with a large garden, six acres of glebe, suitable outhouses, stable, byre, barn, turnip shed, etc., all in good order. There is a cottage in the north end corner of the glebe recently remodelled, with inside water supply and sanitation. The rent of the manse in 1949 was £30:15/-; glebe £25; house on glebe £3:10/-, but these figures have been slightly increased following the recent improvements. The minister's man and beadle occupy the Glebe Cottage.

St John's Episcopal Church, Drumlithie, has as its pastor Rev. J.D. Bisset, incumbent of Drumtochty, no resident minister being attached to the charge at Drumlithie. Less than fifty years ago the Episcopal Church had a fairly large membership, but today it is down to a score of adherents. The Church, a beautiful building, is in the Gothic style and consists of a nave and chancel, with vestry and organ chamber attached. The east window of three lights was placed there as a special memorial to the Very Rev. Robert Kilgour Thom, Dean of Brechin, formerly clergyman of the church, who died in 1874.

HORTICULTURE

Keen interest is manifested in horticulture and demands some reference to the founding of the local society. Previous to 1888 Glenbervie combined with the parishes of Arbuthnott and Fordoun in holding a joint display, but there were certain obvious disadvantages to all the parishes in this arrangement. Accordingly a public meeting was called to decide as to holding a local show. This was agreed upon, and the following persons formed the original Committee:— Rev. R.M. Boyd, president, Mr Alex. Cruickshank, vice president, Mr D. Dunbar, secretary, and Mr Alex. Edwards, treasurer, Mr John Grant and Mr John Ferguson, the last-named being one of the strongest supporters of the society. Mr James Badenach Nicolson very generously threw open the policies of Glenbervie to visitors, a privilege highly prized and continued by the present proprietor, Mr A. B. Nicolson. The club is very efficiently carried on by an enthusiastic and hard working Committee, chosen annually from amongst the members. The present secretary (Mr Alex. Murray) was appointed on the 9th February 1904.

PLOUGHING ASSOCIATION

The Glenbervie and District Ploughing Association is another enthusiastic body. Their annual ploughing match is held on some local farm, horse ploughing and tractor ploughing being witnessed by an interested crowd from the surrounding districts.

OTHER ACTIVITIES

The W.R.I. has a large membership and meets every month. Boy Scouts and Cubs meet weekly. A Dramatic Society has its winter entertainments. Difficulty is experienced in getting talent for the plays, most of the young people being employed in Stonehaven and Aberdeen. The village possesses a splendid hall, built in 1926, equipped with electric light and heating. During the winter months, whist drives, socials and dancing are engaged in, the proceeds being devoted to some charitable object. In the schools there is lodged the County Library, which is taken advantage of in the winter.

WAY OF LIFE

The farm servant's lot has improved considerably this past 50 years. Houses have been modernised, with inside water supply and bathrooms. Tilley and paraffin lamps are in use, also paraffin cookers. Farm buildings have been improved and labour-saving devices installed. Oil engines do the threshing and tractors are in use. The farmer's 'gig' has disappeared and in its place, a nice car now emerges from the farm buildings, taking the farmer and his wife to church and market. Most farm houses are equipped with telephones. Difficulty is experienced in obtaining domestic servants. Most girls prefer to work in shops, offices, etc., where they get off early and are free to go to the pictures and so on, farm girls being too much tied to the farm. Milking machines are used, as no girl will undertake byre work.

BURNS'S ANCESTORS

Warm interest is shown by Burns enthusiasts in the tombstones in Glenbervie Churchyard. Quite recently, the Glenbervie Burns Memorial Committee had the stones of Burns's ancestors attended to. One bears the dates 1715 and 1719 and marks the resting place of William Burnes (great-grand-uncle of the poet) and his wife, Christian Fotheringham. The other commemorates James Burnes, tenant, Brawliemuir, and his wife, Margaret Falconer, the great-grand-parents (with the dates, 1743 — aged 87; 1749 — aged 90 years). The stones were laid on flat cradles, exposed to 'decay's effacing fingers' and to every atmospheric agency. It was proposed to build a mausoleum to protect the stones, but this proved too expensive. In 1951 the Committee had the stones removed to the yard of Mr Fenton Wyness, Aberdeen, an expert in the restoration of ancient monuments. He had the stones cleaned, lettering renewed, and all small crevices filled. The stones were restored to their original place, being preserved for all future ages, enclosed in cement casing, where they lie on a bed of fine sand.

Visitors come from all parts of the world to learn about Burns's ancestors, whose last resting place is in Glenbervie Churchyard.

A new cemetery will be opened soon near Glenbervie Church. Workmen are busy laying out the ground.

March 1952

THE PARISH OF INVERBERVIE

by the Rev. Thomas Nicholson, M.A.

EXTENT

The parish takes its name from the river which flows along its northern boundary. The township at the mouth of the river is, naturally enough, Inverbervie. Commonly known simply as Bervie, it is a royal burgh, having received its charter in 1342.

The parish is bounded on the south-east by the North Sea; on the south and south-west by the parish of Benholm; on the north and north-west by the parish of Arbuthnott; and on the north-east by the parish of Kinneff. Its length (E. and W.) is 3 miles and its breadth between 1 and 2 miles. The landward area is 2124 acres; that of Inverbervie is 206.5 acres. From the coast to the ridge on which the burgh is built there is a gradual rise to 100ft. above sea-level. On the north is the Craig David hill, which overlooks the burgh, known also as Bervie Brow. It is in Kinneff parish, but only just so. From this, descending to the south and east, there is much flat land. A fertile valley passes along the northern boundary and through it Bervie Water runs to the sea. Gourdon Hill on the Benholm border, near the coast, is a landmark seen far out at sea.

POPULATION

The population of Bervie parish rose steadily from 1068 in 1801 to 1459 in 1851, then still more rapidly to 2523 in 1901, since when there has been an unbroken decline, as follows:— (1911) 2391; (1921) 2153; (1931) 2116; and (1951) 1909, females outnumbering males by 1036 to 873. The burgh of Inverbervie, in 1951, accounted for 885 (386 males: 499 females), as compared with 1031 in 1931 and 1200 at the end of the nineteenth century. Gourdon village, which claimed almost 1200 inhabitants in 1901, has likewise dwindled, the whole landward population of the parish (outside Inverbervie burgh) now totalling little over 1000.

A possible reason for this decrease is that young people often remove from the parish as there is not great scope. The war also has had an effect, not so much because of casualties but on account of employment, this being found elsewhere and so necessitating severing of connections. There never has been an influx of people from other areas. At present more of the population are engaged in industry than on the land and the people are more industrially-minded, no doubt because of the immediate sources of employment. With the greater ease of transportation, more people travel to Aberdeen and Stonehaven than formerly. Several young people have gone into nursing. With the compulsory service of youths in H.M. Forces, young men are being kept away from home and occasionally as a consequence find employment in different spheres on being released. For the most part the life of the community is not greatly affected, though by no means so static as during last century.

GOURDON VILLAGE

The present inhabitants of Gourdon are mainly children of the old inhabitants, and this is why Gourdon is so much a place apart. A very strong community feeling exists here. But again there is the modern influence filtering through. Young people, especially girls, when married tend to return to their village and their husbands, though belonging to other parts, settle here for a time at least. The percentage of population is interesting from this angle: 75 per cent of inhabitants are natives of Gourdon and 25 per cent were born outwith the village and of these 12 per cent from other counties. Many of the inhabitants of Gourdon have friends and relatives in England and other parts of Scotland, but very few have connections in other countries. The incidence of immigration is extremely slight. There is a gradual rise in the number of people who have to leave the village because of the lack of employment. In this connection it is remarkable that there are several who work during the winter in casual employment and in summer work at salmon-fishing, lobster-creels and crab-fishing.

WATER SUPPLY

The water supply is adequate for all the needs of the population, as quite recently a new tank has been installed. Several springs contribute to the supply of water for the burgh. These come from Montgoldrum, Three-Wells and Pitcarry. Recently, on excavation, a wooden pipe was found in one house. Nowadays these are seldom found and certainly never installed.

SANITATION

Great strides have been made in sanitation. The old methods of cleansing have been superseded. All the new Town Council houses have baths and toilets. The sewage system is modern, with pipes that run the refuse and waste to the sea.

ROADS

The main road of the burgh is an arterial roadway, the main highway to Aberdeen and the north from Dundee, on the coast route. The streets are well covered with good metal and are kept exceptionally clean. Often the impression created is of much paper lying about. This is because of the wind from the sea, which seems always to be blustery.

ELECTRICITY

A few years ago new electric standards were provided and this has made a creditable difference in the illumination of the burgh. These lights are visible for miles around. The electricity is supplied by the North of Scotland Hydro-Electric Board and in this part we are singularly fortunate in not suffering from many cuts in power. The price of a unit is 5½d for the ordinary dwelling house, and after a fixed number of units have been consumed at this rate the price is greatly reduced.

GAS

For the most part, gas is used in cooking, the gasworks providing a very good supply. It is not a large works and employs only a few men. This is controlled from Stonehaven through a manager and engineer. The meters installed are capable of taking coins, such as a shilling and a penny. This method of 'pay as you burn' has been a help to the users, as it eliminates quarterly accounts.

TRANSPORT

Public transport is by bus. (The branch railway from Montrose to Inverbervie closed to passenger traffic in 1952). Inverbervie is on Alexander's Dundee-Aberdeen route (hourly service daily) and is also connected with Montrose (13 miles) *via* Gourdon.

HOUSING

The burgh suffers from no acute shortage of houses. There are a few people who seek houses, but on the whole most of the pressing needs have been met. The different types consist of:— semi-detahced villas: flatted: cottages: tenements: bungalows: and the latest, the Archon, better know as prefabricated. The complete number of houses is 326, which includes:— ordinary 207: sublets 12: Council 100: and tied 7. The extent of overcrowding in the burgh is very small. The building societies have not had a great influence in Inverbervie. Very little has been heard of them and because of the Second World War no private houses have been built. There is a very fine sense of community here and everyone feels a part of the whole. Every good cause is very well supported and the people do feel themselves to be in the life of the whole burgh.

In Gourdon many radical changes have been effected during the past years. Thirty years ago houses were built and at that time great difficulty was experienced in finding tenants, partly on account of inability to pay the rent demanded. But in these days there is a better proportion and there is more money available. It has been the practice to build houses near the waterfront in order to be near the sea, as most of the men were fishers. Most of the houses there are now very old. Many of them are now being renovated and made modern, the people preferring to remain at these sites, to be near their business. The County Council has built new dwellings and, though some of the fishermen removed from the lower levels of the village to these houses on the hill, they have in many instances removed back to the waterfront. In Gourdon there was not much planning; but the second wave of house building rectified this and now there is much better order. In the new housing area the planning is satisfactory.

The average number of people per room in Gourdon is 2. In all probability the amount of overcrowding is much the same as in Bervie, viz. 3 per cent. It is more difficult to obtain information regarding the different sizes of houses, but they range from single apartment to 4 and 5 apartments. Like other fishing villages, Gourdon has picturesque dwellings and idiosyncrasies, peculiar to such communities. Gourdon is very quaint and is an old fashioned fishing village, with a coast-guard station, which has a strip of the coast from St Cyrus to Dunnottar Castle to watch. There are two men on duty on alternate shifts.

AGRICULTURE

The soil in the parish is exceptionally good, especially on the low land, and is most fertile. It is a fine loam on gravel, which is pervious. The sandstone conglomerate on which the gravel is superimposed is the type of sandstone that prevails in the parish. Where it can be obtained, it is used for building. The beach is shingle and is composed of pebbles of jasper, porphyry, slate and agates. The upper fields are mainly strong soil on an impervious clay bottom.

The loam of the low land is very productive. Root crops, corn, wheat and barley are all grown and the farmers are well rewarded for their labours. This is not a cattle-rearing parish. There is grazing land, but for the most part it is crop-growing that is engaged in. Labour seems to be obtainable and satisfactory and each farmer seems to keep his workers for some seasons at least. This is different from former days when there was a change, often every six months at term time. The agricultural worker's state has altered considerably within the last ten years. In 1938, he received in some cases £1/14/- and perquisites, but now there is a minimum of £5 per week and often perquisites are given with this. The conditions are also greatly changed in regard to hours of work. In the past the farm labourer worked early and late for much the same wage, but today fixed hours are observed and remuneration is made for each additional hour, and work ceases at noon on Saturday. There is no Sunday work, unless contracted for.

The cottar houses are now dwellings worthy of the people and this has resulted in making labour more easily obtained and farmers can keep good workers for longer periods. The farm buildings are not the leaky places they often were, as farmers are having more favourable conditions themselves and are in the more happy position of expending money on their property. So, from appearances, the farms in the parish are places of prosperity, and everyone is more happy and contented.

INDUSTRIES

In these days the chief industries are flax-spinning, furniture assembling and mattress making. Some years ago there were several mills for flax-spinning, but these are now reduced to 1 in Gourdon and 2 in Bervie. These mills are up-to-date and the workers number about 100 in each mill. The raw material comes from Norway and after spinning is sent to Dundee for the finishing processes. In these mills the conditions are as good as it is possible to obtain. There is modern ventilation and everything that can make for efficiency and good health. A five-day working week of 44 hours is in force. The workers are now paid for an annual holiday of two weeks' duration. Each day, morning and afternoon, time is set apart for a cup of tea. In summer and winter the workers are entertained by the owners at functions; between workers and employers there exists much good-will. The employers are men of benevolent moods and have done many fine and commendable things for the parish. There is personal contact here by the mill owners and it means a great deal to the community in fostering friendship and has done much to give the community spirit which is necessary in a burgh of this size. At the mattress-making works some furniture assembling is done. This factory gives work to a considerable number of people. Great difficulty is experienced at present in obtaining material, and very often places abroad, like Holland, are tried to find the right material for the matresses. The manufacture of gas within the burgh is a great boon, but so far it has not been possible to supply Gourdon or any other village with gas. There is also a quarry.

FISHING

The fishing industry is confined almost solely to Gourdon village, the only exception being the salmon fishing at Bervie, which is small and employs only a few people. Two types of fishing are found in Gourdon, seine netting and line-fishing, the latter being the more popular. Each line takes 1200 hooks. There are usually 4 or 5 men to a boat, depending on its size. The women of the village who have fisher husbands bait these lines, which takes about five hours to complete. Herein lies one of the main difficulties and probably the chief reason for the decrease in the number of fishermen in Gourdon. The women nowadays are not willing to undertake the work. The usual wage is 12/6 per line per day. The bait is obtained from Montrose and, at the time of writing (1954), this is very expensive and much is said about it in the village. The fleet of boats is not more than 22. This is much smaller than in former years, but would be increased if boats were not so high in price and if labour were more easily obtained.

Where there are fishing boats, there must also be merchants. In Gourdon there are 6 fish-merchants, all employing at least 4 workers, mainly females. The fish is sold far and wide and the village has long had a reputation for its line fish. There is prosperity in the trade at present. While the fish are not too plentiful, the prices are good, and this makes it profitable enough. The task of fishing is less arduous now than it was years ago. The introduction of motor-propelled boats has revolutionised the work and the fishermen are able to go further out to sea. Fewer lives are lost in storms.

SHOPS, ETC.

Other merchants must be mentioned, e.g. 3 bakers, 3 butchers, several grocers, including the largest establishment, the Cooperative Society, a branch of Brechin United Cooperative. There are two each of the following:— ironmongers, plumbers, joiners, masons, coal merchants, drapers, shoe-repairers, hairdressers, chemists, fried fish restaurants; and there is also a local labour exchange. Inverbervie has 5 licensed hotels and Gourdon 1. Each has a sub-post office and a railway station.

COMMERCE

Owing to the situation and the needs of the burgh, not much can be traded outwith its bounds. The only commodities are what is sent from the mills and factories. The tradesmen in the area round about and the merchants have vans which supply the landward area with goods. Fish is the only edible that travels far, the other supplies having only a limited range.

CHURCH

The membership of Bervie Church is 904, of which number 340 reside in Gourdon village. The attendance average for Sunday is 230 for the whole parish. At communion that number is increased to 340. This part of the country for some reason is not an area where people are church-conscious. Some say that the influence of the Disruption of 1843 did not reach the north east, but there was a Free Church (later United Free Church) in the burgh until 1929. As in other parts of Scotland the parish church itself is too large for the congregation and the number at public worship at any time looks small in such a size of building. But the proportion of faithful members is as high as elsewhere. At any rate it can be said that the real and faithful members are in their places regularly sabbath by sabbath. The eldership numbers 21 and this is adequate for the size of the congregation.

The Sunday schools provide the religious education for the young which is now more than ever necessary for the upbuilding in the Christian faith of the boys and girls. The bible class meets the needs of the youth of the church and its membership includes the portion of the 'teenagers' to be expected from a community of this size. During the past winter a group was formed for the study of the bible. While only a few, usually 8, met for this purpose, it was agreed that it was most useful. Also in the congregation, to help the literary side, there is the church fellowship. Its membership is approximately 60 and it satisfies a want for many in the congregation.

In Gourdon, for many years, there was a branch of the Scottish Coast Mission. When this organisation became incorporated in the British Sailors' Society, that body decided that, since Gourdon had ceased to be a seaport, it would relinquish its hold there. The Church of Scotland was invited to take over the work carried on by that society, and this it has done since 1949. In 1950 the first missionary of the Church of Scotland began his work in the Mission Hall, under the guidance of the parish minister of Bervie.

An Episcopal Church in the parish has a membership of 80 approximately. The preacher comes from Montrose to conduct services in the small corrugated-iron building. Along the coast at Catterline, many years ago, was a stronghold of Episcopalianism, and many of the inhabitants of that village have come to live in Bervie. This accounts, in great measure, for having a church of that denomination here.

It should also be mentioned that there is a branch of the Christian Brethren. The adherents number 12 and they meet once a week in the Y.W.C.A. hall.

EDUCATION

In Gourdon is a primary school, with four teachers, 3 female and one male, who is headmaster. He lives in the schoolhouse while two of the other teachers travel from outwith the parish. The number of children attending is about 90, all belonging to the village. The school teachers are very interested in giving the best possible service under difficult circumstances, owing to the high cost of text books, writing materials and pencils, etc. The village takes great pride in the school. In recent years the number who proceed to university and for higher education from Gourdon is increasing. This, in good measure, is due to encouragement from the headmaster and also, in part, because of the greater realisation of the value of education, with the help of bursaries from the government.

In Bervie, until a few years ago, six buildings were in use by the Education Authority to accommodate the scholars. These were the available halls in the burgh. But within the past 10 years this has been remedied by a fine new junior secondary school being built. Now ample room is available for everyone in the new building. Accommodation is being provided for chemistry, handicrafts, domestic science and manual subjects. The school has a first-class gymnasium and twice a week a teacher comes to give training. The staff consists of 5 male and 6 female teachers. The number of pupils is about 240, some of whom come from Arbuthnott, Kinneff, Johnshaven, St Cyrus, and the surrounding countryside. At the moment several of the teachers live outwith the parish, which is unfortunate in some aspects, as their influence is not felt in other activities. The scholars from these parts who are not proceeding to a senior secondary school are retained until the age of 15.

A few classes during the winter evenings are held in the school. Whether because of the relatively small population or the lack of interest in adult education, there is no great demand for these. This is unfortunate as some who are serving apprenticeships in electrical and mechanical engineering have to travel miles to a larger centre. At present there are 3 persons attending university and this is about the usual number.

At school, meals are provided at a very moderate charge, in a special canteen with facilities and employees for the purpose. Kincardine County Council prepare the food in their canteen in the burgh and it is conveyed to the other primary schools in the surrounding districts.

HEALTH SERVICES

The surrounding districts, from Kinneff to St Cyrus and Arbuthnott, are well served by 2 doctors and 2 district nurses. Under the National Health Service the needs, optical, dental and medical, are adequately met. The two chemists dispense and one gives optical services. In many cases people travel to Stonehaven for optical services, yet it is quite unnecessary as this is performed by a capable optician here.

YOUTH ORGANISATIONS

The voluntary social services form an important part of the activities of the parish in the winter months. Among those especially for youth is the Army Cadet Force, which is organised locally by two lieutenants, men of standing in the burgh. The Girl Guides organisation is excellent and is heartily supported and enjoyed by the members. As usual, these organisations depend so much on leaders of the right type and we are fortunate at present in having fine people as leaders. The Brownies have a pack in Gourdon and one in Bervie. These too have been successfully carried on for years now because of the leaders' efficiency. Until last year there was a youth club in the parish. At the moment this is in abeyance, but it will be revived in due course when the hall which is being constructed from the former Free Church is available. (It was completed in 1952).

WOMEN'S ORGANISATIONS

Some years ago a Townswomen's Guild existed and earned much praise. This was incorporated in a branch of the Women's Rural Institute of Scotland, which is well attended and most popular in the parish and round about. A branch of the Order of the Eastern Star, whose membership is composed not only of local people but of some from outwith the parish, meets in the masonic hall periodically. The leader of the local branch has been head of the Y.W.C.A. for the past 60 years. Its weekly meetings during the winter months are well attended and it has been of great influence over the years.

The church plays an important role in the life of the burgh. Of several organisations within its orbit, one is the Woman's Guild. There is a general improvement at present in the life of the organisation. The latest activity is the development of a dramatic section, which is enthusiastically supported by some members.

RED CROSS

Each year an effort is made to raise funds in the burgh on behalf of this worthy cause. The Red Cross is responsible for transport for those who have to go to hospital in Aberdeen and Stracathro. No ambulance is available and the Red Cross does the valuable work of providing a conveyance where possible.

BRITISH LEGION

Just after the Second Word War, there was an influx in the membership of the branch of the British Legion in the burgh, but of late there has been a decrease, so much so that it is not possible to have regular meetings. Yet the branch is in being and has been of great service from time to time.

MASONIC ORDER

This Order has a fine response, drawing its membership from the surrounding district. The regular meeting is held once per month. It has been in existence for at least 60 years.

POLITICAL PARTIES

This is a stronghold of National Liberal sympathies. It never has been Labour, though the candidates of this party have received a fair proportion of votes, enough to ensure that the 'deposit' has never been lost.

WAY OF LIFE

Life in this burgh goes on like a meandering stream; past its youthful best, it flows on quietly, with scarcely ever a spate of enthusiasm.

Support is always given to such social events as concerts, parties, etc., but there is never a great wave of enthusiasm. This is probably explained by the fact that we are not near enough a big centre of habitation. Montrose holds little of interest for the people. Aberdeen (24 miles) is too far away to have any influence. Stonehaven, which is nearest (9½ miles) has not much to offer, except as a shopping centre; most of the life there is in groups, which are as separate, one from the other, as Bervie is from towns north and south of it. Transport makes it difficult for people here to have much evening activity outwith its boundaries. So people have largely to develop their own pool. It is not, however, stagnant, and that largely because of some few people who have ideas. But altogether life is quiet and with little excitement.

This even tenor of life is seen throughout. There is undoubtedly more family life, from the point of view of families being at home together, than in many other centres. Yet it is not that each member does much in his or her leisure hours to knit the family together in games or other interests. Many people have hobbies, such as handicrafts, and take an interest in the wireless programmes. There is no sign of lethargy, just as at the other extreme there is no great driving interest. Here and there, little groups meet for an evening and indulge in card-playing, like bridge or whist. It is a welcome change from the usual activities to attend a concert or children's party promoted by one of the various organisations. Another source of social life is the evening classes provided by the Education Authority. There are sessions when classes are well attended; then, after one or two sessions of the same class, the membership falls off.

In civic affairs, scarcely ever does an election contest take place; rather, difficulty is experienced in finding people who will stand for the Town Council. This is very annoying to the zealous merchants who see how different affairs would be if there was remote control of the burgh's affairs from Stonehaven, that is, by the County Council. So very guardedly is this watched that likely people are approached with a view to entering municipal life. Not many people are inclined for public life in a community of this size.

The same spirit is to be seen in church life. The majority in the burgh are definitely interested and good people, but here again the faithful, keen workers number anything up to 300. This is by no means a reflection on the congregation, but rather is a true perspective on the present state of affairs. There is no great insight into spiritual realms, sufficient to make people consider making great efforts to evangelise the whole area, something which could easily be done by half-a-dozen people. But the same attitude, as in civic life, has been prevalent for many generations in the church. At the present time there is a rise in interest, whipped up by the fresh ideas presented and by the infiltration of methods used elsewhere. The economic situation has made necessary the introduction of the freewill offering scheme.

This has been in operation in towns for 20 or 30 years, but only now in this congregation has it been realised that financially something must be done to keep buildings in repair, sustain obligations, etc. There has been a response, and it is gratifying to realise that lassitude is not one of the reasons for this congregation not being a real power in the religious life of the Mearns. The point is that there is no burning fire of zeal, though the interest is there if only it could be fanned into flame.

In the realm of education and culture, where possible pupils are helped, and a good proportion each year proceed from Gourdon and Inverbervie to the senior secondary school at Stonehaven. There is a strong desire here in parents to give the best possible mental equipment to their children. A fair percentage of young people pass on to university and training colleges, pre-apprenticeship schools and commercial colleges. A branch of the Montrose Library, open each week, provides good reading material for all levels of thought.

Delinquency and crime are little seen and the burgh must have an exceptionally high place on any list of law-abiding communities. Life flows on sweetly and with little change, and this is something in itself for gratitude. Leisure is utilised in many minor interests. In summer the youth play tennis and the older people play bowls. There is a happiness among the people which is good to see. There is, too, a community spirit. Gourdon people will wholeheartedly support any effort for a village cause. Bervie likewise will rally for its own. But seldom is the effort made to travel from one place to the other — a little over a mile — to give a demonstration or have a second night of the same show or concert. A friendly rivalry exists. But this is really a healthy friendship, and in reality there is a gradual closing of a gap that has existed from time immemorial between the sections of the parish as represented by Gourdon and Bervie.

December 1951 (probably revised in 1954)

THE PARISH OF KINNEFF

by the Rev. James N. Macpherson, M.A.

EXTENT

Kinneff, in the Mearns, is a coastwise parish, with which Catterline was conjoined by the Court of Teinds in 1719. With Barras to landward, the parish falls into three clearly marked areas. The coast is rugged, the cliffs rising to 150 feet, interspersed with small and often lovely coves, with beaches of shingle without sand. To the south of Kinneff, where it adjoins Bervie, rises the noble contour of Craig David, or Bervie Brow, under which David II landed when returning from France in 1341. He founded a chapel (discernible at the time of the *First Statistical Account*, but long since obliterated) in thanksgiving for deliverance from the peril of English pirates at sea. Narrow at this southern extremity, the parish opens irregularly to its extreme width where it abuts on the Perth-Aberdeen highway. Bruxie Hill (710 feet) on the north-western border, is the highest point in the parish, and was for long a landmark for the fishers of the coast. The boundary returns again to the sea, along the Burn of Uras. The parish is roughly triangular, about five miles in length (N and S) and four in extreme breadth. The area is 7180 acres. The adjoining parishes are Dunnottar (north), Bervie (south) and Arbuthnott (west).

GEOLOGY
(This section has been contributed by Dr Campbell, M.A., D.Sc., F.R.S.E., Reader in Petrology, Edinburgh University).

The solid rocks in the parish are all of Lower Old Red Sandstone age and constitute part of the eastern limb of the Strathmore syncline, so well known from the writings of Sir Charles Lyell. The magnificent coastal cliff sections give unrivalled opportunities for studying the fluviatile conglomerates and sandstones of that period. The conglomerates, as at Hallhill, are often exceptionally coarse, containing boulders up to 12 feet or more in their greatest diameter. Sometimes the boulders are dominantly of volcanic origin and indicate a former much greater extension of lavas of Old Red Sandstone and Siberian age along the southern flank of the lofty Caledonian mountain chain, the denuded core of which forms the present Grampians. Other conglomerates are made up largely of Highland metamorphic rocks and those found near the mouth of the Bervie water are of particular interest, since they contain rounded fragments of fossiliferous limestones and cherts of pre-Old Red Sandstone age. No fossils have been recorded from the sandstones of Kinneff but, just beyond the parish boundary, at Three Wells, sandstones which are on approximately the same horizon as those at St John's Hill have yielded specimens of *Cephalaspis Lyelli*.

Contemporaneous vulcanicity is evidenced by the occurrence of lavas and tuffs at several horizons. The youngest lavas, mainly hypersthene andesites and basalts, appear in the Barras district from Leys Hill northwards; they are part of the north-easterly extension of the lava belt of the Sidlaws and the Ochils. Lower in the series basalts with unique petrographical characters can be studied on the foreshore at Crawton. The outcrop of these Crawton basalts is shifted inland by a powerful fault, which can be traced south-westwards from Braidon Bay, and they re-appear near the Bellfield road, a short distance south of the Fernyflatt crossroads and extend southwards to Kirkcorner. There the outcrop is faulted westwards to the line of the Wardhead road and, after a small displacement further to the west by a fault near Grange, it continues as the lower of the two crags of Bervie Brow and reaches the parish boundary at the Bervie Water. At a lower horizon andesitic lavas and tuffs occur on the cliffs opposite Whistleberry Farm and still older is a basaltic flow near the Todhead Lighthouse. Minor intrusions are represented by dykes of quartz porphyry and porphyrite and by thin sills of andesite and dolerite.

Admirable examples of contemporaneous denudation of the lava flows can be studied at the Crawton shore and in the Whistleberry Wood quarry, where not only may one find rounded boulders of Crawton basalt in the overlying conglomerate, but one can detect remnants of deep potholes cut in the lava by the rivers of the Old Red Sandstone period. At Crawton also may be seen, in contrast with the above, marine potholes in process of being eroded in the same lavas at the present day.

Throughout the parish the solid rocks are in large part concealed beneath a thick mantle of glacial drift, deposits of red boulder clay and fluvio-glacial gravels and sands. The boulder clays are the bottom moraine of a great ice-sheet which traversed the district in a N.N.E. direction early in the Great Ice Age. Fluvio-glacial sands and gravels occur conspicuously as two terraces with steep fronts facing seawards, which extend from Temple almost as far as the Catterline burn. The formation of these, and of an Esker at Fawsyde, may be ascribed to the melt waters set free during the retreat of the ice-sheet at a time when the land in the Kinneff area was nearly ice-free, while the sea and a narrow fringe of land adjacent was occupied by dead ice. Evidence of the direction of the ice-movement is revealed by glacial erosion furrows particularly well seen as one looks southward from the Slains road and views the skyline of Bervie Brow and the intervening landscape.

HISTORY

The centre of the parish in all historic time has been Shieldhill, where in a sheltered dell above a tiny harbour, the old parish church stands, neighboured by no fewer than four castle sites. Here Arnty, possibly Adamnan, had a cell near a spring; it stood in a line between the church and the castle of Kinneff. Arnty, or Arne, was associated with the famous Culdee centre of Brechin, and had at Kinneff a suidhe or seat, a word similar in meaning to cathair, which suggests a possible derivation for Catterline. This sacred site has seen successive churches. David de Bernham, Bishop of St Andrews, to which see Kinneff belonged, though Catterline pertained to Brechin, in August 1242 dedicated the church of Kinneff. Did his wide activity signify the end of Culdee influence and the open assertion of Roman supremacy?

The present church stands on the site of its predecessor, in which the Regalia of Scotland were hidden from 1652 till the Restoration in 1660. The edifice was a very old fabric, the walls thereof being supported with eight strong buttresses, and the roof by pillars of wood, so that probably it is the oldest country church presently possessed and in use, of any in Scotland (Macfarlane's *Geographical Collections*, Scottish History Society). The edict for building the present fabric is dated 1735, and until it was ready for use services were variously held in the manse and in Catterline Church, which apparently fell into decay after this time. Within the present church are several monuments of historic interest:— to the memory of James Grainger, the minister who, with his wife, preserved the Regalia; to Sir George Ogilvie of Barras, Captain of Dunnottar Castle during that period; to the Honeyman family, four of whom in succession were ministers of the parish, a very notable record; to the men of the parish in the wars of 1914-1918 and 1939-1945. In 1876 the Rev. Dr Mearns added a wing, which greatly altered the fabric, but the six fine windows towards the sea and the small windows in the gables are of interest. Several courses of the ancient foundations are visible. The bell, founded in Holland, bears the initials of James Honeyman (the second) and the date 1679.

The importance of this small central area of the parish is further attested by the presence of four castle sites in close proximity. Kinneff Castle, reputed to have been founded as a hunting lodge by Kenneth II, is the best known, though only one mass of rubble remains to mark it. Cadden Castle, on an easily defensible promontory, lay to the north-east. Whistleberry Castle, a little further north on a similar site, is still indicated by a curtain wall on which, in season, wallflowers flourish. This marked the moat or ditch which cut off access from landward. Adam's Castle, most northerly of all, has no remaining vestiges; the site, both of castle and garden, is now under the plough, but the water of Adam's Well still flows clear and sweet. No traditional lore or authentic history appears to attach to these castles; they could hardly be contemporaneous, but they do suggest the need for vigilance, even in so close neighbourhood to Dunnottar, on a coast fronting Europe's western seaboard.

THE REGALIA OF SCOTLAND

The outstanding event in parish history was the concealment of the Regalia within the church of Kinneff and its successful protection for eight years within that sanctuary. These symbols of royalty were coveted by Cromwell's government and every effort was made to seize them. By the intrepidity of a woman, Mrs Drummond of Moneydie, they were conveyed safely to Dunnottar Castle and entrusted to the safe-keeping of the Governor. George Ogilvie of Barras was a heritor and a recently appointed elder in Kinneff. He had fought in the continental wars under Gustavus Adolphus and he may well have answered to the character of Dugald Dalgetty as Sir Walter Scott depicts him, save that he was actuated by a high conscience and a more enlightened sense of honour.

Dunnottar Castle was in no case to resist siege, but Ogilvie was put in command and with zeal and haste endeavoured to secure a garrison, armaments and provisions. It was besieged in September 1651, and Ogilvie faced the English troops with a confident front. The besiegers were held off until, after delays caused by the incredibly bad roads, heavy artillery was brought from the south and mounted. It became evident that no real resistance could be offered to siege artillery and Ogilvie prepared to capitulate. Before this, however, he had sent a son of the Earl Marischal, who was among the garrison, to the Continent and the story was set afoot that he had carried the Regalia with him to Charles II at Paris. Actually, a plot was concerted between his wife and Christian Fletcher, the wife of the Rev. James Grainger, minister of Kinneff, that without the knowledge of Ogilvie, lest afterwards he might disclose the hiding place under torture, the Regalia should be smuggled out and hidden in a safe place. This daring plan was successfully carried through, whether the method was, as Mrs Grainger after asserted, by herself hiding the sword and sceptre in hards of lint for making napery and the crown on her person or, as local tradition avers, by her maid going as dulse wife to Dunnottar

Bay and becoming a familiar and unsuspected figure to the soldiery. She is supposed to have received the precious emblems of kingship lowered over the cliff and to have carried them to the manse hidden in her creel. Grainger received them and, under cover of the dark, buried them in the kirk, where they remained in safety, despite rigorous search, till the Restoration. To the widow of the Earl Marischal, he wrote: 'I, James Grainger, minister at Kinneff, grant me to have in my custody the Honours of the Kingdom of Scotland, viz., the Crown, Scepter and Sword ..... For the Crown and Scepter I raised a Pavement Stone and dig'd under it a hole and put them (the Crown and Scepter) in there, and fill'd up the hole and put down the Stone, just as it was again, and remov'd the Mould that remain'd that none would have decerned the Stone to have been rais'd at all; the Sword again at the West end of the Church among some common seats that stand there, I dig'd down in the ground betwixt the two foremost of the seats, and laid it down within the case of it and covered it up, so that removing the superfluous Mould, it could not be decerned by anybody; and if it shall please God to call me by death before they may be called for, your Ladyship will find them there. To the Countess Marischal, March 31st 1652.'

Ogilvie had been twice summoned to surrender in November 1651 and had defiantly refused, but in May 1652, at a sufficient interval after the spiriting away of the Regalia, he accepted terms. The third article of the terms of capitulation runs: 'That the Crown and Scepter of Scotland together with all other Ensignes of Regalitie be delivered unto me or a good account thereof, for the use of Parliament, etc.' He marched out with flying colours, drum beating, match lighted, completely armed. There were five and thirty soldiers in the garrison. The English had expected a far larger number. The 'good account' of the Regalia was unsatisfactory and involved Ogilvie and his wife in close surveillance and house and later local arrest. The early death of his wife is attributed to the severity of siege conditions and the ensuing confinement and vexation.

This gallant story had an unromantic sequel. The Countess Marischal claimed the sole credit of preserving the Regalia and her son was created Earl of Kintore by Charles II. Ogilvie, seeing himself forestalled, presented his claim and was created Knight Baronet of Barras. In the long and unseemly controversy Grainger appears to have been harried by both principals, favouring first Ogilvie and then turning to the Countess. By this time his health was broken, and it must be remembered that he had sustained the onerous and anxious charge of the Regalia for eight years in close secrecy, and he appears to have died unrewarded, in 1663. The final irony of the unhappy story was that his wife, re-married, made a claim in her turn to have been the sole saviour of the Regalia. She received a small money reward, made payable from local vacant stipend, of 200 merks.

POPULATION

During the last hundred years the population of the parish has steadily declined. The most recent figures show a rise, but it is premature to envisage lasting increase. The long marked drift to urban areas still persists. The figures available follow:— (1755) 858; (1801) 937, (1851) 1069; (1901) 899; (1911) 835; (1921) 814; (1931) 713; (1948) 784. The year 1851 shows the highest recorded figure and 1931 shows the lowest. There was no census in 1941 owing to the war and the figure given for 1948, though reasonably accurate, has not the authority of a census. An interesting comparison of age groups is possible under the 1948 figures:—

Under 10	Over 10 and Under 21	Over 21	Total
193	135	456	784

Looking at war conditions and their influence on population, we have:—

Under 10	Over 10	
101	282	Male
92	309	Female

giving support to the contention that in time of war male births exceed female, while in peace female exceed male. (The census of 1951 recorded a population of 803, consisting of 408 males and 395 females).

AGRICULTURE

Kinneff is almost wholly agricultural in its economy. There is lobster fishing on the coast, and a few men engage in forestry and trades, but farming is the staple industry. In the *Second Statistical Account* the writer, Dr T. Brown, reckons the wage of the married farm worker at 12 guineas per annum or roughly 5/- a week. The married worker today receives about £5 a week. This is an extraordinary advance and the largest increase is within the last ten years and derives from war conditions. The qualification has to be made that perquisites have altered and often disappeared. It would be a safe allowance to say that today the value of house, coal, potatoes, oatmeal and milk would be around £1.10/- per week. As to the improvement in wages, conditions of employment and hours of work there can be no question, though many cottar houses are still below a reasonable standard for comfort and health, but other amenities have developed that were formerly unknown, including bus travel and entertainment. The cost of labour is now a ruling consideration with the farmer; it has made the winter feeding of cattle, once remunerative, less widespread.

CATTLE

Up to the beginning of this century Aberdeen Angus was the predominant breed of cattle and the standard of quality was high. Nowadays very few beef cattle are bred in the parish and the quality has considerably deteriorated. Farmers buy Irish bullocks and the dairy farms provide a number of steer calves, mainly Ayrshire and Friesians. None of these produce best quality beef. Dairy farming became a major interest in this parish some 25 years ago and now there are several excellent dairy herds, both Ayrshire and Friesian. This has tended to the improvement of steadings, which in general are in good order. The double shift system of labour, with three milkings a day, is practised by some farmers.

Land reclamation has recently been attempted: a knoll south of Kirk Croft and a field on the road to Slains Park have been broken in from whin in 1949. Former *Accounts* remark on the absence of hedges: fencing is still mainly by post and wire but recently concrete is replacing wood for posts, owing to the scarcity of larch, the only suitable wood for fencing. Dykes are few.

The revolution in farming caused by the use of machines is here very complete. Whole farms are entirely mechanised and have no horses: there are fewer and fewer at work. An early but not permanent use of the steam engine for ploughing in the parish is interesting; two engines were used, one at each side of the field, and a cable revolving on a drum drew the ploughs across the field; three or even more ploughs could be used.

The balance between arable and pasture land has been reasonably maintained, but the need to grow more grain and the reduction in animal husbandry has tended to impair the fertility of the soil. The reduced number of feeding cattle has meant the return of less dung to the land, and that has been of inferior quality owing to the lack of concentrated feeding stuffs. On the other hand greatly increased quantities of artificial fertilisers are being used. Methods of silage-making have improved, bringing an economy in the use of hay and a tendency to displace the growing of turnips, a crop which requires more labour.

Poultry farming on a scientific basis is increasing, and experiments in the growing of crops like raspberries and rhubarb are being made.

CROPS

Tables of production in the parish are appended, showing the contrast created by the Second World War.

	Acres 1939	Acres 1949
Wheat	230½	86½
Oats	1440	1640
Barley	425	810½
Potatoes	212	389¾
Sugar Beet	21¼	4
Turnips and other cultivated crops	760	658
TOTAL	3088¾	3588¾

LIVESTOCK

	1939	1949
Horses	150	60
Dairy Cattle	463	624
Beef Cattle	1131	1428
Sheep	4299	1058
Pigs	312	156
Poultry	11297	15421

The above sections dealing with agriculture are based on information supplied by Mr Gordon Watt, B.Sc.

FISHING

Formerly there were three stations of the fishing industry in the parish. Gapul, or Gaphill, is now hardly known even by name. Shieldhill is deserted, having one inhabited house tenanted by a fisherman of advanced years, who has long been beadle at Kinneff Church and who may be the oldest beadle in the country. Catterline has about 20 houses, some of them built for the coastguard service and in good condition: most have been bought by the tenants. There are 4 boats engaged in lobster and crab (partan) fishing. It is fully fifty years since herring fishing ceased. Salmon fisheries extend along the coast from Montrose and a proportion of men in the parish are thus employed. There is a pier at Catterline, built by Viscount Arbuthnott over a century ago, when the Catterline estate belonged to that family. When the estate changed hands some twenty years ago, the pier also was sold. It was bought by a lady in memory of her son, an artist who often painted beside it and who was killed in the bombing of London during the war. She has given it to the fishermen of the village, who have formed an association for its management and upkeep.

HABITATIONS

In addition to Catterline, already referred to, the only considerable group of houses is at Roadside of Kinneff. (It is thus named on the Ordnance Survey 1925 popular edition and in Bartholomew's revised 1946 half inch maps). Here there are about 40 houses, comprising the old type in rows, with large gardens; council houses, with indoor sanitation and electric light; and prefabricated houses, with these conveniences and electric cookers and refrigerators.

Four houses were built in 1910, called Coronation Cottages, and the new houses at Roadside abovementioned: the most recent is a group of 4 at Barras intended for agricultural workers. But many cottages have been allowed to decay and there is still a real shortage of accommodation. Further housebuilding is in prospect at Catterline but, as at Kinneff, adequate water supply is difficult to provide.

A fine specimen of a castellated residence is Castle of Fiddes in Barras, which bears the date 1603 and has been well restored and is now again inhabited. There is no other house in the parish that can be called ancient. The House of Barras, in which Sir George Ogilvie lived, is marked by a low wall. Fawside House is an enlarged farm with grounds.

HALL

The village hall was erected in memory of those who fell in the First World War.

LIGHTHOUSE

Todhead Lighthouse was built in 1897, after a series of wrecks on this perilous seaboard. It has a half-minute flashing light, visible for 17 miles, and an automatic siren, much in use in prevalent fogs.

CHURCHES

Between the *Second Statistical Account* and 1900 much building was done. The Free Church, of which Dr Brown, who wrote the *Account*, was founder and first minister, was built in 1843 and is now, since the Union of the churches in 1929, the main centre of the Church of

Scotland's spiritual work in the parish. In 1848 an Episcopal Church was erected at Catterline and a school built. Catterline, owing to the presence of the coastguard station and perhaps because of the old tradition carried forward from the Reformation period in the north east, has always had a special inclination to episcopacy, while the rest of the parish has been stoutly presbyterian. The charge of St Philip is worked from Stonehaven. The other schools of the parish were all built about this time, Kinneff in 1865 and Barras in 1881, in both cases superseding inferior and antiquated buildings. In turn they now all fall below present standards and require improvement.

EDUCATION

There are 3 schools in the parish and all, by population standards, should be two-teacher schools. Kinneff and Barras have each 2 teachers; Catterline has 1 teacher, the older age groups under twelve attending Dunnottar School in Stonehaven. There is only one male teacher in the parish, at Kinneff school. A number of younger children, as well as all over twelve years, go out of the parish for schooling, to Bervie or to Stonehaven, totalling 46 boys and 36 girls in all. Attendance at primary schools in 1948 was:—

	Kinneff	Catterline	Barras	Total
Male	29	9	26	64
Female	19	13	25	57
Total	48	22	51	121

ANTIQUITIES

The parish abounds in traces of of early man and at Auchendreigh, Cosy Corner, St John's Hill and elsewhere prehistoric burials have been disinterred. In the Museum of Antiquities, Edinburgh, are relics uncovered in 1831 on the glebe at Shieldhill and presented by the Rev. A. Stewart, the writer of the *First Statistical Account*. The find consisted of two armlets of bronze, penannular, with the ends tightly joined, and a food vessel, classified by Childe as type C.2. (*The Prehistory of Scotland*, Kegan Paul, 1935), together with a bronze spear head, which Joseph Anderson judged not to belong to the burial. The ring and the urn are illustrated in Anderson, *Scotland in Pagan Times, Bronze and Stone Ages*, pp. 59 and 60.

A century later, in 1923, a burial was exposed at Catterline, under the direction of Rev. Joseph Frazer. Here the urn was a beaker and a unusual feature was a cover stone with pecked spirals, a decoration of which other examples are found widely separated in locus. There were three layers of smaller stones superimposed above the cist covering proper, and in the second was a stone with a countersunk perforation. This cist has been re-erected in Marischal College Museum and is perhaps the finest example of a bronze age burial found in the N.E. of Scotland. The skull is of a male over forty years old and has a cephalic index of 1600cc., or about 120cc. in excess of the average Scottish skull of today. The height must have been from 5 ft. 7¾ ins. to 5 ft. 10 ins. and is well above the average measurement from such interments of 4 ft. 4 ins. (*Proceedings of the Society of Antiquaries of Scotland*, Vol.X, Fifth Series).

WAY OF LIFE

All rural parishes have seen a complete revolution in the way of living, and Kinneff is no exception. Though no railway runs through the parish, it is well served by motor buses, being traversed by the main road from Dundee to Aberdeen. A frequent demand from farm workers is now a house near the bus route and accessibility to school. As farmers travel by car, the farm worker travels by bus, and wants increasingly more time off. This explains a preference for tractors over horses on the part of younger men — not just love of machinery, but desire for more leisure and especially a free weekend.

A further feature is the travelling shop with groceries, etc., a development of the vans that bring meat, bread, fish, and now milk, to the door. A travelling chemist is not unknown. In the homes excellent oatcakes are still largely eaten and the girdle is in regular use. In this parish there are few shops — a post office and a general shop at Kinneff Roadside; a combined store and post office at Catterline roadside, with a licence; and public houses at Kinneff and at Catterline. Much shopping is done at Bervie and Stonehaven.

March 1950

THE PARISH OF LAURENCEKIRK

by Alexander Laing, M.A., Ed.B.

EXTENT AND BOUNDARIES

The parish of Laurencekirk lies in the Howe o' the Mearns, a continuation of the valley of Strathmore. It is 4 miles long (south west to north east) with an extreme breadth of 3 miles. Its total area is 5615 acres, of which the burgh of Laurencekirk occupies 569 acres. Its boundaries with the neighbouring parishes of Marykirk (to the west and south-west), Fordoun (north and north-west) and Garvock (east and south-east) have been partly determined by nature: for instance, the Gauger's Burn and the Black Burn, both tributaries of the Luther Water, divide it on the south-west from the parish of Marykirk, and the Burn of Leppie divides it on the north-east from the parish of Fordoun. The boundary between the parishes of Garvock and Laurencekirk was in bygone days the northern limit of the forest of Garvock, the old Rae or Deer Dyke, parts of which can still be traced.

LAURENCEKIRK

The parish has a gently rolling topography, and is drained by the Luther Water, which flows southwards through the middle of it to join the River North Esk. Of its total population (1951) of 1,935, fully three-quarters were resident in the burgh. The burgh itself lies on the main Brechin to Aberdeen highway, and also on the main railway line from Perth to Aberdeen. In pre-nationalisation days this line was part of the London, Midland and Scottish Railway system; before that, it was part of the Caledonian Railway, and at the outset of its career, in 1849, it was the Aberdeen Railway. From the main Brechin-Aberdeen road radiate roads to Montrose, Fettercairn, Garvock and the coast, and Auchenblae.

HISTORY

Little is known of the history of the parish prior to the Reformation. Its name in those days was Conveth. Laurencekirk is usually designated 'Conveth' in the records of the Presbytery of Fordoun up to the end of the 17th century. The name also appears in the first entry of the extant kirk session records of the parish church (dated 26th April 1702), but from the first two decades of the 18th century the name 'Laurencekirk' comes into general use. The name 'Conveth' survives in the names of two farms in the parish, Mill of Conveth and Conveth Mains, and also in one street name, Conveth Place.

In medieval times the village of Conveth consisted of a small group of dwellings clustered round the kirk of Conveth on the lands of Haulkerton, and known as 'kirk-toon of Conveth'. The kirk is said to have been dedicated to St Laurence of Canterbury (successor of St Augustine), who is believed to have visited the Mearns between 600 and 605 A.D. In 1914 one interesting link with the past was broken, for in that year the tenth Earl of Kintore sold the 4,000 acres of land in the parish belonging to him - lands which had been acquired by his ancestors from medieval times onwards.

HAULKERTON

Haulkerton (or Hawker's Toon) is mentioned very early in the history of the parish as the residence of the King's falconer. The first Falconers of Haulkerton were descendants of Walter de Lunkyir (Lumgair in the parish of Dunnottar), whose son Ranulph was appointed falconer by William the Lion, who bestowed upon him by royal charter the lands of Luthra (presumed to be Haulkerton, which borders the Luther Water), Balbegno (parish of Fettercairn) and other lands near the castle of Kincardine (parish of Fordoun), the residence of William and his successors when they hunted in the Mearns. The ruins of the castle are still to be seen: they lie within a mile of the western boundary of Laurencekirk parish. Ranulph assumed the name of Falconer, and he and his descendants appear to have acted as falconers to the kings of Scotland on their hunting expeditions in this area. By intermarriage and other ways the Falconers extended the lands they owned in the parish, e.g. in 1539-40 they obtained by charter the lands of Middleton. In 1647 Sir Alexander Falconer was created first Lord Falconer of Haulkerton. The fourth Lord Falconer (died 1727) was the last of his family to reside in the castle of Haulkerton. By 1790 the castle was a ruin, and the stones were used partly for repairing the dykes round Haulkerton plantation, partly in buildings of the farm of Mains of Haulkerton, and partly in rebuilding the parish church in 1804. Today the site of the castle is covered by Haulkerton Wood. In 1778 Anthony Adrian, eighth Lord Falconer, succeeded to the estate and earldom of Kintore, becoming the fifth Earl of Kintore. At that time, and indeed up till 1914, when the tenth earl disposed of all his lands in the parish, nearly four-fifths of the parish belonged to the Kintore estate.

THE NEW VILLAGE

The history of Laurencekirk as we know it today really began in 1760, when Francis Garden, sheriff of Kincardine (later Lord Gardenston, a Lord of Session) purchased the estate of Johnston, and set about founding a model village. By this time the village, which lay at the eastern boundary of the Haulkerton estate, had begun to extend into the neighbouring estate of Johnston. It was still very small. Dr Webster in his 'State of the Population of Scotland' gives the population of the whole parish as 757 in 1755, and the *First Statistical Account* gives the population of the village as under 80 in 1730, and as having decreased to 54 by the time Lord Gardenston purchased the Johnston estate. Lord Gardenston set about building a new village in 1765. He leased out land cheaply and encouraged a variety of craftsmen to settle in the village, among them several handloom weavers and Charles Stiven, maker of snuff-boxes. By 1801 the population of the parish had increased to 1,215. In 1779 the village was erected by royal charter into a burgh of barony, and the burgesses were given the right to elect triennially a bailie and four councillors for administering its affairs. The new burgh was granted the right to hold a weekly mart and an annual fair. Among the buildings for whose erection Lord Gardenston was personally responsible were the Boar's Head Inn (known today as the Gardenston Arms Hotel), a masonic temple and an Episcopalian chapel (the first chapel having been destroyed by Cumberland's army in 1746).

HANDLOOM WEAVING

From the end of the 18th century the number of weavers grew steadily, until by 1838 (*Second Statistical Account*) 147 persons were engaged in weaving, besides a few married women. The weavers in general worked about 15 hours a day, and the more able and industrious seldom earned more than 7/- or 8/- a week. In addition, there was a spinning mill at Blackiemuir with seven spinning frames, employing 7 men and 25 women. This mill was closed in 1842. By the time Fraser published his *History of Laurencekirk* (1880) the number of weavers had declined to 34. The average weekly wage at that time was 12/-, and the main fabrics produced were sheeting, towelling and winceys. By 1906 only five weavers remained actively engaged in the craft, three of them over eighty years of age and one aged seventy-nine.

The craft, however, has not completely died out. One handloom weaving shop was continued by a local shopkeeper, William Walker, and later by his successor, William Winter. When Mr Winter died in 1939, the business was acquired by a Dundee firm, which still owns it.

To keep the craft going, Mr Winter brought over William McIlwaine, a weaver from County Down, Northern Ireland, in 1920. During his life-time in Laurencekirk, William McIlwaine trained two or three apprentices. One of these, William Taylor of Luthermuir, carries on the craft today. Except during the years 1940-48, the clack of the weaver's shuttle has been a familiar sound in Gardenston Street. In the shop today there are five looms, two for weaving table-cloths (1½ yard and 2 yard respectively), two for towels, and one for napkins. Each loom is fitted with a Jacquard machine for putting in the patterns. There is a strong prospect that the craft will be kept alive, and the number of weavers increased.

STIVEN'S SNUFF-BOXES

The most notable artisan Lord Gardenston brought to Laurencekirk was Charles Stiven, the snuff-box maker, like Lord Gardenston himself a strong Episcopalian and Jacobite. He came to Laurencekirk from his native Glenbervie in 1783. At one time there were three establishments producing snuff-boxes in Laurencekirk, one run by C. Stiven & Son, and the others by apprentices of Stiven. The distinguishing feature of the Stiven products was a concealed hinge with a wooden pin. The firm of Stiven also produced tea-caddies, napkin rings, pin-boxes, glove-boxes, totums, etc. Older residents in the burgh still recall the 'totums' produced by Stiven, whose four sides bore the letters 'A', 'D', 'N' and 'T' respectively. 'A', which stood for the Latin 'Accipe unum', was rendered in Mearns dialect as 'A, tak ane'; 'D' (Donato alium) as 'D, duntle doon ane'; 'N' (Nihil) as 'N, nickle, naething'; and 'T' (Totum) as 'T, tak a'! In 1848 C. Stiven & Co. were appointed box-makers to Her Majesty the Queen. With the death in 1874 of Alexander Stiven, son of the founder of the firm, the business came to an end.

DEVELOPMENTS 1841-1951

Throughout the first three-quarters of the 19th century Laurencekirk continued to expand. By 1871 the population of the parish was 2,174 (the maximum ever recorded), of whom 1,521 were resident in the burgh. In 1841 gas lighting was introduced into the burgh. In 1849 the opening of the Aberdeen Railway made it feel less remote from the rest of the country and facilitated the export of livestock and agricultural products. In 1854 the first bank opened its doors. The opening of the St Laurence Hall in 1866 provided a new focus for its community-life and leisure interests. Changes, too, were made in municipal administration. In 1889 the General Police and Improvement (Scotland) Act of 1862 was adopted and Police Commissioners for the burgh elected. With the coming into force of the Burgh Police (Scotland) Act 1892 the Police Commissioners were superseded by a Town Council consisting of a Provost, 2 bailies and 6 councillors.

In 1901 a piped water supply and sewage disposal system were introduced into the burgh. The source of water was a copious spring on the shoulder of Strathfinella Hill, on the Glensaugh estate. Hitherto, water had been obtained from Garvock Hill, on the Johnston estate, and the inhabitants had had to collect their daily supplies from 'walls' erected at various points in the streets. During the past fifty years the Town Council has taken an active part in improving the amenities of the burgh. One notable addition to these amenities was the Memorial Park, gifted to the town at the close of the First World War by Mr. R. B. Pearson, a member of the family which for close on 150 years had owned the Johnston estate, on which most of the burgh lies. In 1927 the storage capacity of the local reservoir, which had hitherto only held 24 hours' supply of water, was increased to hold 3 to 4 days' supply. Electric lighting began to be introduced into houses in the burgh in 1939, but electric lighting in the High Street was only introduced in 1942, and in the side streets in 1945. Between 1901 and 1951 the number of houses in the burgh increased from 444 to 501. This increase over-taxed the existing sewage disposal plant. A new plant and one or two new sewers were completed in 1951, at a cost of £17,000. Today every home in the burgh has sewage disposal facilities except three large houses (two of them rather remote from the town) which have septic tanks.

THE TOWN TODAY

To the visitor passing through it by car the little town of Laurencekirk seems bigger than it actually is, for it has spread itself for about a mile along both sides of the main road from Brechin to Aberdeen. There has not, however, been a corresponding development of houses to the east and west of the High Street. Most of the houses on the High Street have their front walls flush with the pavement, and their gardens behind. The majority of houses in the burgh are built of stone, but a few built of clay from the claypit, the 'Brickells', in what is now Kinnear Square, still survive round Kinnear Square and in the High Street. Council houses are now being built of brick.

POPULATION

The population of Laurencekirk parish rose without a break from 1215 in 1801 to 2125 in 1851. In 1871 it was 2174, the maximum recorded. Since then there has been a downward trend, with slight fluctuations. From 2011 in 1901 the figure fell to 1921 in 1911, recovered to 1956 in 1921, and dropped heavily to 1713 in 1931. The 1951 Census showed a total of 1935 - an increase of 222, or 13 per cent higher than in 1931. The burgh, with a population of 1,485 in 1951, had the lion's share (169) of this gain, but the landward part, unlike so many rural areas, also participated with an increase of 53. In 1851 the town had 1611 inhabitants - a figure never since equalled. By 1881 it was down to 1454 - about the same as today - and in the present century it registered: (1901) 1512; (1911) 1438; (1921) 1461; (1931) 1316. It is noteworthy that, whereas in the burgh today females outnumber males by 819 to 666, in the landward part males predominate by 258 to 192.

There may be more than one reason for the recent growth in population. Perhaps the chief one is the increase in the number of houses in the burgh. Other factors may be the post-war bulge in the birth-rate and the fact that old people are living longer. It should be noted that the mechanisation of agriculture has not led to a decrease in numbers employed on the land: on the contrary, there has been an increase.

HOUSING

In 1951 there were 501 houses in the burgh and 108 in the landward part of the parish. Between 1919 and 1951 the Town Council built 74 houses; 12 in 1919, 12 in 1924, 16 between 1930 and 1935, 30 between 1946 and 1948, and 4 in 1950-51. Of these 12 are three-roomed houses, 58 are four-roomed, and 4 are five-roomed. The majority of these have been built in Cairnview Place. A further 12 houses will be ready by the end of 1952. These are being built in Gardenston Street: 8 have three rooms, and 4 have four rooms. The Council's total for the years 1919-52 is thus 86. By the end of 1952 only 6 houses will have been erected by private enterprise during the years 1945-52. The County Council built 8 Cruden houses for agricultural workers in 1949 and have another 6 in course of erection, all of them within the burgh. At the end of 1952 the total number of houses in the burgh will be 523, as against 501 in 1951. Of the houses in the burgh, 21 are 'tied houses', i.e. houses purchased by farmers to accommodate their own workers. At present only 12 out of the 21 are occupied by agricultural workers, as the sitting tenant has still to find alternative accommodation. Comparisons between the costs of building Council houses before and after the war are interesting. In 1919 the average cost per house was £1,196; in 1924, £402; between 1930 and 1935, £415; today, a three-roomed house is costing £1,524, and a four-roomed house, £1,744.

SHOPS AND BUSINESSES

The life of the town of Laurencekirk depends upon its agricultural hinterland. For that reason the town probably has more shops than some towns of comparable size. Classification of the shops and other businesses is rather difficult, for one finds that many shops in the town have a variety of lines, e.g. a baker is also a grocer, a butcher is also a greengrocer, a draper also sells crockery, a chemist sells cigarettes, or a tobacconist and confectioner is in effect a general merchant. The following classification is as accurate as possible in such circumstances.

Bakers and Grocers	3	Hotels (Public Houses)	5
Blacksmiths	1	Ironmongers	1
Building contractors	1	Joiners	2
Butchers	5	Newsagents & Stationers	2
Chemists	2	Painters & Decorators	2
Cycle agents	1	Plumbers & Electricians	2
Confectioners, Tobacconists	4	Printer	1
Drapers	3	Radio Shops	2
Drapers and Grocers	1	Saddler & Ironmonger	1
Electricians	1	Shoemakers	3
Fish Merchant	1	Slaters	2
Fish & Chip Shop	1	Tailors	1
Grocers	7	Tractor Depots	6
Garages	4	Watchmakers	2
Hairdressers	4	Potato Merchants	2

Practically all the above are private enterprises. The Brechin Cooperative Society has a branch in Laurencekirk with bakery, grocery and butchery departments. From the local printing office comes a weekly paper, the *Kincardineshire Observer*, widely known as the 'Squeaker', which reports news from Laurencekirk and the surrounding parishes and serves as an advertising medium for local firms. It was first published on 11th April 1902, by the grandfather of the present editor. The town has 2 banks, branches of the Commercial Bank and the Clydesdale and North of Scotland Bank respectively. The local post office serves a much wider area than the parish of Laurencekirk. It has a staff of one postmistress, 3 counter assistants, 7 postmen, 3 telephone exchange operators and one telegraph boy. Most of the legal business of the parish and the neighbouring parishes is dealt with by a local firm of solicitors and by a Stonehaven firm, which sends a representative to the town on two days a week. The parish now has 2 doctors, but for several years between the wars it had only one.

Changes in commerce

Some idea of the changes that have taken place in the commercial life of the town may be gauged from the following facts. In 1906 there were 7 blacksmiths in the parish: today there is only one, and he spends his time, not shoeing horses, but mending agricultural implements. The old forge has yielded place to electric welding. There are, however, 6 tractor depots, the largest a branch of the Reekie Engineering Co. Ltd., Arbroath, employing 11 men. At the outset of the century there were 8 or 9 tailors in Laurencekirk, as against only one today, and each of the 3 drapery establishments had its staff of milliners and dressmakers. Today the majority of the people go to Aberdeen, Montrose or Brechin to buy their new suits or dresses. Before the First World War each of the local inns was a coaching establishment, with 10 or 12 horses and 4 men. Little did Laurencekirk realise when a local garage proprietor brought the first motor-car into the parish in 1906 that the new invention was to effect a radical change in its community-life, and that by 1952 agriculture in the parish would be as highly mechanised as any in the country.

Auction mart

A focal point of the commercial life of the town and its rural environs is the local auction mart, which brings farmers and buyers from a wide area to its weekly sales each Monday. Since 1780 Laurencekirk has had the right to hold a weekly market, and this market has grown in importance with the passage of the years. The Kincardineshire Auction Co. was set up in 1890. In 1910 it was registered as a society under the title of the Kincardineshire Auction Mart Co. Ltd, and in 1947 it acquired both the Stonehaven and Banchory Marts from the Stonehaven Auction Mart Co. Its average sales in recent years have been: 19,000 cattle, 34,600 sheep and 3,300 pigs. Of these, 12,300 fat cattle, 22,000 fat sheep and 1,700 fat pigs are taken over by the Ministry of Food. The balance are store stock sold through the cattle ring. In addition to its weekly sales of cattle and pigs, the Company holds sales of all classes of store lambs, drawn from the whole of Kincardineshire, on the second and last Thursdays of August, and a sale of breeding and feeding ewes in September. Each April and October it holds special sales of store cattle and calves, and it also has occasional sales of pedigreed and non-pedigreed pigs, in conjunction with the North East of Scotland Pig Breeder's Association. Its premises have now been converted for the holding of attested cattle sales, and the first of these sales will be held before the end of 1952. The average prices of livestock in August 1952 were: milk cows, £50; bullocks. £70.15s; heifers, £55.5s; stirks £47.17.6d;

young pigs, £9 to £13; young calves, £14.5s; store lambs, £5.10s; fat cattle, £77 to £93; fat sheep, £8; fat pigs, £25.

AGRICULTURE

Agriculture in the Mearns has witnessed many changes since the time of the last *Statistical Account*, but none so sweeping as the change-over to mechanisation which has largely taken place in the last two decades. This change is reflected in the following statistics of the number of horses in the parish: (1807) 143; (1832) 205; (1870) 160; (1890) 198; (1912) 197; (1918) 202; (1930) 151; (1939) 95; (1943) 82; (1950) 19. Another index of the speed of mechanisation is the fact that the largest tractor depot in the Mearns has sold over 800 tractors since it opened in 1947. The Second World War speeded up the process of mechanisation, especially as the war years brought prosperity to the farming industry. Not only have tractors replaced horses, but all the horse-drawn implements have been superseded by mechanical implements specially designed for work with tractors — manure spreaders, improved potato diggers, hay-loaders, hay-balers, combine-harvesters, etc. Many steadings have been electrified.

There are 45 farms in the parish, 23 of them small-holdings which came into existence after the First World War. Not all these farms lie completely within the parish. Almost all are owner-occupied. The largest is Bent-Kilnhill (730 acres), a fusion of what up till 1930 were two farms of 560 and 170 acres respectively. The total land acreage of the parish is 5,615 acres. Of this, 3,069 acres were under tillage, 1796 under grass, and 337 were rough grazing in 1950: a total of 5,202 acres. A soil scientist, Dr. R. Glentworth of the Macaulay Institute for Soil Research, makes the following comments on the soils of the parish: 'a thick covering of till or clay loam derived largely from the Ednie beds — marly strata of the Old Red Sandstone formation — blankets the area and forms the parent material of the soils. Broad flat spreads of loam to sandy loam alluvium flank the Luther Water and its tributaries. Before the Christian era began (possibly about 2,000 years ago) the area supported a broad-leaved deciduous forest. The soils have a characteristically red colour, and a naturally high supply of plant nutrients. Generally the texture of the subsoil is richer in clay than the top layers. This results in imperfect drainages and necessitates the use of tile drains in the fields'.

TILLAGE AND CROPS

The acreage under tillage rose from 2,709 acres in 1912 to 3,395 in 1918. It decreased to 2,488 acres in 1939, but the stress of war caused it to rise to 3,391 in 1943. The following statistics show the changes in acreage of main crops over the last 100 years.

	1807	1866	1912	1918	1930	1939	1943	1950
Oats	1275	1348	1080	1606½	1501¼	1284½	1419¼	1392½
Barley	590	668	575¾	326½	170½	82½	323	455½
Wheat	100	179	150	405	119	188½	51 3¼	281½
Potatoes	50	170	257¼	513¼	161¼	378¾	532½	555½
Turnips, Swedes	268	869	621	524¾	559	460	516	358½

Oats has always been the main cereal crop in this area. Both wars led to marked increases in the acreages under wheat and potatoes. On some farms, however, there has been over-cropping with potatoes, and this has led to an increase in the eelworm pest. Experiments with the rotation of crops may pay immediate dividends, but they have also their liabilities. The figures for cattle production in 1950 were the highest ever recorded: 1,743. The poultry population, too, has greatly icreased: the figure of 12,443 is considerably more than double the 1943 figure.

NOTABLE FARMS

Two farms merit special mention. The first is the Bent (one of the most highly mechanised farms in the whole of the United Kingdom), which has applied most of the recent scientific inventions in dairy-farming, arable farming and poultry farming. As early as 1937 it was experimenting with the combine harvester. In 1940 it introduced an attested herd of Ayrshire cows, and electrical milking machinery in 1941. In 1948 it started egg-production in a big way. Now it has 2,000 to 3,000 hens arranged in six hatcheries with several hundred hens in each. The birds are in wire cages. Every 1¼ hours an electrically operated food trolley passes round the battery and each bird is allowed 4½ minutes for feeding and 2½ minutes to get grit and water. Each hen is given two months' probation as an egg-layer. If at the end of the two months, it is not laying sixteen eggs a month, it is sent to the poulterer. When the present tenant, Mr John Mackie, took over the farm in 1930, there were 16-20 employees on the two farms, Bent and Kilnhill. Today, on the amalgamated farm there are 35 employees, 4 on supervision, 3 on poultry-keeping, 10 on dairying, 16 on arable farming and 2 in the office. In place of 9 cottages and 2 bothies there are now 14 cottages and 2 hostels. All these have hot and cold water, electric light and indoor sanitation.

The second farm whose name is known beyond the bounds of the parish is Burnton, which specialises in the breeding of Shorthorn cattle and is also experimenting with the breeding of cross-Highland cattle (one-half Aberdeen Angus: one-eighth Highland: three-eighths Shorthorn). It was the first farm in the county to have an attested beef herd. This farm also employs more men than it did before the days of mechanisation, 13 today in contrast to 8 in 1929. Burnton also goes in for sheep-rearing on Garvock Hill in the parish of Garvock, in which part of the farm lies. As a result of reseeding part of the hill it is now possible to maintain 5 times as many sheep there as it was before reseeding was carried out.

EFFECTS OF PROSPERITY

The prosperity of the farmer today is in sharp contrast to the hard struggle he had in the late 20s and early 30s, when prices slumped. In 1929 the price of potatoes at the rail-head was 7/6 per ton. It was not uncommon at that time to see heaps of potatoes left to rot in woods about the parish. In those days the market was largely a free one: today it is more or less controlled. The farmer is assured of a good price for his milk, livestock or grain. He is now freer to concentrate on the business of production and does not need to expend so much time and energy on dealing. Moreover, since in this area the farmer is usually the owner of his own land, he is much readier than he used to be to spend his profits on improving his land, on buying implements or on improving conditions for his workers. Prosperity has made him less conservative, and much keener than he was in pre-war days to experiment and to apply the latest findings of the experts in animal and plant nutrition and soil sciences. But he is still a strong individualist. Politically, the majority of farmers in the parish are Conservative. One notable exception, however, is Mr John Mackie of Bent, who stood as Socialist candidate for the constituency of North Angus and Mearns (within which the parish lies) at the general election of October 1951. He lost to his Conservative opponent by over 8,000 votes.

WORKING CONDITIONS

The lot of the farm worker has also improved enormously. In the old days his working day for nine months of the year began at 6 a.m. and did not finish till 6 p.m. (7.30 a.m. till 5 p.m. during the winter months). He had a break from 11 a.m. to 1 p.m., but during this break he usually had his horse to feed. Today his working day does not exceed 8¾ hours (8 hours in winter). He earns much more than his predecessors, his wage-scales now being laid down in Agricultural

Schedules. Quite frequently he now has a house with indoor sanitation, electric light, hot and cold water and a Rayburn range. Since on
some farms there is no adequate water-supply, an attempt is being
made to find houses for agricultural workers in the burgh of
Laurencekirk; hence the increase in the number of 'tied houses', and
the 14 Cruden houses built by the County Council, referred to above.
In pre-war days the offer of an extra £2 a year was often sufficient to
induce a man to move. Today the first enquiry made by the farmservant's wife is about the house. Better wages, improved housing
conditions, and the scrapping of the yearly and half-yearly engagements now mean that farm-hands are staying longer and that there is
less migration from farm to farm or county to county. Farm-servants
are now engaged direct by the farm or through a registry office. Gone
are the days of the old 'feeing markets' at the Whitsun and Martinmas
terms, when the crossroads at the northern end of the High Street of
Laurencekirk were thronged with farmers and farm-servants haggling
over terms. The general improvement in the living and working
conditions of the farm worker is reflected in his children. Cottar
children are on the whole cleaner and better dressed than they were in
pre-war days. Families, too, are smaller. At the Bent the average
number of children in 15 families is two and one-third. In general,
farm workers today show a keener interest in the education of their
children than they used to do, but the majority have little interest in
either politics or religion. Most of them only go to church at
communion time.

CHURCHES

The parish has two Presbyterian (Church of Scotland) congregations,
one Episcopalian congregation and a small company of Plymouth
Brethren. Of these, the largest is the congregation of the East Church,
the parish church. This church was erected in 1804, on the site of the
post-Reformation church of Conveth (built 1626), and was enlarged
in 1819. It has a membership of 855, a Sunday school with 108 pupils
and a Woman's Guild with 115 members. The West Church has 237
members. Prior to the Union in 1929, this church was the Laurencekirk United Free Church, and before that the Free Church. The
Free Church began its life in Laurencekirk in November 1843, and the
first recorded meeting of its Kirk Session was held on 8th January
1844. Up to 1867, when the present church was built, the congregation worshipped in a church in Farquhar Street.
    St Laurence Episcopal Church has 120 members on its roll. For at
least 260 years there has been an Episcopalian congregation in
Laurencekirk. When the Presbyterian Church was confirmed as the
established church of Scotland in 1690, the Rev. William Dunbar, an

Episcopalian and Jacobite, who had already been ejected from the charge of the parish church, became minister of an Episcopalian congregation in the village. By 1746 the congregation apparently had a chapel, for it was burned down by Cumberland's soldiers in that year. After the Rebellion the Episcopalians continued to meet at different spots in the parish, until Lord Gardenston, himself an Episcopalian, erected a chapel for them in 1791. The present church was erected in 1871 and consecrated in 1873.

The only other religious sect in Laurencekirk is the Plymouth Brethren, with 16 members in all. They meet for worship every Sunday morning and evening, and have a prayer meeting every Monday evening and a Bible reading every Wednesday evening. Their meeting house in Johnston Street was acquired in 1913. Prior to that, Plymouth Brethren in the parish of Laurencekirk worshipped with their co-religionists at Luthermuir or Auchenblae.

Attendances at both the Presbyterian Churches and the Episcopalian Church are small. At the West Church there is seldom more than 20% of the total membership at any diet of worship, and at the East Church and the Episcopalian Church the percentage is considerably less. The morning services are usually better attended than the evening ones. The East Church discontinues its evening services during July and August. Though the majority of people in the parish are not church-goers, there are few among them who would declare themselves atheists or agnostics, if put to the test. The majority still turn up at the twice-yearly communion services and call upon the services of a minister at the major crises of life — birth, marriage and death. They still maintain these slender links with the Church as a sort of insurance policy against a possible Hereafter, but are not prepared to pay the premiums. All three churches depend for their continued existence upon a loyal and active minority of their congregations whose sincere and simple faith finds an outlet in devotion to the Church and its activities. Most of them belong to the older generation. It is doubtful whether an adequate number of the younger generation are coming forward to take the place of the older folk. Perhaps the youth of the parish would respond to a new and challenging presentation of the Church's message in the light of the needs of 20th century society, and to a more active pastorate.

EDUCATION

Within the parish of Laurencekirk there are 2 schools, Laurencekirk Junior Secondary School, which lies within the burgh, and Redmyre School, a rural primary school, which stands at the north-eastern limit of the parish.

A parish school certainly existed in Laurencekirk in 1683, for the

records of the Presbytery of Fordoun show that on 10th July 1683 the
schoolmaster's salary was '40 merks from the heritors of the paroch,
ten bolls of meal from the tenants and 20 mks as session clerk with the
common casualityes'. Thomas Ruddiman, author of the Latin Gram-
mar used in many English and Scottish schools until well into the 19th
century, was schoolmaster in Laurencekirk from 1695(?) to 1700. The
Kirk Session records show that the school had a fairly continuous
existence throughout the 18th century, though for some unaccou-
ntable reason it was not mentioned in the *First Statistical Account*.
James Beattie, author of 'The Minstrel' and professor of Moral
Philosophy at Marischal College, Aberdeen from 1760-1803, who was
born in the parish in 1735, proceeded from the parish school at the age
of 14 to begin his studies at Marischal College. By 1838 (*New
Statistical Account*) there were, in addition to the parish school (with
about 70 pupils), 7 private schools, 3 conducted by male teachers (with
about 100 pupils in all) and 4 conducted by female teachers (with
about 70 pupils in all). In 1865, seven years before the passing of the
Education Act of 1872, the parish had four schools — the parochial
school (with 162 pupils), the Free Church school (with 105 pupils), the
Episcopal school (with 72 pupils), and a private venture school (with
20 pupils). The parochial school and the Free Church school were
handed over to the newly constituted School Board in 1872. The
private venture school continued for a number of years, and the
Episcopal school remained up to the passing of the Education Act of
1918, when it was handed over to the newly constituted Kincardineshire Education Authority. This school's two classrooms were used to
accommodate two primary classes from Laurencekirk Public School
from 1919 to 1933, when the Town Council acquired the building
and converted it into what are now the Burgh Buildings.

LAURENCEKIRK SCHOOL

At the beginning of 1920 Laurencekirk Public School was housed in
three different buildings — the main building at the north end of the
town (to which science, domestic science and woodwork rooms had
been added in 1912), the old 'Pisky school', which housed two classes,
and the infant school, halfway down the High Street which housed
(and indeed still houses) the two infant classes. The post-primary
department of the school at that time was merely an 'Advanced
Division'. Parents who wanted secondary education for their children
had to send them to Stonehaven or Montrose. Agitation for a higher
grade department at Laurencekirk started early in the century. In
response to local demand, the Education Authority decided in 1920 to
make Laurencekirk a Higher Grade School, and it began functioning
as such in August 1923. In 1933 five classrooms, two staff-rooms, a

headmaster's room and a clinic were added to the main buildings, and the two classes at the 'Pisky school' were transferred to the 'big school'. Two years later four additional classrooms and a gymnasium were built, and the four antiquated classrooms of the old building were converted into a dining-hall and rooms for art and technical subjects. A Horsa hut with two additional classrooms was built in 1949. Plans for the building of two new science rooms and two domestic science rooms have been approved; and an additional classoom at the infant school to accommodate the increased number of children now entering school — the effect of the post-war bulge in the birth-rate — is also to be built shortly.

Today Laurencekirk Junior Secondary School (it has been so called since 1939) has about 450 pupils on its roll, 200 of them in the secondary department. The policy of the Kincardineshire Education Committee being to centralise post-primary education, the secondary department at Laurencekirk has steadily grown over the past twenty years, as the rural primary schools have ceased to keep children beyond the age of 12. Of the pupils in the secondary department about 40% are from the parish of Laurencekirk; the remaining 60% are from the neighbouring parishes of Marykirk, Garvock, Fettercairn and Fordoun. The majority of pupils in the primary department are from the parish of Laurencekirk. The school has a staff of 20, of whom 9 are graduates. The headmaster and the principal science teacher are honours graduates.

SECONDARY DEPARTMENT

When they enter the secondary department, at the age of 12, the pupils are divided into three classes, 'A', 'B' and 'C', on the basis of teacher's estimates and the results of the County Promotion examination, which is now based on the results of two standardised tests of intelligence, standardised attainment tests in English and arithmetic, a test in problem arithmetic, and a test in composition. Parents' wishes are also taken into consideration. The 'A' class (12 to 18 in number) takes a literary course, which in addition to the core subjects includes one compulsory foreign language (French) and either Latin or Commercial Subjects. Pupils can proceed at the end of the three-year course to a senior secondary school. The average number who do so is 5. Of these 5, perhaps one will proceed to university. The 'B' class (about 30 pupils) does no foreign language. The boys take a full technical course, with Mathematics and Technical Drawing, and the girls a full Domestic Science course. It is also possible for pupils to proceed from this course to a continuation of their studies in a senior secondary school at the end of their third year. For the 'C' class, the duller pupils (numbering over 30), the course consists of the basic subjects, plus science with a rural bias, i.e. gardening for the boys and domestic science for the girls. Visits to farms and industrial undertakings have been made an integral part of the courses for 'B' and 'C' pupils.

On leaving school, the majority of the boys go to agricultural jobs. Some go to local tradesmen. An increasing number, however, are now going to the pre-apprenticeship school in Aberdeen. Of the girls, a proportionately large number go to the nursing school. Some go to commercial schools or directly into offices. A decreasing number are going in for domestic service. A few go to Craibstone, and thence to work in dairies, the school meals' service, canteens, etc. Craibstone is sometimes the finishing school for the farmer's daughter in preparation for her entry to the marriage market.

ATTITUDE OF PARENTS

The present headmaster is trying to foster a closer relationship between the school and the community it serves. Parents' days are held once a year, and the parents see the school under normal working conditions; the school produces an annual concert in the St Laurence Hall; and since 1950 there has been a local magazine, edited by senior pupils, to which children from every class in the school contribute. It is hoped to start a parent-teacher association in the near future. The majority of parents in the parish (at least 95%) appreciate the value of education. Though some were hostile to the raising of the school leaving age in 1947, most of them now accept the extra year. An increasing number of pupils are now staying at school to complete the three-year course. All the 'A' stream and most of the 'B' stream complete the course, but about 60% of the 'C' stream leave as soon as they reach the age of 15.

SCHOOL MEALS

Laurencekirk has been, since 1946, the centre of a School Meals' Service which daily provides meals for 800 pupils, distributed over 12 schools in the parishes of Laurencekirk, Garvock, Fettercairn, Fordoun and Marykirk. The meals are prepared in a central kitchen, situated near the infant school and manned by a staff of 7 under a supervisor. Two motor-vans deliver the food in insulated containers to the schools.

REDMYRE SCHOOL

Near the north-eastern boundary of the parish stands Redmyre School, a primary school with 74 pupils on its roll at present, under a headmaster and 2 assistant teachers. It was opened in December 1875 to cater for the educational needs of children living in the north-eastern part of the parish of Laurencekirk, the village of Fordoun, and the south-eastern part of the parish of Fordoun, and neighbouring parts of the parishes of Arbuthnott and Glenbervie. Today it still draws its pupils from these four parishes. Before this school was built pupils in this part of the county attended a school at Waterlair in the parish of Garvock, which had been established by the Free Church. The population of the school varies with the migrations of farm workers from, and into, the area: for instance, the numbers in the top class have varied from 5 to 14. At the end of their primary course the majority of pupils go to Laurencekirk Junior Secondary School. Occasionally, a pupil who shows promise of benefiting from a senior secondary course proceeds direct to Mackie Academy, Stonehaven.

LOCAL DIALECT

During and since the war years the population of Laurencekirk has changed considerably. It is difficult to say, without actual statistics, where all the newcomers have come from, but one is fairly safe in saying that a majority of those who have come into this parish in the last 25 years have come from the north, especially Aberdeenshire. Certainly most of the incoming shopkeepers and farmers have come from the north. Both in the burgh and in the rural part of the parish one frequently hears what the *Scottish National Dictionary* calls Mid-Northern Scots dialect, the dialect of Aberdeen, Banff, Moray and Nairn, in contradistinction to South Northern Scots, the dialect of Mearns and Angus. In the dialect of the Mearns boots are 'buits'; shoes are 'schune'; moon is 'mune' and good is 'gude', whereas in the dialect of Aberdeenshire the corresponding equivalents are 'beets'; 'sheen'; 'meen' and 'gweed'. The latter are not infrequently heard in the parish today. Speakers of pure Mearns dialect are not easy to find: indeed, the searcher has difficulty in finding men and women over 70 who have spent all their lives in the parish. Altogether, the community is becoming more and more mixed, and this commingling of people from different airts, together with the influence of education, radio and cinema, is leading to a rapid decay of the local dialect. In addition, this mixture of people is having its effect on the community-life of the burgh, since many incomers do not have the same interest in, and attachment to, Laurencekirk as persons born and bred in the parish.

SOCIAL LIFE

Ease of travel by bus, train and motor-car, machine-made amuse-ments, the decay of religious belief, indeed the general intellectual climate of the 20th century, have had a marked effect upon the social life of Laurencekirk. The keen community spirit of the 19th century and first two decades of the 20th is no more. Community spirit manifests itself only sporadically and is seldom sustained; or it tends to express itself only in the activities of certain groups within the community. Seldom is it an expression of the life of the whole community. The Laurencekirk of Victorian and Edwardian times was much more of a self-contained community. Families were larger, and family spirit stronger. The town made its own amusements: it had a thriving Mutual Improvement Association, a town band, and a choral society; it evinced a strong interest in municipal politics, especially the deliberations of its Town Council and its School Board which, in the years before the First World War, were reported in great detail in the local paper. Today families are smaller; not more than eight families in the burgh have more than five children. The family goes out as a unit much less frequently than it used to do, even as late as the 20s. Some local associations show strong signs of life, but usually they owe their vitality to the enthusiasm and leadership of older folks in the burgh, not on the whole to the younger folk. This is partly due to the fact that for many years now Laurencekirk has been losing its ablest sons and daughters who, when they reach adolescence, tend to migrate to urban areas where vocational opportunities are greater; but even more potent factors in producing the rather passive attitude of the youth in the burgh today are the causes listed at the outset of this paragraph. Interest in local politics is at a low ebb at present. In the past two years (1951 and 1952) there has been no municipal election in Laurencekirk. This year the Town Council had to coopt two citizens to fill vacancies on the Council.

CLUBS AND SOCIETIES

One or two societies in the town are still strong. The local Masonic Lodge, which dates from 1775, has 247 members. A branch of the Townswomen's Guild has been active since 1934, and today has a membership of between 50 and 60. In 1952 the Howe o' the Mearns Horticultural and Industrial Society was revived after 13 years of inactivity and held the first show of its new career in August of that year. It will undoubtedly continue. Until the late 30s this Society ran the Laurencekirk Highland Games on the same day as their annual Flower Show. There is, however, little prospect of their being revived. The Laurencekirk Lodge of the Loyal Order of Ancient Shepherds (founded 1893), though it has an adult membership of 219 and a juvenile membership of 76, has ceased to make the contribution to the social life of the village it used to make in pre-war days, and is now little more than a collecting institution. One notable development of the post-war years was the formation in 1946 of an Old Men's Club to bring together the over-seventies in the burgh. At its inception it had a membership of 40, but many of the original members have died and their places have not been filled by others, so that today the membership has fallen to 15. The Club meets each afternoon in the old Council Chamber during the winter months, and in the Pavilion at the Memorial Park during the summer, to play dominoes or cards or simply enjoy each other's company. The community from time to time shows some concern for its old folks. Local business men club together to give the Old Men's Club an annual outing and the Townswomen's Guild give an annual party to the ladies in the burgh over 60.

A link between the burgh and the landward parts of the parish was forged in 1945 by the formation of the Howe o' the Mearns Agricultural Club. Its aims are: to bring together master and man in a sociable way; to foster agricultural education among the farming community of the Howe; and to provide a round table for the discussion of topics of interest to agriculturalists. Its committee, which is elected annually, consists of 12 members representative of farmers, farm workers and people interested in agriculture in the town of Laurencekirk and the parishes of Laurencekirk, Garvock, Fordoun, Marykirk and Fettercairn. The majority of the lectures and debates are on agricultural topics (these always excite the strongest interest) but occasionally a distinguished speaker who is not an agriculturalist is invited to talk about his own special subject, e.g. 'Modern Education', 'Art', 'Public Speaking', 'Plastics' (to cite one or two of the topics from syllabuses of recent years). Though the initial enthusiasm for the club has waned, it still had 87 members on its roll in session 1950-51.

YOUTH ORGANISATIONS

Among youth organisations in the burgh the Boy Scouts, Girl Guides, Wolf Cubs and Brownies have had fairly continuous histories since the end of the First World War. The present Boy Scout troop, with four patrols and a strength of 26, meets weekly in the Scout Hut at the foot of Garvock Hill. The Girl Guide Company is meanwhile 22 strong, and has three patrols; it meets every Tuesday in the school gymnasium. Both the Scouts and the Guides have annual camps. The Brownies and Wolf Cubs are 25 and 20 in number respectively. During the war years a Youth Club was formed in the burgh, but it died out a year or two ago for want of an enthusiastic leader. One other activity deserves to be noted here, though it does not fall under the heading of youth organisations. It is the annual children's concert or pantomime produced by one or two enterprising local ladies.

DRAMA AND MUSIC

Laurencekirk had a Dramatic Society before the First World War, but records of its productions have not been kept. The present Dramatic Society began its life after that war, and has kept going except during the Second World War and the immediate post-war years. In the 20s it was doing *Mains Wooin*, *The Kye Amang the Corn*, etc., but it has given up 'kailyaird comedy'. In 1951 it presented *The Strange Case of Blondie White*. Before the First World War Laurencekirk had a choral society. In the early 20s some of its members and others came together to form the Laurencekirk Musical Society which for several years, under the capable direction of an ex-member of the D'Oyly Carte Opera Company, gave an annual performance of a Gilbert and Sullivan opera. Later, under another producer, the Society ventured further and produced *Lilly of Killarney*, *Maritana*, etc. The Society went out of existence before the last war, and has not been revived.

RECREATION

Laurencekirk has a thriving Bowling Club, with about 70 members, ten of them ladies. Bowling has had a strong following in the burgh since the 90s. Today, however, it has become a young men's as well as an old men's game. This is partly due to the fact that Laurencekirk no longer has either a golf or a cricket club. Prior to the recent war there was a golf club, which played over a nine-hole course on Garvock Hill. This was ploughed up and reseeded during the war. Unfortunately local interest was not sufficiently keen to revive the club. Now it is defunct, its pavilion demolished, and its course a grazing ground for cross-Highland cattle. The few remaining golfers go to Edzell, Montrose or Brechin for a game. Before the Second World War the town had a cricket team, but so far no attempt has been made to revive it. On the other hand, interest in football is still keen, and the town gives strong support to its juvenile team, West End, and its junior team, St Laurence. The teams play during both the winter and summer months.

One thriving recreational activity of the winter months is a Scottish country dancing class, run by a local school teacher. It has nearly 50 members. The youth of the parish usually turn up in large numbers to Saturday night dances in the St Laurence Hall, especially if the dance-band is a well-known one. Modern ballroom dancing predominates in the programme, but a few Scottish country dances are generally included. The majority of the young folk, however, seldom do these dances as they should be done. Quite often the Eightsome Reel and the Dashing White Sergeant amount to little more than 'birling', i.e.

swinging and yet more swinging. There is little art about the dancing; many youths seem intent only on trying to swing their partners off their feet.

The local cinema, opened in 1916 in the building which up till 1913 had been the local Congregational Church, is well patronised. Two shows are given each Wednesday, Friday and Saturday. There is a different programme on each of these nights. The building has seats for 234. The average attendance per evening (i.e. two shows) is about 300. Of these about 60 are children. Laurencekirk has had 'talkies' since 1931.

THE FUTURE

What of the future of Laurencekirk? In the days when it was a growing village an unknown Aberdeen professor penned the rhyme:

> Frae sma' beginnings Rome of auld
> Becam' a great imperial city,
> 'Twas peopled first, as we are tauld,
> By bankrupts, vagabonds, banditti.
> Quoth Tammas, 'Then the time may come
> When Laurencekirk will equal Rome.'

Doubtless the satire of the professor's lines is more apparent today than perhaps it was to the local inhabitants when it was written. Laurencekirk is still a very small town — small enough indeed to be frequently designated a village. It is probable that the downward trend in the population both of the burgh and of the landward parts of the parish is now at an end, and that the population figure will remain about 1900. No industrial developments are likely in the burgh itself. There is little likelihood that farms in the parish will be amalgamated into large farms of 1,000—2,000 acres, unless perhaps a wave of adversity hits the farming industry. This is improbable, since the nation seems to have realised that it needs everything that the land can produce. The Mearns farmer today, like his fellow-farmers elsewhere in the kingdom, can look to the future with a sense of security he did not have in the past. For the past twelve years he has prospered. It is to be hoped that in their prosperity the farmers of the parish will not forget that the prosperity of the burgh depends in no small measure on their continuing to spend their money in it.

August 1952

THE PARISH OF MARYCULTER

by James Irvine-Fortescue of Kingcausie

NAME

It is well established that the name *CULTER*, spelled *CULTYR* in the 14th century, is geographical in origin, deriving from the Gaelic *CU'L-TIR*, the 'back land', that is, for a person travelling north from the Howe of the Mearns, the land lying behind the low outrunner of the Grampians which forms the southern boundary of the parish of Maryculter. The division of the district into the two parishes of Peterculter and Maryculter, separated by the river Dee, dates from an arbitration of the year 1287, when permission was granted for the Templar Chapel of St Mary to be used as the parish church of those persons living on the Templars' lands south of the river. Thus it is the footnote, not the text, on page 189 of the Kincardineshire volume of the *New Statistical Account* that is correct.

BOUNDARIES

These have remained unchanged for centuries, apart from the addition to the parish of approximately 44.2 acres lying to the north-east of Mains of Maryculter — the Inch of Culter — which was formerly part of Culter estate within the Shire of Aberdeen. Due to the river changing course to the north, the Inch had become isolated, and the draft order made by the Boundary Commissioners under the Local Government (Scotland) Act 1880 transferring the land from Aberdeenshire to Maryculter parish in Kincardineshire took effect on 15th May 1892.

CLIMATE

Of recent years there has been a tendency for the winters to become milder, but the severe frosts of the winter of 1981-82 caused considerable damage to water pipes. The prevailing winds are south east and south west, which is why the great (north-west) gale of 1953 caused such devastation to woodlands in the parish. The Dee was frozen over in the winter of 1896-97.

HYDROGRAPHY

The river Dee is still subject to sudden floods, the worst since the Muckle Spate of 4th August 1829 being that of 25th January 1937 when the carriageway of Maryculter bridge was under four feet of water at the height of the flood, the 6600 volt electricity cable suspended under the bridge was severed, and the central piers seriously damaged. The farmer at Inchferry lost all his pigs and the cottage at Waterside was flooded to the eaves.

The Dee has changed its course *ex adverso* Maryculter several times during the last 300 years. Already by 1774 the Inch of Culter had become separated from Culter estate and joined to the south bank. The Kingcausie (Powberry) Island has expanded greatly to the north in the last 50 years, and the river has cut through a long section of the protective embankment and is steadily moving towards the heugh at Mains of Murtle. The Ewe Haugh, an island until after 1850, had already become joined to the north bank by 1902, but still remains part of Blairs estate. The Inch of Auchlunies, now called the Inch of Heathcot, an island in 1774, had become joined to the north bank by 1850 and is now part of Bieldside golf course (Deeside Golf Club) though remaining within Maryculter parish.

SOILS AND GEOLOGY

The remarks in the previous accounts are still valid. There is much evidence of the last glaciation including large deposits of boulder clay, random boulders and the terminal moraines of small streams. One of the latter near the confluence of the Blaikiewell and Crynoch burns, was long known locally as 'Pestie Knap', because it was believed to mark the site of a cottage all of whose inhabitants had died of the plague, after which the local population covered the whole building with stones and earth to seal off the infection.

PLACE NAMES AND FOLKLORE

The farm of North Burnside used to be called 'Scushelgutter' — was this the place where lint was 'scutched'? On the site of the modern house named Blair Crynoch stood an ancient red-tiled cottage with clay walls known as Futtret Neuk. There were many futtrets (weasels) living in the drystane dykes near the cottage but local gossip would have it that the cottage was so named because its inhabitant had a face like a futtret. The small farm of Pamphle Mou (Pinfold Mouth) was inhabited in the early 1800s by one Andrew Cadenhead who had the 'second sight'; he used to tell how, on the night of the full moon, the fairies would come down the chimney and dance on his hearthstone.

HISTORICAL MONUMENTS

Antiquities in the parish are few. The stones on the farm of Standing Stones, and the boundary stones inscribed with the Cross of the Knights Templar referred to in an early 15th century description of the boundaries of the parish, have unfortunately all disappeared, though a rock which formed the base of one of the latter can still be seen just above the 500 foot contour beside the dyke which forms the western boundary of the Clochandighter plantation. The foundations of the Templars' Chapel of St Mary which served as the parish church from the middle of the 16th century until the present church was built in 1787 remain, as do those of the Templars' mill dam across the Crynoch Burn, restored in 1637. The 16th century building at Templars' Park which now houses the Scout Headquarters, incorrectly believed by some to have been the old manse of Maryculter, was simply an estate house of the Menzies family, the old manse having been demolished in 1762, when the 18th century manse (demolished in 1972) was built at the rear of the present manse. The original church bell cast in 1786 which fell in 1896 and was cracked, reportedly after violent ringing for a funeral, is preserved on a plinth near the door of the church hall. The war memorial in the churchyard commemorates sixteen men of the parish who gave their lives in the First World War and four killed in the Second World War. Mention must also be made of an ancient chapel site on Blairs estate, adjacent to Craigingles (CREAG EAGLAIS = Chapel crag) Wood. The drystane and lime-pointed dykes with triangular or square dressed stone copes on the farm of Swellhead built in the 1830s and 1840s by workmen from Fife are noteworthy.

The parish church was enlarged in 1882 by the addition of an organ transept on the south side which contains four double stained glass windows presented by Mr A.J. Kinloch of Park and Altries in 1887 in memory of his wife. The pulpit was presented by the widow of Mr Alexander Gordon of Fyvie and Maryculter in 1886, and the communion table in 1908 in memory of Mr A.J. Kinloch by his family. The present church bell, purchased from Messrs Mears and Stainbank of London in 1896 at a cost of £15.12.0 plus carriage 10/- was unfortunately found on arrival to have been inscribed, without reference to the Kirk Session, with the words 'Sancta Maria, Ora pro nobis'. The Session minute briefly records that 'the Session disappro-

Plate 12. At work in the stackyard, possibly at Uras, around 1900. (*Photo: By permission of the National Museums of Scotland*).

Plate 13. An aerial view of Catterline: a traditional cliff-top fishing village. (*Photo: By permission of Van Werninck Studio, Montrose*).

Plate 14. The opening of the Inverbervie paddling pool in 1959. (Photo: By permission of Clark Photographers, Laurencekirk).

ved, and agreed that the objectionable inscription should be erased'. Mr Kinloch, after ascertaining that no harm would come to the bell by the deletion, arranged for the erasure by a workman from Messrs Shirras and Laing of Aberdeen. In 1939 two tablets commemorating the Rev. George Ogilvie and and Rev. William Selbie were removed from the Free church when it was dismantled and affixed to the south wall of the parish church. Five volumes of the Session records covering the period 1719-1907 were deposited for safe custody in the Register House in Edinburgh in 1964.

MANSION HOUSES

Of the four mentioned in the 1833 account, Maryculter is now a public house and restaurant; Kingcausie was embellished in 1853 by the addition of wings, dormer windows and an oriel to the designs of David Bryce; Heathcot, which for some years served as a hydropathic establishment, was demolished and replaced by a modern house in the late 1950s; and Auchlunies, which was purchased from the Duguid family in 1970 by the church benefactor James Nicol of Clashfarquhar and given to the Church of Scotland, is now sub-divided into four flats.

The main portion of Altries House, seat of the proprietors of that estate, was built in 1840, with later additions. Shannaburn and Kincairn (formerly Marybank) date from the 1850s. Apart from farmhouses which, with the exception of a few older structures such as Eastland, date mostly from the 1870s and 1880s, houses of any importance are modern. There are twenty buildings of architectural and historic interest, eleven in Category B and nine in Category C(S). There are no ancient monuments, and there are nine archaeological sites identified by the Grampian Regional Council archaeologist

It may be mentioned that, of the five sub-divisions of the Hospitallers' lands made in 1535, only Kingcausie remains in the hands of the descendants of the original proprietors, having been passed on in unbroken succession for fourteen generations.

The letters from James VI to Sir John Boswell of Balmuto, and the portrait of Sir John's grandfather, David Boswell of Balmuto (1498-1582), painted in 1578, referred to at page 806 of the *New Statistical Account* of Fifeshire 1845 (Kinghorn Parish), are preserved at King-causie. For a list of the most important documents preserved at Kingcausie, see National Register of Archives (Scotland) NRA (Scot.)/801. Many of the Blairs archives are preserved in the Scottish Catholic Archives at Columba House, 16 Drummond Place, Edinburgh, and the library is now in the National Library of Scotland on a long-term loan basis.

R

ZOOLOGY AND ORNITHOLOGY

As stated in the *New Statistical Account*, there is a considerable population of roe deer in the Kingcausie and Blairs woods. Foxes have reappeared in recent years, after a long absence, and two badgers were caught in fox snares on the farm of Blaikiewell some years ago. The rabbit population, formerly very numerous, is at present well under control, due firstly to the outbreak of myxomatosis in the early 1950s and, secondly, to the intensive follow-up action taken by the Maryculter and Banchory Devenick Rabbit Clearance Society — the second to be formed in Scotland — which is unfortunately no longer in being due to the ill-advised action by the Government in terminating the grant to such societies. A red deer stag which had strayed from higher ground was shot at Kingcausie in 1922 and another in 1957. Grey squirrels, formerly unknown in the parish, have appeared in recent years, possibly escapees from the now defunct Aberdeen Zoo, and for a time red squirrels almost disappeared. Both species, however, appear now to be living quite happily together and even interbreeding.

Before the Great Gale of 1953, a few pairs of capercailzie bred in the old Scots Pine wood of Kingcausie (= Ceann-Guithsaich, Pinewood head or end) but have now moved elsewhere. For many years three or four pairs of herons nested in high larches in the same wood. After the gale, the birds moved down the hill and nested in old beech trees, but these were unfortunately too accessible to egg hunters, and the nests were abandoned. Herons have now taken refuge on the Kingcausie Island in the Dee where they are reasonably safe until after the nesting period. A wide variety of low ground resident and migrant birds are present in the parish; there has been a considerable increase in the number of jays and magpies in recent years; among the more unusual birds in the district may be mentioned the green woodpecker (nesting at Kingcausie for the past ten years), the goldfinch and the blackcap. Kestrels, sparrowhawks and owls are quite common, and the buzzard has been seen occasionally. Kingfishers breed beside the river.

BOTANY

Paris quadrifolia and *Gymnocarpium dryopteris* (oak fern) still grow in the woods of Kingcausie, as does *Arum maculatum*, believed to have been introduced by the Knights Hospitallers, but the Linnaea has not been noted for some years. Corbie Den was a 'classic' botanical locality close to Aberdeen and was well-known and well-worked by academic botanists and amateurs from the Aberdeen Working Men's Natural History and Scientific Society in the nineteenth and early twentieth centuries. The Den was noted as one of the most eastern lowland localities for upland plants. It also possessed the relatively rich, ungrazed flora of humid gorges, and the surrounding woodland appears to be an intact ancient wood though much modified by planting. This belief is supported by a recent study of seedbanks in the area, when it was found that Corbie Den lacked any clear indicator of previous land use. The other important sites within the parish are the ash-alder-willow woods of the river Dee and the Kingcausie Island, the latter also celebrated for its lupins. Readers are referred to William MacGillivray's *Natural History of Deeside and Braemar* and George Dickie's *The Botanist's Guide to the Counties of Aberdeen, Banff and Kincardine* (1860).

AGRICULTURE

At the time of the last statistical account in 1833, the parish was divided between five estates, Auchlunies, Heathcot (formerly part of Auchlunies), Blairs, Kingcausie and Maryculter. In 1839 the greater part of Maryculter estate was sold to Mr James Kinloch's Trustees and renamed Altries. Apart from two home farms retained in the hands of the proprietors, all the farms in the parish were let on the landlord and tenant system, the customary six-course shift — oats, turnips, barley or oats undersown with grass seeds, followed by three years in grass — being strictly adhered to in accordance with estate regulations. The years after the 1923 Agricultural Holdings (Scotland) Act witnessed a gradual relaxation of this practice. With the slump of the early 1930s came bankruptcies and the break-up of Maryculter estate, with the new phenomenon of the owner-occupier. Some of the land was sold for as little as £10 per arable acre. Grazing rents fell to rock bottom. In 1933 a sixteen acre field at Kingcausie let for £2.00 — or 12½ new pence per acre — for the six months' grazing period May to October. (In the post war boom of 1920-21 grazing rents reached as high as £10 to £12 per acre).

With World War II came the compulsory breaking-up of grass parks and old grass on the poorer farms under the direction of the Agricultural Executive Committee, a case of 'up corn, down horn'. Meat rationing was inevitable until livestock herds were re-built after the war. Prior to 1952 a number of farms on the estate of Altries were sold to the sitting tenants. According to the current valuation roll, there are now 24 owner-occupiers including one mink farm. In addition, the farm of Millbank is now devoted to rose nurseries, and the lower valley of the Crynoch Burn has been converted to a 'story book glen' with the aid of a £50,000 grant from the Scottish Tourist Board, thus curtailing the area available to wild life. The number of tenanted farms is 17. According to the Department of Agriculture, in June 1982 there were 38 'statistically significant' holdings in the parish;

the discrepancy with the valuation roll total of 42 holdings (above) presumably arises from holdings farmed together. These 38 holdings are subdivided, according to the new European Economic Community classification, into 19 less favoured area farms (one sheep and cattle, thirteen mainly cattle and five cattle and arable), one cropping, two dairy farms, one intensive horticulture and fifteen part- and spare-time holdings. There was a tendency in the 1950s for estate proprietors to take land into their own hands; with the easing of restrictions on rent increases this situation may be reversing itself, though there are exceptions. Fiscal considerations have a considerable influence in landowners' and farmers' decisions. A good deal of the land suitable for cattle rearing has been put down to grass, and until recently there were three cattle dealers with substantial businesses active in the parish. However, while the land is mainly regarded as suitable for cattle rearing, one farmer has successfully cultivated winter barley on quite a large scale. This crop was formerly thought to be unsuitable for the district and it remains to be seen whether others will follow this lead. The advent of mains water has enabled many field drinking troughs to be installed; formerly water had to be carted to a number of fields. Turnips for stock feed still represent more than 10% of the land in crop; sheep in relation to cattle are relatively few. There has been a sharp decline in the number of men working full-time on the land; this is partly due to mechanisation (work horses have practically disappeared within the last forty years) but mainly to the fact that the farmers' returns have not been keeping pace with the compulsory increases in agricultural wages.

The 19th century witnessed a large scale reclamation of waste ground in Maryculter, notably John Irvine-Boswell's reclamation of the Bog of Swellhead in 1834-1841, for which he received the Gold Medal of the Royal Highland and Agricultural Society.

George Robertson (*A General View of the Agriculture of Kincardineshire or the Mearns*, London and Edinburgh, 1813) says (p.311) 'This great proportion of wastes (being 3 parts in 7) should not raise very sanguine hopes of a speedy subjugation by culture were it not that the energetic exertions of the husbandmen in that quarter may lead us to expect anything. Having already brought much of their present arable land from a state of the most forbidding sterility into a high state of production; these hardy *stony-culturists* will not long suffer a reclaimable waste to exist'.

Robertson gives the following figures for cropping and livestock in Maryculter in 1807:—

Wheat	1	Milch Cows	200
Bear (bere)	145	Calves reared	160
Oats	642	Draught oxen	20
Peas	8	Other cattle	540

Turnips	90		
Potatoes	24	Total cattle	920
Flax	2		
Gardens	14		
Sown grass	376	Riding horses	4
		Horses in husbandry	56
Total cultivated	1302	Foals reared	6
		Sheep	400
		Swine	6
Wood	350		
Improvable by Tillage	1502		
Waste	4619		
Total	7773	English acres	

By 1833, about 400 acres of this waste ground had been brought into cultivation. Robertson estimates (p.418) that in 1801 there were 696 persons either employed in or dependent on agriculture in the parish and only 13 in trade.

A French writer on agricultural subjects, Count Conrad de Gourcy, visited Maryculter in 1847, and there follows a translation from his little-known volume *Journal du second voyage agricole en Angleterre et en Ecosse*, Lyon, 1849. He writes (page 54):

Kingcausie extends to 2000 acres (about one half in Banchory Devenick parish), of which about a quarter has still to be reclaimed in order to become productive; this part is thin heathland covered with enormous stones or depressions which only afford the very poorest pasture. In order to reclaim the heath it is broken up by spade or pick, and stones are torn up and those that are too big to be moved are blown up with gunpowder, the large and medium stones being used for enclosure walls or farm buildings while the smaller ones are used for bottoming drainage trenches. The enclosure walls, four feet high without the cope-stones, cost three shillings a running yard if built with lime and sand; drystane walls with sand and lime coping cost one shilling a yard if the material is delivered to the site.

This reclamation work costs on average £16 an acre; the parts that are too stony or where the soil is too shallow are planted with conifers after draining but part of these plantations, planted without the land having been reclaimed sufficiently to destroy the iron pan which is always present in the subsoil of damp heathlands, is not thriving.

The complete draining of peaty marshes is a work of giants; the water channels must cross through the whole bed of the peat which is sometimes ten feet thick and they fill with water as soon as made. The peat has no firm base, so it is necessary to support it by means of planks or props, then the stones have to be brought which are to fill the bottom of the trench, and that becomes very costly; it would be better to replace then with strong terra cotta tiles (pipes). These peaty places have then got to be refilled with earth, preferably if possible of a clayey type. At the end of it all, very good meadows have been created, but at enormous cost.

Mr Boswell has already constructed nine farms; they replace about a hundred hovels which formerly housed as many miserable small farmers who, despite paying hardly any rent, frequently died of hunger and misery.

Each of these farms has cost between £600 and £1,200 to construct according to their importance. This estate was yielding an annual income of £250; it now produces ten times as much.

As Mr Boswell has put down the greater part of his land in hand to grass, he has now only eight very strong work mares of the Clydesdale breed: some of them are worth £60, because work horses are very dear because of the present railway construction works. It is said that they are worth fully 50% more than their price ten years ago; in addition, Mr Boswell rears three or four work colts every year. One of his mares twenty years old and still very fine and sound gave birth last year to a good colt foal. He told me that he had a foal from one mare when she was 28, and another from her the following year.

There follow detailed observations on farm livestock, cultivations, farm buildings and the improvements of neighbouring proprietors.

In 1834 the parish minister counted 34 farms and 36 crofts. According to the 1907-1908 valuation roll, with a slightly different classification, there were 48 farms and 29 crofts. The reduction to just over half that number of agricultural holdings today arises from amalgamations.

As a result of the continuing reclamation of waste ground throughout the 19th century, the land capable of being tilled or under rotation grass must have been by the early 1900s very similar to what it is today. The figures for the June 1982 agricultural return were as follows (hectares in brackets):

Wheat	Nil		Cattle	
Spring barley	784	(371·40)	Dairy cows in milk	134
Winter barley	49½	(20·00)	Dairy cows in calf	2

Oats	142¼	(57·60)	Dairy heifers in calf		12
Early potatoes	0¼	(0·10)	Dairy heifers for breeding		21
Main crop potatoes	16½	(6·70)	Beef cows in milk		479
Turnips, etc. for stock feed	123	(49·80)	Beef cows in calf		72
Kale and cabbage	6¾	(2·07)	Beef heifers in calf		67
Other crops for stock	22¼	(9·00)	Beef heifers for breeding		200
Rose and rose stocks	60	(24·30)	Bulls for service		16
Other nursery stock	2½	(1·00)	*Beef cattle*		
Bare fallow	5	(2·00)	2 years old—Male		279
Rotation grass			2 years old—Female		79
Under 5 years old:—			1 year old—Male		776
For mowing	785	(317·70)	1 year old—Female		849
Not for mowing	1527¾	(618·20)	Under 1 year—Male		457
			Under 1 year—Female		569
Sub-total	3524¾	(1426·50)	Total cattle		4012

			Sheep	
Grass over 5 years old			Breeding ewes	498
For mowing	591¼	(239·20)	Rams for service	28
Not for mowing	1031¾	(417·60)	Other sheep	781
Rough grazings	1022¾	(413·90)	Total sheep	1307
Woodland including shelter belts	94	(38·00)		
Roads, buildings, etc.	150¾	(61·00)		
Total	6415¼	(2596·20)	Pigs	4
			Poultry	197

Labour
Occupiers and spouses	37
Regular staff	52
Part-time, casual and seasonal workers	78

Glasshouses — 648 square metres.
There were also about 40 goats in the parish (not in the returns).

As is to be expected, due to sales off the grass of fat cattle and large stores and the fact that the majority of hill cows are spring calvers, fewer cattle are carried through the winter, the number of animals at December 1981 being 3,090. However the number of sheep at that time was 1,570.

The most striking change in the agriculture of the parish between 1807 and 1982 is the very large increase in the number of cattle ($4\frac{1}{2}$ times), made possible by the reclamation of waste ground which has also resulted in a more than trebling of the number of sheep, a 25% increase in cereals, a 30% increase in turnips but, significantly, a decrease in the acreage of potatoes. The message is clear: the land in the parish is much more suitable, on the whole, for livestock rearing than for growing cereals, and too poor for potatoes on any scale. In the words of a local: 'land on Deeside needs a shoor o' rain during the day and a shoor o' shite at necht'. If one assumes that in 1807 one-third of Robertson's figure of 376 acres was cut (by scythe) for hay, the acreage of grass conserved for winter keep in 1982 ($1376\frac{1}{4}$ acres of hay and silage) will be seen to have increased tenfold. Such an increase has only become possible through mechanisation. The items of farm machinery most commonly in use are tractors, often more than one per farm, tractor-mounted hydraulic loaders, general purpose elevators, mowers and silage cutters, but no separate machinery figures are available at parish level. The 1904 Ordnance Survey map shows no less than fifteen farm mill dams in the parish for storing water for driving threshing mills; these are no longer in use, having been superseded by the combine harvester.

As regards breeds of cattle, the Shorthorn was paramount in the 19th century, followed by the Aberdeen Angus. The Hereford became popular in the 1950s, and at the present time the Charolais has quite a following, with interest being shown also in other continental breeds — Simmental, Limousin, and Romagnolas. Galloway and Highland cattle are rather too slow maturing for this district.

The area of the parish given in the 1904 Ordnance Survey, 7978 acres, is believed to be correct, and is made up of 6415 acres per the 1982 agricultural returns, 1152 acres of forestry woodlands, about 120 acres of scrub and potential woodland, 142 acres of water and a balance of approximately 150 acres unaccounted for, including public roads and verges.

FISHINGS

There are now seven salmon fishings in the parish on the river Dee, the estate of Maryculter having been divided since the last statistical account, extending in all to six miles on the south or right bank of the river and approximately 3300 yards on the north bank. As noted in the previous accounts, fishing by net and coble was becoming uneconomic and by 1871, when the Dee Salmon Fishing Improvement Association was formed, most netting stations had closed down. Since that time, fishing in Maryculter has been entirely by rod and line and catches and financial returns have shown wide fluctuations, with a downward tendency in recent years. Two cases may be cited: at Kingcausie, 333 salmon were taken during the 1958 season, while the average for the same beat for the six years 1977-1982 was only 22 fish. At Altries 425 salmon were taken in 1963 and only 12 in 1973. Various factors account for this: sea netting by Greenlanders and Faroese and, more especially, off the Northumberland coast; intensified netting activity inside Aberdeen Harbour; disturbance of the estuary at the river mouth by shipping related to North Sea oil business; the advent of ulcerative dermal necrosis, a fatal salmon disease of unknown cause, in the 1960s; a tendency towards milder winters causing the salmon to run through to the middle and upper reaches; and, lastly, disturbance of the river bed due to the construction of four oil and gas pipelines between 1973 and 1982 and the rebuilding of Maryculter bridge, all causing silting of holding pools along the Maryculter river frontage. Increased extraction of water for Aberdeen city is almost certainly also a contributory factor.

It may be mentioned that in the three years 1980-1982 the Aberdeen Harbour nets took annually approximately eight times as many salmon and grilse as they did on average during the first decade of this century. On the other hand, despite a large increase in the number of anglers, the average total of fish taken on rod and line in the Dee has, if anything, declined, resulting in a diminution in the status of the whole Dee as one of the great salmon angling rivers. The effects of sewage entering the river at Banchory are negligible at Maryculter.

FORESTRY

The principal woodlands are situated in the eastern half of the parish where conditions are more favourable to the growth of timber than in the rather cold and hostile western corner. The total area under trees extends to approximately 1152 acres (466 hectares), of which 361 acres (146 hectares) belong to the Forestry Commission. The compulsory fellings of the two World Wars, followed by the Great Gale of 31st January 1953, in which approximately 250,000 cubic feet of timber were blown down on Kingcausie estate alone and considerable damage was done to the Blairs and Auchlunies woodlands, left the parish much denuded and presented a formidable re-stocking problem. The Forestry Commission plantations at 'Old Man' (Allt Monadh) wood were unaffected by the gale, being then only fifteen years old and well below the wind susceptible height. The replanting task has now been overtaken and the woodland area has not only been restored to its maximum size in the 19th century but a few additional acres have been planted. There has been a tendency to plant conifers rather than hardwoods. In the Forestry Commission sector (Auchlunies planted 1960-62, Old Man Wood 1938-40 with more recent planting under larch overstorey now mostly removed, and Tilbouries 1982) the proportions of species planted are Pines, mainly lodge pole, 24%, Spruces, mainly Sitka, 60%, Larches, mainly Japanese and Hybrid, 7%, Douglas Fir, Silver Fir and Western Hemlock 7%, and Hardwoods (Beech and Sycamore) 2%.

Already thinnings have been taken from the post-1953 plantings but the present market is very depressed, and a net return to the grower, after all expenses, of only 50 pence or 60 pence per tonne has been quite usual for several years. At this level there is no incentive either to thin woodlands or to plant. The advent of wood-burning stoves may result in a rather better return from disposals, but time will tell. Estate sawmills have long since ceased to be economic. The mean annual increment of the Sitka spruce plantations is about 12 cubic metres per hectare (135 hoppus feet per acre) and for pines approximatley 6 cubic metres per hectare. The traditional markets for fish boxes and pitprops have decreased steadily over the past two decades. The main markets today are for pulpwood, pallet wood and saw logs. The pulpwood is exported from the port of Montrose to Sweden, whilst the pallet wood and saw logs are converted at well equipped sawmills at Banchory and Aboyne. Plans are in hand for the development of larger processing facilities to meet the increasing quantities of timber becoming available from the large areas of post-war planting in the country generally.

It can be stated that the pattern of land use in the parish is now well-established, with agriculture claiming the better sites, whilst managed forestry plantations occupy those areas which are too steep or where the terrain is too rough for agricultural use. Apart from a small area of older beech at Auchlunies, all the Forestry Commission land was either rough grazing or felled woodland at the time of acquisition.

NOTES ON INDIVIDUAL SPECIES

Deciduous trees: Oak, Ash, Beech, Wych Elm, Norway Maple, Sycamore (known locally as Plane), Lime, Horse Chestnut, Holly, Hornbeam, Gean, Rowan, Hazel, Alder, Birch, Bird Cherry and various Willows have grown in the parish, in most cases for centuries. Among recent introductions may be noted a few specimens of *Nothofagus*, which appear to be growing well. A specimen of *N. obliqua* planted at Kingcausie in 1965 is now two feet four inches in girth at breast height and over forty feet high. Some fine beech planted around 1880 which survived the gale occupy the sides of the Shanna Burn at Auchlunies. These have been retained in the interest of amenity. Natural regeneration of Turkey oak occurs at Kingcausie.

Conifers: The European silver fir, *Abies pectinata (Abies alba)* introduced by John Irvine-Boswell in 1815, regenerates naturally and grows well in mixtures. The largest specimen blown in the 1953 gale measured 430 cubic feet. Since the gale, Sitka spruce, Douglas fir, Western hemlock, Thuya, Japanese and Hybrid larches, *Abies grandis* and *Abies nobilis*, have been planted in small stands and mixtures in the private woodlands. European larch has been grown since the 1790s; a tree of boatskin (the external planking of a wooden boat) quality measured 190 cubic feet in 1953. The Norway spruce has been grown for two hundred years; the Scots pine is indigenous. The yew hedges at Kingcausie, ascribed to the late 17th century, are noteworthy.

ECCLESIASTICAL STATE

The parish church is as described in the *New Statistical Account* except for the addition of an organ transept on the south and church hall on the north in 1882. A kitchen and toilet facilitiies were added in 1963. Burials in the churchyard, apart from those for existing lairholders, have ceased, and the cemetery below the manse, consecrated in 1938, has ample ground for the foreseeable future. Burials in the old churchyard beside the Dee ceased in 1906, apart from those of members of the heritors' families.

In 1972 the parish was linked with the adjacent parish of Banchory Devenick and as from 1st December 1982 a union of Maryculter and Cookney parishes (the latter geographically a part of Fetteresso) was approved by the Presbytery. In the last eighty years, while the Established Church roll has remained fairly constant at between 270 and 310 members, church attendances have slowly declined, but there are some signs that this trend is beginning to be reversed. As long ago as 1913, the Session minutes recorded that only 179 out of 270 members communicated that year, so poor church attendances are not a new feature. Following the Disruption of 1843, a Free Church and manse were built near the southern boundary of the parish. In the churchyard of the Established Church is a stone in memory of Alexander Cockie, servant at the manse for 43 years, who died on 19th February 1859 aged 71 years. Jervise (*Epitaphs and Inscriptions*, vol. II, page 124) writes: 'Sandy took a deep interest in church politics at the time of the Disruption; and the farmer of Whitestone (pronounced Fyte steen) having allowed the Free Church party to meet upon his premises, Sandy celebrated the event thus:—

There cam' a bletherin' f'uter
T' the parish o' Maryculter,
An' frae the Kirk he took a swarm
An' skeppit it in Fytie's barn.

However, as the farm of Whitestone was in the hands of the
proprietor, John Irvine-Boswell, in 1843, the writer thinks it more
probable that 'Fytie' refers to the farm at Whiteside, just over the hill
(Berry Top) from the Free kirk which was dismantled in 1939. The
farmer at the adjacent farm of Strypeside was known as 'Strypie'. But
these farms lie just south of the parish boundary. The majority of the
inhabitants of the parish belong to the Established Church. There are
thirteen wholly Roman Catholic families, and in seven other households at least one person is a member of that communion.

The Roman Catholic parish of St Mary's, Blairs (Diocese of
Aberdeen) includes the entire area of the civil parish (plus that of
Banchory Devenick and parts of Durris). It is distinct from Blairs
College, but its congregation has its own services at Blairs College
chapel, and a member of the College staff is appointed as part-time
parish priest. Its present roll is 71 including children.

Maryculter church is entirely self-supporting. In 1911, the annual
budget, excluding a stipend of £250 paid by the heritors, was under
£40. In 1982 the budget exceeded £7,000, and the stipend proposed
for 1983 for Maryculter-Cookney linked with Banchory Devenick
was £6,700 plus manse and car allowance, reflecting the inflation of
the last thirty years. A comparison between primary school rolls and
admissions to the church may have some validity despite the time lag
of four or five years between leaving the local school and joining the
church. From 1917 to 1963 young communicants averaged eight or
nine per annum, the primary school leavers about 14; from 1965 to
1981, out of ten primary school leavers annually, five or six joined the
Church of Scotland, so it would appear that the proportion of young
people joining the church has not varied appreciably in the last sixty
years, nor has the completion of secondary education outside the
parish affected the position. Church endowments include the Mollison
Trust for the provision of school prizes for religious education, and
the Burnett and Angus Fund and Kingcausie Mortification for the
relief of persons in need in the parish. However funds from the latter
were used in 1731 for the purchase of two silver communion cups, in
use today.

EDUCATION

The parochial school referred to in the *New Statistical Account* became
a school for boys only between the ages of 8 and 12 years in 1875 and

was finally closed in 1894. It was sold by public roup on 23rd October 1896 for £340 and has since remained a private house. Following the Education (Scotland) Act 1872 a School Board was elected in 1873, and after various meetings and discussions two new schools were planned. The West School and teacher's house were built in 1875 on land feued by Mr Kinloch of Altries near Pepperhillock at a cost, net of Government grant, of £521.4.3d. Miss Anderson, mistress of the girls' school at Stobhall (Mar Lodge), which had a roll of 36 in 1873, became the first teacher and the Stobhall School was closed. The East School was built in 1876 and Miss Jemima Stephen was appointed teacher from October in that year at a salary of £20 plus school fees, which averaged about ten shillings per pupil per annum plus half the small Government grant and a yearly cleaning allowance of £2.10.0. Outdoor pumps were installed at each school for the water supply. In November 1878 the school rolls were: Kirkton School 54, West School 49 and East School 38. In 1921 the rolls numbered 75 (East School) and 55 (West School) and declined to a low point of 23 (East School) and 31 (West School) in 1951, since when, helped by the post-war births, they have been on a gently rising trend. Since in 1833 there were 77 children in the parochial schools and 40 in the private elementary schools, it seems a reasonable deduction that the average family differed little in size from that time till 1921 but that since then families have become smaller. The present (1983) rolls are: East School — boys 16, girls 15, total 31, and West School — boys 18, girls 16, total 34, in both cases up to the age of 12. Secondary education has been continued at Cults Academy for the last five years and before that at Banchory and Mackie Academies after the closing of Port-lethen Secondary School in 1969. It seems probable that when the projected new Portlethen Academy is completed, secondary education for Maryculter children will again be afforded there. An extension was built at the West School in 1979.

It appears from the schoolboard minutes that in the 1870s and 1880s considerable difficulty was experienced in getting all the children of school age to attend school. Thus in 1879, out of 194 children in the parish of school age, 69 were not attending school. Due to strenuous efforts by the inspector, the number of non-attenders was reduced to 56 one year later, and to 47 by 1882. Out of that 47, 12 children under 13 were already working. Non-attendance was partly due to the inability of some parents to pay the fees. From the school minute books it is possible to trace the gradual improvement in conditions. Illnesses, including a number of cases of diphtheria, were a problem in the 1920s and 1930s. Nurses' visits were commenced in 1938, and dental inspections soon after. At the outbreak of war 15 evacuees from Dundee and two from Edinburgh were accommodated in the East School but these did not stay long in the parish. The school meals service commenced in 1946. Electricity was installed to both schools in

1954. Educational instruction at Blairs College is noted under that heading.

THE BLAIRS ESTATE

The estate of Blairs lies south of the river Dee with the exception of the 8 hectare (22 acre) Ewe Haugh in the bend of the river's older course. It marches with Kingcausie to the west and with Auchlunies and several smaller properties to the east. Its highest point, in Craigingles Wood, is 155m (510 feet) above sea level.

Since 1827 Blairs has been in the hands of Trustees holding it for the Roman Catholic Church in Scotland to provide education for candidates for the priesthood. Blairs College, the raison d'etre and administrative centre of the estate, has a granite boarding school building (opened 1897) of three storeys, three-quarters of a kilometre south of the river, a fine neo-Gothic church with a spire (1901) and a small burial ground and, now used for recreational purposes, a section of the former college (1829-1897) which incorporates the mansion-house of John Menzies ('Menzies of Pitfodels') (1756-1843) who donated the estate. About ten hectares (25 acres) including tennis courts are used as sports grounds near the College building. A walled garden of 1.5 hectares (3½ acres), now partly in rough pasture but with some fine fruit trees, was laid out by Menzies.

The crofts of Strypeside and Cannycreich were long ago combined with Kintewline and Maidenfold respectively. The latter was in turn recently incorporated into the home farm, which has 131 hectares (315 acres) under cultivation, and a herd of 120 dairy and 50 beef cattle (including calves). Five home farm workers (three full time) occupy estate houses.

There are four other (tenanted) farms or smallholdings, viz. Greenloaning (incorporating Merchants' Croft and Patonslaw), Kintewline, Fernybrae and Netherlands.

The Ewe Haugh is let as rough grazing.

One hundred and twenty hectares (300 acres) are forested, mostly under Forestry Commission control. A granite quarry within the southern margin of Craigingles Wood is leased out but has not been worked for many years.

The estate holds fishing rights over 1.5 km. of the right bank and a somewhat shorter length of the present left bank of the river Dee. By a riparian owners' agreement there is a limit of four rods. The rights to two rods are retained by the College for members or guests, and the remainder leased to a small syndicate. The average recorded annual catch is twelve salmon of average weight 10 lbs., and twenty sea-trout of average weight 2¼ lbs.

Fourteen houses are let to tenants. Three have special status under a

Land Court ruling. Four others have been feued to private owners and there is a small block of local authority housing on feued land near the East School. Some properties are only recently derelict, for example, Braeside Cottage, ¾ km. SSW of the College, which was occupied into the late 1960s; within the last eighty years nine have become uninhabitable.

The College has accommodation for 200 students, and a present roll of 110 boys of secondary school age, from all parts of Scotland. There is a resident staff of sixteen priests, fourteen of whom teach full-time. Attached to the College is a convent of seven Sisters of St Joseph of Annecy who assist, one as a full-time teacher, the rest with domestic work. Two full-time and four part-time teachers, two full-time maintenance men, and some twenty-five other part-time (mainly catering or cleaning) staff are non-resident. The College's water supply is piped from its own springs; this is now supplemented, in emergency, from the Regional mains, and was formerly supplemented from the river Dee; an iron pipeline and a small pump-house on the bank still exist. The home farm supplies milk and potatoes, and some vegetables and fruit in season come from the walled garden.

Perhaps half of the tenants can trace back their residence on the estate, if not in their present house, for several generations. The College as an educational establishment was housed from 1715 to 1799 at The Scalan, a property now maintained as a small museum, situated 2 km. above Chapeltown of Glenlivet in Banffshire, and families from 'The Braes' have, so to speak, followed the College to Deeside even into the present century. The estate revenues were originally sufficient to support the students; several tenants supplied their needs; Davidson at Salmon Croft was the shoemaker, another Davidson at Burnside the tailor, and the smithy opposite the lodge was repairing implements until 1967; indeed the present garage is the direct descendant, so to speak, of that business, and its owner is the son of that tenant. Part of the Smithy Croft has been absorbed into the home farm, but the croft house and the shop attached are leased to the local postmaster or postmistress, and at present this business functions as a flourishing 'village shop'.

LOCAL GOVERNMENT

The recommendation of the Royal Commission on Local Government in Scotland, Cmnd.4150, 1969 (the 'Wheatley Report') that the ancient county and Sheriffdom of Kincardineshire or the Mearns should be split between the North East (Grampian) Region with its centre at Aberdeen and the East (Tayside) Region with its centre at Dundee was made without adequate investigation at local level, Kincardine County Council not having even been visited by a

member of the Commission, and was strenuously opposed by the
local authorities, press and population. The effectiveness of the
opposition and the sound case put forward were recognised in the
ensuing Government White Paper Cmnd.4583, 1971, paragraph 47,
which states that 'the whole of the county looks to Aberdeen as its
regional centre.' However, despite the reference to the whole of the
county in the White Paper, the north Kincardine parishes of Nigg,
Banchory Devenick and Maryculter were shown in that document,
without any explanation given, as included not in Kincardine-Deeside
District but in Aberdeen City District. This arbitrary proposal, made
centrally without reference to local opinion, belied the lip service paid
to the concept of local democracy in both the Wheatley Report and
the White Paper, and was vigorously opposed by the Lower Deeside
District Council, comprising the three parishes affected, with the
backing of Kincardine County Council, the Member of Parliament
and the local electors. The arguments against the White Paper
proposal were set out in detail in a letter dated 26th April 1971 from
the District Clerk to the Secretary of the Scottish Development
Department, to which readers are referred. Following on a local
enquiry, the Secretary of State decided that the parishes of Maryculter
and Banchory Devenick should remain part of the Kincardine and
Deeside District, so the 'consistent philosophy of local democracy'
referred to in paragraph 4 of the White Paper was finally vindicated.
Had the District Council not been vigilant in their duties to the
electorate, this ill-conceived proposal would have gone through by
default.

The parishes of Maryculter and Banchory Devenick jointly elect a
District Councillor to the Kincardine and Deeside District Council,
and Maryculter sends five members to the North Kincardine Rural
Community Council which meets regularly and circulates a
newsletter.

PUBLIC AND SOCIAL SERVICES

A public water supply was introduced to Maryculter for the first time
in the late 1950s by the former Kincardine County Council, pumping
water, under agreement, from Aberdeen City to Clochandighter
Reservoir, from where it gravitated north and north-west in 3' and 4'
asbestos cement pipes. Up to that time water was available only from
individual private wells and springs, or from burns. At about the same
time Kincardine County Council commenced a regional water
scheme with a source on the Water of Dye and a treatment works
near the village of Strachan to supply the north east part of the
county. From 1968 to 1975 the North East of Scotland Water Board
was the statutory water undertaking for the area and completed a

Plate 15. A country postie on his rounds. (*Photo: Scottish Ethnological Archive, National Museums of Scotland*).

Plate 16. Clatterin' Brig, at the southern end of the Cairn o' Mount road. (*Photo: Scottish Ethnological Archive, National Museums of Scotland*).

Plate 17. Baiting the lines at Gordoun in the 1940s. (*Photo: by permission of* The Scotsman *and the National Museums of Scotland*).

Plate 18. A Farmtoun team.

network of 3', 4' and 6' P.V.C. and 12' spun iron (a type of wrought iron) pipes with tanks at Bogfon and Stranog. Water services are now administered by a department of Grampian Regional Council. There is no public drainage system within the parish, and each property is served by its own private tank. These can be emptied annually, free of charge if required, by the water services department.

In 1931 the parishes of Maryculter and Banchory Devenick were connected to the public electricity supply provided then by the Aberdeen Corporation electricity undertaking. It was reported in 1933 that 'the compulsory overhead and underground mains under the Department's special order (1930) have been laid down to Kirkton, Maryculter and are now available for supply in the district.' The distributing mains along the South Deeside road were completed in 1934 as far as Linn Park and in 1938 extended to a transformer at Tilbouries Lodge on the western boundary of the parish. The North of Scotland Hydro Electric Board took over responsibility for the supply of electricity to Maryculter parish in 1948, since when electricity has been taken to all premises requiring a supply. There are still a few older properties which have not yet been connected to the mains.

A high pressure gas main crosses the Dee at Maryculter bridge. Only two consumers are connected and bottled gas is used where required.

POSTAL SERVICES

There was a post office at Blairs smithy from 7 June 1869 and a second from 1895, first at Smithy Corner, Altries and then at North Lodge, Kingcausie from 1908 to 1977. The letter box at Kirkton bears the V.R. monogram. In the middle of the last century letters were collected weekly by private individuals on visits to Aberdeen from Farquharson's shop in the Castlegate. Later came deliveries by 'Postie' Mackenzie who went round the parish on horseback. Deliveries by bicycle were introduced during World War I, and by van when deliveries were transferred, temporarily, to Milltimber in 1956. There is a public telephone at Blairs, now the only post office in the parish.

The former police station at Ardoe is now a private house and the nearest stations are at Cammachmore and Peterculter.

COMMUNICATIONS

Until 1895 there was no bridge across the Dee between Aberdeen and Durris apart from the footbridge, Morrison's Bridge, known as the Shakkin Briggie, at Banchory Devenick, so communications were

mainly in an east and westerly direction up and down the Dee valley.
There were fords practicable only in low water in Tilbouries and just
below the confluence of the Crynoch Burn, and ferry boats at
Inchferry ('Boat Meg') and Blairs ('Ferry Bell'), the latter continuing
to the mid-1960s. Maryculter bridge was built to facilitate access to
Milltimber station on the Deeside railway. There was public transport
twice a day by open wagonette drawn by two horses on the South
Deeside road as far as Blairs until 1920. Strachan's Deeside Bus Service
was started in 1925. The motor car made its appearance in the early
1920s and by 1925 there were six or seven in the parish including a
taxi at the Mill Inn. Gigs and pony traps were used by the farming
community. The South Deeside turnpike road was completed in the
years 1837 to 1842, and the Netherley turnpike about the same time,
though certain sections of the former followed the route shown on
William Garden's map of 1774. By 1850 there were, in addition to just
over 8 miles of turnpikes, $14\frac{1}{2}$ miles of commutation roads. The roads
from Millbank to Smithy Corner and from Newlands to Redmire are
not shown on the commutation map of 1850 so they must have been
added to the list of highways at a later date, as were the private road
from Bogfon to Nether Muirskie in 1966, and the short link road at
Backmains of Altries in 1967. With these exceptions, the roads remain
as they were in the middle of the last century, apart from the re-
alignment in the 1930s at Altries bridge. The Maryculter bridge was
re-decked with a wider carriageway in 1972. It remains to be seen
whether, in the event of a spate of similar proportions to that of 1937,
the much heavier steel beams used to support the road will obstruct
the flow of the water. There are no public rights of way in the parish,
except for the ford at Blairs ferry where farmers used to wash their
carts, and collect water for dairying in times of drought.

POPULATION

The population of the parish from 1841 is as follows:

	Males	Females	Total
1841	505	486	981
1851			1055
1861			1055
1871			1110
1881			1072
1891			1024
1901			951
1911	469	392	861
1921	524	426	950
1931	523	402	925

1951	554	373	927
1961	496	322	818
1971	418	288	706
1981	483	295	778

The preponderance of males since 1911 is largely accounted for by the clergymen and students (all male) at Blairs College. There were 70 students at Blairs in 1891 and 114 in 1983. The February 1983 voters' roll shows 285 males in the parish including 31 at Blairs College and 233 females. From Miss C. Wyllie's extract of marriages in Maryculter 1783-1855 in the hands of the Session Clerk, it is noted that out of the total of 200 marriages between 1804 and 1855, in 126 cases both spouses were resident in Maryculter, 45 were between a Maryculter resident and a spouse from an adjacent parish, 27 between a Maryculter resident and a spouse from adjacent parishes but one, and in only two cases did the spouse come from further afield. The inadequate means of communication was certainly an influence in the general tendency to choose marriage partners from near at hand. With the general increase in mobility, this tendency is now less evident. Marriages in church have averaged between two and three per annum over the last fifteen years. There were in addition 27 marriages at Blairs (23 local — 4 not local) in the years 1965-1981. Baptisms from 1965 to 1981 totalled 132 in the Established church including 19 adult baptisms and four sets of twins, and 42 at Blairs including 34 local and one set of twins, so total births have averaged between nine and ten per annum. There has been a relatively small influx of dormitory population working in the oil industry and related jobs, and the majority of the population are descendants of marriages noted in the 1783-1855 list, although most of the parents of children of primary school age were born outside the parish. Approximately half the primary schoolchildren were born in the parish. This seems to indicate a certain amount of immigration of younger parents into the parish. While no precise figures can be stated, it would appear that the population under 18 years of age — approximately the difference between local population and the number on the voters' roll — can be divided almost equally between three categories with about 60 children in each, viz. (a) children under primary school age, (b) children of primary school age, and (c) children of secondary school age, the remainder, about 90 in number, being pupils under 18 years at Blairs College.

Many of the surnames of last century remain in the parish today. Within the last sixty years, one centenarian is recorded, and several nonagenarians. The health of the population is good, as might be expected from the favourable surroundings of a country area, and the general prosperity.

HOUSING

From the list of occupations compiled by the minister in 1834, and making an adjustment for cottar houses not included, it is estimated that at that time there were between 150 and 160 houses in the parish (population 1831 — 960). The 1907-1908 valuation roll shows a total of 194 houses, of which 19 were vacant and five were ruinous. The occupied houses at that time included 48 farmhouses, 29 croft houses and four cottar houses. Fifteen cottar houses were vacant, a fact which seems to tie up with the dip in population in the 1911 census. The 1982 valuation roll shows 242 houses, of which 157 have garages, ten are vacant and four are uninhabitable. Of the 228 occupied houses, 108 are owner-occupied and 120 rented. There are eight local authority houses — two semi-detached at Sunnyside, Altries, four semi-detached at Fernieslack, Craigingles and two at Millbank. Of these two have been sold to the occupants. A further four local authority houses are planned at the Kirkton. A house for the Durris and Maryculter District Nurse was built in the 1950s. Since 1975 planning permission has been granted for 32 houses in Maryculter, one being a conversion of a farm steading. It thus appears that, allowing for houses which have become ruinous, some of which have been replaced by entirely new buildings, not more than about 30 houses were built between 1908 and 1975, eight of these being local authority houses. Oil fired central heating has been installed in most new houses. The tendency to block up existing fireplaces in older houses appears to be reversing itself, and open fires or wood-burning stoves are gaining ground, partly due to the high cost of heating oil. The 1833 account notes that coals were then found to be cheaper than peat. In 1901, 2 tons of coal for the church boiler cost £1.0.6d per ton delivered to Milltimber railway station. In 1962 household coal cost £12 per ton delivered and in 1982 £84 per ton. Firewood, stacked and cut into metre lengths, costs approximately £16 per ton in the wood.

Sixty-seven of the houses are in the larger category, rated at £400 gross annual value and over; there are 39 medium sized houses rated at £300 to £399, and the remaining 136 are small houses rated at under £300.

The number of inhabitants per house has declined from about six early last century to a little over three per house. There is no overcrowding.

According to the preliminary census for 1981, out of 195 households in Maryculter, 190 had the exclusive use of a bathroom and W.C., 29 houses had 1-3 rooms, 128 had 4-6 rooms and 37 had 7 or more rooms, but even allowing for 11 vacant houses, the houses (households) enumerated in the census fall short of the figure in the valuation roll, namely 242, which in the personal knowledge of the writer can be taken as accurate. The total number of rooms in the parish is stated to be 1,001 but for the reason stated this figure is certainly less than the actual. No other meaningful figure applicable to Maryculter can be deduced from what are, in any case, obviously incomplete returns.

In November 1972 the farm of Blaikiewell was purchased by a building company, a small housing project of 100 to 150 houses having been proposed there as part of Kincardine County Council's contribution to an estimated 16,000 new houses required in the counties of Aberdeen, Banff and Kincardine and in Aberdeen City for the rapidly expanding North Sea oil industry. However other companies joined in the project and purchased farms in the Upper Crynoch valley, and the ambitious concept of a 'Maryculter New Town', equal in size to Stonehaven and with an eventual target of 2,700 houses, took shape. Kincardine County Council supported the plan but after local government reorganisation in 1975 planning permission was refused by Kincardine and Deeside District Council. Refusal was supported by Grampian Region, one reason being that 'a development of the magnitude proposed would involve the Region and District authorities in expenditure which could not be met under the current financial restrictions.'

Housing development is now very strictly controlled in Maryculter, as the entire parish lies within the green belt in the Kincardine Suburban Area Local Plan (now finalised), except for three housing areas and one specially protected area. In any case the estimate of houses required for the oil industry is now seen to be excessive, as conditions in that business have stabilised.

INDUSTRY, COMMERCE AND OCCUPATIONS

Throughout the 19th century and until the 1930s the parish was very much a self-contained and self-sufficient community. This was partly due to the difficulty of communications and the slow pace of life. At page 82 of the *Old Statistical Account* there is a short and incomplete list of occupations of the people in 1790; these included four tailors, ten weavers, three wrights (carpenters), one Norfolk ploughwright, four sailors, four shoemakers and four gardeners. The parish minister compiled in 1834 a useful list of occupations which he recorded in the Session minutes. Agriculture has always been the principal occupation in the parish, and besides the 34 farms and 36 crofts noted under that heading, the other occupations at that time were five blacksmiths, three wrights, three shoemakers, three merchants, two tailors, three gardeners, one miller, one dyker, one carrier, three overseers or ground officers, one schoolmaster (school-mistresses not being judged worthy of comment), one constable, one innkeeper and one kirk officer. There were four smithies, at Blairs, Burnhead, Cockley and

Stobhall, the latter employing two blacksmiths and sited at 'Smithy Corner' near the present garage and showrooms. It appears that weaving in the parish had ceased by 1834. In 1907, the valuation roll shows the Burnhead smithy as vacant, and there is no mention of Cockley or Stobhall, but the Blairs smithy has two blacksmiths. Other occupations in 1907 were one wright, two carpenters, two masons, two shoemakers, one merchant, four tailors, eight gardeners, one miller, three coachmen, two schoolteachers, one innkeeper, one ferryman, two gamekeepers, besides farmers, crofters, labourers and roadmen. Only four persons worked outside the parish. Many girls found employment in domestic service; it is estimated that even as late as 1939, about sixty may have been employed in this manner in houses and farmhouses ('kitchie deems'). The three quarries at Craigingles, Parkhead and Wetshaw are no longer worked, and the Crossley quarry, apart from the fish pond, is now a local authority roads depot.

Business premises entered in the 1982 valuation roll include five garages, five stores and workshops, one caravan site, one meat-cutting establishment (now closed), one hotel, one restaurant, one mink farm, two boarding kennels and one shop and post office at Blairs. There is a Ministry of Defence wireless station at the summit of Clochandighter, the highest hill in the parish (544 feet). There are about 120 persons employed in non-agricultural businesses within the parish, including fourteen proprietors, and of these no less then ninety travel to work in Maryculter from Aberdeen and neighbouring parishes. Of the 518 adult residents on the voters' roll, no less than 70 are retired persons and approximately 270 are persons working in the parish, including wives working full- or part-time and housewives not working outside the parish. There are about 40 students or young people undergoing training and between 130 and 140 working in neighbouring parishes, Stonehaven or Aberdeen. The advent of the motor car has certainly encouraged mobility of the population so far as jobs are concerned. The general opinion among those coming to work in Maryculter is that they like doing so and find working conditions more pleasant than elsewhere. The majority of those travelling for work outside the parish are either professional people, clerical staff or persons working in oil-related businesses, for whom jobs do not exist locally. The nearest doctors' surgeries (health centres) are in Portlethen and Peterculter. The flourishing village shop at Blairs can supply many of the community's needs, apart from fresh fruit and vegetables which can be bought at the farm shop at Altries. The general picture is one of a thriving, prosperous and independent community.

LEISURE ACTIVITIES, RECREATION AND SPORT

As early as 1882 there was a young men's Mutual Improvement Association in the parish, which developed into a discussion group in the 1920s. The local Volunteers met from the 1870s onwards in the East School. A branch of the Scottish Girls' Friendly Society met regularly in the 1920s and a Dramatic Club was formed in the 1930s and flourished again after World War II.

Maryculter companies of Boy Scouts and Girl Guides were formed in 1921; the Guide company was carried on continuously till 1939. The Scouts were re-started in 1952, and both have met regularly ever since. There were in 1982 twenty-six Scouts, twenty-four Cubs and eight Venture Scouts, most of them from Maryculter where a new Scout hut has been built, with a car park, on part of the glebe. Companies of Guides and Brownies were recommenced in 1977, with (1983) 11 Guides and 24 Brownies. They meet regularly in the Scout premises. The City of Aberdeen Scouts have a hostel and camping ground at Templars Park.

A playgroup for children under school age was formed in 1974 and meets four mornings per week in the church hall. The Ladies' Work Party is active for the church and the Maryculter branch of the Scottish Women's Rural Institute has been in existence over fifty years. After the First World War games were organised annually in Maryculter by the Games Committee. Their activities were inter-rupted by the Second World War but in 1953 the field named Corbie Park on the east side of the Crynoch Burn was bought by the Maryculter Recreation Trust. Games were held for several years and the ground is now used by the local football club, which raised the money to build the pavilion, and is administered by trustees. The Stonehaven and District Angling Association own the fishings in Crossley Quarry. The Lower Deeside Young Farmers' Association now meets at Cookney.

WAY OF LIFE — CONCLUSION

As will be seen from the foregoing paragraphs, Maryculter is a community where a sturdy individualism flourishes. It was noted in 1790 that the people were 'sober, industrious and oeconomical' — that is, thrifty. The same is true today; those working on the land are industrious, inventive and adaptable to new methods; and the number of small independent businesses which have sprung up are character-ised by the energy and initiative of their proprietors. There are several small units, not recorded in the valuation roll, run from the owners' residences. The parish shop, a family business open for 73 hours per week, may be cited as typical of the attitude to work of the small entrepreneurs. The incentives introduced by the fiscal relaxations of recent years have encouraged this attitude and increased prosperity. Despite the population being distributed fairly evenly throughout the parish — the Kirkton is only a small hamlet — there is a strong sense of identity as a separate and distinct community conscious of its local obligations. Recent examples include the support given to the appeal for funds to build the new Scout hut, and the special appeal in 1978–79 which raised £1,814 for the overhaul of the church organ. The parents' committees of the East and West schools, the playgroup and senior citizens committees, the church organisations, the football club, Women's Rural Institute, uniformed organisations and Community Council all provide means of contact between different age groups and emphasise the importance of family life and the spirit of service and co-operation in the parish. As might be expected in such a happy and prosperous community, there is no unemployment, delinquency or crime.

With a population of approximately one person per ten acres, Maryculter can be described as a predominantly rural community verging on the sparsely populated, completely different in character from the suburban built-up areas north of the river Dee which form part of the city of Aberdeen district. As such, the parish is more effectively administered at district level from the administrative centre of the rurally orientated Kincardine and Deeside District authority rather than from Aberdeen city, and this continues to be the strongly held wish of the inhabitants of Maryculter who, as in 1971, remain firmly opposed to any alteration of their boundaries.

The writer wishes to record his thanks to all who have helped in the preparation of the above account and in particular to the Rev. Peter A. Moran of Blairs College for his valuable assistance.

May 1983

THE PARISH OF MARYKIRK

by the Rev. William Eadie

PHYSICAL BASIS

The parish is bounded on the south by the river North Esk, at this point the boundary between Angus and Kincardineshire; on the east by the parishes of St Cyrus and Garvock; to the north by Laurencehirk and Fordoun; on the west by the parish of Fettercairn. The neighbouring parish on the other side of the North Esk is Logie-Pert. The area is 9855 acres. Marykirk parish is irregular in shape. At its widest (east to west) it is about 6 miles and it extends to approximately 5 miles north and south. It lies only some 3 miles inland from the coast and, situated as it is in the very south of the Howe o' the Mearns, it is relatively flat. There is, however, a comparatively steep gradient, the Barns Brae, from Marykirk northwards, almost to Laurencekirk. In addition to the North Esk and its tributary the Luther, which enters the North Esk within the parish, there are several small streams and numerous springs.

The soil generally is now very good, as successive generations of farmers have done much to improve it. The parish has no outstanding flora or fauna and no minerals or special geological structures of any interest.

HISTORY OF THE LOCAL COMMUNITY

While this is still the civil parish of Marykirk, it is now the ecclesiastical parish of Aberluthnott, as the local congregation has reverted to the old name. In the time of David II it was the Thanedom of Aberluthnot. In 1540 Cardinal Bethune feued to David Barclay of Matheris the church lands and mill of Aberluthnot, and Queen Mary confirmed this in 1543 and constituted the town and lands a free burgh of barony, with certain privileges. No municipal use was ever made of the privileges, except the erection of a market cross, part of which is to be seen (in the Marykirk Hotel grounds) to this day. Further evidence of the old name, and the change to Marykirk, is found in the communion cups still in use. Two of these were presented 'to the Kirk

of Aberluthnott' in the year 1715, and appear to have been made by
John Walker, a silversmith in Aberdeen from about 1713 to 1730. The
other two were presented 'to the Parish of Marykirk'. These cups
were made by Thomas Johnston, a silversmith in Montrose from
approximately 1740 to 1760. The date ascribed to these cups in
Jackson's reference book is 1752.

There have been many changes in the parish in the last one hundred
years. Of the industry mentioned in the *Second Statistical Account*
(1842), for example, not a trace remains. The flax-spinning mill, the
weaving sheds and the hand-looms in the homes are gone as if they
had never been. Hand-loom weaving in the home was discontinued in
Luthermuir about forty-five years ago and only two links with the
past remain. A young man resident in the village today is working as a
hand-loom weaver in Laurencekirk, while the bell which now calls
the people to worship in the village church once called the weavers to
their work in the weaving sheds. This complete obliteration of a once
busy, if not always prosperous, industry makes the Marykirk of today
a one hundred per cent agricultural parish, the only traces of industry
left being those associated with, and dependent upon, agriculture. No
history of the parish has ever been written and little information about
it is to be obtained from works covering Angus and the Mearns.
Mention is made of Aberluthnott Church as a possession of St
Germains, the one definite foundation in Scotland of the Crutched
Friars (see *The Crutched Friars*, part II, p. 14, by the Rev. James
Bullock B.D.). The congregation of Aberluthnott parish is within the
bounds of the Presbytery of Brechin and Fordoun and the Synod of
Angus and the Mearns and is represented therein annually by its
minister and one elder.

ESTATES

Of the estates mentioned in the *Second Statistical Account* only one is
still, more or less, as it was then, the estate of Thornton, and in the
interval it has had numerous owners. For over five hundred years,
until 1720, it was owned by the Strachans. In the next one hundred
and seventy-three years, it changed hands a number of times, being
bought in 1893 by the late Sir Thomas Thornton LL.D., Town Clerk
of Dundee, who vowed as a boy that he would one day own this
estate bearing the family name. It is still in the possession of this
family. Sir Thomas's grand-daughter is Mrs Thornton-Kemsley, wife
of the sitting member of Parliament for the local constituency of
North Angus and the Mearns, Mr C.N. Thornton-Kemsley, O.B.E.,
T.D., M.P.

Inglismaldie Castle, once the seat of the Earls of Kintore, after having various owners has been bought by a member of a branch of the Kintore family, Major Keith-Falconer. The estate, however, has been broken up to a large extent, much of it having been bought by the Department of Agriculture and turned into smallholdings and part of it having been bought by the Forestry Commission, which has planted trees here and elsewhere in the parish. In all they have planted almost 1200 acres.

Kirktonhill estate was bought by the Department of Agriculture and turned into smallholdings. The mansion house has been almost completely demolished, because of dry-rot. The other estates have been broken up and most of the farms are now owned by the present occupiers. There are a number of crofts, which are also, in the main, owned by their occupiers.

ADMINISTRATION

The affairs of the parish are administered by the County Council, partly through the District Council but largely from Stonehaven, the county town. There is one Justice of the Peace in the parish, a lady, and the local Registrar is also a lady, residing in Luthermuir.

CHURCH

There is now only one church in the parish, with a Communion Roll of 440. It unites all three major denominations found within the parish bounds in former days, the Auld Kirk, the Free Church and the United Presbyterian Church. The congregation worships, and the Sunday Schools (total number of scholars 62) meet, in the former Auld Kirk building in Marykirk and in the former United Presbyterian building in Luthermuir. The former Free Church building, Crosspoles, was sold some years ago. The manse is the former Auld Kirk manse (over two hundred years old) at Marykirk. A few years ago the manse barn was converted into a small hall by the office-bearers and the Boys' Club. The glebe (about four acres) is let and there has already been some very slight encroachment upon it in the interests of housing. The Kirk Session records, from 1699 onwards, are almost complete: two volumes have been lost. A small amount of charity money is still disbursed annually, obtained from legacies in the possession of the congregation.

MEN OF MARK

The parish has not nurtured many men or women of note in the past one hundred years, though some of its sons have made their mark.

One family alone, the Eatons of Luthermuir, produced a schoolmaster
and a Doctor of Divinity. James Bennet Peace (1864-1923), the son of
a former parish schoolmaster, became a Fellow and Bursar of
Emmanuel College, Cambridge. Marykirk's most outstanding son in
this period, James Blyth, M.A., LL.D., F.R.S.E., was Professor of
Natural Philosophy in the Royal Technical College, Glasgow. Professor Blyth (1839-1906) was one of the pioneers of electricity. He did a
great deal to develop the theory of the microphone receiver and was
an early worker on the telephone. One of the first to demonstrate
successfully the conversion of electric energy into useful work in
driving wheels, he set up in the garden of his house in Marykirk (still
known as Blyth House) a windmill generator with which he lit, by
means of arc lamps, a portion of the village. It is rather ironical that at
this later date the village has no street lighting! Professor Blyth wrote
articles for the *Encyclopaedia Britannica*.

POPULATION

The population of Marykirk parish today is less than half of what it
was in 1841, at the time of the *Second Statistical Account*. At that date it
reached a total of 2387 — the maximum recorded by Census —
having mounted steadily from 1530 in the year 1801. The 1851 figure,
viz. 2232, marked the beginning of an equally steady decline — to
1461 in 1881 and to 1209 in 1901. In the present century the total has
remained much the same:— (1911) 1167; (1921) 1285; (1931) 1163;
(1951) 1162 (590 males: 572 females).

Whereas in 1841, for example, the population of the village of
Luthermuir was about 1090, today it is about 200. In 1841 the
population of the village of Marykirk was almost 300: today it is
about 80. Over the past thirty years the rolls of the schools in
Luthermuir and in Marykirk have also declined rapidly. Whereas in
1920 there were 108 scholars in each school, all of whom lived within
the parish, in 1952 there were 61 scholars in Luthermuir and 28 in
Marykirk, of whom 12 came from outwith the parish.

The most obvious cause for this decline in the population is, of
course, the shift of industry. The introduction of the power-loom and
the decline of handloom weaving was the initial cause and the
mechanization of agriculture has carried the process a stage further in
our own day. Better roads and more convenient methods of travel
have also played their part. The break-up of the estates where
numerous servants — some of whom at least had families — were
employed in former days, and the much smaller families today are
further contributory causes. As will be seen from the section on the
'Way of life' of the people, all this affected the parish as a self-
contained unit and this, in turn, caused further depopulation.

As is the case generally throughout the land, the average age of the population is on the increase. Indeed, there is a very high percentage of old age pensioners in the parish, the oldest parishioner being a lady of 92. The number of baptisms in the past six years was 80. There is quite a movement of population within the parish. The farm servants do not settle. Not more than 30% of the population was born within the parish.

PUBLIC SERVICES

Until the year 1950 the parish enjoyed little or nothing in the way of modern amenities. Since then, however, things have improved. Both villages now have a gravitational water supply, a sewage system and electric power, though neither has street lighting. The County Council have built houses in Luthermuir — they were first occupied in 1952 — and they are at present building houses in Marykirk, which may be occupied this year (1953). Not all of the householders in the village, however, have taken advantage of these amenities. Some of them can't afford to, and in any case few of the houses are really worth the expense involved.

ROADS

The roads in the parish are in a poor state of repair. Some of them are second-class roads (or worse) for which no government subsidy is available and the County Council cannot afford to keep them in good repair.

SCHOOLS

There are 3 schools, all administered by the Education Committee of the County Council. The parish school, known locally as Dunthill School, is now a one-teacher school, with 32 pupils; Luthermuir school, built in 1840 by local people and endowed by the Society for the Propagation of Christian Knowledge, is at the moment a two-teacher school, with 63 pupils; the Napier School in the village of Marykirk, built and endowed with money left for this purpose by David Napier, a labourer who pitied the children their long walk in wintry weather to Dunthill School, is also a one-teacher school, with 17 pupils. All are primary schools. The pupils in Luthermuir and Dunthill are transferred at the age of eleven or twelve to Laurencekirk Junior Secondary School. Most complete their schooling there at the age of fifteen: a few, desiring their Higher Leaving Certificate, go on to the Mackie Academy, Stonehaven. Some of the children within the parish attend Montrose Academy, others Brechin High School. School dinners are served in all three schools. This is a great boon to scholars coming from a distance, some of whom are brought, from outwith the parish bounds, by car.

HEALTH

There is no resident doctor within the parish, no chemist's shop and no resident dentist. These needs are supplied from the neighbouring burghs. A District Nurse resides in the village of Marykirk and serves part of the parish, the remainder being covered by the District Nurse from Fettercairn. There is no hospital within the parish, but the parishioners are well served in this respect by Stracathro Hospital, located just outside the parish bounds on the main Forfar-Aberdeen road, and by Charleton Maternity Home near Montrose.

No policeman is resident within the parish. Police services are supplied, if required, from Laurencekirk, Fettercairn and St Cyrus. The nearest fire-fighting facilities are located at Montrose, Laurencekirk and Brechin.

There are two licensed hotels in the parish, one in the village of Marykirk and the other in Sauchieburn, near Luthermuir.

SOCIAL ACTIVITIES

1. YOUTH ORGANISATIONS

All the youth work in the parish is centred on the church. The minister's wife runs a Girls' Club and the minister a Boys' Club, both in the village of Marykirk. There is also an active Youth Fellowship which meets on Sunday evenings.

2. WOMEN'S ORGANISATIONS

The church has a branch of the Women's Guild which meets alternately in the villages. Two branches of the Women's Rural Institute, one in each village, meet monthly and are both very active.

3. MIXED CLUB

The church has a Social Club, which meets weekly throughout the winter, alternating between the villages. It is social, cultural and educational in aim and is very well attended, with approximately 60 members.

4. SPORT

A football team in Luthermuir plays in the Kincardineshire Junior League. Few of the players are locals. Two hard-courts for tennis in Luthermuir are open in summer but are not well patronized.

5. CONCERTS, ETC.

Each village possesses a fairly good hall in which local functions are held — concerts, whist drives, dances and country dancing classes being popular forms of entertainment during the winter months.

6. LIBRARY

Library services in the villages are now supplied by the County Education Committee, but both libraries are of long standing and are much older than the County service. The Marykirk library was founded and endowed by a one-time owner of the estate of Kirktonhill, Mrs Adamson, who also paid a major share in the expense of the erection of the village hall.

HOUSING

Housing in the parish is very mixed. It varies from the 'clay biggins' (houses with clay walls, variously faced) in Luthermuir to the new council houses in both villages. Many of the houses are, by modern standards, condemnable and many indeed have been listed by the county authorities for condemnation when the present housing shortage is overtaken. Some of the houses in the villages, especially in Marykirk, have been modernised and some of the farm cottar houses also have been brought as far up-to-date as possible. Almost all the farm-houses have been modernised. In Luthermuir most of the houses have fairly large gardens and many of the people there market their fruit, in the season. At one time the Luthermuir strawberry was famous, but it is not now so good as it was.

INDUSTRY

Of industry in the technical sense of the word there is, we may say, none in Marykirk. The parish is an agricultural one and this accounts for the occupation of almost one hundred per cent of those of employable age. There are 2 blacksmith's shops, both dependent on farm work; 2 joiner's shops, also dependent on farm work; one slater's and plasterer's business (a family business employing two brothers) finding work locally; a general contractor's business finding work further afield as well as locally; a firm engaged, also more or less locally, on ditching and draining; and a sawmill at Spearmill.

A local bus firm, centred on Luthermuir, runs a regular service to Brechin and Montrose and also runs tours in the summer from Brechin.

FARMING

At the end of the 18th century the horse had superseded the ox in this parish for general farm purposes. Today the horse in its turn has been superseded by the tractor. Farming is now almost fully mechanized. The sole exception is at Marymill, where the meal-mill (the only one left in the district) is still water-driven, but even here the sound of the tractor is now to be heard in the fields. Some of the larger farms own their own combine-harvesters, and one owns a number which travel as far afield as the south of England at harvest time, complete with teams to operate them.

Much of the farming here is on the usual rotation system, but one farm, Dykelands, has a wide variety which includes cropping, dairy farming, poultry, market gardening (fruit, daffodils, tulips — flowers and bulbs both being sold) and pig breeding. This farmer employs a staff of almost 40 all the year round. There are 2 other large dairy farms and one smaller one in the parish and one fairly large croft specialising in poultry alone. A number of the farmers are experimenting with the deep-litter system of poultry farming. Little or no sheep farming is carried on in the parish.

On the whole the standard of farming is fairly high.

WAY OF LIFE

As is only to be expected, the way of life in the parish has been considerably changed in the past one hundred years. Marykirk parish was at one time a more or less self-contained unit. The village shops supplied all the basic needs, clothing, footwear, groceries, bread and general merchandise, and after the introduction of the penny stamp postal facilities. One shop in Luthermuir actually ran quite a profitable side line in photography. All this was necessary, of course, because travelling was difficult. The railway station is fully a mile from the village of Marykirk and fully 3 miles from Luthermuir. Roads were far from good. Inter-marriage, especially in Luthermuir, was by no means uncommon. Social life was not highly organized. The advent of the petrol engine changed all this. Travel became easy as roads and buses improved. The decline in the population, previously explained, and the easy access by bus to centres like Montrose, Brechin and Laurenckirk, made many of the village shops redundant and they disappeared, one by one, until today there are only 2 shops of the general merchandise type, one of which is also the sub-post office, in Marykirk, and 4 shops in Luthermuir, of which again one is the sub-post office. All the licensed premises, except the two hotels, have been closed.

Bus travel, too, had its effect upon inter-marriage. Young people from outwith the parish come to dances held in the village hall. Young people from the parish travel to dances in neighbouring towns and parishes and some of them work outwith the parish. In this way their acquaintanceship is widened and inter-marriage has become a thing of the past. Modern inventions, such as the films, wireless and now television, have brought old and young alike into close touch with a much wider world than that of former days, enclosed as it was within the parish boundary. The almost inevitable result, of course, is that the cleverest and most ambitious of the young people leave the parish to find work elsewhere. In spite of all this, one thing has changed little. Life still proceeds at a much more leisurely pace than in the towns and it is not so dominated by the clock! Meetings, concerts, dances and other entertainments rarely start at the appointed time, and even then there are late-comers.

The people are, on the whole, kindly, industrious folk, going quietly about their business, though on occasions, like many others, not always minding their own. There is little drunkenness in the parish, certainly nothing by comparison with days gone by, and the people are very law-abiding. They have, however, most of them at any rate, been caught in the meshes of the prevailing form of gambling, football pools.

Church attendance varies, naturally, with the weather. It has been improving for some years past, though slowly. For the past year or two it has, in reasonably good weather, totalled approximately 60 at Marykirk in the morning and about 45 at Luthermuir in the afternoon. That is roughly 25% of the congregation. At the sacrament of the Lord's Supper and at special services, the percentage is much higher. Many of the parishioners are quite indifferent, and some actually hostile, to religion. The farmers, particularly, are indifferent. There is only one farmer on the Kirk Session at present and one more is a member of the Congregational Board. Another farmer who attends irregularly is, nevertheless, quite generous to the church.

During the summer most organizations and the schools have summer outings, some of them to places far outwith the parish boundary, and in addition private individuals sometimes organize bus trips, mainly on a Sunday. The social life of the parish revolves round the church organizations and the Women's Rural Institute branches, with an occasional dance, usually to raise funds for some good cause. Public Saturday night dancing is intermittent.

The Liberal-Unionist Association has an active branch but there is little activity on behalf of the Labour party. This is understandable, as the local Member of Parliament is a parishioner.

While poverty is no longer a problem and a challenge to the social conscience, a new problem is arising which is not easily solved. Old people, especially those without near relatives (in both meanings of the word 'near') reach a stage where they can no longer look after themselves. Even if there were places where they could be cared for (and such places are severely limited in number) few of them are really willing to leave their home. It is almost impossible in this parish to find a suitable house-keeper or home-help for such cases. This problem has already risen in an acute form and is likely to arise increasingly in the future.

In their quiet undemonstrative way, the people of the parish look forward to the future, waiting to see what it will bring but doing little to influence the course of events.

March 1953

THE PARISH OF NIGG

by the Rev. Laurence J. Matthews, B.A., B.D.

Three possible derivations of the word 'Nigg' have been suggested:—
1) From a Gaelic source meaning 'peninsula'. The parish has a peninsula-like shape, as it lies between the North Sea, the River Dee and the foothills of the Grampian mountains. There is a Nigg in Ross-shire which has a similar peninsula-like shape.
2) From the Gaelic 'niuc', meaning a 'corner' or 'recess'. The parish was the north-east corner of the ancient Celtic province of the Mearns and, later, of Kincardineshire.
3) From the Gaelic 'n' eig', meaning 'the notch'. This may refer to the shape of the Bay of Nigg.

BOUNDS

In earlier times the name Nigg simply referred to the substantial area on the south side of the River Dee opposite the Royal Burgh of Aberdeen. It was the locus of a considerable population from pre-historic times, living mainly along the coast, on the banks of the Dee and its estuary, and near the confluence of the Burn of Leggart and the river. The interior was wild heathland and bog, and generally uninhabited.

The bounds of the parish were precisely defined in 1242 A.D. under the ecclesiastical arrangements initiated by David de Bernham, Bishop of St Andrews. The northern boundary was the River Dee, the eastern was the North Sea, the western was the Burn of Leggart, and the southern was a line one mile south of Cove Bay running from Hare Ness, on the coast, to Bothiebrigs. Its greatest length, north to south, was about four miles; and its greatest breadth, east to west, about three miles.

This continued to be the area of the parish from 1242 A.D. until the end of the nineteenth century, and it was entirely within the county of Kincardine. The rapid expansion of the burgh of Aberdeen during the nineteenth century caused the city to look southwards, and gradually, piece by piece, the lands of Nigg were absorbed, until by the late 1970s, the whole parish became a dormitory and industrial suburb of

the City of Aberdeen. Inevitably, the whole character and way of life
has been transformed by this gradual process of urbanization and
industrialization, and the parish has changed from being a predominantly farming and fishing community into being an industrial and
residential suburb of Aberdeen.

PHYSICAL FEATURES

The foothills of the Grampian mountains form a ridge of high land,
running west to east across the parish, and terminating at the sea,
where the cliffs are vertical and much indented, reaching 100 feet or
more in height. This ridge of high land, locally called 'The Gramps',
reaches its highest point at Kincorth Hill, 345 feet above sea level. It
then descends eastwards to form a gap near Nigg Kirk, about 200 feet
above sea level, then rising again to 277 feet at Baron's Cairn and 233
feet at Doonies Hill, before dropping to the sea. This ridge is about 3
miles long and is now designated 'Loirston Country Park' by
Grampian Regional Council, some paths and picnic-places having
been laid out on the westerly portion, though the eastern end is at
present used as a municipal refuse tip.

The rocky coast-line forms three natural harbours — at Cove,
Burnbanks and Altens — and in former times these served as havens
for the fishing communities who lived there. The Bay of Nigg is
about ¼ mile in diameter, roughly semi-circular, but exposed to
easterly gales, which often prevail. It is flanked by the dangerous cliffs
and rocks of Girdle Ness and Greg Ness, and in the days of sailing-
ships was often a death-trap for ships blown by easterly storms. The
main municipal sewage outfall reaches the sea at Girdle Ness, and a
new sewage outfall is at present being constructed at the southern side
of the bay. Erosion by the sea has washed away much of the soft clay
and gravel at the southern end of the bay, and in 1963 the coast road
was threatened and had to be moved inland alongside the railway line.
In 1965 the Corporation began to strengthen the sea defences, some
500 tons of material being dumped into the sea, of which the hard
core consisted mainly of demolished air-raid shelters. The sea-defences
continue to require strengthening to the present day.

There are two principal water-courses in the parish. The Burn of
Leggart rises in the Loch of Loirston and flows roughly north-west
until it reaches the River Dee; and the Tullos Burn, which rises from
springs at Stoneyhill — now the site of the housing development at
Redmoss — flows north and then east into the Bay of Nigg. Much of
this burn is now carried through culverts. The only considerable
expanse of water is the Loch of Loirston, which covers about 27 acres,
and is supplied with water by underground springs.

The coastal plain, the low land round the Bay of Nigg and in the

Vale of Tullos, and the broad haughs forming the banks of the Dee, consist of more recent alluvial deposits, forming good arable soil. The higher ground is of clay and peat, often filled with stones of varying sizes, and with the occasional outcrop of granite. It is generally covered with furze, moss and heathland, and is arable only with difficulty. There was once a good supply of peat in the parish, but this has now been worked out or built upon; and there are some deposits of sand.

CLIMATE

The air is healthy and bracing, and reasonably unpolluted. The temperature is above the average for this latitude, the sea modifying the heat in summer, and making the frost less intense in winter. Snow rarely lies for long on the ground. The east wind brings moisture, and there are frequent sea-mists in summer, useful in preserving crops from drought. Yet it is not a damp climate, the rainfall averaging no more than 27 inches annually. Much of the parish is exposed to northerly and easterly winds, though on the other hand, westerly winds are usually dry, warm and balmy. There is a fickleness about the weather, which can change in a few hours from mild air to cold and bitter winds.

PLANTS AND ANIMALS

The natural habitat shows considerable variety, ranging from the coastal strip to the high heathland; and from suburban gardens to river banks, enabling an interesting variety of birds, animals and plants to exist. It is true that natural open space has been progressively encroached upon by building developments and the provision of new roads in recent years, but sufficient natural habitat remains still to support a flourishing natural life.

There is a scarcity of mature trees and hedges in the parish, which makes its appearance rather bare and windswept, and reduces the cover for birds and small mammals. These are also harassed by predatory birds, such as magpies, kestrels and herring-gulls. The local authority has recently followed a policy of planting young trees along the roads and around industrial and housing developments, and one hopes that more will be done in this way by providing plantations of both conifers and deciduous trees where there is shelter from the wind. The benefit for the future, environmentally, in creating wind-breaks and relieving the bare appearance of the landscape, would be considerable. In former days, the parish was much more wooded than it is now, with attractive woodlands near the Bay of Nigg and in the

Vale of Tullos, and plantations of conifers on Tullos Hill. Peat-bogs have revealed the stumps of birch and oak trees, proving that these species of tree, now almost non-existent in this area, once flourished here. There are some mature beech and elm trees around Nigg Kirk and Hall, and these provide a nesting-place for magpies, which in the last few years have increased in numbers and spread over a wider area. There is a similar small wood at North Loirston which has a small rookery. The great gale of 31 January 1953 blew down many trees, and almost levelled the 6 acre wood then growing in the glebe opposite the church.

In suburban gardens the blackbird is very common, followed in frequency by the mistle-thrush and song-thrush, robin, chaffinch and occasional blue-tit; small flocks of starlings roost in winter. In spring and summer the sky-lark, golden plover and curlew inhabit the higher ground; house-martins visit from May to September. Herring-gulls are prevalent everywhere, and oyster-catchers are heard day and night in spring and summer, piping as they fly inland. The Loch of Loirston is an important refuge for swans and various species of water-fowl; but the birds have to compete with visiting fishermen, and more recently, with wind-surfers.

Roe deer are occasionally seen in the vicinity of Kincorth Hill, sometimes in hard winters approaching the houses in Redmoss Road for food. The rabbit and brown hare are not numerous, though they are sometimes seen invading suburban gardens and lawns. The hedgehog, mole, shrew and field-vole are fairly common.

ROUTES AND COMMUNICATIONS

The parish was relatively isolated and remote until modern times, because of the difficulty of crossing the bogs, peat-mosses and heathlands which cut it off from the south, and the barrier of the River Dee and its estuary on the north. Within the parish, the few roads and tracks were of poor quality, the interior being hardly accessible until the end of the eighteenth century, when agricultural improvements began to open up the centre of the parish and the Charleston area was developed.

Until the nineteenth century, the only route south followed the Burn of Leggart, climbing steeply over Tollohill in Banchory-Devenick to cross the Mounth via the Causey Mounth pass towards Stonehaven. The modern road following the coast southwards was not constructed until the nineteenth century. New techniques then enabled the bogs and peat-mosses to be drained and crossed and between 1800 and 1810 the much more convenient Stonehaven Road was made along the western edge of the parish. In 1838 Wellington Road was made as a second 'turnpike' road through the middle of the parish to join the Stonehaven Road at the Checkbar.

Communication to the north of the parish was only possible by crossing the River Dee via one of the fords or ferries, and this was dangerous and often impossible when the river was in spate or storm conditions prevailed. There were long delays for travellers waiting to cross the Dee and tragic accidents were not uncommon. Prior to 1527 when the first bridge was built, there were three historic crossing-places:—

1) The ferry across the Dee estuary from Torry to Footdee.
2) The ferry at Craiginches below Ferryhill.
3) The ancient ford opposite Ruthrieston just down-stream from the present Bridge of Dee.

The opening of the first bridge in 1527 was doubtless a great blessing to travellers and traders, but it resulted in most of Nigg being by-passed, though the hazardous ferries at Craiginches and Torry continued to be used for another three hundred years, especially by the fisher-folk carrying their fish to sell in Aberdeen.

Within the parish itself, roads and tracks were poorly made until comparatively modern times, and the high interior was almost inaccessible. The most substantial road was the coast-road from Cove Bay via Burnbanks, Altens and Nigg Bay to Torry. From Torry a second road ran westwards along the banks of the Dee to the Burn of Leggart. A third well-used track, later to become Wellington Road, ran through the centre of the parish from Cove Bay to the ferry at Craiginches, and along this track carts passed carrying peat to the burgh from Redmoss, and fisherwomen walked with their creels to and from Aberdeen.

Today four bridges link the ancient parish with the north side of the Dee:—

1) The Bridge of Dee opened on All Fools' Day 1527. Begun by William Elphinstone, Bishop of Aberdeen, it was completed 18 years later by his successor, Gavin Dunbar. It was widened in 1841. This bridge cannot carry the weight of modern heavy vehicles and there is a proposal to build a new bridge up-river capable of meeting modern requirements.

2) The Wellington suspension bridge was built in 1830 by the heritors of Nigg parish church, partly for the benefit of members travelling to the church from the city. Wellington Road was also improved at the same time, and the total cost to the heritors of these beneficial works was about {10,000. The Town Council reconstructed Wellington Bridge to carry the increasing volume of traffic in 1930.

3) In 1881, the Victoria bridge was opened, linking Torry with the city.

4) In 1941, the King George VI bridge was opened. This provided an alternative route southwards out of the city, and made possible the development of the lands of Kincorth into a suburb of Aberdeen.

A new bridge is now under construction at Craiginches, a short distance down-river from the Wellington suspension bridge. It is expected to be ready in 1984.

Apart from the sea-route which for centuries linked Aberdeen with Leith and London and the ports of northern Europe, communication with the south was immensely difficult until the nineteenth century, when roads began to improve. Around 1590, for example, the official postman, clad in a blue uniform with the burgh's coat-of-arms on his sleeve, walked to Edinburgh with the mail via the Causey Mounth pass. In 1667 he was provided with a horse. A hundred years later relays of horses made an almost daily journey to Edinburgh and on to London with mail. For ordinary travellers, the Aberdeen and Edinburgh Fly began to make coach journeys in 1794, taking 34 hours to reach Edinburgh and carrying passengers at a charge of 2 guineas each.

The coming of the railway in 1850 made a big change for both travellers and trade, the line from the south crossing the parish via the once-beautiful Vale of Tullos, and having a station at Cove Bay.

In the last 100 years communications have steadily improved, and to complete the picture the first telegraph was installed in Aberdeen in 1854; the first telephone in 1881. In 1908 a motor-car went to London in 24 hours; in 1910 the first radio message was received; and today Dyce Airport is the second busiest airport in the United Kingdom. The problem now is no longer one of isolation and remoteness; rather it is one of traffic congestion as the inhabitants of the new suburbs on the south of the city hurry about their daily labours.

ARCHAEOLOGY

Important evidence about the first inhabitants of Nigg was discovered in 1866, indicating that about 4000 B.C. a nomadic group of food-gatherers came to the Bay of Nigg. They were 'strandloopers', so called from their custom of journeying from one sandy beach to another, sometimes using frail dug-out canoes, and living mainly on shell-fish and fish from the sea or rivers. Essentially a sea-shore people, they also made expeditions inland to hunt deer, wild boar and other animals, using dogs to help them in the chase. They made harpoons for fishing and spears for hunting from bone or deer-horn.

Ample evidence of 'strandloopers' was discovered at the Bay of Nigg in 1866 in the form of midden heaps containing quantities of periwinkle, limpet and mussel shells as well as some fish and animal bones. Probably no more than one or two families of these primitive nomads came to the Bay of Nigg, living for a time in caves or hollows in the sand covered by skins. The 'strandloopers' were eventually absorbed or exterminated by a more advanced race of people, who came across the North Sea from Holland and the Rhine Delta. These were the late Stone-Age people, who settled in this parish about 2000 B.C. and became the first real settlers and colonists here. Three round cairns on the Hill of Tullos provide clear evidence of their existence.

The most easterly of these cairns is the 'Tullos Cairn'. The cairn itself was approximately 20m in diameter and 2.5m in height. Inside was a short-cist grave containing a beaker about 15cm high.

The middle of the three cairns is known as the 'Baron's Cairn'. It is approximately 18m in diameter and 1.7m high, characteristically situated on top of a knoll.

Further west is the 'Cat Cairn' which was approximately 22m by 19m and 2.5m high. There may have been a stone platform originally as a base for the cairn.

Unfortunately, all three cairns are now badly mutilated and vandalised, and no attempt has been made to preserve them. The municipal authorities at present use the area around the cairns as a refuse tip, with scant concern for archaeological remains or the environment.

These Neolithic settlers were farmers, keeping sheep and cows, and planting barley, and they lived in small communities in wigwam-like tents of skin set on a low wall of stones. They believed in life after death and buried their dead in short cists of stone along with a clay 'beaker' containing food for the after-life. They are said to form the basic strain of the original rural population — short, sturdy build, square jaw, oval face and long skull.

Roman fish-hooks were discovered in the River Dee on the north-west boundary of the parish in 1950. These almost certainly date from the period 208 to 211 A.D., when a Roman army under Septimius Severus made a marching-camp at Normandykes, near Peterculter. Simultaneously, the Roman fleet sailed up the east coast and anchored in Aberdeen Bay before advancing northwards into the Moray Firth, parallel to the army, probably turning back at Elgin. There is no evidence that the Romans set foot in this parish, but it seems they had an appetite for our Dee salmon.

CELTIC PERIOD

Nigg fell within the ancient Celtic provice of the Mearns, ruled by its Mormaer or chief. The province was divided into districts, each with a stronghold located at some important strategic site. Nigg constituted one of the ancient Celtic districts and had a stronghold on raised ground at Balnagask. Here a 'motte-and-bailey' fort once stood, controlling the land routes and the ferry crossing at Torry. A mound of earth in the grounds of Balnagask House, now an old people's home, is all that remains of the Celtic stronghold. Originally it would have consisted of a flat-topped mound of earth crowned by a wooden palisade within which was a tower built of timber. This was the 'motte'. Beside it there was probably a second mound of earth with a wooden palisade containing the various ancillary buildings necessary for the working of the fort. This was the 'bailey'. These wooden superstructures have, of course, long since disappeared.

The Celtic period probably lasted from the 8th to the 12th centuries, gradually giving way to the more highly organised structure of Norman feudalism. Towards the end of the period, Viking incursions along the coast left their mark on the parish in the adoption of the Norse word, 'Ness', meaning a headland, found in local place-names such as Girdle-Ness, Greg Ness and Hare Ness.

Celtic society was based on the tribe or clan and there was a strict system of social grades within the paternalistic aristocratic structure. To this day, the Scot's family ties and pride of ancestry and clan may be a relic of Celtic times. In the 12th century, the lands of Nigg were held by Cormac de Nug, one of the Celtic nobility, whose name suggests that Norman influence had already reached this district.

By the end of the 12th century, Saxon was generally the spoken language here. In Aberdeen, the literate classes had begun to speak Saxon about 1100 A.D., according to Alexander Keith in *A Thousand Years of Aberdeen*, as a result of the considerable immigration from northern Europe to the mouth of the Dee during the 11th and 12th centuries. Flemish immigrants settled mainly in Aberdeen itself, introducing the manufacture of textiles, and then becoming the merchants and craftsmen of the community. Saxon and Norse immigrants tended to join the fishing and farming population, many settling in the villages of Torry, Burnbanks and Cove in this parish, thus diluting the native Celtic population. It was this newly-formed population that offered such sturdy resistance to the attempts of Edward I and the English to dominate Scotland, when they occupied Aberdeen Castle in 1290 A.D., often being at variance, in this and other matters, with their still-Celtic neighbours in Buchan and Deeside.

MEDIEVAL TIMES

Norman feudalism, with its closely integrated class system descending from the King down to the landless serf or peasant, gradually replaced the paternalistic Celtic social order. In 1178 A.D. King William the Lion founded the Abbey of Aberbrothock or Arbroath; and his son, Alexander II, gave the lands of Nigg to the Abbots, who thus became both the feudal and ecclesiastical superiors of the parish. The Abbot of Arbroath had a seat in St Fittick's Church by the Bay of Nigg, and a dovecote nearby. Two fields near the Bay of Nigg were long afterwards known as the 'Upper and Lower Doocot Fields'. The dovecot was a typical symbol of medieval feudal authority, not only providing food but also great quantities of pigeons' eggs for stone building operations. The egg albumen and shells were an essential ingredient of the mortar used by early masons and may be the reason why so many early buildings still stand despite the severities of the climate. Probably the first stone church at Nigg was built about this time, and the east gable-end of St Fittick's Church is said to date partly from the thirteenth century. The Abbots had a villa in Nigg close by the ancient fording-place opposite Ruthrieston. It was a favourite summer residence with them, and near to it was a small chapel or shrine, and a hospice for the use of travellers waiting to cross the Dee at that point. Evidence of an old burial ground has also been found at the site, and a silver coin of the reign of Queen Mary was unearthed there. The Ruthrieston Burn across the river was known by the local name of the 'Spital' Burn, no doubt a reference to the hospice near the Abbot's villa. The name 'Abbotswell', once given to a farm on the site and now to a road and a crescent in the vicinity, is really a corruption of Abbot's Wall — the ruined walls of the villa still being visible in the seventeenth century.

SAINT FITTICK

Christianity was brought to Nigg about 650 A.D. by Saint Fittick, who was a Franco-Scottish missionary. Unlike most of the Deeside apostles of Christianity he had no apparent connection with Whithorn or Iona or any of the Celtic centres of missionary enterprise, but came independently from France to work in Pictland, landing at the Bay of Nigg after a storm. Saint Fittick was a Scot of royal blood, born at Dunstaffnage in Argyll, which was an ancient royal seat, and in his youth went to France where he became celebrated as a miracle-working hermit. In 622 A.D. he refused the prayers of a deputation of priests and chiefs from Scotland to return and accept the crown and rule his own people, preferring the life of a hermit in France, where he became famous for his garden at Meaux, near Paris, in which he grew herbal plants for the benefit of the poor. For this reason he became the patron saint of all gardeners, his saint's day being observed on 30th August. In France he is known as Saint Fiacre, while in Gaelic his name is 'Fiachrach' which means a 'raven' — a manner of naming which was common in early times. There are various versions of his name in old documents, the commonest being Fiacar, Fithack and Fittick. Sometimes the Gaelic prefix 'mo-', which is a title denoting holiness, is attached to his name, for example, one old map refers to the Bay of Nigg as 'Sanct mo-Fithack Bay'. Paris taxi-cabs were sometimes known as 'fiacres' owing to the fact that the Hotel de S.

Fiacre in Paris was the first stand for hackney-cabs in the city. Saint Fittick or Fiacre was sent by the Bishop of Meaux to take the Gospel to Pictland, and he endured the rigours of life at the Bay of Nigg and the initial hostility of the natives to found the church which bears his name. Afterwards he returned to his garden in France, and died about 670 A.D. at Breuil, being buried at Meaux. This Franco-Scottish saint must have been a truly remarkable man, and he is commemorated in sites and customs connected with the Bay of Nigg. Saint Fittick's Well at the south-east corner of the bay was for centuries a place of pilgrimage and venerated for its curative properties. Mothers used to bring their sick children to the well believing in its healing powers. That ancient well has now disappeared as a consequence of work by the local authority to strengthen the coast at that point to prevent erosion by the sea.

CHURCH HISTORY

We look back with gratitude and admiration to Saint Fittick, who brought Christianity to Nigg in heathen and barbarous times. Information about the ensuing 500 years is meagre in the extreme, and we can only assume that the church he founded followed the customs of the ancient Celtic Church in being independent of Rome, worshipping in the Gaelic tongue of the people, having a non-celibate priesthood, and being democratic in government and discipline. By the 12th century its purity and missionary zeal had so declined that the organised rule of the Roman Church inevitably began to absorb it. The change in church order corresponded with a change in civil affairs from the paternalistic aristocracy of Celtic times to the imposition of Norman feudalism.

In 1242 A.D. the church by the Bay of Nigg was consecrated as a parish church, according to Roman Catholic rites, by the Bishop of St Andrews, David de Bernham — although it had already existed for over 500 years. The dedication to Saint Fittick was retained. A Vicar of Nigg was appointed and provision made to maintain him and the church from teinds and glebe-land. This important episode is recorded in David de Bernham's 'Pontificale' or 'Book of Ceremonies', where 'Nigg-on-the-Dee' is mentioned as one of 140 parish churches, mainly along the east coast, consecrated by him between 1240 and 1249. This industrious and able bishop made excellent rules for the proper keeping of churches and churchyards, the safety of sacred vessels, and the good repute of the clergy. Each parish was visited regularly through his 'Deans of Christianity', reports being made about their spiritual and material well-being. The first stone Church of Nigg probably dates from this time, built of surface stones gathered locally and bound with a mortar containing pigeon eggs — hence the importance of the near-by dove-cote. Previous church buildings would be of the customary 'wattle and daub', that is timber and clay, with a thatch of heather or reeds — a rather fragile structure but easily repaired after storm damage. The 'lepers' squint', a vertical narrow slit in the north wall of Saint Fittick's Church, is still visible in the ancient ruin, a reminder that lepers, untouchables from the Burgh of Aberdeen, inhabited the wild uplands of the parish for centuries. Loirston, the local name for a large area of land inland from Cove Bay, is said to be derived from 'lobhars' town', the Gaelic 'lobhar' meaning a leper. These lepers were the object of charity, food and clothing being left for them, while one peat in ten was supposed to be left by the roadside at Kirkhill for their use. Through the 'lepers' squint' in the church wall they would see the elevated chalice and hear the intoning of the priest without mixing with the people. For 300 years the Roman Catholic Abbots of Arbroath dominated ecclesiastical affairs, but prior to the Reformation of 1560 there is evidence of the increasing worldliness of the clergy. One Vicar of Nigg attempted to exact a teind of all fish caught by his parishioners for his own use, but without success, for he was deposed by his bishop for his avarice. Another enjoyed the material benefits of plurality, bolding both the Vicarage of Nigg and the Rectorship of Durris.

The Reformation probably brought little immediate change to the parish. The Menzies family of Pitfodels, who dominated politics for over a hundred years in the neighbouring Burgh of Aberdeen, acquired the lands of Nigg on the dissolution of Arbroath Abbey, leasing them for a time to Forbes of Monymusk. Locally the people accepted the new order while continuing to respect the past. Only once, in December 1559, a fanatical mob of reformers mainly from Angus and the Mearns passed through the parish into Aberdeen where they sacked the monasteries and despoiled St Machar's Cathedral, though their attempts to pull down the spire of St Nicholas Church were frustrated by the citizens. In 1573, at the Bay of Nigg, retribution fell on some who had sought to profit from the spoils of the Reformation when a ship on its way to Holland, heavily laden with lead from the roof of St Machar's Cathedral and three bells from its towers, was wrecked on the Girdle — a dangerous rock off the Ness which bears its name. The tolerant local attitude towards the Reformation is illustrated by the fact that Sir Thomas Menzies, who owned the lands of Nigg and was Provost of Aberdeen at this time, was made an elder of the Reformed Church even though he never renounced his allegiance to the Roman Catholic faith. John Knox must have passed through the parish in 1564 when he spent six weeks in the burgh, though little is known about his visit. The first reformed minister of Nigg was David de Menzies, appointed in 1567. Owing to the desperate shortage of ministers following the Reformation he also had charge of most of the parishes on the south side of the Dee with the help of two lay readers. By a cruel irony the Reformation, intended at its outset to abolish superstition, found itself witnessing the superstitious persecution of witches in the closing years of the 16th century, Aberdeen being notorious for the number of its witch-burnings and drownings, doubtless pleasing to King James VI and I. It is said that some of these poor demented women fled across the Dee to find refuge in the wild interior of Nigg, which over the centuries provided a place of safety for escapers from the burgh.

Within fifty years of the Reformation religious opinions hardened with the rise of the Covenanters, and Charles I attempted to impose the English ecclesiastical system upon Scotland; though Nigg Church remained contentedly Episcopalian within the Church of Scotland until 1716. The beneficent influence of that remarkable group of ministers and Professors known as the 'Aberdeen Doctors', led by Bishop Patrick Forbes and his son, Dr John Forbes of Corse, doubtless found acceptance here. Their tolerance, piety, erudition and catholicity of spirit stand in marked contrast to the bitter intolerance and cruelties of that period of Scottish ecclesiastical history, providing a model for the solution of contemporary religious disputes.

The 'Killing Times' came to this parish in March 1639. James Graham, Earl of Montrose, arrived with an army of Covenanters to compel Aberdeen's surrender to the Covenanting cause. He camped at Tollohill in Banchory Devenick, with 9,000 men 'wel armit both on horse and futt', on a site known afterwards as 'Covenanters' Faulds' — a name preserved today in street names in the suburb of Kincorth. After the Battle of the Bridge of Dee the burgh surrendered, paid 10,000 merks and signed the Covenant. Worse followed five years later when Montrose returned, having meanwhile changed sides from ardent Covenanter to fervid Royalist. This time his army of 'wild Irishes' plundered, slaughtered and burnt in the streets of Aberdeen. One of their victims was the tenant-farmer of Kincorth, William Mylne, whose gravestone in St Fittick's graveyard bears an inscription in Latin, which translates:—

'William Mylne, tenant of Kincorth, slain by his enemies on the 10th July, 1645, for the cause of Christ, here rests in peace from his labour, this man whom piety, probity and God's holy Covenant made happy fell by the sword of a savage Irishman — I am turned to ashes.'

The Covenanters found little support in Nigg, and the church here continued to be Episcopalian until support for the Jacobite cause resulted in the then minister, Richard Maitland, being deposed in 1716, ostensibly for praying for the Old Pretender. He had been minister of Nigg for 42 years, and his initials are carved on the base of the bell-tower of the old church which was added in 1704 to house an iron bell of 18 pounds Amsterdam weight. His name also appears on two silver communion cups made in 1703 by George Walker of Aberdeen for Nigg Church — beautiful examples of this local craftsman's art. These were acquired by Aberdeen Art Gallery in 1974.

The first Presbyterian minister of Nigg was James Farquhar, appointed in 1717 to succeed Richard Maitland. There was a violent demonstration by a section of the congregation when he was about to take his first service, and an attempt was made to prevent the bell being rung. The new minister was a man of considerable stature and strength who quickly put the demonstrators to flight, and Presbyterianism was established.

The original Reformation documents allowed considerable room for freedom of thought and practice, and Episcopalian ministers, like those of Nigg, regarded themselves as within the Church of Scotland. They accepted bishops and in their public worship used the Lord's Prayer, the Apostles' Creed and the Doxology after Psalms — liturgical items eventually dropped by the Presbyterians to the severe detriment of worship. They did not use a set liturgical book, unlike the later Scottish Episcopal Church which did not come into being until 1766. Presbyterian discipline has left an interesting relic outside the entrance to St Fittick's Church in the form of a rusted iron chain, which is all that is left of the 'jougs' by which offenders were fastened for public ridicule. In 1757 a larger bell was installed, cast in bronze by John Moat of Old Aberdeen. This bell was removed from the ruined church in 1960 and is now on display at the present church. A manse was built beside St Fittick's Church in 1759 and was demolished in 1965.

Greater prosperity came to church and parish in the nineteenth century with the agricultural improvements and the advent of a new farming community. Practical concern for the welfare of the parish was combined with an evangelical outlook. A number of Sunday Schools existed in 1801, not only giving religious instruction but the elements of reading, writing and arithmetic. Schemes for small savings and insurance were organised by the church particularly for the fisherfolk, and local support was given to the Royal Infirmary. Smallpox vaccination was promoted enthusiastically by the minister, who himself went round vaccinating many of the babies of the parish in a worthy attempt to stamp out the scourge of smallpox. Discussion about the building of a new parish church more centrally situated began about this time.

The new parish church was opened on the first Sunday in June 1829, during the ministry of Alexander Thom, A.M., a former distinguished Headmaster of Robert Gordon's Hospital and College. He was 68 when he was ordained to the parish, and was described as 'a little spare man who lacked flesh between the skin and the bone', being nevertheless a forceful character and noted disciplinarian. The ancient church was abandoned, roof and interior woodwork being removed, and the congregation transported to Kirkhill where the heritors had built the new church on a splendid site overlooking the city and 'not more than $2\frac{1}{2}$ miles distant from any part of the parish'. The church was designed by John Smith, the first official city architect, often known as 'Tudor Johnny' because of his admiration for Tudor architecture, though most of his massive granite buildings are in a well-proportioned Classical or Gothic style. Nigg Church is in his granite-Gothic style, the cost being £1800. The heritors performed another valuable service to the community in the following year when they built the first Wellington suspension bridge over the Dee at Craiginches and improved Wellington Road at a cost of £10,000. In 1906 a set of halls were built near the church at a cost of £635, while the grave-yard beside the present church was opened in 1877 and extended in 1896. The church still stands in excellent condition, celebrating its triple jubilee in 1979, having been recently redecorated with some internal alterations and the addition of a toilet-block.

The Disruption of 1843 left the church undivided within the Auld Kirk — in sharp contrast to the bitterness of division experienced in the city and surrounding parishes. Patronage, long vested in the Crown, was not an issue in Nigg, for the people had been well-content with the ministers appointed: and patronage was abolished in the Auld Kirk in 1874.

The rapid expansion of the city during the nineteenth century in both area and population, and the improvements made to the harbour, meant its inevitable encroachment into Nigg, particularly in the area of Torry, which became part of the city in 1891. About that time, the then minister of Nigg, Hugh Smith, M.A., began to hold mission services in a wooden hall at Pierhead, Torry, and a committee was set up to plan the building of a church. On 24th November 1899, a church was opened in Walker Road and named St Fittick's, Torry. It had 65 members and operated as a mission church of Nigg, then as a chapel-of-ease, eventually gaining the full status of a parish church in 1914.

As the city expanded south of the Dee the original parish of Nigg was reduced in area, as follows:—

1) Torry St Fittick's was disjoined from Nigg in 1914.

2) Torry Victoria Road was allocated part of Nigg parish in 1929. This church was formerly a United Free Church formed by Footdee Free Church.

3) Kincorth South St Nicholas Church was allocated a portion of Nigg in 1955.

4) Torry Victoria Road Church was allocated a further portion of Nigg in 1965 following the creation of the Balnagask local authority housing scheme.

By the mid-1950s Nigg was left with about half its original parish area, and at that time the larger part of its population resided in that part of the Kincorth local authority housing scheme still within the parish bounds.

In the 1970s, new housing developments began in the Redmoss and Cove Bay areas, and at the same time the city boundary moved south in stages, encroaching into Kincardineshire, until the whole of Nigg parish was absorbed into the city in 1975.

Nigg Church has a continuous history from the 7th century A.D. of serving a predominantly agricultural and fishing community, but now finds itself facing a typical suburban and industrial situation, though retaining some links with the remaining farming community. Urbanisation and industrialisation have transformed the face of the parish, and a new network of roads tends to divide it into separate communities. In the Altens and Cove Bay areas, church members have played a leading part in establishing youth organisations and community projects. Nigg church had for long held Sunday services in the old Mission Hall at Cove Bay, originally for the fisher-folk, and when that hall was sold the services were transferred to the old Cove school. More recently, Sunday services have been started in the Loirston primary school which is centrally placed. Once again in its long history the church is adapting to social changes. What pattern this will take in the future cannot clearly be seen in this time of transition.

Churches other than the Church of Scotland have not proliferated in this locality. An Episcopal mission and school was opened in Cove Bay in 1864, primarily for English families moved there with the Coast Guard and preventive services. Roman Catholic churches exist in Torry and Kincorth; Torry also has a United Free Church formed in 1929 and a number of gospel halls. Many of the new families moving into the parish retain their membership of churches in other parts of Aberdeen.

EDUCATION

For over 300 years education was the responsibility of the Church of Scotland, and prior to the Education Act of 1873 Nigg church did its best to provide schooling for the parish. The earliest mention in church records of education is in 1726 when a Mr Andrew Bonner was appointed teacher at Nigg, also serving as lay reader and Session Clerk, though the history of schooling in the parish is probably much older than existing records indicate. Church records refer to a school existing in Cove Bay in 1758, and Miss Janet Murray in her excellent book, 'Schooling in the Cove' mentions a byre near the inn being converted into a sessional school in 1771. The parochial schools at Nigg and Cove Bay, erected in the last century, still stand and are now used as community centres. Nigg parochial school was erected in 1849, described as 'a neat and commodious building' with a house and garden for the schoolmaster. It was opened 'in the presence of

members of the Presbytery, the minister Rev. Mr Fairweather, and
the heritors', the latter being thanked for their generosity. This
building continued as a school till 1939. The parochial school at Cove
was erected in 1865, enlarged in 1880, and continued as a school till
1981, when the pupils were transferred to the new Loirston primary
school. Charleston had a sessional school from 1813 to 1898; and there
was a sessional school in Torry village. St Mary's Episcopal School in
Loirston Road, Cove, was opened in 1864 and continued for 30 years,
closing as numbers declined in 1894. There were also 'dame schools' in
various parts of the parish, these being house-schools run by ladies —
at least five existed in 1792, and in that year Dr David Cruden,
minister of Nigg, reported that virtually everyone in the parish could
read and write.

In the 1950s, the Kincardineshire portion of the parish used the
primary school at Cove Bay, and for secondary education the pupils
travelled to Mackie Academy, Stonehaven. The Aberdeen section
endured a variety of ad hoc arrangements until new schools were built
in the Kincorth suburb. In the 1960s, Rosewood infant school and
Kirkhill primary school were opened, and Kincorth Academy ten
years later. As the school population had declined Rosewood infant
school closed in 1982, and all pupils in the present parish now attend
either Loirston primary school or Kirkhill primary school and proceed
to Kincorth Academy for secondary education.

THE PAST ERA

For many centuries life in the parish changed little, being dominated
by hard physical toil to extract a meagre living from the soil or the
sea. Events in the neighbouring burgh only marginally affected life in
the group of isolated and self-contained villages and hamlets of Nigg.
In the fishing villages, the men battled with the North Sea, the tiny
harbours giving little shelter in the worst conditions of storm and tide;
and there was little spare capital for repairing or replacing boats and
nothing to provide for dependents when tragedies occurred. The
women baited lines, gutting, salting, smoking the fish and carrying it
to market in Aberdeen. The farming folk struggled with stony land
and a fickle climate, handicapped by farming customs that were
unhelpful to the point of absurdity. The antiquated 'run-rig' system
with adjacent strips of land cultivated by different tenants; the failure
to rotate crops so that the land bcame exhausted; the use of the
cumbersome 'twal-ousen plough', a huge timber-built plough pulled
by twelve oxen and held in communal ownership; short leases and
insecurity of tenure — all combined to make farming a poor and
insecure occupation. Quarrying provided employment at Cove Bay
and Tullos Hill from about 1760, round pebbles and causeway stones

being shipped from the Bay of Nigg in large quantities to pave the
streets of London, Maidstone, Ramsgate and elsewhere, some 400 tons
annually being exported. About this time the women could supple-
ment their income by gathering sea-weed at Nigg Bay for kelp-
burning; and by knitting and making salmon nets in their cottages.

In that past era the people were poor, hard-working, conservative
in habits, and mingled little with the outside world except for the
purpose of buying and selling. There was much intermarriage so that
many in Cove Bay, Burnbanks and Torry were related. But hardships
breed sympathy, and the parish minister, Dr Cruden, stated in 1792,
'the parishioners, though very poor, were always willing to help
others' and there is ample evidence of generous help being given to
victims of disaster and misfortune. Many a nameless sailor cast lifeless
on the shore was given Christian burial in St Fittick's graveyard, and
as recently as 1813 forty-two of the crew of the whaling-ship 'Oscar',
which was wrecked at Greyhope Bay, were buried in a communal
grave in the old kirkyard. The sea which provides a living also claims
the lives of those it supports, and this is as true in these days of North
Sea oil as it has been in fishing communities for centuries.

The way of life here took a different turn in 1495 when Torry
village was granted a charter by James IV making it a free Burgh of
Barony. That corner of the parish might have become a thriving
commercial community as a result, for the charter gave it the right to
hold weekly markets; to have a annual fair on 30th August — St
Fittick's Day — and for six days following; to charge tolls and duties;
and to appoint bailies and burgesses. But nothing came of it; the
opportunity was not grasped; and with the opening of the Bridge of
Dee in 1527 both trade and travellers could travel easily into the
burgh, by-passing Torry and its ferry, and rendering the charter
worthless.

An event which did change life in Nigg considerably was the
partitioning of its land by arbitration in 1798 and the accompanying
agricultural reforms. The ancient 'run-rig' system was abandoned and
arbitration gave the burgh the lands of Torry and along the coast,
while the Menzies family obtained the lands beside the Dee and in the
interior. This enabled fields to be enclosed and let to tenant farmers,
and the land to be drained and improved with lime and fertilisers.
Oxen were replaced by horses, and more efficient ploughs were
introduced. Centuries-old heathland and bogs were reclaimed for
cultivation and the interior of the parish began to be developed. In
1813, the farm-lands of Charleston were created when Mr John
Menzies portioned out 5 and 6 acre lots for improvement and
cultivation. The 2000 sheep that had grazed freely on the uplands
disappeared as the land was enclosed, and crops and cattle proved
more profitable than sheep. An increase in population of some
hundreds followed these land improvements, and in the 19th century a

new era of more prosperous farming came to the parish.

Despite increasing prosperity, Nigg was never able to hold all its population. Emigration became a feature of the parish in the nineteenth and twentieth centuries, many enterprising families and ambitious young men seeking a better life in the dominions and colonies, America and the Far East. To this day the parish has strong links with many lands, and every summer visitors come seeking the homes and graves of their ancestors and worshipping in the parish church which they see as their spiritual home. Others left the parish for more lucrative employment in the industrial towns of the south; yet others joined the Merchant Navy and the Royal Navy, and during the Napoleonic Wars were occasionally seized from the fishing villages by the press-gangs. Unemployment, especially after the First World War, was a major cause of emigration, Canada being a favourite destination as it offered free land and housing in its undeveloped territories.

ABERDEEN EXPANDS SOUTH

Following its phenomenal growth during the 19th century, Aberdeen began its encroachment into this rural Kincardineshire parish in 1891 with the absorption of Torry. In the second half of the century, Torry itself had grown from a fishing village of 400 inhabitants into a thriving industrial and commercial community based on ship-building and the fish trade. People moved into Torry from the fishing villages along the coast and, as a consequence of the herring industry, from the ports of north-east England. One result was the emergence of a 'Torry dialect' compounded of native Scots and north east English dialects, and a local sense of identity. The opening of the Victoria Bridge in 1881 made the incorporation of Torry into the city almost inevitable and the Corporation Act of 1891 completed the process.

The city's second southward leap arose from the need to rehouse those living in the Victorian slums in overcrowded and often insanitary conditions. Prior to the Second World War it was estimated that 8000 families required rehousing, and the prevalence of tuberculosis gave urgency to the task.

The Kincorth lands were purchased by the city in 1920, and by 1955 a well-planned suburb, mainly of conventional granite houses, occupied the south-west portion of the parish.

A second municipal housing scheme was built some ten years later at Balnagask, overlooking the ruins of St Fittick's Church. Completed in 1967, this new scheme had its share of multi-storey blocks and flats, then becoming the fashion; while granite had become too expensive to use and was replaced by artificial granite facing.

The lands of Tullos, Craigshaw and Middleton were designated for industrial development, advantageous concessions being offered to attract new businesses in the 1960s. Industry was, however, very slow to move into the east and west industrial estates until, in the 1970s, the 'oil boom' ensured their completion.

NORTH SEA OIL

October 1970 is the significant date when British Petroleum announced that the 'Forties Field', 120 miles off Aberdeen, was commercially viable and would be developed. A new chapter began in the history of Nigg, accelerating its transformation into a dormitory and industrial suburb of the city. The exploitation of oil created employment offshore on rigs and platforms, and with firms supplying equipment and services to the oil industry, and building pipe-lines. One of the first visible manifestations locally of the 'oil boom' was the building of the Shell (U.K.) exploration and production headquarters on a site in the green belt near the church, first as a temporary building — so uncertain were the early days of the North Sea oil enterprise — and then expanding into a permanent building dominating the landscape and employing some 1000 persons. On the lands of Redmoss farm, also in the green belt, the French Michelin Tyre Company erected a large factory employing some 300 men, the large quantities of water required for cooling being brought by pipe-line from the Dee. Natural gas was brought to the city by pipe-line in the late 1970s, the branch pipe-line crossing the parish via Kincorth Hill to the gas terminal at Tullos. Land values rose in the parish in the 1970s by some 300% to 400%, as the demand for land for industry and housing increased. The second half of the 1970s was a period of feverish development, the best farm land in the parish being taken for industry and houses. It is reasonable to speculate that without the 'oil boom' Nigg would have remained a largely rural parish apart from the housing developments at Kincorth and Balnagask, while the southern section, designated as green belt by both the city and Kincardineshire, would have stood unaltered, preventing any further expansion of the city southwards.

In fact, the city pushed its way south, taking in the lands of Altens and North Loirston and eventually the whole of the parish. Altens was laid out as an industrial estate with the help of funds from the European Economic Community, rapidly filling up with mainly oil-related enterprises, three major multi-national oil companies making their headquarters there. Some of the firms taking up large areas of land employ very few people, being mainly for storage and warehouse purposes. On the lands of North Loirston another municipal housing scheme was built, in the late 1970s, mis-named 'Altens' by the local authority. Private housing developments took place in the grounds of Loirston House, and on the lands of Mains of Loirston and South Loirston, near Cove Bay, and are not expected to be completed until well into the 1980s, when some 8000 people will be living in that area.

THE PRESENT ERA

The parish of Nigg was moved into the modern urban and industrial age with such startling rapidity that its past history tends to be forgotten, while the present way of life and social structure has not yet achieved the status of a true community. Few appear to regret the passing of the old days, when this was a fishing and farming community, some remembering the physical hardships and economic uncertainty of former times and contrasting them with the comparative affluence and comfort of today.

Disadvantages exist, and the local authority, so eager to increase the population south of the city, is slow to recognise that new communities require more than houses. Even schools and community centres are provided as a kind of afterthought, while the provision for shopping is very inadequate, as is that for parks and recreation spaces. No doubt this is partly due to the high value of land. The new Loirston Country Park has never been properly developed, part being used as a municipal refuse-tip, while noisy motor-cycles destroy the peace of what was intended as a pleasant and quiet environment. Unemployment affects old and young, and the relative prosperity of Aberdeen has not prevented the unemployment rate rising to about 6.3% in this area, which compares favourably with rates as high as 16% on the north side of the city. School-leavers do not find it difficult to obtain temporary employment which is in fact poorly paid and has no long-term prospects. The contrast between the more and the less affluent, those in regular employment and the unemployed and the elderly, is clearly evident, and the possession of a motor-car is a visible symbol of relative prosperity.

The further expansion of the city southwards is already being planned. The lands of Moss-side and Blackhills, south of Cove Bay, are provisionally designated for yet another industrial estate; while those of Cove Farm may become a residential area. The city appears ambitious to produce a Greater Aberdeen by expanding into Findon, Portlethen and Banchory-Devenick. Oil-related affluence will not last for ever, however, and no attempt has yet been made to build up any kind of reserve capital fund for use in the future to revive older industries and finance new ones — a short-sightedness that may one day be greatly lamented.

TRUTH, LEGEND AND CUSTOM

Tradition tells that in St Fittick's churchyard not even worms disturb man's last resting place, for a portion of sacred soil was brought from Ireland after St Patrick had banished snakes and worms from that land, and ever since no worm has been found in the sacred precincts.

A limb of Sir William Wallace, hero of the Scottish Wars of Independence, is said to be buried in the south-east corner of St Fittick's churchyard. In 1297 A.D., Wallace is said to have attacked the English in Aberdeen from Torry, destroying 100 English ships in the harbour and expelling the English garrison from Aberdeen Castle. In 1305 A.D. he was betrayed, and beheaded in London, and in revenge the English sent one of his limbs to Aberdeen to be exposed on the Justice Port, but this was removed by the citizens and given decent burial in St Fittick's churchyard.

St Fittick's Well or Downies Well was a place of pilgrimage for many centuries. It was a pool of clear water fed by a spring, and situated at the south-east corner of Nigg Bay until destroyed in recent years by sea erosion of the coast. People from town and country laid down simple offerings at the well — a pin, a nail, or even a rag — to seek some favour or benefit. The well was also supposed to possess healing powers, mothers visiting it with their sick children or leaving articles of clothing in the desperate hope of curing the afflicted. It was for long the custom of people from the burgh to cross by the Torry ferry on May Day or on Sunday afternoons in summer to picnic at Nigg Bay and visit St Fittick's Well. The young people would walk along the Downie cliffs, crossing the narrow neck of land known as the 'Brig o' ae Hair', and carving the names of their loves in the smooth turf. The 'Brig o' ae Hair' was unfortunately despoiled by rubbish tipped over it when the railway cutting was made in the last century. Many efforts were made by kirk session and even town magistrates to curb what they saw as superstitious practices. On 8th May 1603, two kirk elders and a bailie were appointed to watch the ferry on the Sabbath to note the names of those going to the Downies Well and to punish them for Sabbath-breaking. In 1630, Margaret Davidson was fined £5 'to be paid to the collection' for taking her sick child to St Fittick's Well 'for recoverie of her health'. In the early 19th century it was reported that a mother took her sick child and washed it in the well water, leaving two slices of bread there 'tae the fairies' — and the child fully recovered.

The coast road round the Bay of Nigg crosses the Tullos Burn by a bridge formerly known as the Bridge of Nigg, and here funeral processions used to stop on their way to the old churchyard, the men doffing their hats for no apparent reason. It is said that long ago, prior to the Reformation, a shrine to the Virgin Mary stood by this bridge at which passers-by used to uncover their heads — old customs die hard.

A persistent local tradition tells that at one time the River Dee used to flow into the Bay of Nigg through the Vale of Tullos — although there is not the slightest geological evidence to support this claim. Another belief foretells that one day the River Dee will flow from Allenvale down the Vale of Tullos into the Bay of Nigg. Certainly it is true that at one time the Bay of Nigg came much further into the Vale of Tullos and the Tullos Burn was much larger and affected by the tides.

The last duel fought for honour in the Aberdeen area took place at the Bay of Nigg in the grey light of dawn on 16th June 1808. It was between two military men, one from the Stirlingshire Regiment, the other from the 1st Aberdeen Volunteers, and the latter was mortally wounded, to the great indignation and grief of his friends.

From the fisher-folk at Cove Bay come many beliefs and customs from the past. For instance, a baby born in a membrane was known as a 'sealy'un' and the membrane was kept valued as a charm or talisman against disaster at sea.

When lines were being baited in the fishing cottages it was considered very unlucky if the minister called or even passed nearby. It was also considered unlucky if a heather-brush or besom was used to sweep the earthen floor while the lines were being baited.

On Saturdays, it was the practice for the bowls to be washed and piled up; for the earthern floor to be sanded 'with bonnie brown sand', and for the bottom of the walls to be 'limed' or white-washed — the latter being done by the men. No fishing was done on Saturdays or Sundays.

Chimney fires were not uncommon in the thatched cottages where fish were smoked over a peat fire, and the Rev. Dr David Cruden, minister of Nigg from 1769 to 1826, in his 'Commonplace book' gives this quaint advice on 'How to quench a fire in the chimney': — 'From water in a vessel, with the hand throw water on the fire but not so much as to injure it, and the steam produced thereby will within a few minutes put out the fire by passing it with the current of air up the chimney'.

The hazards of journeying in the past are illustrated by a tragic accident which occurred in 1876 — only 5 years before the Victoria Bridge was opened at Torry. On a Sunday afternoon the Torry ferry, which was pulled by chains, sank with the loss of 32 lives, most of those drowned being young people crossing over to Nigg to enjoy themselves by the Bay and on the Downies cliffs.

April 1983

THE PARISH OF ST CYRUS

by Michael A. Grant

TOPOGRAPHY

St Cyrus, the southernmost parish of Kincardineshire, is bounded on the south-east by the North Sea; on the south-west by the river North Esk, which separates it from Angus (parishes of Montrose and Logie-Pert); north-west by Marykirk parish; north by Garvock; and north-east by the parish of Benholm. Some 5 miles in length (NE to SW) and 2 to 3 miles in width, St Cyrus parish is roughly rectangular in outline, with a land area of 8279 acres, nearly 13 square miles. The old name for the parish was Ecclesgreig. In the *First Statistical Account* (1794) it is called 'Ecclesgreig *alias* St Cyrus'; in the *Second Statistical Account* (1841) it is 'St Cyrus or Ecclesgreig'. The later *Account* derives Ecclesgreig from the Gaelic meaning 'the church of the rock' and dismisses the earlier *Account's* assertion that it is an abbreviation of *Ecclesia Gregorii*. Others identify Greig with a ninth century King of the Scots, Grig or Girig, 'liberator of the Scottish Church'.

The Garvock hills, to the north-west, separate the parish from the agricultural valley known as the Howe o' the Mearns, which continues to the Grampian foothills further west. The physical contours of the parish are strangely inconsistent, giving an impression of slopes and small hills, although the area is very well cultivated with few exceptions. The southern sector from the North Esk slopes gradually to Commieston and Stone o' Morphie, rising in the extreme west of the parish, at Canterland, to 500 feet. Behind Commieston, the Hill of Morphie rises to a summit of 500 feet also, whereafter it slopes down to a valley caused by the Criggie Mill Burn, thence up again to slightly over 500 feet on Canterland Moor and to the farm of Hospital Shields. The centre sector, from Kirkside to Kaim o' Mathers, is bounded on the sea by cliffs varying from 80 to 180 feet. From the cliff tops, contours rise irregularly to the Ecclesgreig estate, where the mean height above sea-level drops to the Criggie Mill Burn, then rises again to the slopes and the summit of Brandshill, at over 600 feet, thereafter crossing the parish border on the upgrade to Garvock.

The sources of water supply are rapidly becoming insufficient for the vastly increased consumption of the community. There are six dens in the parish, all with their own burns, but to date these have been inadequately harnessed as sources of water supply. Unfortunately they are all situated far from the densest centre of population and this has made their possible utilisation a costly consideration. Four of these burns flow into the North Esk, and two into the North Sea. The most picturesque den, Fenella, has a waterfall of 72 feet drop, immediately below the road bridge on the Montrose/Aberdeen coast road (highway A92). The North Esk is a clean, fast flowing river with a discharge of approximately 3 million cubic feet daily.

GEOLOGY

Coastal rocks are of the igneous type, except for the Milton promontory, which is of red sandstone. Much whinstone is to be found further back from the coast. It is quarried very extensively by the County Council at Taylorspark, where a large electric crushing plant has just been brought into operation.

SOIL

The soil over the main area of the parish is very fertile, and on the uplands there is a very deep stratum of heavy clay under the top soil. Woodston Hill and Canterland Moor, with Brandshill, are the exceptions, both having a peat stratum intermingled with poor, acid-ridden, sandy soil as the top layer. Even timber production on these two hills would be a dubious venture. There is very little soil in the remainder of the parish not ideal for intensive cultivation.

FLORA AND FAUNA

The flora and fauna have diminished seriously in the last thirty years. The indirect effect of two major wars, involving maximum tillage of land, heavy felling of wooded areas, the demand for game as food and the gradual replacement of the old aristocracy by numerous smaller utilitarian landowners have ravaged the countryside of wild flowers, birds and animals more than the casual onlooker would really have expected.

WOODLANDS

Plantations have been sadly depleted by the heavy demand for timber during the two wars. By far the largest plantation is Woodston Hill, of about 130 acres, the property of the Forestry Commission. The timber on this hill is larch and conifer, all planted about 1935. Other than some very small coniferous woods in outlying districts and two strips of beech at Kirkside and Den of Fenella, there is the estate of Ecclesgreig, which contains some magnificent beech specimens. The policies of this estate are well wooded, with beeches, oaks, elms and most of the common hardwoods. There are outlying woodlands of birch, conifer and some young plantations of larch. Due to what is considered unsatisfactory forestry encouragement from the Government, few woods are being replanted by private owners.

HISTORY OF THE LOCAL COMMUNITY

LANDOWNERS

Of those given in the *Account* of 1841 only one name now stands, that of the Forsyth Grants of Ecclesgreig, then known as Mount Cyrus. All the other big established families have sold their estates and left the district, although a trusteeship over the Morphie lands is still exercised from Dundee. Other than the Morphie Trustees and Captain Grant of Ecclesgreig, there is no single individual owning over 200 acres in the parish. Prominent owner-occupiers of small properties are Miss Mitchell Thomson, Kirkside, Mrs Singleton, Scotston and Mrs Scrymgeour Wedderburn, Bridgeton. The mansion houses of Ecclesgreig, Kirkside and Bridgeton are all occupied by their owners and are in a good state of preservation.

ANTIQUITIES

Lauriston Castle, although no longer under single ownership, stands in memory of a historic past. The estate of Lauriston itself, at the time of its break-up the largest unit in the parish, was liquidated as such in the late 1920s. The Kaim of Mathers, described in detail in the 1841 *Account*, has remained in a good state of preservation, as has the Stone of Morphie. The site of the old fountain of St Cyrus is near the farm of Stone of Morphie.

POPULATION

During the last eighty years there has been a gradual decline in the population of the parish. Census figures are as follows:— (1801) 1622; (1811) 1664 — the maximum recorded; (1851) 1579; (1871) 1585;

(1901) 1228; (1911) 1222; (1921) 1306; (1931) 1173. (The 1951 Census showed virtually no change, with a total of 1178. Of these 578 were males and 600 females). The decline was probably due to a drift from the rural areas to the towns, where employment was better paid and more plentiful. Up to the outbreak of war in 1939 agriculture was in a depressed state, and as that was the greatest single source of employment within the parish it was bound to affect the population and cause a drift to the towns. Since 1942 agriculture has flourished universally, and it is possible this will be reflected in the next census of population, although it is offset to a high extent by the present age of mechanisation. There is only one village in the parish, no other group of houses amounting to over 20 souls.

HOUSING AND PUBLIC SERVICES

Nearly all new dwellinghouses in the parish have been built by the local authority. Not since 1914 has private building been carried out to any extent, with the exception of a few cottar houses. The present trend appears to be brick and mortar houses, with Welsh slates, the exterior walls being finished with cement and harling. The latest houses are being constructed of breeze block, which is a mixture of hardened concrete interwoven on spent clinkers. A few prefabricated houses, built chiefly of asbestos, have been erected to deal with the temporary housing shortage.

SANITATION

Little improvement in hygiene appears to have been effected between 1900 and 1936, about which date St Cyrus had its first taste of properly organised public authority water, and a new sewer was laid, emitting its effluent into the sea south of Kaim of Mathers. Since the inception of these improvements great strides have been made with water sanitation. A number of local authority houses were erected in the early 1930s in the village, all having electric light and modern sanitation. It is estimated that in 1949 not more than one third of the privately owned dwelling houses in the village had modern sanitation or electric light. More council houses were constructed in 1947-48, and it is estimated that at least one third of the village population are thus housed. Over 80 per cent of dwellings are now believed to be covered by water sanitation.

Until around 1945 no steps were taken to any extent to modernise farm workers' houses, nor yet the smaller tenanted farms and freeholdings. However, due to the boom in agriculture, these houses are now more highly modernised than most private property in the village. Moreover, a number of excellent new cottar houses have been built by private enterprise, this being the only form of private building that is permitted meantime. A subsidy also attaches thereto.

WATER

Water for the village precincts is supplied by the local authority from Morshil Den. It is pumped by electricity, and is only just sufficient for current consumption. In the outlying districts and farms, water is almost exclusively obtained from small springs in the holdings, and supply for domestic needs is chiefly by gravitation. The quality of the water is good and it is comparatively free from contamination.

ELECTRICITY

Electricity is supplied by the Hydro Electric Board, and the village itself is well covered by the network. Outlying farms are not well supplied, and it is apparent that it will be a number of years before complete electrification is effected. Materials for this have been in very short supply since the Second World War.

The farm cottar houses are not electrified. Paraffin lighting is the most common, but rural gas is gaining in popularity. There is no public authority gas in the parish. Some time ago Ecclesgreig had its private gas works, but this was discontinued after the First World War. There has never been any other source of gas in the village.

HEALTH

There is no resident doctor, but a district nurse stays in St Cyrus.

ROADS

Roads in the parish are good. Most of the road metal and the whinstone is quarried from Taylorspark, St Cyrus. The roads are all paid for out of county revenue, except the main north-south road (highway A92), which bisects St Cyrus. Part of the upkeep of this is accountable to the Ministry of Transport.

A street refuse collection is made once weekly by motor. This service was inaugurated in 1948 by the county sanitary authority. Street lighting off the grid was initiated in the middle thirties. It is extinguished normally at 11.30 p.m.

AGRICULTURE

Agriculture is the most widespread activity, the soil being some of the finest in the county for that purpose. Arable and mixed farming are the most prominent, but three large farmers, two of whom have won mention in recent national shows, are worthy of note. They are Mr Andrew Spence of Commieston, Mr W.L. Anderson of Morphie and a recent arrival from Ayrshire, Mr Hourston of Nether Woodston. From 1928-1937 agriculture was very depressed indeed, and about 1937 farms were selling at as low as £5 per acre. Today, over £65 an acre is more common.

With the exception of Mr Spence's Commieston farm, famous for its preponderance of horses, all the farms are highly mechanised. Many farms have no horses at all, and rely entirely on tractors. Root harvesting is still done chiefly by hand labour, but combine harvesting of grain and pick-up baling of straw are becoming more frequent. An elevator digger which leaves potatoes in neat rows is also an innovation.

Principal crops are wheat, barley, oats, potatoes and sugar beet. Of the larger pedigreed herds in the district, Friesians, Shorthorns and Ayrshires are most prominent. A number of mixed farms fatten Irish store cattle and sell them after a time as fat cattle for slaughter. Poultry and pig farming are treated as a sideline.

FISHING

Salmon fishing in the sea, by fixed engines, is the next most important industry. The sea, *ex adverso* the parish, and the River North Esk are famous for their annual yield. The salmon season lasts seven months in the year, employing upwards of 70 men, and the capture of salmon is effected by bag and fly nets. The fisheries are operated by two different companies, both domiciled outwith the parish. The only sea salmon fishery within the parish owned by a private individual is probably the best fishing of all. This is Rockhall, on Milton Ness, and is owned by Captain Grant of Ecclesgreig and leased to a company.

OTHER OCCUPATIONS

The two foregoing are by far the major industries. In the parish there are 3 blacksmiths, 3 joiners, 2 tailors, 5 bakers (operating under a company), a garage employing 5, 3 postmen, 7 roadmen and 8 employed on the railway. A number of people, although resident in St Cyrus, work in Montrose (5 miles away) as builders, clerks, operators in a jam factory, in forestry and so forth.

CHURCH

The parish church, in the village of St Cyrus, is under the charge of the Rev. Mr Douglas. The church was erected about a hundred years ago and has a lofty spire. A Free Church was built in 1844.

SCHOOL

St Cyrus primary school (headmaster, Mr Alexander Pirie) takes children up to the age of 12. Thereafter they are sent to Inverbervie (7 or 8 miles to the N.E.)

WAY OF LIFE

Since the *Account* of 1841 the era has been conspicuous for the levelling of incomes and property generally, and whereas at that date by far the major portion of the parish was owned by five big landowners, this is no longer true. The only large estate now is Ecclesgreig. Most of the farms, all of which are under 250 acres, are owned by freeholders.

Weekly wages of farm labourers average £5.2/-, with free house; salmon fishers, £6; most other manual labourers, £4/10/-; gardeners, gamekeepers and so forth usually earn over £4. Few women in the parish are dependently engaged in commerce; those that are earn about £3.10/- in agriculture and the jam factory in Montrose.

Entertainment in St Cyrus is backward. There is no cinema, and a village hall is the mainstay, where whist drives, public meetings and dances are held. Of the two public houses, one is in St Cyrus and the other at Lauriston. Three trains run daily in each direction from St Cyrus and Lauriston stations on the Inverbervie-Montrose branch line, and an hourly bus service across the parish connects to Aberdeen and Dundee and intermediately. A Young Farmers' Club in the village, a Youth Movement (Girls) and an Army Training Corps occupy part of the leisure of the local youth.

The community on the whole may be said to have prospered in recent years. Practically no unemployment exists among the labouring classes. A number of people have settled in the village after retirement from business. There are also a few of independent means. In conclusion it may be said that the parish has probably enjoyed a period of prosperity since 1940 not widely shared by other communities, chiefly due to the prosperity of those industries which are most locally concentrated.

June 1950

THE PARISH OF STRACHAN

by G.W.Anderson

Strachan parish is in the west of Kincardineshire. It is bounded by the counties of Forfar and Aberdeen and by the parishes of Banchory-Ternan, Durris, Glenbervie, Fordoun, and Fettercairn. Its length north-north-eastwards is 13 miles and its greatest breadth is 9 miles. On the most westerly point of the western boundary Mount Battock soars to an altitude of 2,555 feet above sea level. Two broad ranges of heights, forming over all the south and centre of the parish a sea of wild uplands, slightly diverge at Mount Battock from the great central mountain range of Scotland and bear away in the direction respectively of Stonehaven and Girdleness. Their chief summits, Cloch-na-ben and Kerloch, have altitudes respectively of 1,935 and 1,747 feet above sea level and these as well as some of the smaller summits command extensive and very brilliant prospects.

The arable land of the parish lies all in the north and is tolerably fertile, but comprehends only about 2,240 acres; the extent of the surface under wood is almost 2,200 acres, and all the rest of the parish is either pastoral or waste. The predominant rock is granite. The chief rivers are the Dee on the northern boundary, the Feugh running in the north east to the Dee, and the Aven or Aan and the Dye running from the south-western border north and eastwards, to join the Feugh about ¼ of a mile west of the village of Strachan. The land covered by the parish of Strachan and divided by the river Feugh is held mostly by two proprietors. The Forestry Commission purchased Blackhall estate in 1940 and started planting in 1941, and the portion south of the Feugh known as Glendye estate was bought by Sir Thomas Gladstone from Sir James Carnegie in 1856. The remainder belonged to Mr Thomas Bentinck but was sold in 1949 when most of the tenants bought their own farms and crofts.

POPULATION

There has been no great change in the population of the parish during the last number of years. Change of course has come, but it has been slow and gradual. 80 to 90 years ago there was a bobbin mill at the

Bridge of Dye employing 7 or 8 men making birch bobbins, which continued until the birch was exhausted. There was also a wool mill at Bogendreip but it ceased working 50 or 60 years ago. This, along with the union of several small farms into one, the smallness of modern families and the fact that several of the inhabitants are elderly, partly explains the decrease of population. The overall decrease is no doubt due to the mechanised methods of farming, the lack of facilities for employment and the attraction of better opportunities which town and city life offer to ambitious and enterprising youth.

The movement of the population has been largely local. For the most part it has been a coming and going between neighbouring parishes and counties.

The village of Strachan consists of a school, two churches, a post-office and general merchants' business combined, a large dairy farm and 18 houses which include the schoolhouse and the manse. Eight of these houses have been built by the County Council within the last 20 years. The village is 3½ miles from Banchory and is situated on the South Deeside road which runs from the Brig of Feugh to Ballater. Since the Forestry Commission acquired part of the land a number of new houses have been built at Blackhall in the north-east corner of the parish, and 2 cottages at Castlehill in the centre. The farm houses are substantially built and all have installed hot and cold water. Cottar houses have also been renovated and enlarged and equipped with all modern conveniences.

PUBLIC SERVICES

The water supply of the parish is not very satisfactory. The houses built by the County Council are provided with an adequate water supply and all modern conveniences. But the majority are supplied from springs and in dry weather these often fail and entail quite a lot of hardship. There is an adequate supply at the manse, but the school, post office house and quite a number of others are on very short supply in dry weather.

ELECTRICITY

This was brought to the village by the North of Scotland Hydro-Electric Board two years ago and now they are in process of extending it throughout the parish, so that all the houses will be supplied with electricity within the next few years.

The main roads are good apart from a few bad corners, but some roads leading from the main road to the farms are very unsatisfactory. There are three main roads in the parish. One runs from east to west between the Brig of Feugh and Aboyne bridge. The other branches off to the south between the church and the dairy farm known as Bowbutts and crosses the Feugh by a bridge which was rebuilt in 1954. The road continues for about a tenth of a mile to where it branches off to the south-east towards Stonehaven, while another branch goes west to Glendye School and south over the Cairn o' Mount. Although the Cairn o' Mount road is an old road (King Edward I of England used it in 1296 when on his tour of the north east of Scotland) it was only a sand and gravel road until shortly before the Second World War when it was tar-macadamised. It is now a good road but very liable to be blocked with snow-drifts during the winter.

The part of the parish named Glendye has been in the hands of the Gladstone family since 1856. It consists mainly of moor and woodlands. Most of the woodlands were planted by them, but the acreage of wood has been greatly reduced by felling during the two wars and by the gale of 31 January 1953. At present a Glasgow firm with three large saw mills, and at times up to 90 employees, is engaged in removing the blown timber. The proprietor, Sir Albert Gladstone, is steadily replanting the felled area and has a nursery at Bridge of Dye for rearing young plants. For a time there was difficulty in getting labour but during the last two years most of the estate cottages have been renovated and modernised.

The moor for a considerable time was a grouse moor and deer forest, but three years ago the proprietor commenced to stock it with black-faced sheep. At one time this was reckoned to be one of the largest grazings in the north-east of Scotland.

SCHOOLS

There are two schools in the parish. The one in the village is staffed by a male head teacher and two female teachers. There are 76 pupils at present on the roll. The other in Glendye was built by Sir James Carnegie about 1839 and was taken over by the Kincardineshire Education Authority about 20 years ago. They built a new school house and the old school was renovated and lavatories and hot water circulation installed. But owing to the scarcity of teachers and the small number of pupils at present in Glendye both school and schoolhouse are not in use meantime, except by a company of girls along with their teacher from St Margaret's School in Aberdeen, who stay in the school during the spring and summer weekends for nature study.

The children outwith a radius of 2 miles are conveyed to and from Strachan school by bus and cars. They are given a bottle of milk in the forenoon and a meal at mid-day for which they pay a small fee. They are taught up to the age of 11 or 12 years, then they proceed to

Banchory Academy, free transport being provided by the Education Authority. The public library is situated in Strachan school. The books are provided by the County Library and changed frequently, and it is used by a section of the people.

There are two churches — both in the village. The Free Church was built in 1853. In 1929 both congregations agreed to unite but the union was not consummated until 1950. Then it was agreed that the Free Church should be used as a church hall and the parish church should be the place of public worship. The parish church stands on the north side of the road and was built in 1865, being gifted by Lady Gladstone. It is a lovely building and in very good condition.

There are 8 elders in the Kirk Session, 17 members in the Woman's Guild, 28 scholars in the Sunday school and 8 members in the bible class. There are 167 members on the Communion roll and the average attendance at the Sacrament of the Lord's Supper is between 90-100 members.

SOCIAL LIFE

Up to 30 years ago, the social life of the community was centred on the school, but in 1927 a public hall was built by public subscription. The feu charter was granted by Baroness Bentinck. The hall has been a boon to the community. One of the first agencies to be formed was the Women's Rural Institute under the presidency of Lady Douglas residing at Larachmore. It has been a source of education, practical help and entertainment ever since, and still grows and expands in influence. Following it other societies were formed, the dramatic society, whist club, youth club, Girl Guides and Brownies. A picture house was built in Banchory a little over a year ago and, travel facilities being fairly convenient and there being greater numbers, the Banchory company of the Boys' Brigade and Boy Scout troop have militated against the attraction of the village hall, with some boys and girls of the parish attending organisations in Banchory.

Nevertheless an active social life still exists. A local committee under the name of the Strachan Children's Fund invites dramatic societies and concert parties from the neighbouring parishes in the county to present plays and entertainments, by which money is raised to provide a free gift and Xmas party for all children in the district under 15 years of age and an annual outing during the summer. The hall is used two days a week by the Education Authority for physical instruction of the children.

There is a Post Office and general merchant's business in the village and a small grocer's shop at Colmack. Up until three years ago there was a blacksmith's shop in the village, but owing to the decrease in the number of horses in the district the blacksmith is at present engaged in

other employment. The parish is however liberally supplied with a
wide range of tradesmen's vans. Two baker's and two butcher's vans
call twice a week. There is only one inn in the parish, the Whitestane
Inn situated on the western boundary close to the bridge built in 1939
by Donald Stewart, Aberdeen. This connects the main road at the
west end of the parish with the Cairn o' Mount road. Strachan's bus
service provides four buses to and from Aberdeen each day during the
summer and three into Aberdeen and four out in winter.

AGRICULTURE

This is the main employment, there being no industry within the
parish bounds. There were two meal-mills but the last one ceased
work about two years ago.

There are 20 farms, two of them being large dairy farms, and 11
crofts. Of these 5 farms and 5 crofts are owner-occupied, the
remainder being worked by tenants. The leases of the farms are 14
years with a break at 7 years. Apart from a few people who find
employment in Banchory the remainder work with the Forestry
Commission and are busy planting the waste ground. Probably the
most important change in farming recently has been the substitution
of tractors for horses. The average farm used to be worked by two or
three pair of horses; now only a few of the farms retain one horse for
doing odd jobs. With the amount of work that can be done with
tractors, government subsidies being given for marginal land, and
better prices for farm produce, most of the old arable land which had
been in permanent pasture for over fifty years has now been cultivated
and is producing good crops and pasture.

The outbreak of myxomatosis disease among rabbits last year has
almost wiped them out. This has made a big difference in production
on the farms bordering moors and woodlands. Many farms and crofts
have poultry in deep litter during the winter months and find it
profitable.

The use of machinery has inevitably reduced the number of regular
employees on the farms. Casual workers are in great demand during
harvesting and potato lifting and are almost impossible to find, but
school children assist with the potato gathering. The farmers did good
work during the war, and are still doing it. The farms in the parish
reveal a high standard of husbandry. They are awake to the benefits
accruing from the more adequate use of lime and artificial manures
and the sowing of permanent grass seed mixtures.

The breed of cattle has been improved and most of the farms carry
a stock of attested cattle. Farms which have a number of acres of hill-
grazing receive government subsidies for cows and calves with the
result that they are fully stocked. Half of the farms rear cattle, the
others feed for beef production.

DAIRY FARMING

Perhaps the greatest advance has been made in dairy farming. Within living memory a great change has taken place in the production of milk. Formerly milk was produced by the individual farms for their own use; nowadays it is produced and supplied by two specialist dairy farms. Lorries and vans deliver it daily throughout the parish, and also in Banchory and the surrounding district. Dairymen possess attested herds from which they secure a safer and purer supply of milk. Their premises are modernised and equipped with the latest machinery. Milking is done by machines, and the whole process of milk production is carried out by the most hygienic methods.

HISTORICAL MONUMENTS

There are three circular and evidently artificial mounds, which may have been used as fences for bowmen when practising arrow-shooting. A farm-house in the neighbourhood is called Bowbutts. Another is named Castlehill, but no remains of a castle are to be seen, nor is there any tradition of its existence. There are two stone cairns about a mile apart on the farms of Letterbeg and Ardlair. Their form is circular and almost 300 feet in circumference. The Bridge of Dye on the Cairn o' Mount road was built about 1680. There was a toll on it for a time, but there is no record when it was stopped. It is the oldest bridge in the valley of the Dee except for the Brig of Dee at Aberdeen. It was scheduled as an ancient monument some years ago, so will now be preserved.

One of the most interesting things in the parish is the Kettle-holes around Bogarn. They are understood to have been formed during the Ice Age when the glaciers were melting; detached portions of ice were surrounded by gravel brought down by melting water from higher up, and when the ice melted the holes were left scattered throughout the gravel.

NATURE NOTES

Few districts used to be better supplied with game, but grouse are very scarce on the moors now owing to an outbreak of disease called 'tick' some years ago. There are still plenty of deer and mountain hares, and on the lower ground pheasants and partridges are fairly plentiful. There are no wild animals peculiar to this parish. The most common are foxes, badgers and a few wild cats, and otters are occasionally seen by the rivers.

Scarcely any plants which can properly be called rare are found in the parish. The hollows and valleys of the streams are filled with varieties of ferns, foxgloves, brambles and wild rasps and in parts where trees have been cut there are beds of willow-herb. The principal trees are spruce, fir and larch.

WAY OF LIFE

No outstanding change has taken place in the parish during the last 100 years. Those who earn their livelihood from the cultivation of the land are not subject to the dramatic changes that sometimes take place in industrial communities. Nevertheless, with the change-over from horses to tractors in farming some of the well-known figures of former generations are gradually disappearing, such as drainers, ditchers and dry-stane dykers.

Labour on the farms and in the households has been greatly lightened, and with improved living conditions, increased wages and shorter working hours the people generally have now more time for leisure. Most of the farms own a private motor car and public bus services provide easy facilities for travel, bringing entertainment and education within easy reach of all. The wireless and public library have been a great asset in this way.

The church and public hall still play an active part in the life of the community, being the chief means of fostering and maintaining the friendly spirit of neighbourliness and co-operation. Although the people are still interested in religion a certain amount of apathy towards the ordinary diets of public worship on the Sunday is to be found in a section of the community. The continued advance in moral and social welfare has opened the way to a higher and healthier life.

(Undated: probably 1955)

BIBLIOGRAPHY

The Bibliography is select rather than comprehensive, but the aim has been to include all the books and articles of major relevance to Kincardineshire, as well as some minor but interesting items. An attempt has been made to check every title either by examining the book or by comparing more than one entry in bibliographical sources. Where no confirmation has been found the entry has been marked with an asterisk (*): these entries should perhaps be approached with caution. Any remaining errors or omissions are the responsibility of the editor.

Where appropriate a title may be entered under more than one heading. No entries have been included for the Torry district, which was transferred from Kincardineshire to Aberdeen city in 1891. The Bibliography is arranged as follows:

SUBJECT: General
   Geology and landforms
   Natural history
   Agriculture
   Fishing
   History and antiquities
   Church history
   Anthropology and folklore
   Genealogy
   Planning and statistics

Politics and administration
Education
Sports
Miscellaneous
Bibliography
Literature

TOPOGRAPHICAL
PERIODICALS

SECTION 1: SUBJECT

GENERAL

Allan, John R.: *North-east lowlands of Scotland*, London 1952, second edition London 1974
Around and about Aberdeen and Grampian area by car, Aberdeen 1974
British Association for the Advancement of Science (eds. A. C. O'Dell and J. Mackintosh): *The north-east of Scotland*, Aberdeen 1963
   Douglas, Francis: *A general description of the east coast of Scotland from Edinburgh to Cullen*, Paisley 1782, reprinted Aberdeen 1826
Duncan, W.: *Description of the coast between Aberdeen and Leith*, Aberdeen 1837
Edwards, David Herschell: *Around the ancient city in six circular tours, historical and descriptive, with notes on the ancient superstitions, folklore, eminent men and curious characters in various districts of Forfar and Kincardineshire*, Brechin 1895, second edition Brechin 1905
[Eeles, Francis Carolus]: *Stonehaven historical and descriptive, being a guide-book to the town and surrounding district, with an introductory sketch of Kincardineshire*, Aberdeen 1897

Fraser, Duncan: *Discovering Angus and Mearns*, Montrose [1967]
    : *Discovering east Scotland*, Montrose 1973 1974
    : *Glen of the rowan tree, and other stories*, Montrose 1973
    : *Guide to the glens of Angus and Mearns: their beauty spots, history and legends*, Montrose 1961, new edition Montrose 1963
Geography of the county of Kincardine, (Collins' county geographies) Glasgow 1875
Graham, Cuthbert: *Portrait of Aberdeen and Deeside, with Aberdeenshire, Banff and Kincardine*, London 1972, second edition London 1980
Illustrated tourists' guide to the Mearns, Laurencekirk [1909]
Inglis, J.: *Oor ain folk: being memories of manse life in the Mearns and a crack aboot auld times*, Edinburgh 1894, fourth edition Edinburgh 1909
Kincardine County Council: *Official guide to the county of Kincardine*, Dundee Aberdeen various editions
Kincardine and Deeside District Council: *Kincardine and Deeside district official guide*, Gloucester 1980— various editions
Kinnear, George Henderson: *Kincardineshire*, (Cambridge county geographies) Cambridge 1921
Macfarlane, Walter (ed. Sir Arthur Mitchell): *Geographical collections relating to Scotland made by Walter Macfarlane*, (Scottish History Society, vols 51-53) 3 vols Edinburgh 1906-1908
M'Michael, George: *Notes on the way through the counties of Perth, Clackmannan, Forfar and Kincardine*, Ayr [c.1889]
The New Statistical Account of Scotland vol xi: Forfar-Kincardine, Edinburgh 1845
Ogilvie, Wilson: *Car tours from Stonehaven*, Aberdeen [1977]
Paterson, J. S.: *Sketches of scenery in Angus and Mearns, drawn from nature and upon stone*, 3 vols, Montrose 1824
Peck, Sir Edward: *North-east Scotland*, Edinburgh 1981. A gazetteer
Pictorial Kincardineshire, Aberdeen [1905]
Sinclair, Sir John (ed.): *The Statistical Account of Scotland 1791-1799*, new edition, vol xiv: Kincardineshire and south and west Aberdeenshire, Wakefield 1982
Tranter, Nigel: *The eastern counties: Aberdeenshire, Angus and Kincardineshire*, London 1972
Watt, Archibald: *Highways and byways around Kincardine*, Aberdeen 1985
Wyness, James Fenton: *Kincardine: official guide*, Aberdeen [1955] [1956]

GEOLOGY AND LAND FORMS

Anderson, J. G. C.: 'The stratigraphical order of the Dalradian schists near the Highland border in Angus and Kincardine', in *Transactions of the Geological Society of Glasgow*, 1937-1944, vol. xx, 223-37
Barrow, George: 'On the occurrence of Silurian (?) rocks in Forfarshire and Kincardineshire along the eastern border of the Highlands', in *Quarterly Journal of the Geological Society of London*, 1901, vol. 57, 328-45
    : 'On the geology of lower Deeside and the southern Highland border', in *Proceedings of the Geologists' Association*, 1912, vol. 23, 274-90
Bremner, Alexander: 'The glacial geology of the Stonehaven district', in *Transactions of the Edinburgh Geological Society*, 1915-1924, vol.xi, 25-41
Campbell, Robert: 'The geology of south-eastern Kincardineshire', in *Transactions of the Royal Society of Edinburgh*, 1913, vol.xlviii, 923-60
    : 'Preliminary note on the geology of south-eastern Kincardineshire', in *Geological Magazine*, 1911, new series vol. viii, 63-69

Friends of the Earth (Aberdeen): *A promise to move mountains: the search for uranium on Deeside*, Aberdeen [1977]

Imrie, [Ninian]: *A description and section of the strata of the Grampian mountains from the plain of Kincardineshire to the summit of Mount Battock*, Edinburgh [1811] (reprinted from *Transactions of the Royal Society of Edinburgh*, vol. vi)

Jamieson, Thomas F.: *List of altitudes in the counties of Aberdeen, Banff and Kincardine*, Aberdeen 1860

Macgregor, D. Ronald: 'The Kincardineshire Plateau', in *Scottish Geographical Magazine*, 1948, vol.64, 81–89

Ritchie, William, Rose, N., and Smith, John Smart: *Beaches of northeast Scotland*, [Perth] 1978

Stamp, Laurence Dudley: *Kincardineshire* (The land of Britain: report of the land utilization survey of Britain, part 28), London 1946

University of Aberdeen, Department of Geography: *A landform inventory of the Grampian region*, Aberdeen 1978

NATURAL HISTORY

Crichton, George M.: *The birds of Angus, including south Kincardineshire*, Brechin 1976

Dickie, George: *The botanist's guide to the counties of Aberdeen, Banff and Kincardine*, Aberdeen 1860

Edlin, Herbert L. (ed.): *Forests of north east Scotland* (Forestry Commission guide), Edinburgh 1963, new edition Edinburgh 1976

Ewan, Lorna A.: *A palynological investigation of a peat deposit near Banchory: some local and regional environmental implications*, Aberdeen 1981

MacGillivray, P. H.: *A catalogue of the flowering plants and ferns growing in the neighbourhood of Aberdeen*, Aberdeen 1853

MacGillivray, William: *History of the molluscous animals of the counties of Aberdeen, Kincardine and Banff*, London 1843

Marren, Peter: 'The History of Dickie's fern in Kincardineshire', in *Botanical Society of Edinburgh Transactions*, 1983, vol. 44 part 2, 157–64

Simpson, A. Nicol: 'Contribution to the ornithology of Kincardineshire', in *Annals of Scottish natural history*, 1900, vol.ix, 147–53, 197–202

Staines, B. W.: 'The management and dispersion of a red deer population in Glen Dye, Kincardineshire', unpublished Ph.D. thesis, University of Aberdeen 1967

AGRICULTURE

Carter, Ian: 'Dorset, Kincardine and peasant crisis', in *Journal of Peasant Studies*, 1975, vol.ii, 483–88

——: *Farmlife in northeast Scotland 1840-1914: the poor man's country*, Edinburgh 1979

——: 'Lewis Grassic Gibbon, "A Scots Quair" and the peasantry', in *History Workshop*, Autumn 1978, issue 6, 169–85

Donaldson, James: *General View of the agriculture of the county of Kincardine or the Mearns*, London 1795

Gourcy, Conrad, comte de: *Journal du second voyage agricole en Angleterre et en Ecosse*, Paris 1849. Pages 52–81 describe impressions gained during his stay at Kingcausie

Kinnear, George Henderson: *Agriculture in the Mearns one hundred years ago*, Montrose 1895

Lawson, Thomas: *A report on the past and present agriculture of the counties of Forfar and Kincardine*, Edinburgh 1881

Macdonald, James: 'On the agriculture of the counties of Forfar and Kincardine', in *Transactions of the Highland and Agricultural Society of Scotland*, 1881, fourth series vol. XIII, 53-173

Robertson, George: *A general view of the agriculture of Kincardineshire or the Mearns*, Montrose [1807] London [1808], etc. Apparently several editions
   : *Rural recollections: or, the progress of improvement in agriculture and rural affairs*, Irvine 1829. Includes 'Part II — Kincardineshire', 401-522

FISHING

Anson, Peter F.: *Fishing boats and fisher folk on the east coast of Scotland*, London 1930

Christie, William: 'A fisherman's diary' [Robert Lees of Stonehaven, 1809-1831], in *Scots Magazine*, February 1966, new series vol.84 no.5, 483-88

Hay, Edna R. and Walker, Bruce: *Focus on fishing: Arbroath and Gourdon*, Dundee 1985

HISTORY AND ANTIQUITIES

Anderson, James: *The black book of Kincardineshire, containing lists of Covenanters confined in Dunnottar Castle in 1685* . . . , Stonehaven 1843, new edition Aberdeen 1879, 1893

Chisholm, J. M.: 'A preliminary survey of the monuments of the county of Kincardine', unpublished B.A. dissertation, University of Leicester, 1977

Coles, Frederick R.: 'Report on stone circles in Kincardineshire (north) and part of Aberdeenshire', in *Proceedings of the Society of Antiquaries of Scotland*, 1900, vol.xxxiv, 139-98
   : 'Record of the excavation of two stone circles in Kincardineshire . . . ', in *Proceedings of the Society of Antiquaries of Scotland*, 1905, vol.xxxix, 190-218
   : 'The stone circles of the north-east of Scotland', in *Transactions of the Buchan Field Club*, 1902-1903, vol vii, 205-38

Davidson, Flora and Davidson, John: *An inventory of the seventeenth century tombstones of the Mearns*, Arbroath 1979

Davidson, Patrick Leslie: *Records of the 5th (Deeside Highlanders) Volunteer Battalion, Gordon Highlanders*, second edition [Inchmarlo] 1898. Originally published in 1892 as an appendix to a bazaar book.

Diack, Francis C.: 'The old-Celtic inscribed and sculptured stone at Auquhollie, Kincardineshire, and ogam in Scotland', in *Proceedings of the Society of Antiquaries of Scotland*, 1924-1925, vol.lix, 257-69

Fraser, Sir William (ed. J. R. N. MacPhail): *Papers from the collection of Sir William Fraser* (Scottish History Society, third series, vol.V) Edinburgh 1924. Includes: Papers relating to the Mearns, pp.47-171

Gordon, James (eds. G. D. Henderson and H. H. Porter): *James Gordon's Diary 1692-1710* (Third Spalding Club) Aberdeen 1949. Gordon was the son of James Gordon, minister of Banchory-Devenick, and an active Episcopalian in the north-east

Illustrations of the topography and antiquities of the shires of Aberdeen and Banff ([First] Spalding Club) 4 vols, Aberdeen 1847-69. Despite the title volumes 2 and 3 contain a good deal of material on the Deeside parishes of Kincardineshire

Jervise, Andrew: *Epitaphs and inscriptions from burial grounds and old buildings in the north-east of Scotland*, 2 vols, Edinburgh 1875-1879
: *The history and traditions of the land of the Lindsays in Angus and Mearns* . . . , Edinburgh 1853; second edition rewritten by James Gammack, Edinburgh 1882
: *Memorials of Angus and Mearns* . . . , Edinburgh 1861; second edition rewritten by James Gammack, 2 vols, Edinburgh 1885
*[Jervise, Andrew]: *Notes and queries on the antiquities of Angus and Mearns*, Montrose 1854
Jervise, Andrew: *Sketch of the history and antiquities of the Mearns: a lecture*, Montrose 1858
Kenworthy, J. B.: 'Nethermills Farm, Crathes: excavations 1978-80: interim report', typescript, University of St Andrews, 1981
Paterson, Hilda Maud Leslie: 'Banchory microliths. By Hilda M. Leslie Paterson and A. D. Lacaille. And, The river terraces near Birkwood, Banchory, Kincardineshire. By Hilda M. Leslie Paterson', in *Proceedings of the Society of Antiquaries of Scotland*, 1936, vol.lxx, 419-34
Peat, Alexander: 'An attempt to explain some antiquities in the counties of Kincardine and Forfar', manuscript 1787. Perth Literary and Antiquarian Society MS 54, now in the custody of Perth Museum and Art Gallery, and described in National Register of Archives (Scotland) report no.1492 item 289
Piggott, Stuart: 'Excavation of the Dalladies long barrow, Fettercairn, Kincardineshire', in *Proceedings of the Society of Antiquaries of Scotland*, 1971-1972, vol. 104, 23-47
Ralston, Ian B. M.: 'A timber hall at Balbridie farm', in *Aberdeen University Review*, Autumn 1982, vol. xlix 4 no. 168, 238-49
and Reynolds, Nicholas: 'Britain's oldest building?: an early timber structure on Deeside', in *Scottish Review*, May 1979, No. 14, 17-22
Reid, R. W. and Fraser, J. R.: 'Short stone cist found in the parish of Kinneff and Catterline, Kincardineshire', in *Proceedings of the Society of Antiquaries of Scotland*, 1923-1924, vol. lviii, 27-40
Reynolds, Nicholas: 'Dark age timber halls and the background to excavation at Balbridie', in *Scottish Archaeological Forum*, 1978, no.10, 41-60
Royal Commission on the Ancient and Historical Monuments of Scotland: *North Kincardine, Kincardine and Deeside district, Grampian region* (Archaeological sites and monuments of Scotland 21) Edinburgh 1984
Royal Commission on the Ancient and Historical Monuments of Scotland: *South Kincardine, Kincardine and Deeside district, Grampian region* (Archaeological sites and monuments of Scotland 15) Edinburgh 1982
Scott, J. Moffat: *The martyrs of Angus and Mearns: sketches in the history of the Scottish Reformation*, Paisley 1885
Sinclair, Donald: *The history of the Aberdeen Volunteers, embracing also some account of the early Volunteers of the counties of Aberdeen, Banff and Kincardine*, Aberdeen 1907
Smith, R. Angus: 'Notes on stone circles in Durris, Kincardineshire, and its neighbourhood', in *Proceedings of the Society of Antiquaries of Scotland*, 1879-1880, vol.xiv, 294-309
*Spence, Stuart: *The Glasgow, Angus and Mearns Benevolent Society: a short sketch of its origin and work*, Glasgow 1895
Watkins, Trevor: 'Excavations of an Iron Age open settlement at Dalladies, Kincardineshire', in *Proceedings of the Society of Antiquaries of Scotland*, 1978-1980, vol.110, 122-64

Watt, James Crabb: *The Mearns of old: a history of Kincardineshire from the earliest times to the seventeenth century*, Edinburgh 1914
Will, William: *The Kincardineshire Volunteers: a history of the volunteer movement in Kincardineshire from 1798 to 1816*, [Aberdeen] 1920

CHURCH HISTORY

Eeles, Francis Carolus: *The church and other bells of Kincardineshire*, Aberdeen [1897]
Scott, Hew: *Fasti Ecclesiae Scoticanae: the succession of ministers in the Church of Scotland from the Reformation*, vol.5: Synods of Fife, and of Angus and Mearns, new edition, Edinburgh 1925

ANTHROPOLOGY AND FOLKLORE

McPherson, Joseph MacKenzie: *Primitive beliefs in the north-east of Scotland*, London 1929. Written by a one-time minister of Rickarton
Small, Alan: 'The small villages of the Howe of the Mearns', in *Folk Life*, 1966, vol.iv, 22-29
Tocher, James Fowler: *Anthropometric observations on samples of the civil populations of Aberdeenshire, Banffshire and Kincardineshire*, Edinburgh 1924

GENEALOGY (see also family histories listed under particular places)

'Copy of a manuscript entitled "A genealogie of the barons in the Mearns of late memory deschending lineally unto the year of God 1578', in *Miscellany of the Third Spalding Club*, 1940, vol. ii, 211-21
Napier, James: *Biographical sketch of the Keiths*, Stonehaven [n.d.], second edition 1870
Nicol, W. E.: *The genealogy of the Nicol family, Kincardineshire branch*, [London] 1909
Peter, David McGregor: *The baronage of Angus and Mearns, comprising the genealogy of three hundred and sixty families . . .*, Edinburgh 1856
Rogers, Charles: *Genealogical memoirs of the family of Robert Burns and of the Scottish house of Burnes*, London 1877

PLANNING AND STATISTICS

Grampian Regional Council. Department of Physical Planning: *Development analysis booklet: Kincardine and Deeside*, January 1980— Aberdeen 1980—. Updated every six months.
Grampian Regional Council. Department of Physical Planning: *Grampian region (part) structure plan: rural area*, 4 vols, Aberdeen 1983-1984
Grampian Regional Council. Department of Public Transportation: *South Kincardine rural area transport survey*, [Aberdeen] [1979?]
Kincardine and Deeside District Council: *Kincardine suburban area local plan*, 6 vols, Stonehaven [1980-1983]
Marr, Norman G.: 'Kincardine and Deeside: the beginnings of conservation', in *Deeside Field*, 1978, third series no.2, 94-103

North East of Scotland Joint Planning Advisory Committee: *Employment and population change in the Grampian region, 1971-1986*, [Aberdeen] 1975
North East of Scotland Joint Planning Advisory Committee: *The regional report*, [Aberdeen] 1975

POLITICS AND ADMINISTRATION

Dyer, M. C.: 'Leadership in a Scottish rural county', in *Political leaders in local government*, ed. G. W. Jones and Alan Norton, Birmingham 1978, 30-50
    : 'The politics of Kincardineshire', unpublished Ph.D. thesis, University of Aberdeen, 1974
Local Government Boundary Commission for Scotland: *Initial review of electoral arrangements for Kincardine and Deeside district*, [Edinburgh] [1979]

EDUCATION

Scottish Education Department: *Education in Kincardineshire: report by HM Inspectors of Schools*, Edinburgh 1972

SPORTS

Etchachan Club: *Rock climbing guide to the north-east coastline of Scotland*, [Aberdeen] 1969. Includes sections on Souter Head and Cove
Turberville, Ruby: 'Kitin's the thing' [the story of Dunnottar Quoiting Club], in *Scots Magazine*, June 1983, vol. 119 no.3, 284-89

MISCELLANEOUS

Annual police report [for the county of Kincardine], Stonehaven [at least 1906-1948]
Annual report upon the health and sanitary condition of the county [of Kincardine], 1890-1911, Stonehaven 1891-1912
Commonwealth War Graves Commission: *The war dead of the British Commonwealth and Empire: the register of the names of those who fell in the 1939-1945 war and are buried in cemeteries and churchyards in the counties of Angus and Kincardine*, London 1959
Dunnottar Parish Church bazaar cookery book, [Stonehaven] 1902
Imperial War Graves Commission: *The war graves of the British Empire: the register of the names of those who fell in the Great War and are buried in cemeteries and churchyards in counties of Aberdeen, Angus, Inverness and Kincardine, Scotland*, London 1931
Kincardineshire exhibition: catalogue of the Kincardineshire exhibition of works of industry and art in the Stonehaven Town Hall buildings, Stonehaven 1881

BIBLIOGRAPHY

Aberdeen Public Library: *Catalogue of the local collection to be found in the Reference Department*, Aberdeen 1914
Johnstone, James Fowler Kellas: *A concise bibliography of the history, topography and*

institutions of the shires of Aberdeen, Banff and Kincardine (Aberdeen University Studies no.66) Aberdeen 1914

and Robertson, Alexander W.: *Bibliographia Aberdonensis: being an account of books relating to or printed in the shires of Aberdeen, Banff, Kincardine, or written by natives or residents* . . . (Third Spalding Club no.12) vol.1:1472-1640, vol.2:1641-1700, Aberdeen 1929-31

Robertson, Alexander W.: *Handlist of bibliography of the shires of Aberdeen, Banff and Kincardine* (New Spalding Club) Aberdeen 1893

LITERATURE

Buchan, David: *The ballad and the folk*, London 1972

Burness, John: *Thrummy Cap: a legend of the Castle of Fiddes*, Brechin 1832, new edition Montrose 1886 (with a memoir of the author)

Colburn, George: *Poems on mankind and nature*, Glasgow 1891. Includes: Home poems, pp.173-271, mainly on Kincardineshire places and personalities

Gibbon, Lewis Grassic (James Leslie Mitchell): *A Scots quair* [comprising *Sunset song, Cloud howe* and *Grey granite*], London 1932-34

: *The speak of the Mearns*, Edinburgh 1982. A fragment of an unfinished novel set in Kinneff

Grant, David: *A Feughside fairy tale*, new edition Finzean 1980. Humorous verse — this and the following item originally appeared in Grant's *Lays and Legends of the North*, Edinburgh 1884

: *The muckle spate of 'twenty-nine*, new edition Finzean 1979

Grant, Joseph: *Kincardineshire traditions*, Aberdeen 1830. Despite the title, a book of original verse.

: *Tales of the glens, with ballads and songs*, Dundee 1834, other editions Edinburgh 1836, Stonehaven 1869 etc.

*Jamie, William: *The muse of the Mearns*, Stonehaven 1844. And other works

Macpherson, Ian: *Shepherd's calendar*, London 1931, new edition Edinburgh 1983. A novel set in the Mearns, and an important influence on *A Scots quair*

Murray, William: *Lilts frae the Mearns: the heather lintie and other lays*, Montrose 1907

Ord, John (ed.): *The bothy songs and ballads of Aberdeen, Banff and Moray, Angus and the Mearns*, Paisley 1930, reprinted Edinburgh 1973

Reid, Alan (ed.): *The bards of Angus and the Mearns: an anthology of the counties*, Paisley 1897

*Walker, James: *Effusions from the braes of Cowie*, Montrose 1850

Will, William: *Song and story of Aberdeen, Banff and Kincardine: an address*, Aberdeen 1939

The works listed above all have specific Kincardineshire connections. Besides these, it may be worth adding a fuller list of writers who either were born in the Mearns or had strong links with the county. Material of local interest may be found in their writings or in writings about them. For a small county the list is not unimpressive

John Arbuthnot (1667-1735), born Arbuthnott, physician, writer and wit

George Beattie (1786-1823), born Hill of Morphie, lawyer and poet

James Beattie (1735-1803), born Laurencekirk, poet and philosopher

John Burness (1771-1824), born Bogjorgan, poet

Gilbert Burnet (1643-1715), born Edinburgh, churchman and historian

James Burnett, Lord Monboddo (1714-1799), born Monboddo, judge, philosopher
  and polymath
John of Fordun (c.1320-1384 or 1385), historian
Sir William Fraser (1816-1898), born Arduthie, historian
Lewis Grassic Gibbon (James Leslie Mitchell) (1901-1935), born Auchterless, Aber-
  deenshire, novelist and essayist
David Grant (1823-1886), born Affrusk, poet and short story writer
Joseph Grant (1805-1835), born Affrusk, poet and short story writer
David Herd (1732-1810), born Marykirk, folk song collector and editor
Cosmo Innes (1798-1874), born Durris, historian
George Ritchie Kinloch (1796?-1877), born Stonehaven, folk song collector and
  editor
John Laird (1887-1946), born Durris, philosopher
Ian Macpherson (1905-1944), born Forres, Moray, novelist
Thomas Reid (1710-1796), born Strachan, philosopher
Alexander Taylor (1805-18—), born Conie, Fetteresso, poet

SECTION 2: TOPOGRAPHICAL

ALLARDICE

Rose, David Murray: *Allardyce of that ilk*, reprint of an article

ALTENS

Ferguson, James: 'Report on the improvement of the Muir of Altens', in *Transactions
  of the Highland and Agricultural Society of Scotland*, 1841, new series vol. vii [= first
  series vol.xiii], 163-80

ARBUTHNOTT (*see also* Allardice)

Arbuthnot, Ada Jane (Mrs P. Stewart-Mackenzie Arbuthnot): *Memories of the
  Arbuthnots of Kincardineshire and Aberdeenshire*, London 1920
Arbuthnott House, near Laurencekirk, Kincardineshire, [Arbuthnott?] [1973]. An ill-
  ustrated guide
Henderson, George Aitchison: *The kirk of St Ternan, Arbuthnott: a Scottish heritage*,
  Edinburgh 1962
The Kirk of Sanct Ternan, Arbuthnott, [Arbuthnott] [c.1970]
*Liber ecclesie beati Terrenani de Arbuthnott: missale secundum usum ecclesiae Sancti Andreae
  in Scotia*, Burntisland 1862. An edition of the missal written and used at
  Arbuthnott around 1500
Mackenzie, A. Marshall: 'Notes on the parish church of Arbuthnott', in *Transactions of
  the Aberdeen Ecclesiological Society*, 1890, vol.i part 4, 41-44
Rose, David Murray: *The lords of Arbuthnott*, [n.p.] [c.1903] (reprinted from the
  Stonehaven Journal, 1902-1903)

302   BIBLIOGRAPHY

Scottish Association of Geography Teachers: *Arbuthnott estate and south Kincardine coast* (SAGT annual field excursion) [Edinburgh] [1983]
Slade, Harry Gordon: 'Arbuthnott House, Kincardineshire', in *Proceedings of the Society of Antiquaries of Scotland*, 1978-1980 vol. 110, 432-74
Spence, Robert Moir: *Arbuthnott parish church: jubilee sermon*, Montrose 1900
Suttie, George Clark: *Arbuthnott, with some reminiscences of the parish sixty years ago*, Montrose 1908. Issued as a bazaar book, edited by A. Mason

AUCHENBLAE (*see also* Fordoun)

Constitution, rules and regulations of the Kincardineshire Ploughman Friendly Society in Auchenblae, instituted June 22, 1812, Montrose 1825
Gove, A.: *The history of Auchenblae*, [Auchenblae] 1967

AUQUHOLLIE

Diack, Francis C.: 'The old-Celtic inscribed and sculptured stone at Auquhollie, Kincardineshire, and ogam in Scotland', in *Proceedings of the Society of Antiquaries of Scotland*, 1924-1925, vol.lix, 257-69

BALBEGNO

Sutherland, Joseph: 'The heraldic ceiling of Balbegno Castle', in *Aberdeen University Review*, Spring 1976, vol.xlvi 3 no.155, 268-73
Wedderburn, L. M. M.: *Excavations at Greencairn, Cairnton of Balbegno, Fettercairn, Angus [sic]: a preliminary report* (Dundee Museum and Art Gallery Occasional Papers in Archaeology 1) Dundee 1973

BALBRIDIE

Ralston, Ian B. M.: 'A timber hall at Balbridie farm', in *Aberdeen University Review*, Autumn 1982, vol.xlix 4 no.168, 238-49
   and Reynolds, Nicholas: 'Britain's oldest building?: an early timber structure on Deeside', in *Scottish Review*, May 1979, no. 14, 17-22
Reynolds, Nicholas: 'Dark age timber halls and the background to excavation at Balbridie', in *Scottish Archaeological Forum*, 1978, no.10, 41-60

BANCHORY — see BANCHORY-TERNAN

BANCHORY-DEVENICK

Cruickshank, Alexander and Copland, Alexander: 'The Blue Hill', in *Cairngorm Club Journal*, 1893, vol.i, 29-45
Henderson, John A.: *History of the parish of Banchory-Devenick*, Aberdeen 1890
Morison, George: *An address to the heads of families in Banchory-Devenick*, Aberdeen 1834

BANCHORY-TERNAN (*see also* Cluny Crichton, Crathes, Hill of Fare, Leys, Tilquhillie)

Banchory: official guide, Aberdeen 1955—, various editions
Banchory and round about, second edition, Aberdeen 1896, and subsequent editions
Bazaar book of the John Watson Guild, Banchory, Aberdeen 1897
[Cowan, W.]: *Banchory to-day*, Aberdeen 1914
Guide to Banchory and neighbourhood, Aberdeen 1907
Moir, John: *Feugh-spray*, [n.p.] [1898], new edition Aberdeen 1903. A book of verse
[Ogg, Charles]: *Banchory-Ternan 60 years ago: reminiscences of bygone days. By an old residenter*, Aberdeen 1870
Murray, William R.: *Banchory-Ternan West parish church: a short history*, Banchory 1981
Paterson, Hilda Maud Leslie: 'Banchory microliths. By Hilda M. Leslie Paterson and A. D. Lacaille. And, The river terraces near Birkwood, Banchory, Kincardineshire. By Hilda M. Leslie Paterson', in *Proceedings of the Society of Antiquaries of Scotland*, 1936, vol.lxx, 419-34
Rundle, John: 'Bouquet from Banchory', in *Scots Magazine*, May 1978, vol.109 no.2, 175-79
*Scots Nordrach-on-Dee: Banchory views, Aberdeen [n.d.]
Steuart, J.: *Report to the Parochial Board of Banchory-Ternan regarding the administration of the poor-law in the parish*, Aberdeen 1869
Walks around Banchory, Aberdeen [1976]
Watt, V. J. Buchan: *The book of Banchory*, Edinburgh 1947

BENHOLM

Bruce, Graham: *Benholm Church: a journey through the ages*, [Benholm] [1982]
Shining lights: memories of Johnshaven and Benholm forty years ago. By A. R. S., Kilmarnock [1940?]

BERVIE — see INVERBERVIE

BLAIRS

St Mary's College, Blairs, Aberdeen, [n.p.] [c.1900]. A book of photographs

CAIRN O' MOUNT

Dryas Octopetala [i.e. Alexander Copland]: *The Cairn o' Mount and Clochnaben*, Aberdeen 1892 [reprinted from the *Aberdeen Journal*]

CATTERLINE

Reid, R. W. and Fraser, J. W.: 'Short stone cist found in the parish of Kinneff and Catterline, Kincardineshire', in *Proceedings of the Society of Antiquaries of Scotland*, 1923-1924, vol.lviii, 27-40

CHARLESTOWN

Blaikie, Provost: 'Report on the system of improvement followed on the muirs of Drumforskie and Drumquhyle, now called Charlestown, in the county of Kincardine . . . by the settlement of crofters on improving leases', in *Transactions of the Highland and Agricultural Society of Scotland*, 1837, new series vol.v [= first series vol.xi], 97-121

CLOCHNABEN — see CAIRN O' MOUNT

CLUNIE CRICHTON

Wyness, James Fenton: 'The castle of Clounie Crichton, Kincardineshire', in *Proceedings of the Society of Antiquaries of Scotland*, 1939, vol.lxxiii, 58-61

COOKNEY

Dickson, Arthur: *The church of Cookney*, Stonehaven 1936

COVE

Aberdeen District Council. Department of Planning and Building Control: *Cove Bay local plan: draft*, Aberdeen 1977
Murray, Janet: *Schooling in the Cove*, Aberdeen [1981]

COWIE

Burnett, J. B.: *The kirks of Cowie and Fetteresso*, Stonehaven 1928
Christie, Elizabeth: *The empty shore: the story of Cowie, Kincardineshire*, [Cowie] [1974]

CRATHES

Ewan, Lorna M.: *A palynological investigation of a peat deposit near Banchory: some local and regional environmental implications*, Aberdeen 1981
Kenworthy, J. B.: 'Nethermills Farm, Crathes: excavations 1978-80: interim report', typescript, University of St Andrews 1981
National Trust for Scotland: *A guide to Crathes Castle and its garden*, Edinburgh [1952—], various editions
Scott, Schomberg: *Crathes Castle: an illustrated account*, Edinburgh 1971, new edition Edinburgh 1979

DALLADIES

Piggott, Stuart: 'Excavation of the Dalladies long barrow, Fettercairn, Kincardineshire', in *Proceedings of the Society of Antiquaries of Scotland*, 1971-1972, vol.104, 23-47

Watkins, Trevor: 'Excavations of an Iron Age open settlement at Dalladies, Kincardineshire', in *Proceedings of the Society of Antiquaries of Scotland*, 1978-1980, vol.110, 122-64

DRUMLITHIE

Prospectus of an agricultural college at Drumlithie, Montrose 1852

DUNNOTTAR (*see also* Stonehaven)

Barron, Douglas Gordon: *The castle of Dunnottar and its history*, Edinburgh 1925
: *For king and country: a record of the fallen* . . . , [Aberdeen] [1919]
(ed.): *In defence of the regalia, 1651-2: being selections from the family papers of the Ogilvies of Barras*, London 1910
'Chamberlain's account, 1650, Dunnottar' [From Sir Patrick Keith Murray of Ochertyre's papers, transcribed in 1910 by the late Dean Christie], in *Miscellany of the Third Spalding Club*, 1940, vol.ii, 183-210
Gibson, Colin: 'Dunnottar', in *Scots Magazine*, January 1965, vol.82, 348-58
Longmuir, John: *A day spent among the ruins of Dunnottar Castle*, Aberdeen 1835
: *Dunnottar Castle: its ruins and historical associations*, second edition Aberdeen 1842 and subsequent editions. The first edition was *A day spent among the ruins of Dunnottar Castle*, listed above
Napier, James: *The preservation of the honours of Scotland (viz. crown, sword and sceptre) and defence of Dunnottar Castle* . . . , Perth 1872
*Ogilvie, James Nicoll: *The tragedy of Dunnottar*, Edinburgh 1915
[Ogilvie, Sir William]: *A true account of the preservation of the regalia of Scotland* . . . , Edinburgh 1701
Sellar, R. J. B.: 'The ladies of the Mearns', in *Scots Magazine*, September 1952, new series vol.57, 466-76
Simpson, William Douglas: 'The development of Dunnottar Castle', in *Archaeological Journal*, 1941, vol.xcviii, 87-98
: *Dunnottar Castle, historical and descriptive*, Aberdeen 1924—, various editions
Turberville, Ruby: 'Kitin's the thing' [the story of Dunnottar Quoiting Club], in *Scots Magazine*, June 1983, new series vol.119 no.3, 284-89
Watt, James Crabb: 'Dunnottar and its barons', in *Scottish Historical Review*, 1905, vol.ii, 389-405

DURRIS (*see also* Balbridie)

Braid, K. W.: 'The last laird of Durris', in *Deeside Field*, 1981, no.17, 96-100
Fraser: *Memorial of the family of the Frasers*, [Edinburgh?] [1904?]. Variously attributed to W. N. Fraser of Tornaveen and Sir William Fraser
Henderson, John A.: *Annals of lower Deeside: being a topographical, proprietary, ecclesiastical and antiquarian history of Durris, Drumoak and Culter*, Aberdeen 1892
Smith, R. Angus: 'Notes on stone circles in Durris, Kincardineshire, and its neighbourhood', in *Proceedings of the Society of Antiquaries of Scotland*, 1879-1880, vol.xiv, 294-309

ELSICK

Bannerman, Sir Donald: *Bannerman of Elsick: a short family history*, Edinburgh 1974
Some account of the family of Bannerman of Elsick, Edinburgh 1812

FASQUE

Binney, Marcus: 'Fasque, Kincardineshire', in *Country Life*, 9 and 16 August 1979,
    vol.clxvi nos.4283 and 4284
Davie, Liz: 'Open house at Fasque', in *Scots Magazine*, May 1979, vol.111 no.2, 124-34
*Two sermons, the first by Samuel, Lord Bishop of Oxford, the second by the Warden of
    Trinity College, Glenalmond, preached in connexion with the consecration of St Andrew's
    chapel, Fasque*, Montrose 1847

FETTERCAIRN (*see also* Balbegno, Dalladies)

Biscoe, Anna Catharina: *The Earls of Middleton, Lords of Clermont and of Fettercairn, and
    the Middleton family*, London 1876
Cameron, Archibald Cowie: *The history of Fettercairn, a parish in the county of
    Kincardine*, Paisley 1899
Edwards, David Herschell: *Historical guide to the Edzell and Glenesk districts*, Brechin
    1876—, various editions. Includes a section on Fettercairn
Walks around Fettercairn, Aberdeen [1976]

FETTERESSO — see AUQUHOLLIE, COOKNEY, COWIE, MERGIE, MUCHALLS, RAEDYKES,
    STONEHAVEN, URY

FINDON

Christie, Andrew: *The 'Finnan haddie': where caught and where cured* (Yachting and
    fisheries exhibition 1897) Aberdeen 1897

FORDOUN (*see also* Auchenblae, Pittarrow)

Buchan, Charles Forbes: *The old chapel of St Palladius and its story*, Montrose 1875 1879
Cramond, William: *The annals of Fordoun*, Montrose 1894
    : *On Stra'finla top: a guide to Auchinblae and Fordoun district*, Dundee 1894
Menzies, John: *Historical sketches in Fordoun. Part I: SS Palladius and Ternan*, Montrose
    [1887]
Mollyson, Charles Alexander: *The parish of Fordoun: chapters in its history*, Aberdeen
    1893
The Story of St Palladius and his chapel at Fordoun, Montrose 1897. Reprinted from the
    Kincardineshire Household Almanac for 1879 with notes and additions

GLENBERVIE (*see also* Drumlithie)

Gairdner, William [i.e. William Macgillivray]: *Glengoyne: reminiscences of the parish and its people*, 2 vols, Edinburgh 1900. A semi-fictional account of Glenbervie
Kinnear, George Henderson: *The history of Glenbervie, the fatherland of Burns*, Montrose 1895, second edition Laurencekirk 1910
Macgillivray, William [see also Gairdner, William above]: *Memories of my early days*, London [1912]. Macgillivray also published several other volumes of reminiscences, set in a semi-fictional Glenbervie
Simpson, William Douglas: 'Glenbervie and its castle', in *Proceedings of the Society of Antiquaries of Scotland*, 1972-1974, vol.105, 255-61
Will, William: *The home of Burns' ancestors*, Aberdeen 1896

GOURDON

Hay, Edna R. and Walker, Bruce: *Focus on fishing: Arbroath and Gourdon*, Dundee 1985

HAULKERTON

Guthrie, Gideon (ed. Christian E. Guthrie Wright): *Gideon Guthrie: a monograph written in 1712-30: [with] notes concerning the family of Guthrie of Halkerton, by H. Paton*, Edinburgh 1900

HILL OF FARE

Innes, Thomas, of Learney: 'The commonty of the Hill of Fare', in *Deeside Field*, 1978, third series no.2, 13-18

INVERBERVIE

Bervie: the story of the kirk, the parish and the burgh, Montrose [1965]
Campbell, James: 'Report on the burgh of Inverbervie', in *Municipal corporations (Scotland): local reports from the Commissioners. Parliamentary Papers*, 1836, vol.xxiii, Command paper 32, 189-92
Inverbervie, Kincardineshire: the official guide, Cheltenham 1935—, various editions

JOHNSHAVEN — see BENHOLM

KINGCAUSIE

Boswell, John: 'Report on the improvement of the farm of Swellhead, on the estate of Kingcausie . . . ', in *Transactions of the Highland and Agricultural Society of Scotland*, 1843, new series vol.viii [= first series vol.xiv], 349-57
Irvine-Fortescue, James: 'Kingcausie', in *Deeside Field*, 1981, no.17, 18-31

KINNEFF (*see also* Catterline)

Rae, Lettice Milne and Gaul, Victoria: *The church of Kinneff: how the honours were saved; and, Kinneff in the Mearns*, Stonehaven 1954

LAURENCEKIRK (*see also* Haulkerton)

Campbell, James: 'Report on the burgh of barony of Laurencekirk', in *Municipal Corporations (Scotland): local reports from the Commissioners. Parliamentary Papers*, 1836 vol.xxiii, Command paper 33, 663-66
Fraser, William Ruxton: *History of the parish and burgh of Laurencekirk*, Edinburgh 1880
Garden, Francis, Lord Gardenstone: *Letter to the people of Laurencekirk, on occasion of presenting the king's charter, by which that village is erected into a free and independent burgh of barony . . .* , Edinburgh 1780, second edition Edinburgh 1823
    : *Plan of a scheme for an academy of useful arts at Laurencekirk*, [n.p.] [1788?]
Lawrie, Thomas: *Laurencekirk, Kincardineshire: the official guide*, Cheltenham 1933—, various editions

LAURISTON

Kerr, Robert: *Copy of memorandum on Lauriston by Mr Robert Kerr AD 1852*, [n.p.] [1852?]
Straton, Charles Henry: *The Stratons of Lauriston and their offshoots*, Exmouth 1939

LEYS

Angus, David: 'The loch of the legends', in *Scots Magazine*, December 1981, vol.116 no.3, 253-60
Burnett, George (ed. James Allardyce): *The family of Burnett of Leys* (New Spalding Club 22), (Aberdeen University Studies no.4) Aberdeen 1901
Burnett, William Kendall: *Genealogical tree of the family of Burnett of Leys*, [Aberdeen] [1893], new edition [Aberdeen] [1901]
R., E. M. [i.e. Elizabeth Maule Ramsay]: *Legends of Leys, collected from oral traditions of the Burnett family; and occasional verses*, Edinburgh 1856
Stuart, John (ed.): 'Court book of the barony of Leys, 1636-1674', in *Miscellany of the [First] Spalding Club*, 1852, vol.v, 221-33

MARYCULTER (*see also* Kingcausie)

Edwards, John: 'The Temple Barony of Maryculter', in *Transactions of Glasgow Archaeological Society*, 1903, second series vol.iv, 195-206
Henderson, John A.: *Annals of lower Deeside: being a topographical, proprietary, ecclesiastical and antiquarian history of Durris, Drumoak and Culter*, Aberdeen 1892
Kincardine County Council and others: *Maryculter: a new community near Aberdeen: final report*, [Stonehaven] 1974

Maxwell, Archibald Strath: *Monumental inscriptions, Templars Park Priory, Maryculter .
. . 1716-1946*, Aberdeen 1971
A Trip to Maryculter, Aberdeen 1851
Wyllie, Mabel Cook: 'Maryculter marriages 1783-1855, from old parochial records . .
. ', typescript, [n.p.] [n.d.]

MARYKIRK (*see also* Thornton)

McClure, James C.: *Marykirk in the olden time: a lecture*, Montrose 1902
Souvenir of Marykirk, [Marykirk?] [1893?]

MATHERS

Barclay, Charles W., Barclay, Hubert F. and Wilson-Fox, Alice: *A history of the
Barclay family*, 3 vols, London 1924-1934

MERGIE

Reid, James: *The chronicle of Mergie*, [n.p.] [1963]

MUCHALLS

Donald, James: *The Seatoun of Muchalls*, Stonehaven [1919], reprinted from the
Mearns Leader
Hill, John Paul: *The Episcopal chapel at Muchalls*, London 1956
Paul, William: *Dr Milne's bequest: notes on the past and present condition of the estate of
Muchalls . . .*, Aberdeen [n.d.]
    : *Muchalls on the Kincardineshire coast: a health resort*, Aberdeen 1896
Walker, Alexander: *Some facts about the estate and castle of Muchalls in Kincardineshire . .
.*, Aberdeen 1902

NIGG (*see also* Altens, Charlestown, Cove)

MacDonald, A. and Philip, J. B. (eds.): *Nigg Bay: a short guide to the north-east corner of
the Kincardineshire coast*, Aberdeen 1923

PITTARROW

Rogers, Charles: *Life of George Wishart . . . and a genealogical history of the family of
Wishart* (Grampian Club 11) Edinburgh 1876
Wishart, David: *Genealogical history of the Wisharts of Pittarrow and Logie Wishart*, Perth
1914

PORTLETHEN

*Tindal, James G.: *Incidents and anecdotes*, Portlethen 1879. Memoirs of the schoolmaster at Downies

RAEDYKES

MacDonald, George: 'The Roman camps at Raedykes and Glenmailen', in *Proceedings of the Society of Antiquaries of Scotland*, 1916, vol.l, 317-59
Ritchie, James: 'Stone circles at Raedykes, near Stonehaven, Kincardineshire', in *Proceedings of the Society of Antiquaries of Scotland*, 1922-1923, vol.lvii, 20-28

ST CYRUS (*see also* Lauriston)

Beattie, George: *Letters, and narrative of facts relative thereto, by the late George Beattie*, Montrose 1823, second edition Aberdeen 1870. The story of the jilted love and suicide of the St Cyrus poet
    : *The life, letters and poems of George Beattie of Montrose*, third edition Montrose 1882. Contains a biography of Beattie and a description of his St Cyrus background
Clark, Robert Douglas: *Memories of my boyhood: or, St Cyrus fifty years ago*, Montrose 1910
Fraser, Duncan: *Portrait of a parish*, Montrose 1970, second edition Montrose 1979
[Peter, David McGregor]: *The Kaim of Mathers: an historical tale respecting Barclay, its lairds, etc., of 1424-38; and verses on Den Finella*, fifth edition Montrose 1880. Mainly verse
Marren, Peter (ed.): *The natural history of St Cyrus national nature reserve*, Edinburgh 1980
Nature Conservancy: *St Cyrus nature trail*, Edinburgh [1969]

STONEHAVEN (*see also* Dunnottar)

Album of Stonehaven views, [n.p.] [c.1890]
Bruce, William Straton: *Reminiscences of men and manners during the past seventy years*, Aberdeen 1929. Includes memories of a Stonehaven childhood in the 1850s
Burnett, J. B.: *The kirks of Cowie and Fetteresso*, Stonehaven 1928
Christie, Elizabeth: *The haven under the hill: the story of Stonehaven*, [Cowie] [1977]
Christie, William: 'A fisherman's diary' [Robert Lees of Stonehaven, 1809-1831], in *Scots Magazine*, February 1966, new series vol.84 no.5, 483-88
*Duff, R. D.: *An address to members of the Working Men's Club at Stonehaven*, Aberdeen 1875
[Eeles, Francis Carolus]: *Stonehaven historical and descriptive, being a guide-book to the town and surrounding district, with an introductory sketch of Kincardineshire*, Aberdeen 1897
Forrest, Vivienne: 'The story of Stonehaven', in *Leopard*, April-August 1979, nos.48-51
Gibb, Andrew: *Views in Stonehaven and environs, taken on the spot*, Stonehaven 1840
Gourlay, Robert and Turner, Anne: *Historic Stonehaven: the archaeological implications of development* (Scottish Burgh Survey) Glasgow 1978
*Greig, A. W.: *Guide to Stonehaven*, [n.p.] [n.d.]
Henderson, I. A. N.: 'Aul' Steenie', in *Scots Magazine*, June 1968, vol.89, 242-49
Horne, H. O.: *Stonehaven Savings Bank, 1838-1938*, Aberdeen 1939
Innes, C.: 'Report on the burgh of barony of Stonehaven', in *Municipal corporations (Scotland): local reports from the Commissioners. Parliamentary Papers*, 1836, Com-

mand paper 33, vol.xxiii, 697-700

McKendrick, John Gray: *Statement regarding the harbour (second statement regarding the harbour)* Stonehaven 1911

Murray, Alfred A. A.: *The history of the lodge of Stonehaven, no.65, formerly no.78,* [Edinburgh] 1922

Napier, James: *Stonehaven and its historical associations: being a guide to Dunnottar Castle and other places of interest,* second edition Stonehaven 1870

Ogilvie, Wilson and Ogilvie, Irene: *Walks around Stonehaven,* Aberdeen [1976]

[Reid, James]: *Picturesque Stonehaven: descriptive guide,* Stonehaven [1899—], various editions

Report by parochial board of Fetteresso on erection of a combination poorhouse, [n.p.] [1859]

The Stonehaven luminary, or literary miscellany. No.1, Stonehaven 1830. No more published?

Stonehaven official guide, Stonehaven 1922—, various editions

Views of Stonehaven, [n.p.] [c.1900?]

Visitor's guide to Stonehaven and surrounding district, Stonehaven 1888—, various editions

Watt, Archibald: *Highways and byways round Stonehaven,* [Stonehaven] 1976 reprinted 1976 and 1978

THORNTON

Rogers, Charles: *Memorials of the Strachans, baronets of Thornton, Kincardineshire . . .* (Grampian Club 27) London 1873

: *Memorials of the Scottish families of Strachan and Wise,* Edinburgh 1877. A second edition of the preceding

Thornton-Kemsley, Colin: *Bonnet lairds,* Montrose 1972

TILQUHILLIE

History of the family of Douglass of Tilwhilly or Tilliquhilly [*Tilliquhillie*], [Bath] [1874]. At least two printings exist, one with additional genealogical tables

Pedigree of Douglas of Tilquhilly or Tilwhilly, co. Kincardine, [n.p.] [1881]

URY

Barclay, Charles W., Barclay, Hubert F. and Wilson-Fox, Alice: *A history of the Barclay family,* 3 vols, London 1924-1934

Barclay, Robert (ed. Henry Mill): *A genealogical account of the Barclays of Urie,* Aberdeen 1740, second edition London 1812

Barron, Douglas Gordon: *The court book of the barony of Urie in Kincardineshire, 1604-1747* (Scottish History Society xii) Edinburgh 1892

Budge, Frances Anne: *The Barclays of Ury, and other sketches of the early Friends,* London 1881

SECTION 3: PERIODICALS

The main local newspapers are:

Kincardineshire Observer, Laurencekirk, 1907—, continuing the *Laurencekirk Observer*, 1902-1906

Mearns Leader, Stonehaven, 1912—

Stonehaven Journal and Kincardineshire Advertiser, 1845-1917

Stonehaven News and General Advertiser for the Mearns, 1904-1906

Many of the periodicals mentioned in the Bibliography contain relevant articles besides those listed here. Particularly relevant are the *Deeside Field* and the three series of Spalding Club volumes.

APPENDIX 1: POPULATION BY PARISH

These figures are extracted from the decennial census of population. An asterisk (*) indicates a boundary change which may have influenced the figures since the previous census.

Parish	1851	1901	1951	1961	1971	1981	1981 as % of 1851
Arbuthnott	1002	698	480	497	366	418	40
Banchory-Devenick	3073	1726*	1380*	1264	1433	3836	125
Banchory-Ternan	2462	3449*	3693	3500	4055	5711	230
Benholm	1641	1426	1028	888	754	683	45
Dunnottar	1949	2533	1512	1180	946	1004	55
Durris	962	884	664	584	504	543	60
Fettercairn	1819	1390*	1323	1115	1602	1392	75
Fetteresso	5720	5409	5696	5739	6796	10086	190
Fordoun	2386	1809	1651	1377	1197	1172	50
Garvock	457	368	259	268	186	158	30
Glenbervie	1239	870	688	559	491	526	40
Inverbervie	1459	2523	1908	1832	1669	1824	125
Kinneff	1069	899	803	719	600	548	50
Laurencekirk	2125	2011	1935	1753	1651	1599	75
Maryculter	1055	951*	927	818	706	621	60
Marykirk	2232	1209	1162	1076	954	883	35
Nigg	1841	1528*	1049*	935	944	1388†	70
St Cyrus	1579	1228	1178	997	815	997	60
Strachan	947	626	546	470	389	336	35
Total	35017	31537	27882	25571	26058	33725	95

† Transferred to Aberdeen

APPENDIX 2: HOUSING BY PARISH

The present-day figures were provided by courtesy of the Grampian Regional Assessor. The 1950s figures are quoted from the relevant parish account, apart from Banchory-Devenick which was calculated from the valuation roll.

Parish	Present number of houses	Number of houses in the 1950s (where available)
Arbuthnott	144	137
Banchory-Devenick	1400	357
Banchory-Ternan	2370	1030
Benholm	366	
Dunnottar	471	512
Durris	220	
Fettercairn	496	
Fetteresso	3803	1541
Fordoun	504	
Garvock	78	
Glenbervie	227	
Inverbervie	828	
(town only)	504	326
Kinneff	233	
Laurencekirk	706	609
Maryculter	241	
Marykirk	384	
Nigg (now in Aberdeen)	904	
St Cyrus	457	
Strachan	154	
Total	13082	

INDEX

Persons and places have been indexed selectively. Where a person or place is mentioned more than once in the same chapter only the first occurrence is noted.